Software Engineering

Software Engineering

Edited by **Cheryl Jollymore**

New York

Published by Willford Press,
118-35 Queens Blvd., Suite 400,
Forest Hills, NY 11375, USA
www.willfordpress.com

Software Engineering
Edited by Cheryl Jollymore

International Standard Book Number: 978-1-68285-195-1 (Hardback)

Printed in the United States of America.

Contents

Permissions

List of Contributors

Preface

Software engineering focuses on the design and development of software. This book encompasses the principles of software engineering. It aims to present a detailed study on software safety, security and risk management. It also brings together various methods of software analysis and designs. This book embraces an interdisciplinary approach and contributes to the new developments in the field. It will help engineers, experts and students to apprehend theories and applications. The researches and case studies presented in this book will be beneficial for everyone associated with this field.

The information shared in this book is based on empirical researches made by veterans in this field of study. The elaborative information provided in this book will help the readers further their scope of knowledge leading to advancements in this field.

Finally, I would like to thank my fellow researchers who gave constructive feedback and my family members who supported me at every step of my research.

Editor

In-depth characterization of exception flows in software product lines: an empirical study

Hugo Melo, Roberta Coelho[*], Uirá Kulesza and Demostenes Sena

* Correspondence:
souzacoelho@gmail.com
Informatics and Applied
Mathematics Department (DIMAp),
Federal University of Rio Grande do
Norte, Natal, Brazil

Abstract

Software Product Lines (SPLs) play an essential role in contemporary software development, improving program quality and reducing the time to market. However, despite its importance, several questions concerning SPL dependability did not get enough attention yet, such as: how the exception handling code has been implemented in SPLs? The characteristics of the exception handling code may lead to faulty SPL products? The Exception Handling (EH) is a widely used mechanism for building robust systems and is embedded in most of mainstream programming languages. In SPL context we can find exception signalers and handlers spread over code assets associated to common and variable SPL features. If exception signalers and handlers are added to a SPL in an unplanned way, products can be generated on which variable features may signal exceptions that remain uncaught or are mistakenly caught by common features or other variable features. This paper describes an empirical study that categorizes the possible ways exceptions flow through SPL features and investigates whether some of their characteristics can lead to faulty exception handling behavior. The study outcomes presented in this paper are helpful in several ways, such as: (i) enhancing the general understanding of how exceptions flow through mandatory and variable features; (ii) providing information about the potential problems related to specific kinds of flows detected in this study; and (iii) presenting how a static analysis tool can be used to support the identification of potentially faulty exception handling flows.

Keywords: Software product line; Exception handling; Static analysis; Code inspection

1. Introduction

Software product line engineering advocates the development of software system families from a specific market segment (Clements and Northrop 2001). A system family is a set of programs that shares common functionalities and maintain specific functionalities that vary according to specific systems being considered (Parnas 1976). A software product line (SPL) is specified, designed and implemented in terms of common and variable features. A feature (Czarnecki and Eisenecker 2000) is a system property or functionality that is relevant to some stakeholder and is used to capture commonalities or discriminate among systems in SPLs. A SPL is developed through of a design of an extensible software architecture and subsequently implemented in terms of reusable code assets that address its common and variable features. The SPL development approach promotes benefits such as cost reduction, product quality, productivity and time to market (Clements and Northrop 2001). However it may bring new challenges to the software dependability.

The Exception Handling (EH) is a widely used mechanism for building robust systems (Goodenough 1975) (Garcia et al. 2001). As EH mechanisms are embedded in most of mainstream programming languages, it is also used in SPL engineering as a way of structuring fault detection and recovery solutions (Bertoncello et al. 2008). Exception signalers and handlers can then be found spread over code assets associated to common and variable features. Hence, intriguing questions arise when developing an exception-aware SPL, such as: How do exceptions flow through both variable and common features of SPLs? How do these exception flows can contribute or lead to a faulty exception handling behavior? A faulty exception behavior may happen when code assets implement common or variable features signals exceptions that are mistakenly caught inside the system. This is an exception handling bug very difficult to detect, known as Unintended Handler Action (Miller and Tripathi 1997).

In a previous study (Melo et al. 2012), we started seeking for answers to these questions. We performed an empirical study based on manual inspection and static code analysis, which presented a first categorization for the ways exceptions were signaled and handled by variable and common features of SPLs. The study was based on two well-known benchmark software product lines: MobileMedia (Young 2005) and Berkeley DB (Kästner et al. 2008). In this study, we have identified common ways in which exceptions are raised and handled inside the SPLs. We could observe that in many circumstances, exceptions raised by variable features were not adequately caught. Some of them were caught by generic handlers defined in the core, and other ones were caught by other variable features with no explicit relation between them.

This paper extends the previous study in the following ways: (i) a new medium-sized product line was analyzed, called Prevayler (Godil and Jacobsen 2005), which implements an open-source memory database configurable system that allows persisting serializable Java objects; (ii) an in-depth analysis of each flow was performed, which besides considering the exception signaler and handler to categorize each flow, also reports about the intermediate elements that compose the exception flows; (iii) a new version of the static code analysis tool was implemented in order to support the in-depth analysis of each flow; (iv) moreover, this work also presents an uncaught exception analysis for each SPL and it discusses about the fault-prone scenarios that may occur in SPL products in the exception handling context.

The contributions of this work allow the developers of dependable SPLs: (i) to consider the potential effects of variable features on the exception flow of SPL products; (ii) to define/use specific variability implementation techniques to deal with such effects; and (iii) to make more informed decisions when defining the possible SPL products. Moreover, it also allows for the designers of Exception Handling policies and strategies to consider improving existing EH solutions to make them more robust and resilient to flaws in the exception handling code.

The remainder of this paper is organized as follows. Section 2 presents the study settings. Sections 3 and 4 present the results of the two study phases. Section 5 provides further discussions and lessons learned. Section 6 describes related work. Finally, Section 7 presents our conclusions. Due to space limitations, throughout this paper we assume that the reader is familiar with SPL techniques and terminology (Clements and Northrop 2001) (Czarnecki and Eisenecker 2000).

2. Study settings

This section describes the configuration of our empirical study in terms of its main goals and research questions, the investigated SPLs (Section 2.1), the study phases (Section 2.3), and the static analysis tool developed to support the investigation of the SPL exception flows (Section 2.4). Section 2.2 uses a code snippet extracted from one of the target SPLs to illustrate the exception handling concepts discussed in this study.

The main goals of our study were: (i) to analyze different Java-based SPL implementations for the purpose of characterizing the exception flows with respect to the code assets responsible for signaling and handling exceptions, and the common and variable features related to them; and (ii) to investigate the fault-proneness of each exception flow category identified in the study.

The research questions that guided this study were the following: (RQ1) How are exceptions signaled and handled through variable and common features of SPLs? (RQ2) Which kinds of exception flows contribute (or may lead) to a faulty (or inadequate) exception handling behavior?

2.1. The target software product lines

One major decision that had to be made for our investigation was the selection of the target SPLs. We have selected three medium-sized well-known benchmark SPLs implemented in Java: MobileMedia (Young 2005), Berkeley DB (Kästner et al. 2008), and Prevayler (Godil and Jacobsen 2005). Such SPLs implement variable behavior and associated features using CIDE (Kästner et al. 2008). CIDE (Colored IDE) is a tool that enables SPL developers to annotate code with feature information using background colors (similar to #ifdefs). All SPLs were used in several empirical studies (Figueiredo et al. 2008) (Brabrand et al. 2012) (Kästner et al. 2008) (Coelho et al. 2008)) (Godil and Jacobsen 2005), and each of them is a representative of different application domains, and heterogeneous realistic ways of incorporating exception handling.

The MobileMedia (MM) is a SPL of applications that manipulates media (e.g., photo, music and video) on mobile devices. There are subsequent Java releases available. All adopt the same architecture style (i.e., model-view-controller), varying in terms of the number of features available and design decisions taken in each version. Our study focused on the 8th release (http://sourceforge.net/projects/mobilemedia).

Berkeley DB (BkDB) is a SPL for embeddable databases of moderate size (42 features) that implements functionalities related to management of memory, logging, transactions, concurrency, and others databases functionalities.

Prevayler (Pvl) is a SPL for the context of in-memory database systems, based on object prevalence. Derived systems of this SPL support plain Java object persistence, snapshots, queries, transactions, and logging. The release analyzed in our study implements five variable features: Replication, GZip, Censor, Monitor, and Snapshot. This release is a subset of the original implementation that was defined in (Prevayler Project 2013).

Table 1 summarizes code characteristics of target SPLs: the number of lines of code (LOC); the number of lines of code dedicated to exception handling (EH LOC); the number

Table 1 Summary of characteristics of target SPLs

Metrics	Software product lines		
	MobileMedia	BerkeleyDb	Prevayler
LOC	3191	39233	5122
EH LOC	614	3028	458
#Throw Clauses	24	127	68
#Exception Flows	111	1522	164
#Classes and Interfaces	51	238	140
#Checked Exceptions	9	22	3
#Unchecked Exceptions	0	3	0
#Variable Features	11	42	5

of throw-clauses; number of exception flows; number of classes and interfaces; number of user-defined checked and unchecked exceptions; and the number of variable features.

2.2. SPL exception handling code example

In order to support the reasoning about the exception handling in SPL context, we illustrate the main concepts of an exception handling mechanism based on an example extracted from MobileMedia product line. Figure 1A presents a code snippet associated to a mandatory feature responsible for creating new albums of a given media (i.e. photo, music, or video) from the `MediaAccessor` class. Besides the normal execution flow, there are two scenarios on which the album cannot be created: either the album name is an empty string (lines 7–8), or if the album name is already in use because there is another album with the same name (lines 11–14). In such scenarios, the normal execution flow should be interrupted and an error message should be presented to the user. These scenarios are called exceptional scenarios, and they are implemented using the exception handling constructs that are briefly described in the next paragraphs.

In modern OO languages such as Java, C++ and C#, such abnormal situations are represented by *exceptions* which are represented as objects. An exception may be raised by a method whenever an abnormal computation state is detected. The *exception signaler* is the method that detects the abnormal state and raises the exception. In Figure 1A, the `createNewAlbum()` method from `MediaAccessor` class detects an abnormal condition and raises the exception `InvalidPhotoAlbumNameException` using the throw clause. Since this method is not annotated (colored in CIDE tool) with any variable feature, we say that such signaler belongs to the SPL core.

Some languages provide constructs to associate a method's signature with a list of exceptions that it may raise (see lines 3–4 in Figure 1A). Besides providing information for the method's callers, this information can be checked at compile time to verify whether handlers were defined for each specified exception. This list of exceptions represents the *exception specification* or *exception interface* of a method. Ideally, the exception interface should provide complete and precise information for the method user. However, some languages, such as Java, allow the developer to bypass this mechanism. In such languages exceptions can be of two kinds: (i) checked exception – that needs to be declared on the method's signature that throws it; and (ii) unchecked exception – that does not need to be declared on the signaler method's signature.

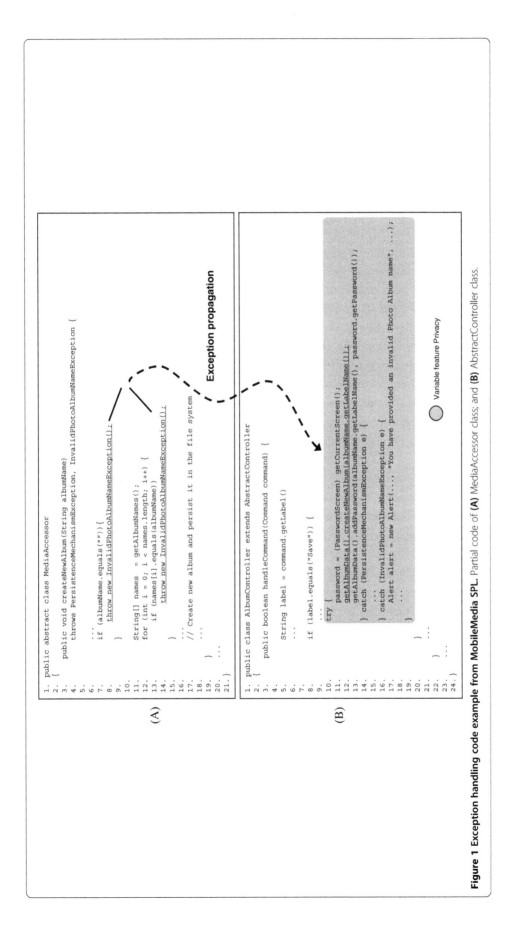

Figure 1 Exception handling code example from MobileMedia SPL. Partial code of **(A)** MediaAccessor class; and **(B)** AbstractController class.

After a method signals an exception, the runtime system attempts to find the block of code that will be responsible for handling it. The exception handler in Java should be defined in the dynamic call chain of the method signaling the exception. In the scenario illustrated in Figure 1B the handler of the exception signaled by the method `createNewAlbum()` is caught by the method `handleCommand()` (lines 16–18) of the `AlbumController` class. In Java programs, a try-catch block represents the block of code responsible for handling exceptions. In this example the handler block is colored using the CIDE tool, meaning that it belongs to the Privacy feature. We call the *exception flow* a path in a program call graph that links the *signaler* and the *handler* of an exception.

2.3. Study phases

In order to provide answers to the research questions – RQ1 and RQ2 – presented before, our study has been organized in two main phases, each of them focusing on one of the research questions stated previously. The study phases were the following: (i) an analysis and characterization of the exception flows in terms of variable and common features responsible for signaling and handling the exceptions; and (ii) a detailed analysis of the exception flows (i.e., method call chains, and handler actions).

There are 3 different approaches to verify a SPL (Apel et al. 2013): (i) the product-based strategy that analyzes every product individually; (ii) the sample-based strategy that focuses on a subset of existing products; and (iii) the family-based strategy that analyzes the design and implementation artifacts of the whole SPL in a single pass. In our exploratory study, we discarded the product-based strategy because it is costly and impractical to analyze the exception flows of every possible product of the target SPLs. The family-based strategy could not be adopted due to the non-existence of static analysis frameworks to support the interprocedural analysis of exception flows of the whole product line at once. Hence we have decided to use the sample-based strategy by focusing on the analysis of products of each investigated SPL that includes all variable features. In our study, it was possible to derive the product of each SPL that includes all the variable features – since the target SPLs do not define alternative features and do not define explicit exclusion constraints between their features. These three products are expressive and representative to be studied in order to characterize the behavior of exception flows in SPLs. We also noticed that during our analysis most of exception flows involved a few number of features, which means that these exception flows are present in all products that include those features.

Phase 1: Characterization of SPL exception flows

The main goal of this phase was to answer RQ1, in other words to explore the possible ways exceptions could flow inside a SPL. We have started this phase by manually inspecting the target product lines but soon such task became infeasible (i.e. the exception flows were too deep and there were too many flows to be inspected). The high cost of manual inspection led to the implementation of PLEA (Product Line Exception Analyzer) tool, which performs a feature-oriented exception flow analysis (see Section 2.4). In this phase, the exception flows of each SPL were calculated using PLEA tool. Every exception flow was analyzed and characterized in terms of the common and variable features of the code assets responsible to throw and handle the exceptions.

Phase 2: In-deph analysis of exception flows and SPL design issues

The main goal of this phase was to refine the answer given to RQ1 in the first phase while looking for answers to RQ2. To do so we manually inspected the exception flow in detail, evaluating not only the signaler and handler information, but also the intermediate elements that compose a flow. In addition, we also investigated the impact of SPL design issues on the types of flows found, and the fault proneness of each of them. Such phase contributes to understand the exception handling policy adopted by each investigated SPL, and which kind of flows can represent a risk for the robustness of the execution of the SPL products. The detailed analysis and results of this phase are presented in Section 4.

2.4. PLEA – a feature-oriented static analysis tool

The PLEA – Product Line Exception Analyzer – tool has been developed to help the analysis and characterization of the SPL exception flows. The main aim of the tool is to calculate the exception flows thrown from the SPL code assets, and to characterize the classes and methods that are part of these exception flows, including the ones responsible to signal and handle the exception. In addition, the tool also distinguishes the classes from each exception flow that are implementing the SPL commonalities or variabilities. Figure 2 shows a package diagram that illustrates the dependencies between the two modules – *Flow Analyzer* and *Feature Identifier* – of PLEA, and the two external tools – *Design Wizard* and *CIDE* – that PLEA is integrated.

2.4.1 PLEA overview

PLEA is structured as two mains modules, which are implemented as Eclipse plug-ins (Eclipse IDE 2012): (i) the Flow Analyzer and (ii) the Feature Identifier. The Flow Analyzer performs an inter-procedural analysis on the SPL bytecode. It implements one of the most used algorithms for call graph construction called class hierarchy analysis (CHA) (Grove and Chambers 2001), in order to build the program dependency graph (PDG) (Ferrante et al. 1987). It traverses the PDG, firstly looking for the checked exceptions, explicitly thrown by the SPL code assets, and then looking for handlers that may handle them. As a result the plug-in reports a set of exception flows. When building the PDG of a SPL, the Flow Analyzer uses the DesignWizard tool (Brunet et al.

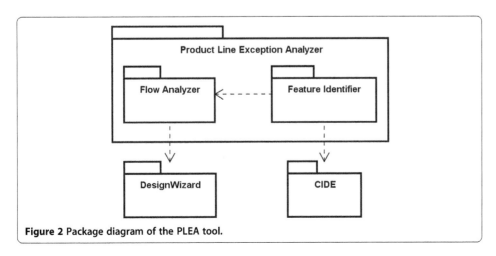

Figure 2 Package diagram of the PLEA tool.

2009), which provides an API that supports the automated analysis and inspection of Java programs.

The Feature Identifier plug-in is responsible for accessing the configuration knowledge (CK) of the SPL to obtain the information concerning the features associated to each exception flow: its signaler, handler and the intermediate methods between them. The CK (Czarnecki and Eisenecker 2000) defines how each code asset (class, interface, method, attribute) is mapped to the specific SPL common and variable features that they implement. The CK format depends on the tool used for the SPL implementation and variability management. The current version of PLEA manipulates the CK defined by CIDE (Kästner et al. 2008), the tool used for the variability management of the analyzed SPLs.

2.4.2 PLEA detailed design

Figure 3 shows a partial class diagram of the main packages and classes of the Flow Analyzer module. The `ExceptionFlowAnalyzer` class defines the `analyze()` method, which parses all the SPL code assets and creates a program dependency graph (PDG) in terms of instances of the `ClassNode` and `MethodNode` classes of the Design Wizard tool. After that, the `DesignWizardUtil` class is used to search the classes of the SPL in order to organize the relevant exceptions (`EAException`) and respective constructors (`EAConstructor`). Finally, the tool obtains the `MethodNode` that represent exception signalers and executes a depth-first search from each of these methods in order to find all the `MethodNode` instances that constitute their respective exception handlers. The depth-first search is executed over the call graph calculated for the Flow Analyzer module. All the information collected regarding exception signalers and handlers is organized in an `EAReport` instance that does not depend on the DesignWizard API.

The Feature Identifier module is responsible for identify the features associated to each signaler and handler methods listed in the `EAReport` instance. Figure 4 shows a class diagram with the main classes of this module. The `IdentifyFeatureAction` class is an action associated to a menu in the Eclipse IDE workspace that activates the execution of the module. It creates an instance of `IdentifyFeatureOperation`

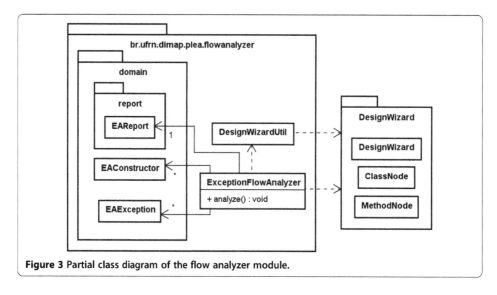

Figure 3 Partial class diagram of the flow analyzer module.

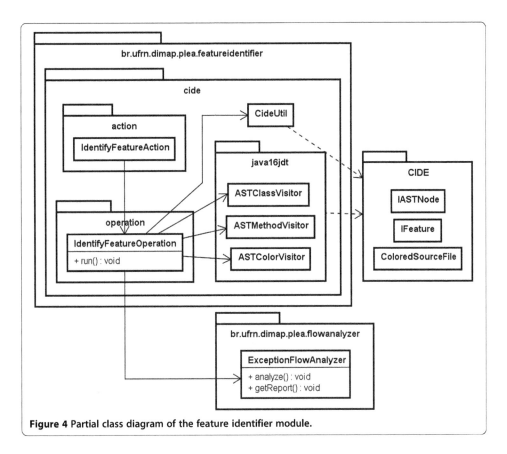

Figure 4 Partial class diagram of the feature identifier module.

and executes its run() method, which is responsible for identify the features of each signaler, handler and the intermediate methods of a flow. The current implementation of PLEA retrieves the configuration knowledge (CK) from the CIDE tool, which stores the features directly related to the code asset in the respective abstract syntax tree (AST) that represents each of them. The information regarding the features is obtained using the CideUtil class. In our implementation, we have extended a Visitor hierarchy (Gamma et al. 1994) that was implemented in the CIDE tool and helps identify the classes (ASTClassVisitor), methods (ASTMethodVisitor), methods call (ASTCallerVisitor), catch clauses (ASTHandlerVisitor), throw clauses (ASTSignalerVisitor) and features (ASTColorVisitor), when the ASTs associated to each signaler and handler class are traversing. The identified features for each method are attached to the same EAReport instance that was created in the Flow Analyzer module.

3. Study results for phase 1: characterization of SPL exception flows

This section summarizes the study results of the first phase, which involves the general analysis and characterization of the exception flows of the target SPLs. These results were collected during the execution of PLEA over Mobile Media, Berkeley DB and Prevayler. Section 3.1 presents the criteria used for exception flow categorization and the number of exception flows found in this study characterized according to these criteria. Section 3.2 compares the exception flow information obtained from the investigated SPLs. Finally, Sections 3.3 and 3.4 discuss about each flow type, presenting real examples extracted from the analyzed SPLs.

3.1 Collected results for the SPL exception flow types

The main goal of this analysis and characterization phase was to explore the possible ways exceptions could flow inside a SPL. We took into account the information concerning which features were associated to the pieces of code responsible for signaling and handling exceptions. The exception flows were characterized according to three attributes:

(i) *The feature associated with the exception signaler.* The piece of code responsible for signaling the exception can be associated to the core (C) or to a variable feature (V);

(ii) *The feature associated with the exception handler.* The piece of code responsible for handling the exception can be associated to the core (C), to a variable feature (V), or the exception can escape from every handler and remain uncaught (E);

(iii) *The exception handling action.* The exception can be caught by a specialized handler (S), a handler whose type is the same of the exception being caught, or by a generic handler (G), a handler whose type is a supertype of the exception being caught.

Table 2 presents the number of exception flows found in our study, characterized according to these attributes. It also shows the percentage of each flow type in relation to all flows found per SPL release. The flow type, first column of Table 2, is an acronym based on the attributes values, for instance: a CC flow is an exception flow on which a

Table 2 Exception flows in MobileMedia, BerkeleyDb and Prevayler

Flow	Signaler	Handler	Handling	Flow occurrences (percentage per release)			
				MM	BkDb	Pvl	All
CC	Core	Core	Any	48 (43%)	413 (27%)	76 (46%)	537 (30%)
CCS	Core	Core	Specialized	22 (20%)	63 (4%)	5 (3%)	90 (5%)
CCG	Core	Core	Generic	26 (23%)	350 (23%)	71 (43%)	447 (25%)
CV	Core	Variable	Any	28 (25%)	210 (14%)	6 (4%)	244 (14%)
CVS	Core	Variable	Specialized	25 (22%)	62 (4%)	4 (3%)	91 (5%)
CVG	Core	Variable	Generic	3 (3%)	148 (10%)	2 (1%)	153 (9%)
CE	Core	Escaped	-	0 (0%)	435 (29%)	62 (38%)	497 (27%)
	Subtotal (CC + CV + CE)			76 (68%)	1058 (70%)	144 (88%)	1278 (71%)
VC	Variable	Core	Any	18 (17%)	183 (12%)	6 (4%)	207 (12%)
VCS	Variable	Core	Specialized	18 (17%)	17 (1%)	0 (0%)	35 (2%)
VCG	Variable	Core	Generic	0 (0%)	166 (11%)	6 (4%)	172 (10%)
VV	Variable	Variable	Any	8 (7%)	19 (1%)	0 (0%)	27 (2%)
VVS	Variable	Variable	Specialized	8 (7%)	19 (1%)	0 (0%)	27 (2%)
VVG	Variable	Variable	Generic	0 (0%)	0 (0%)	0 (0%)	0 (0%)
VaVb	Variable	Variable	Any	9 (8%)	100 (7%)	0 (0%)	109 (6%)
VaVbS	Variable	Variable	Specialized	9 (8%)	13 (1%)	0 (0%)	22 (1%)
VaVbG	Variable	Variable	Generic	0 (0%)	87 (6%)	0 (0%)	87 (5%)
VE	Variable	Escaped	-	0 (0%)	162 (10%)	14 (8%)	176 (9%)
	Subtotal (VC + VV + VaVb + VE)			35 (32%)	464 (30%)	20 (12%)	519 (29%)
Total				111	1522	164	1797

core asset signals an exception and another (or the same) core asset handles it. Depending on the way the exception is caught, this flow can be sub-characterized as: CCS - if the exception is caught by a specific handler; or CCG - if the exception is caught by a generic handler. When the exception signaled by a core element remains uncaught, it was classified as CE. It is worth mentioning the special flow type identified as VaVb in Table 2. It represents the flow on which a given variable feature throws an exception and a different variable feature handles it, and there are no inclusion constraints between them. The VV represents the flow on which the same feature signals and handles the exception. Additionally, Table 3 focuses on the number of flow types signaled only by variable features, and presents the percentage of such flows in relation to all flows originated by variable features.

3.2. Exception flow types across different SPLs

Figure 5 illustrates the proportion of exception flows found in each investigated SPL. We can observe that although proportion of flow types in every SPL differed, most of the flows in all SPLs represent exceptions signaled by core elements. Considering CC, CV and CE flows all together, they represent, 68%, 70% and 88% of all flows found in MobileMedia, BerkeleyDb and Prevayler, respectively. Moreover, we could find exceptions signaled by variable features in all analyzed SPLs. In Prevayler, in particular, most of exceptions signaled by variable features escaped (VE). In MobileMedia, most of such exceptions were handled in the core (VC) or by other features (VV or VaVb).

Considering the way the exceptions were handled (i.e., by generic or specialized handlers) – regardless of whether they represent exceptions signaled by variable or core features – we could observe that most of the handlers in MobileMedia are specialized handlers, while in BerkeleyDB and Prevayler, generic handlers caught most of the exceptions. Figure 6 shows the results for the exception handlers. The high number of specialized handlers found in MobileMedia may give the impression that the exceptions are being adequately handled inside the MM SPL, and they are inadequately caught in other SPLs. However, only a deeper analysis can really show what is happening in the real scenario.

Table 3 Exception flows signalized by variable features

Flow	Signaler	Handler	Handling	Flow occurrences (percentage per release)			
				MM	BkDb	Pvl	All
VC	Variable	Core	Any	18 (51%)	183 (39%)	6 (30%)	207 (40%)
VCS	Variable	Core	Specialized	18 (51%)	17 (4%)	0 (0%)	35 (7%)
VCG	Variable	Core	Generic	0 (0%)	166 (35%)	6 (30%)	172 (33%)
VV	Variable	Variable	Any	8 (23%)	19 (4%)	0 (0%)	27 (5%)
VVS	Variable	Variable	Specialized	8 (23%)	19 (4%)	0 (0%)	27 (5%)
VVG	Variable	Variable	Generic	0 (0%)	0 (0%)	0 (0%)	0 (0%)
VaVb	Variable	Variable	Any	9 (26%)	100 (22%)	0 (0%)	109 (21%)
VaVbS	Variable	Variable	Specialized	9 (26%)	13 (3%)	0 (0%)	22 (4%)
VaVbG	Variable	Variable	Generic	0 (0%)	87 (19%)	0 (0%)	87 (17%)
VE	Variable	Escaped	-	0 (0%)	162 (35%)	14 (70%)	176 (34%)
Subtotal (VC + VV + VaVb + VE)				35 (100%)	464 (100%)	20 (100%)	519 (100%)

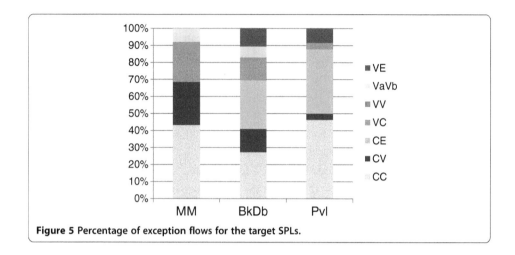

Figure 5 Percentage of exception flows for the target SPLs.

Next sections discuss about each flow type found in this study and presented above. Section 3.3 details the flow types signaled by core elements. Section 3.4 discusses and presents examples of the flow types signaled by variable features. The analysis of the exceptions that remained uncaught in every SPLs (i.e., CE and VE flows) is left to Section 4.

3.3 How the exceptions signaled by core elements are handled

We can observe that most of the exception flows from the target SPLs were signaled by core elements (see CC + CV + CE subtotal in Table 2, 68% in MM, 70% BkDB, and 88% Pvl). From this set, Figure 7 shows that a considerable amount was also caught by core elements (CCS and CCG flows) and a more reduced amount was handled by variable features (CVS and CVG).

The flows on which exceptions were signaled by core elements and handled by a variable feature were found in every SPL (see CV flows in Table 2, 25% in MM and 14% in BkDb and 4% in Pvl). One instance of the CV flows from Prevayler is depicted in Figure 8. The method `run()` that is defined in a variable feature calls a method from the same variable feature, called `CentralPublisher#subscribe()` (line 5). Such method calls other methods from core assets, and one of such methods signals an

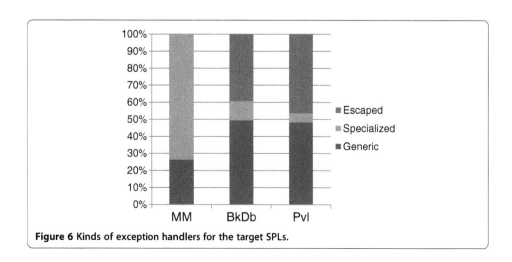

Figure 6 Kinds of exception handlers for the target SPLs.

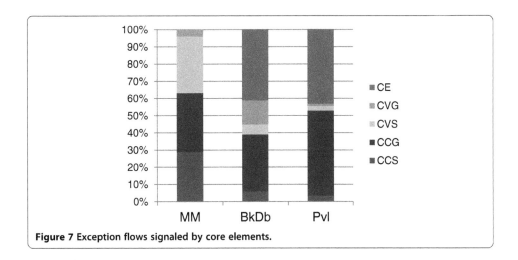

Figure 7 Exception flows signaled by core elements.

exception. Hence, we can observe that such flow happens when a variable feature re-uses existing methods from core assets, Section 4 discusses in more details the causes and consequences of such flows.

3.4 How the exceptions signaled by variable features are handled

Table 2 also shows that a considerable amount of exception flows originated from variable features (32% in MM, 30% in BkDB, and 12% in Pvl). Figure 9 focuses on such exception flows, originated from variable features. From this set, most of them were handled by core elements (51% in MM, 39% in BkDB, and 30% in Pvl). Only part of such flows was indeed handled by the same variable feature that had signaled it (23% in MM, 4% in BkDb, and 0% in Pvl), as illustrated by the VV flows in Table 2 and Figure 10. We also observed flows on which a different variable feature caught the exception (26% in MM, 22% in BkDB and 0% in Pvl, see the VaVb flows in Figure 11). Next subsections present examples of these flow types.

Exceptions signaled by a variable feature and handled in the core (VC)

In BerkeleyDB and Prevayler, most of the exceptions signaled by variable features were captured by generic handlers defined in a core element, while in MobileMedia most of the exceptions signaled by variable features were caught by specialized handlers in the core (see VCG flows in Figure 9). Figure 12 illustrates a scenario on which a method from the core of BerkeleyDB calls methods from different variable features.

The method illustrated in Figure 12 pertains to a core asset and has around 100 lines of code. It contains method calls to 8 distinct variable features (through method calls), which can signal specific exceptions. The code snippet only presents three of such variable features that can signal instances of `DatabaseException` (see colored tags in the code). Moreover, such method also accesses other core methods that can also signal specific exceptions. Although distinct exceptions may flow in such method a single and generic treatment is given for all of them (lines 30–34).

3.4.1 Exceptions signaled and handled by the same variable feature (VV)

In MobileMedia and BerkeleyDB, we found exceptions signaled and handled by the same variable feature (7% in MM, 1% in BkDB). Figure 10 illustrates one of such flows

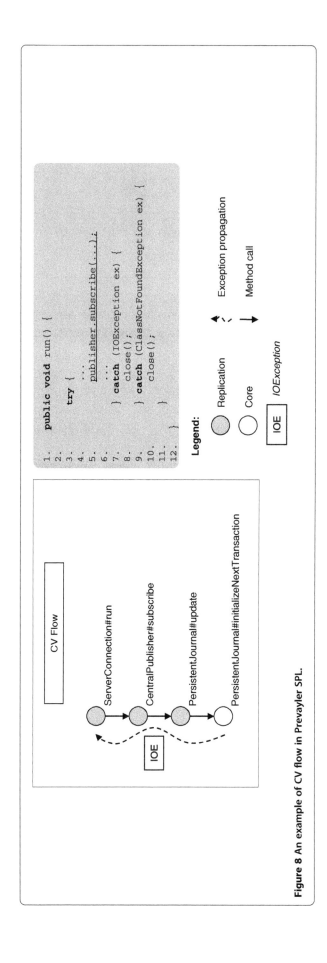

Figure 8 An example of CV flow in Prevayler SPL.

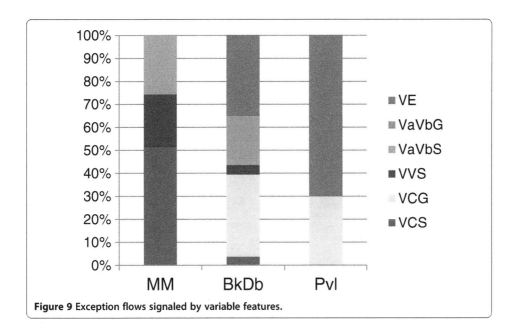

Figure 9 Exception flows signaled by variable features.

found in MobileMedia SPL. Inspecting such flow, we could observe that the intermediate elements (the methods called between the signaler and the handler) were also associated to a single feature, which means that, in such flows, no core functionality were reused.

In addition, considering the handler action associated to such flows, we observed that all flows signaled and caught inside the feature context (the VV flows) were handled using specialized handlers – which can lead to an adequate handling as a single feature can have enough information to handle the exception. An interesting finding was that even in BerkeleyDB, where most of the exceptions were handled by generic handlers (see Figure 6), the exceptions signaled and handled in the context of a single feature were caught by specific handlers.

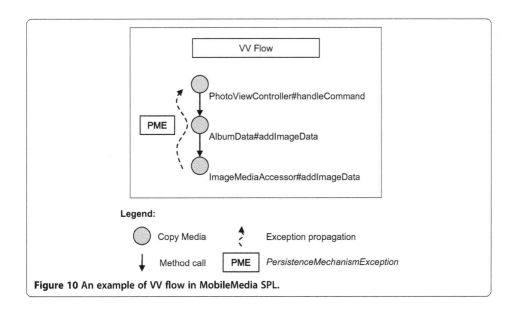

Figure 10 An example of VV flow in MobileMedia SPL.

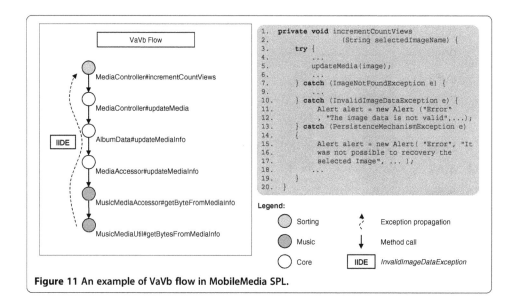

Figure 11 An example of VaVb flow in MobileMedia SPL.

3.4.2 Exceptions signaled and handled by distinct variable features (VaVb)

The exception flows, whose signaler was defined on a variable feature and the handler on a different variable feature, were found in two of the analyzed SPLs (8% in MM, and 7% in BkDb). Such flows bring out an implicit relation between features that may lead to EH faulty behavior as illustrated in Figure 11.

Figure 11 illustrates the code snippet of a method from a variable feature of MM called *Sorting*, which is responsible for sorting lists of different kinds of media. The

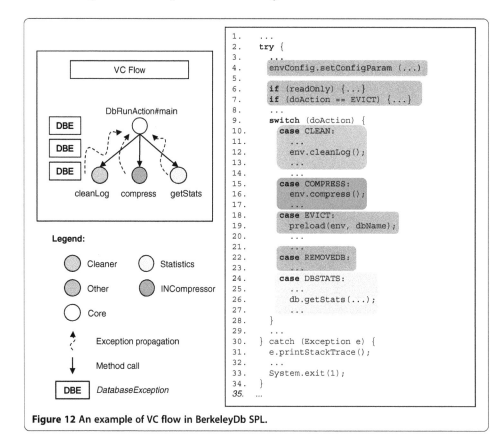

Figure 12 An example of VC flow in BerkeleyDb SPL.

updateMedia() method (line 5) transitively calls other methods as illustrated in the call chain illustrated on Figure 11. One of such methods in the call chain belongs to the *Music* feature (i.e., getBytesFromMediaInfo()), which can signal InvalidImageDataException (represented as IIDE in Figure 11). When such exception is signaled by *Music* feature, it is caught by a specific handler (lines 11–12), and a message related to another feature (i.e., *Photo* feature that may also interact with the *Sorting* feature) is presented to the user. Such exception handling confusion problem is a consequence of the implicit feature interaction in exception handling scenarios.

In the scenarios where VaVb flows were detected, there was no constraint associating the feature that signaled the exception and the feature that handled it. The handler feature does not have enough contextual information to adequately handle the exception. Such scenarios usually happen by mistake. In other words, the exception signaled by the feature would remain uncaught but was mistakenly caught by a handler defined by another feature. This is an instance of the Unintended Handler Action (Miller and Tripathi 1997) problem, a faulty exception handling behavior very difficult to diagnose at runtime. Such kind of interaction, which only happens in exception handling scenarios, was not documented in any of the SPLs analyzed in this study.

4. Study results for phase2: an in-depth analysis of exception flows

In the previous section the exception flows from the investigated SPLs were classified according to their signalers, handlers, and the features associated to each of them. This characterization enabled us to identify patterns related to exceptions signaling and handling while dealing with a high number of exception flows. In order to obtain a more fine-grained view of how exceptions are signaled and handled inside SPLs, we performed an in-depth analysis of each flow on which: (i) we investigated the intermediate methods that composed the exception flows call chains – this analysis was based on manual inspection and guided by results provided by PLEA static analysis tool; and (ii) we analyzed how the flow types that are related could lead to faulty or inadequate exception handling behavior.

Table 4 illustrates the number of flows inspected in this second study phase. All exceptions flows of MobileMedia and Prevayler were inspected, they contain 111 and 164 exceptions flows, respectively. The mean size of EH flows in MM was approximately 5, while in PvL it was 7. Table 4 also presents the mean, minimum and maximum size of exception flows of target SPLs. Since BerkeleyDb product line contains 1522 exception flows, whose mean size is approximately 12, only a few of its flows were evaluated during this study phase, which was strongly based on manual inspection. As a result, most of the findings of our in-depth analysis were related to scenarios found in MM and Pvl.

Table 4 Exception flows information

	MM	BkDb	Pvl
Size of shorter flow (# number of methods)	2	1	2
Size of longer flow (# number of methods)	7	31	12
Mean	4,76	11,91	7,01
Median	5	11	7
Total Number of flows	111	1522	164

4.1. Inspecting the intermediate elements of a flow

During such in-depth analysis, the exception flows were fully inspected and were sub classified according to the following criteria: the presence of variable or core features affecting the intermediate elements on the flow. Table 5 presents the kinds of flows found according to such criteria.

Such in-depth analysis is worth doing because it may reveal new ways of interaction between features which can lead to faulty exception handling behavior, as follows: although the intermediate element of a flow does not catch the exception, during a maintenance task a general handler (e.g. catch `Throwable` clause) can be added to it, and it can mistakenly catch the exception that was flowing through it – leading to the *Unintended Handler Action* (Miller and Tripathi 1997). Next we present examples for some of such sub-categories of flows, and Section 4.2 discusses about their causes and consequences.

CC flows and their intermediate elements

In the first phase of our study (Section 3), we observed that the CC flows was the kind of exception flow with the highest frequency in the analyzed product lines (see CC flows in Table 2, 43% in MM and 46% in Prevayler). However, the in-depth analysis of CC flows revealed that most of such flows was actually affected by a variable feature. Such flows were

Table 5 Amount of flow subtypes in SPLs

Flow Type	Flow Subtype	Description	Occurrences MM	(Percentage) Pvl
CC	Pure CC	All the intermediate elements pertain to the core.	6 (5%)	22 (25%)
	C[V]C	At least one intermediate element pertains to a variable feature.	42 (38%)	54 (61%)
W	Pure W	All the intermediate elements pertain to the same variable feature.	6 (5%)	0 (0%)
	V[C]V	At least one intermediate element pertains to the core.	2 (2%)	0 (0%)
CV	Pure CV	All intermediate elements pertain to the variable feature that handles the exception, or to the core that signals it.	20 (18%)	6 (7%)
	C[Va]V	At least one of the intermediate elements pertains to a variable feature different from the one that handles it.	8 (7%)	0 (0%)
VC	Pure VC	All intermediate elements pertain to the variable feature that signals the exception, or to the core that handles	8 (7%)	6 (7%)
	V[Va]C	At least one of the intermediate elements pertains to a variable feature different from the one that signals it.	10 (9%)	0 (0%)
VaVb	Pure VaVb	All intermediate elements pertain to the variable feature that signals the exception, or to the one that handles it.	2 (2%)	0 (0%)
	Va[C]Vb	At least one of the intermediate elements pertains to the core.	2 (2%)	0 (0%)
	Va[Vc]Vb	At least one of the intermediate elements pertains to a variable feature different from the ones that signals or handles it.	3 (3%)	0 (0%)
	Va[VcC]Vb	At least one of the intermediate elements pertains to the core and other one pertains to a variable feature different from the ones that signals or handles it.	2 (2%)	0 (0%)
Total			111 (100%)	88 (100%)

classified as C[V]C. In this kind of flow, a core element signals an exception that propagates through one or more methods of a variable feature, and it is caught by a core element. We can observe in Table 5 that C[V]C flows represent 87% of the CC flows in MM and 71% in Pvl. Therefore, only a few flows were indeed unaffected by a variable feature, specifically 5% and 25% of all exception flows in MM and Pvl, respectively.

Figure 13 shows an example of a kind of C[V]C flow in Prevayler SPL. We can observe that the initial and final method in exception propagation is related to the SPL core, although there is an intermediate method related to variable feature (i.e. Snapshot).

VV flows and their intermediate elements

Another flow type found in the first phase of our study was the VV flow, 7% in MM and 0% in Prevayler. It gives us the impression that the whole exception flow – from signaler to handler – is composed by methods of a single variable feature. However, the in-depth analysis of the intermediate elements of VV flows revealed that in 25% of them in MM, one or more of the intermediate elements pertained to the core. Such flows were classified as V[C]V, and they represent a scenario on which a variable feature element signals an exception that propagates through a method from the core, and it was finally caught by a method from the same variable feature that had signaled it.

CV flows and their intermediate elements

The first phase of our study also revealed that the CV flows corresponded to 25% in MM and 4% in Prevayler. In MM and Pvl SPLs, our in-depth analysis of CV flows revealed that in 24% of them, one of the intermediate elements related to a variable feature is different from the one that handled it. Figure 14 shows an example of CVaV

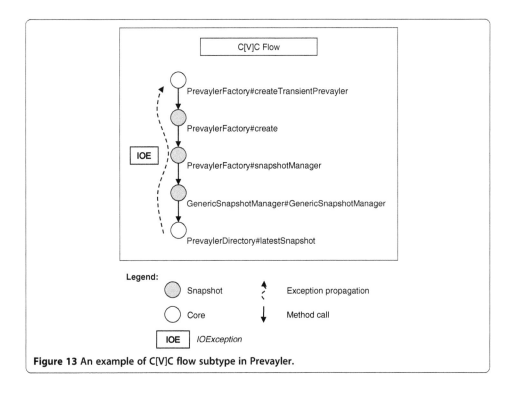

Figure 13 An example of C[V]C flow subtype in Prevayler.

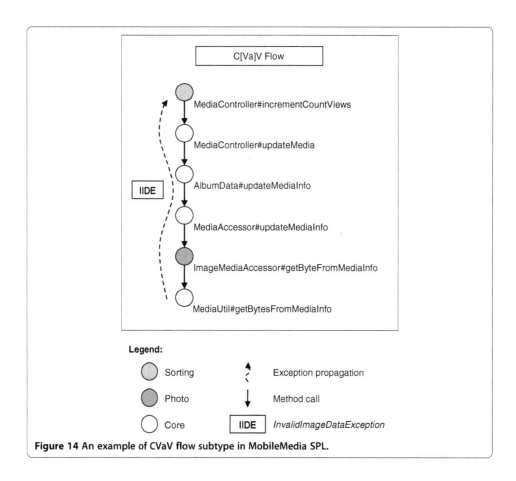

Figure 14 An example of CVaV flow subtype in MobileMedia SPL.

flow in MobileMedia. *Sorting* feature is responsible for sort media using amount views criteria, and for this functionality this code piece requires core information about loaded media. After that, a method of other variable feature is called (i.e. Photo), and, finally, this reuses a core method. Therefore, a signalized core exception propagates by code pieces of different variable features.

VC flows and their intermediate elements

The results of the first study phase also showed that the VC flows corresponded to 17% in MM and 4% in Prevayler. In MM and Pvl, our in-depth analysis revealed that in 42% of these VC flows, similarly to the previous scenario, one of the intermediate elements related to a variable feature is different from the one that signaled the exception. Such flows were classified as V[Va]C.

VaVb flows and its intermediate elements

The VaVb flows represented only a few ones of the analyzed as we observed in our first study phase, specifically 8% in MM and 0% in Prevayler. Our in-depth analysis of VaVb flows revealed others interesting scenarios, which have the following patterns: (1) Va[C] Vb; (2) Va[Vc]Vb; and (3) Va[VcC]Vb. Figure 15 shows an example of call graph in MobileMedia. In this example, three variable features interact by exception flow. Neither initial, final or intermediate methods are related to SPL core, because of that circumstances this flow subtype was classified like Va[Vc]Vb.

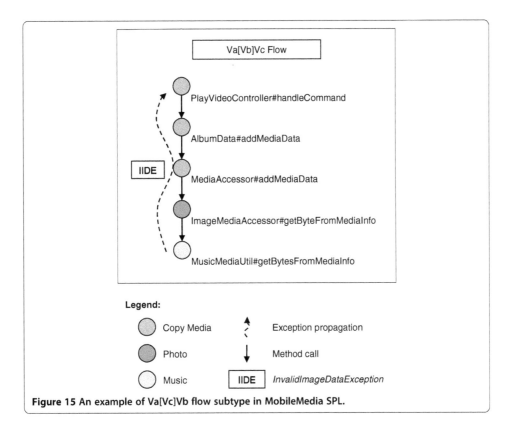

Va[Vb]Vc Flow

PlayVideoController#handleCommand

AlbumData#addMediaData

IIDE

MediaAccessor#addMediaData

ImageMediaAccessor#getByteFromMediaInfo

MusicMediaUtil#getBytesFromMediaInfo

Legend:

◯ Copy Media   ↑↲ Exception propagation

● Photo   ↓ Method call

◯ Music | IIDE | *InvalidImageDataException*

Figure 15 An example of Va[Vc]Vb flow subtype in MobileMedia SPL.

4.2 Causes and consequences of exception handling flow types

When manually inspecting the code, we observed that flows such as C[V]C, V[C]V and C[Va]V were caused by common design strategies adopted by both SPLs: (i) variabilities were added to the SPLs by extending their core classes that implement variation points; and (ii) methods belonging to the core were reused by the classes that implementing some of their variable features.

The first strategy is a well-known design technique to implement framework-based SPLs. In this technique, the core elements are responsible to refer to abstract classes or interfaces that must be implemented by the variable features. Hence, when a concrete class that implements a variable feature extends or implements a framework extension point, all handlers defined to the exceptions signaled by the parent method can be reused. On the other hand using an annotative approach such as CIDE, the code of variable features can be introduced in the middle of methods belonging to the core features. In both cases the exceptions signaled by the new piece of code that are related to an implementation of the variable feature should obey the *Exception Conformance* principle (Miller and Tripathi 1997).

According to the *Exception Conformance* principle when a method inherits or redefines another method this cannot signal a checked exception that is not a subtype of the exceptions defined in the parent method. However, sometimes a new functionality (added due to an inclusion of a new variable feature) may need to throw new exceptions, which are not subtypes of exceptions of the extended method. In order to manage these exceptions, the methods defined in parent class usually use sufficiently generalized exception types, so that any possible new exception that may be signaled by an extension method would be a subtype. However, the generalized exception types may be so general that they have limited value in defining a clear and consistent *exception interface*. The intended benefit for the *Exception Conformance* is that the handlers defined to the parent method can be reused by the methods that will redefine it.

In our study, we observed that although some core methods were overriding by variable features (or modified through the use of annotative mechanism), the errors (exception information) were too specific, thereby the reuse of the same handler of the parent method cannot always be the adequately strategy. We should say that overriding of functionality is acceptable and often desirable, but the overriding of exception information is usually not [a]. We also noticed that the exception handlers defined in the core classes were reused by many flows that were thrown by the code that implements the variable features. Flows such as VC and C[V]C are examples of such reuse, where such problem may happen. This problem could be minimized if the SPL developers adapt the handler code as soon as the code of the variable feature was added. However, the study results have shown that developers usually ignore the way the exceptions signaled by variable features are or not adequately caught (see Section 4.3).

4.3 Uncaught exception analysis

Our study also investigated the number of exceptions that remained uncaught on each one of the investigated SPLs. This analysis is important because uncaught exceptions abort the program's execution, which is one of the main causes of software crashes. Moreover, the number of uncaught exceptions is one way of checking whether the exception handling policy is adequately implemented. The exception handling policy states that when an exception is signaled inside the system, a handler should be defined to deal with it. When this is not the case, the exception flows through the system and may remain uncaught or may be mistakenly handled by any method in the call chain of the exception flows. Another indicative that the exception might be inadequately caught is the number of exceptions that are handled on a general catch clause. This general clause is usually located on the entry point of the system (i.e. main method), which only exists to avoid the exception to remain uncaught. Usually such exceptions handled on main are only logged and abort the program's execution.

Table 6 illustrates the number of uncaught exceptions and exceptions that are only caught on the system entry point. We can observe that considering MM, no exceptions remained uncaught or were caught by a general handler on the entry point. On the other hand, a significant number of flows in the other SPLs represent exceptions that remained uncaught – 46% of all flows in Prevayler (see Figure 16). The number of exceptions that were caught on the main method was also high in this SPL – 24% in Prevayler.

When considering both types of flows as indicators that the exception handling policy might not have been obeyed, we can see that in BerkeleyDb and Prevayler, 68% and

Table 6 Number of unhandled exceptions and exceptions handled on entry point

	Occurrences		
	MM	BkDb	Pvl
Unhandled	0	597	76
Handled on entry point	0	440	40
Total flows	111	1522	164

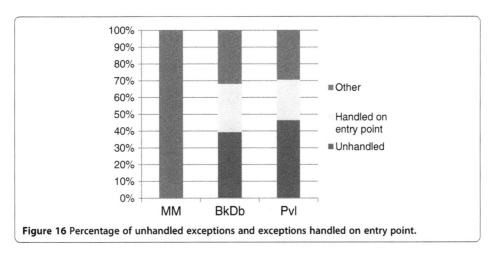

Figure 16 Percentage of unhandled exceptions and exceptions handled on entry point.

70% of the flows, respectively, escaped or was handled inside the main method (see Figure 16). Such impressive numbers raise an alert to the reader that the exception handling policies of such SPLs might not have received enough attention during development.

Although such numbers indicate that the exception handling policies have not been appropriately defined, we cannot ensure this information because the developers of such SPLs have not made them explicit on the SPL artifacts. On the other hand, the MobileMedia implementation has explicitly defined the exception handling as one of the primary concerns (Figueiredo et al. 2008). The quality of the exception handling policy is also reflected by the considerable number of user-defined exceptions in MM (see Table 1) and specialized handler actions (see Table 2), in contrast with BkDb and PvL on which most the exception handler actions were generic (i.e., catch `Throwable` or catch `Exception` clauses) – see Table 2.

After discovering the number of uncaught exceptions and the exceptions handled on the main method, we extended our analysis to include the elements responsible for signaling such exceptions. Table 7 shows the number of uncaught exceptions and exceptions caught in main, that are signaled by core and variable features. We observed that 41% of the BerkeleyDB exceptions signaled by core elements escaped, and 21% of such flows were handled on the entry point. In Prevayler, 43% of the exceptions signaled by core elements escaped and 25% were handled on the entry point (see Figure 17). Focusing on the exceptions signaled by variable features, our analysis showed that in BerkeleyDB 35% of such exceptions escaped and 27% were handled on the entry point. In Prevayler 70% escaped and 20% were caught on the entry point (see Figure 17). As in Prevayler most of the exceptions escaped we could find only few VC flows and neither VV nor VaVb flows.

Table 7 Signaler (core or variable) of unhandled exceptions and exception handled on entry point

	Occurrences					
	MM		BkDb		Pvl	
	Core	Variable	Core	Variable	Core	Variable
Unhandled	0	0	435	162	62	14
Handled on entry point	0	0	314	126	36	4
Total flows	76	35	1058	464	144	20

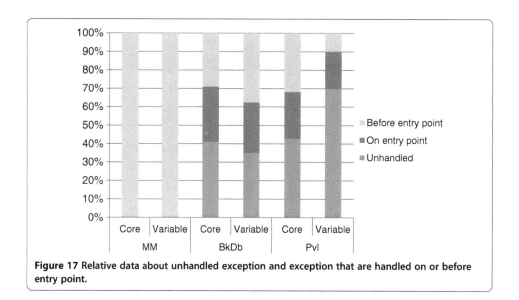

Figure 17 Relative data about unhandled exception and exception that are handled on or before entry point.

5. Discussions and lessons learned

This section provides further discussion of issues and lessons learned while performing this study.

Collateral effects of specific flow types

In our study we classified all exception flows found on three SPLs according to their signalers and handlers. Such characterization enabled us to identify the most common flow types and analyze how the characteristics of such flows could lead to faulty exception handling behaviors. It is known that the exception handling policy of a system or product lines depends on others factors than the intrinsic ones (i.e., software architecture). Design decisions, coding patterns or company-specific policies, and developer's experience (Shah et al. 2010) may also affect the way exceptions are signaled and handled inside the system. Hence, what is an inadequate handling for a system may be a design decision for another. However, it is also known that specific exception handling patterns may lead to faulty exception handling behavior affecting the system robustness (e.g., Unintended Handler Action, and Generic handling (Miller and Tripathi 1997)). In this study, by performing a deeper analysis of specific flow types, we could consistently detect such faulty scenarios in the analyzed SPLs, such as the ones associated to VC, VaVb, and V[C]V flows presented in Sections 3 and 4.

Dealing with feature overlapping

In our study we could find pieces of code associated to more than one feature, which is known as *feature overlapping* (Kästner et al. 2008). There are two main ways of feature overlapping: (i) *AND overlapping* – when a piece of code is annotated with feature A AND feature B, in this case both features should be selected in order to include a given piece of code; and (ii) *OR overlapping* – a piece of code is annotated with feature A OR feature B, and hence at least one of the features should be selected for the piece of code to be included in a product. In CIDE, feature interactions become apparent when colors denote different feature overlap (in this cases the colors are blended in the overlapping region). Such blended colors represent *AND overlappings*. Since all target SPLs were implemented using the CIDE tool, only AND feature overlapping could be found. Considering the feature overlapping on code related to exception signaling or handling, we found the following: (i) in MobileMedia 10 out of 111 (about 10%) flows presented features overlapping on signaling or handling code; (ii) in Berkeley DB 12 out of 1522 (less than 1%) flows presented features overlapping on signaling or handling code; and (iii) none of the flows in Prevayler presented feature overlapping on signaling or handling code. We adopted the following strategy for classifying these specific scenarios: (i) if the signaler was annotated with feature A, and the handler was annotated with feature A AND feature B, we classified such flow as VV; (ii) if the signaler was annotated with feature A and feature B, and the handler was annotated with feature A and feature B, we classified such flow as VV; (iii) if the signaler was annotated with feature A and feature B, and the handler was annotated with feature B, we classified such flow as VaVb; and finally (iv) if the signaler was annotated with feature A, and the handler annotated with feature B and feature C, we also classified such flow as VaVb. In doing so, we could prevent false positives and false negatives on the feature overlapping scenarios found in our study.

Exception handling guidelines for software product lines

The outcomes of our study also emphasizes the need for the definition of EH guidelines for SPLs. Such guidelines could motivate, for instance, application engineers to avoid throwing exceptions from their variable feature implementations to the core assets. In practice, however, there are several technical and organizational factors that impairs the full adoption of such kind of guidelines, such as: (i) the runtime exceptions thrown from by third-party libraries used by the variable code assets; (ii) the difficulty in coordinating the work of product line and application engineers; and (iii) the natural complexity of the dependencies between SPL common and variable code assets. Given such restrictions to the full adoption of an EH guideline, feature-oriented exception flow analysis tools, such as PLEA, would be strongly useful to detect violations of the practices defined on EH guidelines. In addition, the variability implementation techniques must also be considered when defining exception handling guidelines for a SPL.

The implicit feature interaction and its consequences

In our work, we found an implicit relation that arises between features in the exceptional flow (when a feature handles the exception signaled by other feature), and we observed that it could lead to the exception handling confusion problem already mentioned in the context of aspect-oriented development (Figueroa 2011) – the exception intended to be handled by a given component is mistakenly handled somewhere else; because using the current exception handling mechanism embedded in languages such as Java, we cannot prevent one exception from being caught by a general handler on a method in the call chain between the signaling and handling points. The in-depth analysis of the exception flows (phase 2 of the study – Section 3) also showed us that feature interaction can be even more complex and involve many different common and variable features.

Study limitations

One may argue that performing the characterization in a sample of three different SPLs is a limiting factor. Even under such restriction, the study analyzed 47 KLOC of Java source code of which around 4,1 KLOC are dedicated to EH handling. From these base code, 1797 exception flows were found, categorized and analyzed. Another limitation of this study is the fact that it only considered the exceptions explicitly thrown by SPL code assets - excluding exceptions signaled from libraries and Java runtime environment. There are also the limitations inherent to the use of a static analysis tool (i.e., inheritance, polymorphism and virtual calls) (Robillard and Murphy 2003), however the limitations of this study are similar to the ones imposed on the other empirical studies with similar goals (Figueiredo et al. 2008) (Coelho et al. 2008, 2011) (Ferrari et al. (2010). Moreover, one may also argue that during the second phase of our study the exception flows of BerkeleyDB were not analyzed, bringing another limitation to the study. However, the different kinds of flows found represent interesting scenarios that may happen in the exception handling of real SPLs.

6. Related work

This section presents related work organized in three categories: (i) empirical studies investigating the exception handling code of SPLs; (ii) studies on implicit feature interactions; and (iii) exception flow analysis tools and methods.

Empirical studies investigating the exception handling code of SPLs

Figueiredo et al. (2008) present an empirical study that aims to compare AO and OO Java implementations of the MobileMedia SPL. In their study, they have analyzed the stability of the EH feature across the SPL evolution in terms of modularization metrics (on the EH source code). In our study we discovered the exception flows originated from the EH code (manually and automatically through PLEA) and evaluated how such flows differ across different MM releases. Coelho et al. (2008) performed an empirical study considering the fault-proneness of aspect-oriented implementations for handling exceptions. Two releases of both Java and AspectJ implementation of MobileMedia product line were assessed as part of that study. Although the study has analyzed the EH code of MM product line, it neither performed a feature-oriented analysis of the EH exception flows, nor discussed the fault-proneness of specific flow types related to variable features, as we have investigated in our work. Bertoncello et al. (2008) propose a method for refactoring OO product line architecture in order to separate their normal and exceptional behavior into different software components. The proposed method motivates the introduction of variations points in the SPL core architecture to address different choices of exception handlers during product derivation. Our approach can be seen as complementary to the refactoring method proposed. First, the static analysis tool proposed in our work can be used to detect violations in the EH strategies established when evolving a SPL implementation with the introduction of new features or modification of existing ones. Second, our exploratory study also emphasizes the need to establish effective EH strategies to address the design and implementation of the core and variable features.

Studies on implicit feature interactions

Recent research work shows the importance and difficulty to analyze features dependencies in the context of SPL implementations using conditional compilation techniques, or similar approaches like CIDE (Kästner et al. 2008). Ribeiro et al. (2010) propose the concept of emergent interface in order to address the analysis of feature dependencies when evolving a software product line. An emergent interface is used to capture the dependencies between code assets previously annotated and associated to specific features. The Emergo tool (Ribeiro et al. 2012) is used to automatically compute the emergent interfaces on demand based on intraprocedural or interprocedural dataflow analysis. Brabrand et al. (2012) propose and compare three different intraprocedural data analysis to detect the feature dependencies, in terms of undeclared variables, unused variables and null pointer. One of the great benefits of their approach is the capacity to analyze the feature dependencies for the complete SPL implementation instead of analyzing the code assets for each individual product separately. Similar to these works, our work improves the code assets dependency analysis using information about the kind of features (common or variable) they implement. However, such works address neither the analysis of exception flows in the context of SPL implementations, nor the implicit feature relation that comes about in the exceptional control flow.

Exception flow analysis tools and methods

Some research works propose solutions based on static analysis to calculate the exception flows of a system (Fu and Ryder 2007) (Robillard and Murphy 2003) (Coelho et al. 2011) (Garcia and Cacho 2011). None of these tools however perform a feature-sensitive analysis as the one proposed in this study. The tool presented in this study performs a feature-oriented analysis of the exception flows, which allows a more accurate and detailed analysis of how exceptions flow through the code assets implementing the mandatory and variable features of a SPL.

7. Conclusions

This paper reported an empirical study that characterized and quantitatively assessed the ways exceptions flow through SPL features. Moreover, it also investigated fault-proneness of specific exception flow types in SPL implementations. The analysis was conducted in three existing SPLs – Mobile Media, Berkeley DB, and Prevayler – using manual inspection and static code analysis. As part of our study, we also developed a tool that performs an automated feature-oriented exception flow analysis. The tool can be useful to support the developer when implementing the exception handling behavior of variable and common features.

Overall this new study corresponds to 47KLOC of Java source code of which around 4,1KLOC are dedicated to exception handling. From such code base, 1797 exception flows were found and characterized. Some outcomes consistently detected through this study refined the findings of our previous work and also pin-pointed new interesting information about the ways exceptions flow on SPLs, as follows:

- Only few exception flows of each product line were unaffected by their variable features. We call such flows *pure CC* flows. In relation to the other flows they corresponded to 5% of EH flows in MobileMedia, and 25% in Prevayler;
- Most of the flows found on this study were somehow affected by a variable feature: 95% in MobileMedia and 75% in Prevayler. They represent: (i) flows on which exceptions are signaled or handled by a variable feature; or (ii) flows on which the

variable feature did not signal nor handle the exception but affected the method call chain on which the exception flowed.

- Considering the flows that were signaled by variable features, most of them were handled by core elements (51% in MobileMedia, 39% in Berkeley DB, and 30% in Prevayler), and some by the same variable feature that signaled it (7% in MobileMedia, 1% in Berkeley DB, and 0% in Prevayler). The study also identified flows on which a different variable feature caught the exception thrown by another variable feature (26% in MobileMedia, 22% in Berkeley DB and 0% in Prevayler).
- Moreover, a significant number of uncaught exceptions were found in two of the investigated SPLs (39% in Berkeley DB, 46% Prevayler). In general, we observed a high prevalence of uncaught exceptions and exceptions caught by the program entry point (i.e. main method). Specially in Prevayler, most of the exceptions signaled by variable features remained uncaught.
- Finally, we could also detect that some of the flows originated from variable features were caught by a different variable feature (8% in MobileMedia, and 7% in Berkeley DB).

We believe that these and the other study outcomes presented in the paper are helpful in several ways, such as: (i) enhancing the general understanding of how exceptions flow through mandatory and variable features; (ii) providing information about the potential problems related to specific kinds of flows detected in this study (for instance the VaVb flows); and (iii) presenting how a feature-oriented static analysis tool can be used to support the identification of potentially faulty exception handling flows in the context of software product lines.

Endnote

[a] The unchecked exceptions may bypass this principle, but in our study we only focused on checked exceptions.

Competing interests
The authors declare that they have no competing interests.

Authors' contributions
HFM implemented PLEA tool and carried out most of the manual inspections conducted during the empirical study, and contributed with several findings found during manual inspections and during PLEA execution. RC worked on the study design, defined the research questions and hypothesis for conducting the study, as well as analyzed the data generated by PLEA tool and devised some of its discussions. UK also worked on the study design and analysis of data; he was also responsible for comparing the present work with related works. DT worked on the manual inspection step of Prevayler product line, and also contributed on the paper discussions. All authors were responsible for writing the paper and all of them read and approved the submitted manuscript.

Authors' information
Hugo Faria Melo holds a MSc from the Department of Informatics and Applied Mathematics (DIMAp) of the Federal University of Rio Grande do Norte, Brazil (2010–2012). He conducted empirical studies in the context of reliability of the product lines. His research interests include static analysis, model driven development and exception handling.
Roberta Coelho is an Associate Professor at the Department of Informatics and Applied Mathematics (DIMAp), Federal University of Rio Grande do Norte (UFRN). She holds a PhD (2008) from the Informatics Department of the Pontifical Catholic University of Rio (PUC-Rio) and worked as a researcher at Lancaster University, where she conducted empirical studies in the context of reliability of OO and AO applications. Her research interests include static analysis, exception handling, dependability and empirical software engineering.
Uirá Kulesza is an Associate Professor at the Department of Informatics and Applied Mathematics (DIMAp), Federal University of Rio Grande do Norte (UFRN), Brazil. He obtained his PhD in Computer Science at PUC-Rio – Brazil (2007), in cooperation with University of Waterloo (Canada) and Lancaster University (UK). His main research interests include: software product lines, generative development and software architecture. He has co-authored over 120 referred papers in journals, conferences, and books. He worked as a post-doc researcher member of the AMPLE project

(2007-2009) – Aspect-Oriented Model-Driven Product Line Engineering (www.ample-project.net) at New University of Lisbon, Portugal. He is currently a CNPq (Brazilian Research Council) research fellow level 2.
Demostenes Sena is an Associate Professor at Federal Institute of Education, Science and Technology of Rio Grande do Norte. He is also a PhD candidate at Federal University of Rio Grande do Norte. His main research interests are software product lines and empirical software engineering.

Acknowledgements
This work was partially supported by the National Institute of Science and Technology for Software Engineering (INES) - CNPq under grants 573964/2008-4 and CNPQ 560256/2010-8. Roberta Coelho is also supported by CNPq under grant 484037/2010-2.

References

Apel S, Von Rhein A, Wendler P, Größlinger A, Beyer D (2013) Strategies for product-line verification: case studies and experiments, Proceedings of the 35th International Conference on Software Engineering (ICSE 2013), San Francisco. IEEE Press Piscataway, NJ, USA, pp 482–491

Bertoncello I, Dias M, Brito P, Rubira C (2008) Explicit Exception Handling Variability in Component-based Product Line Architectures, Proceedings of the 4th International Workshop on Exception Handling, Atlanta. ACM, New York, NY, USA, pp 47–54, doi:10.1145/1454268.1454275

Brabrand C, Ribeiro M, Tolêdo T, Borba P (2012) Intraprocedural Dataflow Analysis for Software Product Lines, Proceedings of the 11th International Conference on Aspect-Oriented Software Development (AOSD 2012), Potsdam. ACM, New York, NY, USA, pp 13–24, doi:10.1145/2162049.2162052

Brunet J, Guerrero D, Figueiredo J (2009) Design Tests: An Approach to Programmatically Check your Code Against Design Rules, Proceedings of 31st International Conference on Software Engineering (ICSE 2009). New Ideas and Emerging Results, Vancouver, pp 255–258, doi:10.1109/ICSE-COMPANION.2009.5070995

Clements P, Northrop L (2001) Software Product Lines: Practices and Patterns. Addison-Wesley Longman Publishing Co., Inc, Boston, MA, USA

Coelho R, Rashid A, Garcia A, Ferrari F, Cacho N, Kulesza U, Staa A, Lucena C (2008) Assessing the Impact of Aspects on Exception Flows: An Exploratory Study, Proceedings of the 22nd European Conference on Object-Oriented Programming (ECOOP 2008). Cypress, Paphos, pp 207–234, doi:10.1007/978-3-504-70592-5 10

Coelho R, Staa A, Kulesza U, Rashid A, Lucena C (2011) Unveiling and taming liabilities of aspects in the presence of exceptions: a static analysis based approach. Information Sciences 181:2700–2720

Czarnecki K, Eisenecker U (2000) Generative Programming: Methods, Tools, and Applications. ACM Press/Addison-Wesley Publishing Co, New York, NY, USA

Eclipse IDE (2012) Eclipse., http://www.eclipse.org/. Accessed 03 April 2012

Ferrante J, Ottenstein K, Warren J (1987) The program dependence graph and its Use in optimization. ACM Transactions on Programming Languages and Systems (TOPLAS) 9:319–349

Ferrari F, Burrows R, Lemos O, Garcia A, Figueiredo E, Cacho N, Lopes F, Temudo N, Silva L, Soares S, Rashid A, Masiero P, Batista T, Maldonado J (2010) An Exploratory Study of Fault-proneness in Evolving Aspect-oriented Programs, Proceedings of the 32nd International Conference on Software Engineering, Cape Town. ACM New York, NY, USA, pp 65–74, doi:10.1145/1806799.1806813

Figueiredo E, Cacho N, Sant'Anna C, Monteiro M, Kulesza U, Garcia A, Soares S, Ferrari F, Khan S, Castor Filho C, Dantas F (2008) Evolving Software Product Lines with Aspects: an Empirical Study on Design Stability, Proceedings of the 30th International Conference on Software Engineering. ACM Press, Leipzig, pp 261–270, doi:10.1145/1368088.1368124

Figueroa I (2011) Avoiding Confusion with Exception Handling in Aspect-oriented Programming, Proceedings of the 10th International Conference on Aspect-oriented Software Development. Porto de Galinhas, ACM New York, NY, USA, pp 81–82, doi:10.1145/1960314.1960345

Fu C, Ryder B (2007) Exception-Chain Analysis: Revealing Exception Handling Architecture in Java Server Applications, Proceedings of the 29th International Conference on Software Engineering. ACM Press, Minneapolis, pp 230–239, doi:10.1109/ICSE.2007.35

Gamma E, Helm R, Johnson R, Vlissides J (1994) Design Patterns: Elements of Reusable Object-Oriented Software. Addison-Wesley Professional

Garcia A, Rubira C, Romanovsky A, Xu J (2001) A comparative study of exception handling mechanisms for building dependable object-oriented software. Journal of Systems and Software 59:197–222

Garcia I, Cacho N (2011) eFlowMining: An Exception-Flow Analysis Tool for .NET Applications, Proceedings of the 1st Workshop on Exception Handling in Contemporary Software Systems, São José dos Campos., pp 1–8, doi:10.1109/LADCW.2011.18

Godil I, Jacobsen H-A (2005) Horizontal Decomposition of Prevayler, Proceedings of the Centre for Advanced Studies on Collaborative research (CASCON'05). IBM Press, Toronto, Canada, pp 83–100

Goodenough J (1975) Exception handling: issues and a proposed notation. Communications of the ACM 18:683–696

Grove D, Chambers C (2001) A framework for call graph construction algorithms. ACM Transactions on Programming Languages and Systems (TOPLAS) 23:685–746

Kästner C, Apel S, Kuhlemann M (2008) Granularity in Software Product Lines, Proceedings of the 30th International Conference on Software Engineering, Leipzig., ACM New York, NY, USA, pp 311–320, doi:10.1145/1368088.1368131

Melo H, Coelho R, Kulesza U (2012) On a Feature-Oriented Characterization of Exception Flows in Software Product Lines, Proceedings of the 26th Brazilian Symposium on Software Engineering (SBES)., Natal, Natal, pp 121–130, doi:10.1109/SBES.2012.15

Miller R, Tripathi A (1997) Issues with Exception Handling in Object-Oriented Systems, Proceedings of the 21st
    European Conference on Object Oriented Programming (ECOOP 97). Springer-Verlag, Berlin, pp 85–103
Parnas D (1976) On the design and development of program families. IEEE Transactions on Software Engineering 2:1–9
Prevayler (2013) Prevayler., http://prevayler.org/. Accessed 07 June 2013
Ribeiro M, Pacheco H, Teixeira L, Borba P (2010) Emergent Feature Modularization, Proceedings of ACM Conference on
    Systems, Programming, Languages and Applications (OOPSLA 2010). Software for Humanity Onward! Reno,
    pp 17–21
Ribeiro M, Tolêdo T, Winther J, Brabrand C, Borba P (2012) Emergo: A Tool for Improving Maintainability of
    Preprocessor-based Product Lines, Proceedings of the 12th International Conference on Aspect-Oriented Software
    Development (AOSD 2012). Hasso-Plattner-Institut, Potsdam, Hasso-Plattner-Institut, Potsdam, March 2012., ACM
    New York, NY, USA, pp 23–26, doi:10.1145/2162110.2162128
Robillard M, Murphy G (2003) Static analysis to support the evolution of exception structure in object-oriented systems.
    ACM Transactions on Software Engineering and Methodology 12:191–221
Shah H, Gorg C, Harrold M (2010) Understanding exception handling: viewpoints of novices and experts. IEEE
    Transactions on Software Engineering 36:150–161
Young T (2005) Using AspectJ to Build a Software Product Line for Mobile Devices. University of British Columbia,
    Canada, MSc Thesis

2

A mapping study of the Brazilian SBSE community

Wesley KG Assunção[1*], Márcio de O Barros[2], Thelma E Colanzi[1,3], Arilo C Dias-Neto[4], Matheus HE Paixão[5], Jerffeson T de Souza[5] and Silvia R Vergilio[1]

* Correspondence: wesleyk@inf.ufpr.br
[1]Federal University of Paraná (UFPR), DInf, CP: 19081, CEP: 81531-980 Curitiba-PR, Brazil
Full list of author information is available at the end of the article

Abstract

Research communities evolve over time, changing their interests for specific problems or research areas. Mapping the evolution of a research community, including the most frequently addressed problems, the strategies selected to propose solution for them, the venues on which results observed from applying these strategies are published, and the collaboration among distinct groups may provide lessons on actions that can positively influence the growth of research in a given field. To this end, this paper presents an analysis of the Brazilian SBSE research community. We present our major research groups focusing on the field, the software engineering problems most addressed by them, the search techniques most frequently used to solve these problems, and an analysis of our publications and collaboration. We could conclude that the Brazilian community is still expanding, both geographically and in terms of publications, and that the creation of a national workshop focusing on the research field was a keystone to allow this growth.

Keywords: Mapping studies; Bibliometrics analysis; Brazilian SBSE community

Introduction

In the technical literature, we find studies that report an increasing number of works and diversity of addressed Software Engineering (SE) areas in the Search Based Software Engineering (SBSE) field (Harman et al. 2009). By analyzing the SEBASE[a] repository, we observe, as it happens with many other research fields, that the first SBSE works were published in European and North-American conferences: 166 out of 184 conference papers published up to 2005 were reported on European and North-American venues. Research was expanded to Asia and Oceania on the second part of the last decade and 62 out of 454 papers published up to 2009 were reported on conferences held on these places. More recently, a strong participation of South America has been perceived, essentially concentrated on Brazil; only one conference paper was published in a venue in Argentina and we did not identify other South American country in which SBSE papers were published.

A quick scan on SEBASE shows that 6% of its publications (of 1,093 papers as for the date) are accredited to Brazilian authors. This expressive number is mainly due to the organization, in the last three years, of an event in the area: the Brazilian Workshop on Search Based Software Engineering (WESB). Since then (2010), an increase in the number of SBSE papers published by Brazilian authors can be perceived (Freitas and Souza 2011; Colanzi et al. 2012) and the SBSE field is growing rapidly in Brazil.

On the other hand, Brazil has gained international attention due to hosting large scale events, such as 2016 Olympic Games and FIFA World Cup 2014, and has attracted investments from different sources. This aroused interest in Brazilian research. This growing interest and the increasing number of Brazilian works in the SBSE field serve as motivation to this paper, which presents the SBSE Brazilian community and maps its production. This mapping aims to answer two main research questions.

- **RQ1:** What are the research groups working with SBSE in Brazil? This question allows the identification of existing groups: institutions and regions of the country; addressed SE areas; search-based techniques used; and number of researchers;
- **RQ2:** How is the production of the Brazilian community? This question allows acquiring knowledge about the field in Brazil. Collected data are analyzed considering the same categories used in a former bibliometrics analysis of the SBSE field (Liu et al. 2012): publication, sources, authorship and collaboration.

The main contributions of the research and analysis conducted and reported in this paper are presenting the Brazilian researchers and groups working on SBSE and providing an overview of the works produced by them. Furthermore, secondary contributions of this work include: 1) discussing some trends and challenges to this community; 2) contributing to consolidate the area in Brazil; and 3) allowing greater cooperation among its members and international researchers.

The paper is organized in sections. The next section encompasses related work, the methodology adopted to conduct the systematic mapping, as well as the mapping results. The section named Conclusions contains our final remarks.

Review

The systematic mapping is reported in this section. First, we present related work. After, we describe the methodology adopted in our study, including how data were collected and the categories used in the analysis. Finally, the collected data are analyzed to answer, respectively, the research questions RQ1 and RQ2.

Background

The field of SBSE is devoted to the application of search based algorithms to support different Software Engineering activities. In the last years, we observe a growing number of works in this field, reporting the use of such algorithms for software bug fixing (Emer et al. 2002), project management (Barreto et al. 2008; Braz and Vergilio 2004), process composition (Magdaleno 2010), refactoring, software slicing and comprehension (Harman 2007b), cloud engineering (Harman et al. 2012b), software repair (Goues et al. 2013), reverse engineering (Harman et al. 2013), and so on. Some of the former areas already have surveys and systematic reviews consolidating the works performed by researchers in their subfield, among them software testing (Afzal et al. 2009; Yoo and Harman 2012), software design (Räihä 2010) and software requirements (Zhang et al. 2008; Pitangueira et al. 2013).

Considering this interest, a great number of SBSE surveys have been published as bibliometrics analysis, mapping studies, or systematic literature reviews. For instance, in (Freitas and Souza 2011), the authors describe the first bibliometrics analysis to SBSE publications. A bibliometrics analysis is a quantitative analysis that describes patterns of publications within a given field or body of literature. This study covered 677 publications of the SBSE community from 2001 through 2010. They focused in four categories: Publication, Sources, Authorship, and Collaboration. Additionally, estimates for the next years of several publication metrics are given. The study also analyzed the applicability of bibliometrics laws in SBSE.

In (Colanzi et al. 2012), the authors present results of a mapping they had performed in order to provide an overview of the SBSE field in Brazil. The main goal is to map the Brazilian SBSE community by identifying the most active researchers, focus of published works, venue, and frequency of publications. It used the Brazilian Symposium on Software Engineering as a basis to identify works relating optimization and software engineering. Having a broader scope, the analyses presented in the present paper are based on a repository maintained by the international community, in which prediction and clustering works are also included (besides works on optimization). Due to this, different results are obtained when compared to (Colanzi et al. 2012), mainly considering authors and publications, now evaluated by using bibliometrics analysis. Thus, a major contribution of the present work, which was not presented previously, is the identification of the research groups and the collaboration links among them. New authors and groups were also identified, which is very important to expand and consolidate the Brazilian SBSE community.

Systematic Literature Reviews have also been performed in the context of SBSE. A Systematic Literature Review (SLR) is *a means of evaluating and interpreting all available research relevant to a particular research question, topic area or phenomenon of interest* (Dybå et al. 2005). For instance, in (Afzal et al. 2009), the authors present a systematic review that examined existing work into non-functional search-based software testing (NFSBST). They analyzed types of non-functional testing targeted using search techniques, different fitness functions used in distinct types of NFSBST, and challenges in the application of these techniques. The systematic review was based on a set of 35 papers published from 1996 to 2007. The results showed that search techniques have been applied for non-functional testing of several aspects, including execution time, quality of service, security, usability, and safety. A large number of search techniques were found to be applicable to those problems, including simulated annealing, *tabu* search, Genetic Algorithms (GAs), Ant Colony Optimization (ACO), grammatical evolution, Genetic Programming (GP) (and its variants), and swarm intelligence methods. The review reported on different fitness functions used to guide the search for each of the identified aspects.

(Ali et al. 2010) describe the results of a SLR that aimed at characterizing how empirical studies have been designed to investigate search-based software testing (SBST) cost-effectiveness and what empirical evidence is available in the literature regarding SBST cost-effectiveness and scalability. The authors also provided a framework that drives the data collection process and can be the starting point for guidelines on how SBST techniques can be empirically assessed. According to the authors, the intent would be aiding future researchers doing empirical studies in SBST by providing an unbiased view of the body of empirical evidence and by guiding them in performing well-designed and executed empirical studies.

Finally, (Harman 2007a) describes a survey that analyzed a set of works on the application of optimization techniques in software engineering. The paper briefly reviews widely used optimization techniques and the key ingredients required for their successful application to software engineering, providing an overview of existing results in eight software engineering application domains. The paper also describes the benefits that are likely to accrue from the growing body of work in this area and provides a set of open problems, challenges and areas for future work.

Methodology

The main goal of a mapping study is to provide an overview of a research area, identifying the quantity and type of research and results available within it (Petersen et al. 2008). In our case, the goal is to provide an overview of the SBSE area in Brazil. To this end, seven researchers were involved in performing the mapping steps, according to the strategy delineated by (Petersen et al. 2008), in order to answer the research questions presented on Introduction. Next, we describe how these steps were conducted.

Conducting search and screening of works

The search for relevant publications was conducted by using the SBSE Repository SEBASE. This choice is due to two main reasons. The first one is that academic databases, such as IEEEXplorer and ACM Digital Library, may not include all the works from a specific field. The second one is that the chosen repository is considered a comprehensive base in the SBSE field and has been used as a reference by a similar work (Freitas and Souza 2011). It contains publications covering different sources and is frequently updated. However, we think those academic databases are very important, and to avoid significant omissions in our collected data, we conducted a verification step. Such steps and other ones included in our methodology are as follows.

In a first step, we asked the researcher responsible for maintaining and updating the SEBASE repository for a list of papers published by Brazilians. Then, the list was checked, considering a single inclusion criterion: at least one author is a Brazilian researcher. We define a Brazilian researcher as someone who works or studies in a Brazilian research institute, typically a state-held university or a research laboratory for a public or private company. This definition rules out research performed by Brazilians working for companies and universities which reside outside the Brazilian territory, except if those researchers have, in some point, returned to their home country and participated in local research to the extent required to be author in at least one paper. At the end of this step, a list of authors was generated. After this, we conducted a verification step to increase the level of confidence in the collected data. We searched in the DBLP site[b] by other works from each author present in the generated list. In such step new authors were found and also searched.

As a result of all steps conducted and mentioned above, 73 works were obtained. It is important to notice that the search included only papers published before 6th February 2013.

Classification schema, data extraction and mapping

According to our research questions, two analyses were conducted considering a classification schema with different categories. On regard of the first research question, the following categories were considered:

- Research groups: we identify the main institutions appearing in the selected papers and the regularity of publications. From this, we identify the main research groups;
- Software engineering areas: this aspect reports the main interest areas of the identified groups. The areas were identified using the ACM Computing Classification System[c]. Areas containing one or two papers were grouped in the category named Other subjects;
- Search-based techniques: this dimension shows what are the preferences and expertise of each group, and what are the most commonly used search-based techniques in each area. We consider categories such as classical and metaheuristic. We also decided to classify the metaheuristics according to the kind of evolutionary algorithm used and the number of objectives. In this analysis the surveys were excluded, as well as some other papers that do not clearly mention the applied algorithm.

On regard of the second research question, the analysis was based on the same categories adopted in the bibliometrics analysis described in (Freitas and Souza 2011):

- Publications: this aspect reports on the number of publications produced by Brazilian researchers working on the SBSE field;
- Sources: this aspect is related to the venue in which our selected papers were published, including conference proceedings, academic journals, books, and technical reports;
- Authorship: this is related to the number of Brazilian researchers entering or leaving the SBSE field;
- Collaboration: here we address the level of collaboration within the community, measured as the number of papers with more than one author, even from the same institution.

According to this classification schema, the following information was extracted for each paper and copied to a worksheet for further analysis: authors; institutions; publication year and venue; city/state; SE area; search-based technique used, and number of citations at Google Scholar[d]. After this, the data were analyzed on regard of different views to answer the research questions. These views are presented in the next section.

SBSE Brazilian community

This section contains an analysis of the obtained information in order to answer RQ1 (Introduction). First we analyze the main areas and techniques addressed by the Brazilian community and after this we identify the main research groups, as well as their expertise and interests.

Software engineering areas

Brazilian SBSE papers were grouped by SE area according to our classification schema (Classification schema, Data Extraction and Mapping). The selected areas are: Testing, Management, Requirements, Software Design, and Other Subjects. Five surveys about SBSE were published by Brazilian researchers, but these surveys were not included in our analysis on regard of the SE area.

Software testing is the area that receives most attention from researchers: 47% of all works are dedicated to testing. This also happens in the international scenario (Harman et al. 2009). Most works address test data generation. Other works focus on test case prioritization and selection, integration testing, selection of testing strategies, test case allocation and test case selection and evaluation.

Testing is followed by Management (18%) and Requirements (11%). Management is an area in which search-based approaches were applied to optimize both the software development process and the product. Works address different tasks related to project planning, including scheduling, task and resource allocation. Other works are related to selection of project portfolios and software technologies.

Among the works on Requirements, the Next Release Problem has been addressed by Brazilian researchers. The goal is to find an ideal set of requirements for a software release considering different objectives, such as customer's requests, resource constraints, and requirement characteristics. Most recently, requirements prioritization has also been addressed (in 2011 and 2012).

Since 2010 works involving other SE areas have appeared in the Brazilian scenario. However, we can also observe that the interest in Testing, Management and Requirements has not decreased. Therefore, this change only indicates that new application SE areas are emerging. 8% of the papers are about Software Design. In 2010 the first paper on this area was published addressing web services composition. From 2012 other works have addressed architecture refactoring and software module clustering. Other subjects, such as refactoring, software reliability prediction, component search, component clustering, database management and SBSE evaluation, have also been addressed recently. They represent 10% of all selected papers.

Search-based techniques

In this section, the SBSE papers are analyzed to determine the preferred search-based algorithms used by Brazilian researchers. Evolutionary techniques are preferred: Multi-Objective Evolutionary Algorithms (MOEAs), Genetic Algorithms (GA) and Genetic Programming (GP) represent 31%, 22% and 11%, respectively. NSGA-II is the most used MOEA, but SPEA2 and MOCell are also frequently used. Besides evolutionary techniques, 22% of the studies have employed other metaheuristics, including Simulated Annealing, Hill Climbing and GRASP. Furthermore, 4 papers (4%) used Ant Colony Optimization (ACO) and 4 papers employed Pareto ACO (PACO) (4%). Classical techniques are applied by 5% of the papers: in this category Greedy and Branch-and-Bound are the most used.

Figure 1 presents the number of SBSE papers that use some kind of optimization algorithm per SE area. MOEAs were applied in papers of all SE areas. Considering all papers, all kinds of optimization algorithms were used to solve problems related to Testing. In this case, other metaheuristics and MOEAs were the most used. For

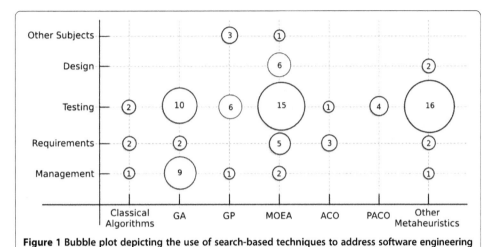

Figure 1 Bubble plot depicting the use of search-based techniques to address software engineering problems as reported by Brazilian SBSE papers.

Management, the most applied algorithm was GA. For Requirements, multi-objective algorithms are generally applied; ACO, GA, Simulated Annealing and GRASP were also applied. Finally, for Design, MOEAs were the most used.

Research groups

To map the research groups working with SBSE in Brazil, we first identified the institution of each author appearing in the selected papers. For each institution, we counted the number of published papers, as well as the frequency and regularity of publications. The result is depicted in Figure 2. This figure presents the institutions, number and percentage of papers published, as well as the year of the first publication. Papers

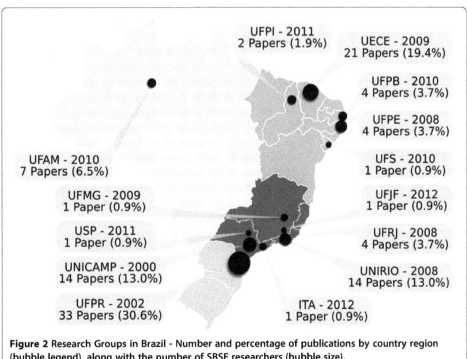

Figure 2 Research Groups in Brazil - Number and percentage of publications by country region (bubble legend), along with the number of SBSE researchers (bubble size).

having more than one author from different groups were counted for all groups. The size of the circles represents the number of authors.

We can observe that the greatest number of authors is in UFPR (in Curitiba/Paraná, with 25 authors) and in UECE (in Fortaleza/Ceará, with 16 authors), the same universities that have the greatest number of publications. In addition, UNICAMP has nine authors, UFPE seven, UNIRIO and UFRJ six, followed by UFAM, UFPB and UFPI with four. ITA and UFMG have three researchers, UFS two, UFJF and USP only one. The first paper was published by the group from UNICAMP at 2000. Three institutions (out 14) published the first paper at 2010, when the first edition of WESB was promoted; they were followed by two institutions in 2011 and two 2012. Six institutions have published only one or two papers. In our analysis characterizing the research groups such institutions were not included, since we consider that they do not have a consolidate group with clear interests in SBSE. Hence, they do not appear in Figure 3 which contains information about the SE areas and techniques addressed per research groups.

Taking into account the SE area, the groups of UECE, UFPR and UNIRIO have publications in almost all areas. For UECE we observe a great interest for Requirements, followed by Testing. Testing is also the most addressed area at UFPR, UNICAMP, and UFAM. UFPR also has interest in other areas, such as Software Design and Management. The major interests of UNIRIO are Management and Software Design. Management is also addressed by UFPB and UFRJ. UFPE has publications only in Management.

Regarding the search-based techniques, we observe that MOEAs are the preferred technique used by UECE and UFPR. ACO is employed only by UECE. UFPR, as well as UNICAMP, also have several publications using Other Metaheuristics. The multi-objective algorithm PACO was only used by UFPR. This institution also has an expressive number of GP-based works. The research group at UNIRIO has concentrated its efforts on GA. UNICAMP, UFPB and UFPE have preference for GA. UFAM also prefers GA, besides Classical Algorithms. Finally, UFRJ published papers only with Classical Algorithms.

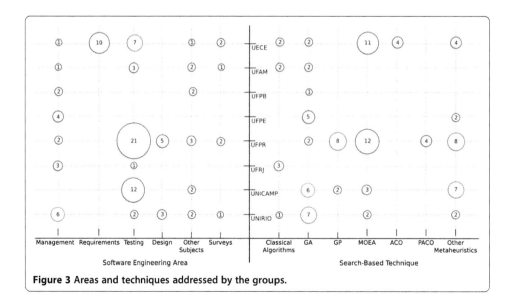

Figure 3 Areas and techniques addressed by the groups.

Production analysis

This section presents a quantitative analysis considering the production of the Brazilian community, using the categories from bibliometrics analysis (Liu et al. 2012), in order to answer RQ2 (Introduction).

Publications

Clearly, the most significant piece of information to characterize the development of SBSE in Brazil relates to the number of SBSE papers published by the community. Table 1 shows exactly the number of SBSE papers published by the Brazilian community, from 2000 to 2012, on a year-on-year basis. Also, it presents the cumulative amount by each year, the contribution of a particular year on the total amount and the growth compared to the previous year.

As can be seen in Table 1, in total, SBSE Brazilian researchers have published, up to 2012, 98 works, which represent 6.67% of all papers reported in the SEBASE repository. That overall result places Brazil as the fourth country with more SBSE papers, behind UK (25%), USA (16%) and Canada (8%). Table 1 shows there was a significant acceleration on the amount of publications in 2010, with more than 70% of the papers being published from 2010 to 2012. That behavior can be at least partially attributed to WESB, which started in 2010 and accounted for 9 papers in that year. However, the other 14 works published in 2010, which represents almost all papers published up to 2008, show this significant growth reached beyond this important national event.

When one considers the languages used in these papers, the analysis showed that 80.62% works were published in English, which accounts for 79 out of the 98 papers. The other 19 papers (19.38%) were published in Portuguese. Those results show that SBSE research in Brazil happens both at national (papers published in the local workshop) and international (papers published in conferences and journals abroad) levels. The local workshop works as leverage for papers in early development stages, engaging

Table 1 Number of works in each year between 2000 and 2012, including cumulative amount

Year	Quantity	%	Growth	Cumulative	%	Growth
2000	1	1.02%	-	1	1.02%	-
2001	1	1.02%	0%	2	2.04%	100.00%
2002	2	2.04%	100.00%	4	4.08%	100.00%
2003	2	2.04%	0%	6	6.12%	50.00%
2004	3	3.06%	50.00%	9	9.18%	50.00%
2005	2	2.04%	−33.33%	11	11.22%	22.22%
2006	2	2.04%	0%	13	13.26%	18.18%
2007	3	3.06%	50%	16	16.32%	23.07%
2008	6	6.12%	100.00%	22	22.45%	37.50%
2009	4	4.08%	−33.33%	26	26.53%	18.18%
2010	23	23.47%	475%	49	50.0%	88.46%
2011	27	27.56%	17.39%	76	77.55%	55.10%
2012	22	22.45%	−18.51%	98	100.00%	28.94%
2000-2012	98	100.00%		98	100.00%	

researchers in discussions with their partners and providing feedback that will ultimately help the paper to reach for larger venues.

Table 2 presents the ranking with the 15 most cited publications, based on Google Scholar. Not surprisingly, 7 out of the 15 most cited papers relate to testing, which is consistent with the ratio of papers published by area. However, the most cited paper tackled a management problem (team allocation). In general, as expected, the overall impact of the papers is still narrow, since the huge majority of the published papers have less than three years.

Source

When considering the venue where those SBSE works have been published, the analysis showed that around 75% (74 papers) of the publications were published in conference proceedings, with 20 articles (20.04%) in journals, 2 posters (2.04%), 1 (1.02%) book chapter and 1 (1.94%) technical report. This result, when compared with the behavior of the overall SBSE world community (Freitas and Souza 2011), which published around 70% of their works in conference proceedings and 20% in journals, shows a local preference to conferences, which, once again, can be attributed to the presence

Table 2 The 15 most cited SBSE works, ordered by Google Scholar

Ref.	Work	SE Area	GS
(Barreto et al. 2008)	Staffing a Software Project: a Constraint Satisfaction and Optimization-based Approach	Management	72
(Bueno and Jino 2002)	Automatic Test Data Generation for Program Paths using Genetic Algorithms	Testing	49
(Oliveira et al. 2010)	GA-based Method for Feature Selection and Parameters Optimization for Machine Learning Regression applied to Software Effort Estimation	Management	47
(Bueno and Jino 2000)	Identification of Potentially Infeasible Program Paths by Monitoring the Search for Test Data	Testing	39
(Costa et al. 2005)	Modeling Software Reliability Growth with Genetic Programming	Testing	36
(Harman et al. 2012a)	Search Based Software Engineering: Techniques, Taxonomy, Tutorial	Survey	32
(Braz and Vergilio 2004)	Using Fuzzy Theory for Effort Estimation of Object-Oriented Software	Management	28
(Costa et al. 2007)	Exploring Genetic Programming and Boosting Techniques to Model Software	Testing	26
(Braga et al. 2008)	A GA-Based Feature Selection and Parameters Optimization for Support Vector Regression Applied to Software Effort Estimation	Management	24
(Costa et al. 2010)	A Genetic Programming Approach for Software Reliability Modeling	Other Subjects	20
(de Carvalho et al. 2010)	A Symbolic Fault-Prediction Model Based on Multiobjective Particle Swarm Optimization	Testing	20
(Emer and Vergilio 2003)	Selection and Evaluation of Test Data Based on Genetic Programming	Testing	18
(Souza et al. 2010)	The Human Competitiveness of Search Based Software Engineering	Other Subjects	18
(Bueno et al. 2007)	Improving Random Test Sets using the Diversity Oriented Test Data Generation	Testing	16
(Freitas and Souza 2011)	Ten Years of Search Based Software Engineering: A Bibliometric Analysis	Survey	16

and value Brazilian SBSE researchers give to WESB, which published almost 25% of all SBSE Brazilian works (Table 3). In addition to this conference, Brazilian researchers have shown a relevant presence in the International Symposium on Search-Based Software Engineering (SSBSE), publishing 14 papers in total. The other four conferences with most works can be seen in Table 3.

In terms of journal venues, SBSE Brazilian publications have been significantly spread with 3 journals publishing 2 articles, and 14 journals publishing a single paper.

Authorship

In Table 4, it is presented statistics concerning the Brazilian SBSE publishing authors. It shows, in different columns, the number of "New" authors publishing for the first time in each year, the percentage participation and growth of these new authors, the number of "Active" authors per year and the numerical relation between new and active authors.

Taking into account the 98 analyzed papers, there are 90 Brazilian authors. The number of authors joining the Brazilian SBSE community increased significantly in 2010, with a growth of 200% compared to 2009. In that year, 21 out of the 41 publishing authors were new. Even with a decrease of authors since then, the national SBSE community had 41 active authors in 2012. Since there is no data available on the number of SBSE active authors in the world in 2012, we can compare the number from 2010 (Freitas and Souza 2011). In that year, there were 168 SBSE active authors overall, which indicates that the Brazilian community contributed with 21.4% of all publishing authors in 2010, representing the 36 active Brazilian authors in that year.

When considering authors individually, as can be seen in Table 5, 38 of those authors published only one paper and 25 of them published two, with only five authors publishing more than 10 papers. This scenario may help to confirm we have a community growing in the last 3 years, as presented in Table 4.

Table 6 shows the Brazilian researchers with more works published, including conference and journal articles, up to 2012. It also presents the number of citations at Google Scholar (taking into account only the papers selected for our mapping study), percentage of participation in relation to all Brazilian SBSE publications, the amount and position of each author concerning only publications in conference proceeding and journal articles. The table shows that the two most prolific authors account for almost half of all publications (36 out of the 73).

Collaboration

In regard of collaboration, which accounts for papers with more than one author, even if those authors are from the same institution, Table 7 shows statistics about the

Table 3 Ranking of conferences proceedings with the most number of SBSE publications

Conference proceeding	#	%
Brazilian Workshop on Search-Based Software Engineering (WESB)	24	24.48%
International Symposium on Search-Based Software Engineering (SSBSE)	14	14.28%
Annual Conference on Genetic and Evolutionary Computation (GECCO)	6	6.12%
International Conference on Tools with Artificial Intelligence (ICTAI)	4	4.08%
Brazilian Symposium on Software Engineering (SBES)	3	3.06%
International Workshop on Search-Based Software Testing (SBST)	3	3.06%

Table 4 Statistics for new and active authors per year (2000-2012)

Year	New	%	Growth	Active	Growth	New/active
2000	2	2.22%	-	2	-	1.00
2001	0	0%	−100.0%	2	0%	0
2002	2	2.22%	-	4	100.0%	0.50
2003	3	3.34%	50.0%	5	25.0%	0.60
2004	3	3.34%	0%	4	−20.0%	0.75
2005	1	1.11%	66.67%	5	25.0%	0.20
2006	0	0%	−100.0%	3	−40.0%	0
2007	3	3.34%%	-	9	200.0%	0.33
2008	14	15.56%	366.67%	18	55.55%	0.77
2009	7	7.77%	−50.0%	14	7.70%	0.50
2010	21	23.33%	200.0%	41	192.85%	0.51
2011	15	16.66%	−28.57%	36	−12.19%	0.41
2012	19	21.11%	26.66%	41	13.88%	0.46
2000-2012	90	100.00%	-	-	-	-

number of authors per paper. Papers with 2 authors represent 29.59% of all published papers. Only 6 works (6.12%) had a single author. Around 35% of the papers had four or more authors, which shows a significant collaborative level. When compared to the collaborative results presented in (Freitas and Souza 2011), where, considering all SBSE publications from 2001 to 2010, only 21.14% of paper had more than 4 authors and more than 13% had only one. Those results confirm a higher collaborative attitude by the SBSE Brazilian community.

Conclusions

The Brazilian SBSE community had been recognized in the last few years as one of the most active in the world. Brazilian researchers have published search-based papers for many Software Engineering areas from 2000 to 2012, including software testing (54 papers), project management (14), requirements (14), and software design (8). They have also used a wide range of search algorithms on their approaches, including multi-objective evolutionary algorithms (26 papers), genetic algorithms (25), genetic programming (10), and ant colony optimization (8). Both in quantitative as well as qualitative terms, this research community has shown a recent and significant growth which qualifies it as an interesting case to be presented and reflected upon. We have identified 98 papers published in the field by 90 different authors from 2000 to 2012, summing up to more than 700 citations on Google Scholar. The number of publications (as well as collaboration between authors and the number of researchers engaging the field) has shown a strong increase since 2010 and more than 70% of the papers were published from this year on. In that sense, this paper discussed this community, by presenting the SBSE Brazilian researchers and groups and providing an overview of the works being produced by them.

Table 5 Number of authors that published each amount of works

Works	1	2	3	4	5	6	7	8	13	21	32
Authors	38	25	5	7	4	2	2	2	2	2	1

Table 6 The ranking of SBSE authors with more than 5 publications in 2000-2012

Rank	Author		Works	%	Citations (rank)	Conference Proc. (rank)	Journal articles (rank)
	Name	Affiliation					
1	Silvia Vergilio	UFPR	32	32.65%	272 (1)	21 (1)	10 (1)
2	Aurora Pozo	UFPR	21	21.42%	181 (2)	11 (3)	9 (2)
2	Jerffeson Souza	UECE	21	21.42%	120 (4)	18 (2)	3 (3)
3	Fabricio Freitas	UECE	13	13.26%	66 (7)	11 (3)	2 (4)
3	Marcio Barros	UNIRIO	13	13.26%	86 (6)	10 (4)	1 (5)
4	Camila Maia	UECE	8	8.16%	52 (8)	7 (5)	1 (5)
4	Thelma Colanzi	UFPR	8	8.16%	26 (10)	7 (5)	1 (5)
5	Arilo Dias-Neto	UFAM	7	7.14%	6 (11)	6 (6)	0 (6)
5	Mario Jino	UNICAMP	7	7.14%	122 (3)	5 (7)	2 (4)
6	Paulo Bueno	UNICAMP	6	6.12%	116 (5)	4 (8)	2 (4)
6	Rafael Carmo	UECE	6	6.12%	45 (9)	5 (7)	1 (5)

This work served to highlight interesting aspects of the community, including the importance of the Brazilian Workshop on Search Based Software Engineering (WESB), which started in 2010 and helped significantly in the increase and consolidation of the Brazilian SBSE community. Other than that, the mapping showed a significant spread in the active SBSE groups in geographical terms, which gives a perspective of an even more dissemination in the future.

This paper may serve as motivation to other national or institutional research groups present their contributions to the SBSE field, which may help the international SBSE community to understand itself and use this knowledge to drive its own evolution. As the Brazilian SBSE community prepares to organize SSBSE in 2014, this work may serve both as a presentation as well as an invitation to this important event, which it is expected to strengthen and consolidate SBSE research in Brazil.

The behavior of Brazilian researchers in the last few year resembles that presented by the international research community in the early-years of the SBSE field: the first studies concentrated almost entirely in the application of heuristic search to software testing; later, some authors moved to address software requirements, design, and project management. While researchers from abroad are exploring these late areas intensively since 2001, each one of them representing about 10% of the world-wide published papers on SBSE from 2001 on, the domestic community caught up around 2008/2009. Comparing samples of very different sizes is always dangerous, but we observe that recent works produced by the Brazilian community tend to be more diverse in application areas than those produced by the international community as a whole. For instance, research in SBSE testing accounts for only 49% of the papers published by Brazilians since 2008, while they represent 61% of the papers published by the international community. Project management has also received more attention of the

Table 7 Authorship pattern in the period 2000-2012

Authors	1	2	3	4	5+
# Works	6	29	28	25	10
%	6.12%	29.59%	28.57%	25.52%	10.20%

Brazilian community (24% of the papers since 2008), while design and requirements receive about the same attention as in the international community.

Regarding the future of the SBSE research and practice in Brazil, we identify some 'hot' trends by analyzing the papers published recently, including high-level design optimization, selection of refactoring strategies, evaluation of SBSE experimental studies, application of SBSE approaches to industrial cases, and using recent heuristic optimization approaches (such as Ant Colony Optimization) to address classic problems (such as the next release problem) in more complex cases. Thus far, no area has shown signs of losing interest from researchers, both in the international and the domestic communities, though research in software testing continues to be the leading trend. The trends discussed above may drive the next steps in research, which may include more interaction with local industry, more collaboration with international partners, a deeper understanding of certain classic problems (such as software module clustering and the next release problem), and customizing problems and their solutions to specificities of the Brazilian industry.

Endnotes

[a]SEBASE SBSE Repository, http://crestweb.cs.ucl.ac.uk/resources/sbse_repository/.

[b]www.informatik.uni-trier.de/~ley/db/. It includes most relevant computer science conferences and journals, published by IEEE, ACM and LNCS, besides important book series.

[c]www.computer.org/portal/web/publications/acmsoftware

[d]The worksheet containing the list of the selected papers and their classification is available at: http://www.inf.ufpr.br/gres/apoio_en.html

Abbreviations
ACO: Ant colony optimization; GA: Genetic algorithm; GP: Genetic programming; GRASP: General responsibility assignment software patterns; MOCell: Mathematical olympiad cell; MOEA: Multi-objective evolutionary algorithm; NFSBST: Non-functional search-based software testing; NSGA-II: Non-dominated sorting genetic algorithm-II; PACO: Pareto ACO; SBSE: Search based software engineering; SBST: Search based software testing; SE: Software engineering; SLR: Systematic literature review; SPEA2: Strength pareto evolutionary algorithm 2; WESB: Brazilian workshop on search based software engineering.

Competing interests
The authors declare that they have no competing interests.

Authors' contributions
All authors carried the bibliometrics analysis, collected, and analyzed the papers. WKGA analyzed the data (publications) per research group, generating the Brazil's map with all identified groups. MOB and ACDN searched for works related to this research to contextualize the contribution. TEC and SRV analyzed publications per software engineering area and search based techniques. MHEP and JTS analyzed publications per year and collaborations among researchers identified in our mapping study. At the end, all authors read and approved the final manuscript.

Author's information
WKGA: is an assistant professor at Federal Technological University of Paraná (UTFPR). He is currently a PhD candidate at the Postgraduate Program in Informatics (PPGInf) of Federal University of Paraná (UFPR). He also holds the MSc degree from PPGInf of UFPR. His main research interests are: model based software reuse, software testing, search-based software engineering, multi-objective optimization and bio-inspired computation.
MOB: is an associate professor at the Applied Informatics Department of the Federal University of Rio de Janeiro State (UNIRIO). He holds a Doctor degree in System Engineering and Computer Science from COOPE/UFRJ. His research concentrates on using optimization and simulation to describe and find (close to) optimal solutions to software engineering problems and bring forth insight about these problems. His main research interests within Software Engineering are software design and project management.
TEC: is an assistant professor at State University of Maringá. She is currently a PhD candidate at the Postgraduate Program in Informatics of Federal University of Paraná (UFPR). She holds the MSc degree in Computer Science and Computational Math from University of São Paulo (USP/São Carlos), Brazil. Her areas of interest are: software architecture, software product lines, search-based software engineering and multi-objective evolutionary algorithms.

ACDN: is an associate professor at Institute of Computing at the Federal University of Amazonas. He holds a Doctor degree in Systems Engineering and Computer Science from COPPE/UFRJ. He leads the Experimentation and Testing on Software Engineering Group (ExperTS) at the Federal University of Amazonas. Additional information can be found at http://www.icomp.ufam.edu.br/arilo.

MHEP: is currently a MSc student at the Postgraduate Program in Computer Science of the State University of Ceará (UECE). His current research focuses on the application of robust optimization to requirements engineering. His areas of interest are: software requirements, search based requirements engineering and evolutionary algorithms.

JTS: is a professor and the dean of graduate studies and research at State University of Ceará (UECE), Brazil. He holds a Ph.D. in Computer Science from the School of Information Technology and Engineering (SITE) of University of Ottawa, Canada. His main research interests are: search-based software engineering, multi-objective evolutionary algorithms, machine learning and software patterns.

SRV: received the MS (1991) and DS (1997) degrees from University of Campinas, UNICAMP, Brazil. She is currently at the Computer Science Department at the Federal University of Paraná, Brazil, where she has been a faculty member since 1993. She has been involved in several projects and her research interests are in the area of Software Engineering, such as: software testing, search based software engineering and software metrics.

Acknowledgements
We should like to thank CNPq, FAPERJ, FAPEAM and INCT-SEC for their financial support.

Author details
[1]Federal University of Paraná (UFPR), DInf, CP: 19081, CEP: 81531-980 Curitiba-PR, Brazil. [2]Applied Informatics Department, Federal University of Rio de Janeiro State, CEP: 22240-090 Rio de Janeiro-RJ, Brazil. [3]Informatics Department (DIN), State University of Maringá (UEM), CEP: 87020-900 Maringá-PR, Brazil. [4]Institute of Computing, Federal University of Amazonas, CEP: 69077-000 Manaus-AM, Brazil. [5]Optimization in Software Engineering Group (GOES.UECE), State University of Ceará, Fortaleza, Ceará, Brazil.

References
Afzal W, Torkar R, Feldt R (2009) A systematic review of search-based testing for non-functional system properties. Inf Softw Technol 51(6):957–976

Ali S, Briand LC, Hemmati H, Panesar-Walawege RK (2010) A systematic review of the application and empirical investigation of search-based test case generation. IEEE Trans Softw Eng 36(6):742–762

Barreto A, Barros M, Werner CML (2008) Staffing a software project: a constraint satisfaction and optimization-based approach. Comput Oper Res 35(10):3073–3089

Braga PL, Oliveira ALI, Meira SRL (2008) A GA-based feature selection and parameters optimization for support vector regression applied to software effort estimation. In: Proceedings of the ACM Symposium on Applied Computing (SAC '08). Butterworth-Heinemann, New York, USA, pp 1788–1792

Braz M, Vergilio S (2004) Using fuzzy theory for effort estimation of object-oriented software. In: Proceedings of the 16th IEEE International Conference on Tools with Artificial Intelligence (ICTAI'04). IEEE Computer Society, Washington, USA, pp 196–201

Bueno P, Jino M (2000) Identification of potentially infeasible program paths by monitoring the search for test data. In: Proceedings of the fifteenth IEEE International Conference on Automated Software Engineering (ASE'00). French, Grenoble, pp 209–218

Bueno P, Jino M (2002) Automatic test data generation for program paths using genetic algorithms. Int J Softw Eng Knowl Eng 12(06):691–709

Bueno P, Wong W, Jino M (2007) Improving random test sets using the diversity oriented test data generation. In: Proceedings of the 2nd International Workshop on Random Testing (WRT'07). ACM New York, NY, USA, pp 10–17

Colanzi TE, Vergilio SR, Assunção WKG, Pozo A (2012) Search based software engineering: review and analysis of the field in Brazil. In: Journal of Systems and Software. Elsevier Science Inc., New York, NY, USA, pp 1–15

Costa EO, de Souza GA, Pozo ATR, Vergilio SR (2007) Exploring genetic programming and boosting techniques to model software reliability". IEEE Trans Reliab 56(3):422–434

Costa E, Pozo A, Vergilio S (2010) A genetic programming approach for software reliability modeling. IEEE Trans Reliab 59(1):222–230

Costa EO, Vergilio SR, Pozo A, Souza G (2005) Modeling software reliability growth with genetic programming. In: Proceedings of the 16th IEEE International Symposium on Software Reliability Engineering (ISSRE '05). IEEE Computer Society, Washington, DC, USA, pp 171–180

de Carvalho AB, Pozo A, Vergilio SR (2010) A symbolic fault-prediction model based on multiobjective particle swarm optimization. J Syst Softw 83(5):868–882

Dybå T, Kitchenham B, Jorgensen M (2005) Evidence-based software engineering for practitioners. IEEE Softw 22(1):158–165

Emer M, Vergilio S (2003) Selection and evaluation of test data based on genetic programming. Softw Qual J 11(2):167–186

Emer M, Vergilio S, GPTesT (2002) A testing tool based on genetic programming. In: Proceedings of the Genetic and Evolutionary Computation Conference (GECCO'02). San Francisco, CA, USA, pp 1343–1350

Freitas FG, Souza JT (2011) Ten years of search based software engineering: a bibliometric analysis. In: Proceedings of the Third International Conference on Search Based Software Engineering (SSBSE'11). Springer, Berlin Heidelberg, pp 18–32

Goues CL, Forrest S, Weimer W (2013) Current challenges in automatic software repair. Softw Qual J 21(3):421–443

Harman M (2007a) The current state and future of search based software engineering. In: Future of Software Engineering (FOSE '07). IEEE Computer Society, Washington, DC, USA, pp 342–357

Harman M (2007b) Search Based Software Engineering for Program Comprehension. In: ICPC '07. Proceedings of the 15th IEEE International Conference on Program Comprehension. IEEE Computer Society, Washington, DC, USA pp 3–13. doi:10.1109/ICPC.2007.35

Harman M, Lakhotia K, Singer J, Yoo S (2012a) Cloud engineering is search-based software engineering too. J Syst Softw 86(9):2225–2241

Harman M, Langdon WB, Weimer W (2013) Genetic Programming for Reverse Engineering. 20th Working Conference on Reverse Engineering (WCRE'13). Koblenz, Germany

Harman M, Mansouri SA, Zhang Y (2009) Search Based Software Engineering: A Comprehensive Analysis and Review of Trends Techniques and Applications. Tech. Rep. TR-09-03, King's College London

Harman M, McMinn P, Souza JT (2012b) Search Based Software Engineering: Techniques, Taxonomy, Tutorial. Empirical Software Engineering and Verification. Springer, Berlin Heidelberg, pp 1–59

Liu Z, Liu Y, Guo Y, Wang H (2012) Progress in Global Parallel Computing Research: A Bibliometric Approach. Scientometrics, Springer, Netherlands, pp 1–17

Magdaleno A (2010) An optimization-based approach to software development process tailoring. In: Proceedings of the Second International Symposium on Search-based Software Engineering (SSBSE'10). Benevento, Italy, pp 40–43

Oliveira A, Braga P, Lima P, Cornelio M (2010) GA-based method for feature selection and parameters optimization for machine learning regression applied to software effort estimation. Inf Softw Technol 52(11):1155–1166

Petersen K, Feldt R, Mujtaba S, Mattsson M (2008) Systematic Mapping Studies in Software Engineering. 12th International Conference on Evaluation and Assessment in Software Engineering (EASE'08). British Computer Society, UK, pp 1–10

Pitangueira AM, Maciel RSP, Barros MO, Andrade AMS (2013) A systematic review of software requirements selection and prioritization using SBSE approaches. In: Proceedings of the V Symposium on Search-based Software Engineering (SSBSE'13). Springer, Berlin Heidelberg, pp 188–208

Räihä O (2010) A survey on search-based software design. Comput Sci Rev 4:203–249

Souza JT, Maia C, Freitas FG, Coutinho D (2010) The human competitiveness of search based software engineering. In: Proceedings of the Second International Symposium on Search-based Software Engineering (SSBSE'10). Benevento, Italy, pp 143–152

Yoo S, Harman M (2012) Regression testing minimization, selection and prioritization: a survey. Softw Test Verification Reliabil 22:67–120

Zhang Y, Finkelstein A, Harman M (2008) Search-based requirements optimisation: existing work & challenges. In: 4th International Conference on Requirements Engineering: Foundation for Software Quality (RE'2008). Springer, Berlin Heidelberg, pp 88–94

3

From project-oriented to service-oriented software development: an industrial experience guided by a service reference model

Marcos Kalinowski[1*], Stefan Biffl[2], Rodrigo Oliveira Spínola[3] and Sheila Reinehr[4]

* Correspondence:
kalinowski@ice.ufjf.br
[1]Federal University of Juiz de Fora,
Rua José Kelmer s/n, Juiz de Fora
36.036-330, Brazil
Full list of author information is
available at the end of the article

Abstract

Introduction: In organizations with software systems in production, new and often unexpected requirements for development come up due to strategic, tactical, and operational customer needs. In this context, it is a strategic advantage for software suppliers to be able to provide software services that meet these demands faster and with less overhead than negotiating traditional value-neutral project-oriented software deliveries.

Case description: This article reports on the industrial experience of restructuring the supplier-side software development process into a value-based service-oriented format, guided by a service reference model. A service level agreement (SLA) was established between supplier and customer reflecting the business needs and values. The report describes the contractual aspects and internal managerial controls employed to facilitate the compliance of the provided services with the SLA, including the integrated use of a managerial spreadsheet, an issue-tracking system, and a Kanban chart.

Discussion and evaluation: The feasibility and results of restructuring software development into a service-oriented format are evaluated. Major results were that only moderate effort was required, around one person month, due to the support of the service reference model and a sufficient level of previously installed capabilities, and that the goals regarding improved quality, productivity, and customer satisfaction were successfully achieved. Additionally we discuss stakeholder needs, the support from the service reference model, the lessons learned, and the success factors for such restructuring.

Conclusions: Restructuring software development in the format of continuous service delivery, guided by a service reference model, is feasible and for suitable contexts can provide significant benefits concerning quality, productivity, and customer satisfaction.

Keywords: Service reference model; Software development as a service; Software process; Software project management; Software quality

Background

In dynamic organizational environments with software systems in production, it is not always possible to forecast and formalize in a contract the requirements for development that will arise over time (Barney *et al.* 2008). Collecting upcoming requirements in formal projects can incur significant overhead and delay to evolving the software that supports mission-critical business processes and analyses.

Therefore, it is common for customer organizations to seek for Information Technology (IT) suppliers who can provide services to efficiently and quickly handle demands according to their business needs, respecting the varying volumes and priority of these demands (Khan *et al.* 2011). However, from the point of view of the supplier, restructuring the software development process to meet such customer expectations is not always an easy task, in particular, if it is not clear whether the supplier software organization process is sufficiently mature to drive towards a service delivery format (Lehman and Sharma 2011).

Treating a customer demand for software development as a request for an IT service is a promising way for addressing the customer value expectations, in line with the definition of services by ISO/IEC (2011), which defines a service as a "means of delivering value to customers by facilitating outcomes customers want to achieve". In practical terms this means migrating software development from a traditional project management format (PMI 2013) to a continuous service delivery management format (TSO 2011).

IT service management can be defined along the lines of the ITIL (Information Technology Infrastructure Library), a model conceived by the British government with a view to provide a consensus on the best IT service management practices, as "a set of specialized organizational capabilities for providing value to customers in the form of services" (TSO 2011).

In the context of providing IT services, it is important to make an effort to establish efficient service management processes (TSO 2011), preferably based on a reference model that supports the best practices for improving service processes and, consequently, increasing productivity and effectiveness of the services provided.

One of the programs available to meet this type of need is the Brazilian nationwide MPS.BR program (Santos *et al.* 2012). In Brazil about 73% of the software industry is constituted of small and medium-sized enterprises (SMEs) (MCTI 2013). Therefore, an effort was made to developed national reference models for software development and IT service delivery, which are compliant to well-established international standards and reference models, in order to provide their suppliers, including SMEs, with more fine-grained steps to define and achieve an appropriate level of software process maturity. Software regulators in other countries with a high share of SME software suppliers can benefit from the lessons learned in Brazil to better support their small-scale software suppliers.

Thus, the main MPS.BR objective is to develop and disseminate reference models that meet the requirements of the Brazilian software and IT services industries, allowing software suppliers, including SMEs, to deliver to customers according to internationally recognized quality standards (Santos *et al.* 2012). The MPS.BR family of reference models currently consists of the MPS-SW for Software (SOFTEX 2012a) and the MPS-SV for IT Services (SOFTEX 2012b). The MPS-SV reference model is a promising basis for establishing service management processes. Another similar and compatible alternative (SOFTEX 2012b) would be following the guidelines of the international CMMI-SVC (CMMI for Services) reference model (SEI 2010).

While the MPS-SW has been established in 2003 and has been widely adopted in Brazil, with 548 official assessments (over 70% of them in SMEs) published by April 2014 (SOFTEX 2014), the MPS-SV model is still very recent and saw its first evaluation published in September 2012. The MPS-SW has already helped on the adoption of good software engineering practices in the Brazilian industry (Kalinowski *et al.* 2010).

There is also objective evidence of positive impacts on the performance of the software suppliers that adopted this model (Kalinowski *et al.* 2008a) (Travassos and Kalinowski 2013), which could be transferred to other countries with a similar software development structure. The MPS-SV model has a broader application scope than the MPS-SW model, since MPS-SV can be applied to support the structuring and improvement of IT service processes in general. These services might include Help Desk and support services (SOFTEX 2012b) or even software development services, as in the experience reported in this paper.

The MPS-SV was developed in conformance to the international standards ISO/IEC 20000:2011 (ISO/IEC 2011), ISO/IEC 15504 (ISO/IEC 2004), being compatible with the CMMI-SVC model (SEI 2010) (SOFTEX 2012b). Therefore, in the context of this paper the MPS-SV can be seen as a representative for international standards. Similar to the MPS-SW model, the MPS-SV is structured in seven maturity levels for assessment (G to A, where A is the highest maturity level), while the CMMI-SVC reference models is structured in four maturity levels (2 to 5, where 5 is the highest maturity level). The compatibility between the MPS-SV and CMMI-SVC reference models is given by the maturity level mapping shown in Table 1.

Software development as a service (SDaaS) started being discussed recently (Lehman and Sharma 2011) and the thematic of applying service reference models to software development has been informally presented at the SEPG North America 2011 (Penn 2011) and SEPG North America 2013 (Penn 2013). However, to the best of our knowledge, there are no published experience reports available on this topic. Therefore, the lack of published work related to moving from a project-oriented to a service-oriented process, and in particular based on a service reference model, leads to uncertainties concerning feasibility, effects, and success and risk factors (pitfalls). An initial effort to bridge this gap was reported in (Kalinowski and Reinehr 2013), the paper we are herein extending. Given this scenario, we investigate the following two research issues (RIs) to shed light on applying service reference models to re-structure software development from a project-oriented to a service-oriented management format from an industry perspective.

RI-1. Survey on perceived utility of structuring software development guided by service reference models

Do software engineering consulting experts see significant utility in adopting service delivery practices for software development? Would these experts consider using a service reference model as a basis for adopting service delivery practices?

Table 1 MPS-SV and CMMI-SVC maturity level compatibility

MPS-SV maturity levels	CMMI-SVC maturity levels
A – In Optimization	5 – In Optimization
B – Quantitatively Managed	4 – Quantitatively Managed
C – Defined	3 – Defined
D – Largely Defined	
E – Partially Defined	
F – Managed	2 – Managed
G – Partially Managed	

To address this research issue, a survey was conducted in the MPS-SV context with software engineering consultants (19 certified MPS-SW implementation consultants from 11 different MPS.BR accredited implementation institutions), who work with software development suppliers helping them to organize their production processes (Jordão and Kalinowski 2013). The survey was structured following the Technology Acceptance Model (TAM) (Davis 1989) to gather the perception on the utility, ease of adoption and intention to adopt from the point of view of those consultants. In a systematic review concerning the TAM, conducted by Turner *et al.* (2010), a correlation between the intention to adopt, as stated in the studies that used the TAM, and actual adoption could be identified, which reinforced the decision of following this model.

Results indicated that the MPS-SW software engineering consultants consider service reference models useful and that they would consider adopting them for providing continuous delivery capabilities to their software industry customers. A summary of these results, which reinforce the motivation for investigating the following research issue, are compiled in the Discussion and Evaluation Section. Further details on the survey planning, operation and limitations are published in a separate paper (Jordão and Kalinowski 2013).

RI-2. Industry experience report on the feasibility and results on restructuring software development guided by a service reference model

What are typical stakeholder needs that trigger software development restructuring? Can a service reference model be helpful to meet restructuring needs in software development? What effort is to be expected? What are the potential effects on quality and productivity? What are the main lessons learned? What are the involved success and risk factors?

To address this research issue a real experience of restructuring software development guided by a service reference model was conducted, analyzed, and an initial report (in Portuguese) was produced (Kalinowski and Reinehr 2013). Main reported results were: (i) the MPS-SV model was found helpful to guide the restructuring; (ii) restructuring required only modest effort; and (iii) significant benefits were perceived in terms of quality, productivity, and customer satisfaction.

However, this initial report only provided an overview of the restructuring and brief indications on effort and on the produced effects on quality and productivity. Therefore, many questions raised in RI-2, to which answers would provide additional insights into structuring software development as a service, remained unanswered. For instance, stakeholder needs that typically trigger such restructuring and how the MPS-SV can support meeting these needs were not described. Lessons learned were also not discussed in depth to allow further understanding the assumptions for such restructuring and possible improvements. Finally, major success and risk factors were not identified.

This paper extends the initial report (Kalinowski and Reinehr 2013) by providing further details on the context and on how managerial skills for handling service requests were established aiming at complying to a Service Level Agreement (SLA) with the customer to satisfy his business needs. Contractual aspects of the restructuring and internal controls used to ensure compliance with the SLA, are described in details. Those internal controls encompass the integrated use of managerial spreadsheets, issue-tracking systems and Kanban charts (Anderson 2010) to monitor the demand prioritization.

Moreover, further analyses of the experience allowed identifying the stakeholder needs and how the MPS-SV supported meeting them. The discussion on lessons learned was extended and success and risk factors were identified. We assume that these additional details, analyses and extensions can provide further insights into the feasibility of applying service reference models to software development, which are relevant for SME software suppliers in Brazil and in comparable international contexts.

The remainder of this paper is organized as follows. Case description describes the case: context of the experience, including the identification of the stakeholder needs, and how the development process was re-structured. Discussion and evaluation presents the discussion and evaluation, including obtained results, lessons learned, success and risk factors. Conclusions concludes and discusses issues for further research.

Case description

This section describes the experience related to investigating RI-2 by restructuring the software development process guided by a service reference model. Therefore, the context is described and further details on how the development was structured as a service are provided.

Context and stakeholder needs

The experience described herein occurred in the context of the companies Kali Software (KS), as the software supplier, and Tranship Transportes Marítimos (TTM), as the customer.

The supplier, KS, can be characterized as a small-sized Brazilian software supplier (20 employees – including the board of directors) that had worked on custom development for almost a decade, providing services for national and international customers in a range of business areas (e.g., naval industry, health insurances, and financial). Despite of its small size the development followed distributed processes, with the development team and their local management were located in the city of Juiz de Fora (Brazil), and directors and requirement analysts located in the city of Rio de Janeiro (Brazil). The previously adopted development process followed a traditional interactive and incremental development life cycle, where increments were included in plan-driven projects (Boehm and Turner 2003), with each project negotiated as a separate development contract.

The customer, TTM, is a medium-sized Brazilian sea freight company (about 400 employees) that provides strategic services to the country. These services include coastal transport and naval support to oil rigs working at the pre-salt layer of the continental shelf. TTM had several software suppliers and internal IT support. The internal support was provided by an IT manager (responsible for supplier agreement management and conducting acceptance tests) and an IT support analyst (responsible for the installed server infrastructure and help desk support).

The software development partnership between the two companies was established in February 2011. The main developed software in this context concerned an Enterprise Resource Planning (ERP) system, involving several modules, such as administrative, operations, allocation of ship crew members, finance, and human resources, which were gradually put into production. In total, 87 use cases were implemented in an overall effort of more than 4000 hours, resulting in a management system of around

83,000 lines of Java code and 167 data tables. At the time of the herein reported experience, 10 of KS employees (1 director, 1 project manager, 1 requirements analyst, 6 developers and 1 testing analyst) were involved – not all exclusively –with the TTM ERP project.

With the modules entering production, the stakeholder's needs started to change. TTM's directors (executive, operations, financial, and human resources), for instance, began needing information and new functions very quickly according to their immediate strategic, tactical, and operational business goals. The contractual model for new development requests was previously structured as separate projects (characterized according to the definition of the PMI (2013) by having a manageable scope, a beginning and an end), in which a new contract had to be negotiated in order to develop new functions. This contractual approach was not adequate for the new scenario anymore. The main problems of this value-neutral approach (Boehm 2006) were the effort of negotiating new contracts and not considering added business value for prioritizing individual demands. As a consequence, fast deployment of the most important new system capabilities from a business point of view, was not achieved.

Table 2 shows an overview on the different stakeholder interests after the system entered production. The interests mainly conflicted with the negotiation of demands to be included in a value-neutral project context. This negotiation effort and not sufficiently considering added business value of individual development requests hindered delivering optimal business value to the customer.

Therefore, the directors of both companies met to define a new and more flexible contractual model to satisfy the new stakeholder needs. They decided on a contractual framework based on the provision of services, in which demands were treated as separate requests for services with different priorities and the billing would be linked to compliance with a SLA (in traditional project-oriented development, contracts usually include terms for incremental delivery and related penalties). By considering a SLA based on the customer's business needs, this contractual framework helps integrating value considerations into software development, as suggested by the Value-Based Software Engineering (VBSE) discipline (Biffl et al. 2006).

The decision of establishing a provision-of-services contract meant that the supplier had to adopt a strategy for delivering such services with internal controls to facilitate the management of individual requests in order to comply with the SLA. The following subsection describes this strategy.

Table 2 Stakeholder interests conflicting with the value-neutral project approach

Stakeholder	Stakeholder interests
TTM - Directors, managers and operational level employees of the different business areas.	Simple contract negotiation; fast definition and deployment of system capability changes or increments; delivery priority according to current added business value.
TTM - IT Manager & IT support analyst	Fast, predictable, and high quality deliveries.
KS – Directors and Project Manager	Simple contract negotiation; steady inflow of system capability changes or increments; translate technical productivity into higher net gains; visibility of team productivity.
KS – Developer& Quality Assurance	Quick customer feedback.

Restructuring software development as a service

Although an official assessment was not in the plans of the supplier, it was decided that the structuring of software development as a service should follow the guidelines of the reference model MPS-SV maturity level G (SOFTEX 2012b). This decision was taken to ensure that service delivery best practices would be incorporated into the new development process. The MPS-SW has contributed to the adoption of good practices by the Brazilian software industry (Kalinowski *et al.* 2010), and the national experts expect that the MPS-SV can do the same for the IT services sector.

Level G of the MPS-SV reference model (SOFTEX 2012b) contemplates five processes: Work Management, Requirements Management, Service Delivery, Service Level Management, and Incident Management. During the experience described in this paper, the practices of Work Management and Requirements Management, already in place at KS in the software development context, were complemented with practices of the remaining three processes directly related to service management. A brief description of these three processes (Service Delivery, Service Level Management, and Incident Management) follows.

The Service Delivery process aims to use a strategy for service delivery in line with the established service agreements. Service Level Management process aims to ensure that the customer's SLAs are fulfilled. Finally, the purpose of the Incident Management process involves capabilities for managing incidents and service requests (SOFTEX 2012b).

MPS-SV's Service Delivery precepts are handled in Contractual aspects Section, in which the contractual aspects that made the service delivery strategy possible and the SLA established in order to meet the customer's needs are described. Service Level Management and Incident Management are addressed in Supplier-side managerial controls Section, in which the internal managerial controls employed for monitoring the SLA and how to operate service requests are detailed.

Contractual aspects

The contractual model had to undergo changes to enable the new service delivery strategy. In this new model, demands for development came to be treated as service requests. Previously, demands had been grouped into increments handled as development projects, billed accordingly as the projects progressed (20% at the outset, 30% after functional specification, and 50% following final delivery).

With the new desired dynamics, requests would no longer be grouped into development projects, but rather handled as work associated with isolated services that should comply with a SLA. The CMMI-SVC reference model (SEI 2010) defines work as "a managed set of people and other resources that delivers one or more products or services to a customer or end user". Thus, in the case of this experience, switching from project management to work management would result in a finer granularity of items to manage.

The strategy that was defined to enable service delivery involved dividing the billing of the contract into two parts, one fixed and one variable. The former included the payment of a full-time requirements analyst in charge of receiving requests from users and specifying them as service requests. In addition to the analyst, the fixed part also included a fee for corrective maintenance services (development effort related to fixing system failures). The variable monthly part, on the other hand, was calculated on a fixed day of the month, based on the implemented requests, according to the SLA. Therefore, higher productivity would directly and intuitively result in a higher monthly net gain for the software supplier.

The strategy for satisfying customer requests is outlined in Figure 1. As shown in this figure, the requirements analyst receives business requests from the system's users. These requests get prioritized according to their added business value and written in the form of requirements to be implemented, in order to become service requests. The priorities are defined together with TTM's IT Manager and other appropriate stakeholders.

The treatment of the service requests was managed to ensure that each request was attended complying with the established SLA. As soon as the developer concludes the technical solution of a request, before it is considered ready for validation, the solution is sent to a test by an independent team. Finally, the delivered requests get validated with the system's users.

The 'Service Level Agreement and Penalties' subsection shows the SLA part of the contract. In this SLA, requests have different deadlines, defined as numbers of days, according to their priority. The priority should reflect the added business value, so that higher added business value has to be treated faster. The following prioritization criteria was adopted:

- *Critical Requests:* these impede the use of the system for the business activities of some sectors or relate to new functionalities that can significantly improve business results.
- *High Priority Requests:* these do not impede the use of the system for the business activities of entire sectors, but hinder the conclusion of some specific business operations;
- *Medium Priority Requests:* these relate to new functionalities that can allow the speedier execution of some business operations;
- *Low Priority Requests:* these relate to new functionalities that enable features of the system to be improved.

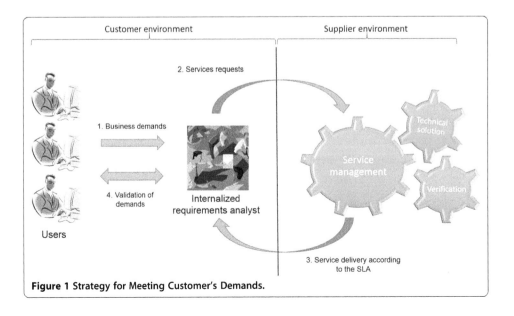

Figure 1 Strategy for Meeting Customer's Demands.

According to this SLA, if a critical request of a new functionality with estimated effort of 40 hours is fully answered on the tenth working day after the request and with a total effort of 80 hours, then only 42 of the 80 worked hours would be billable. This amount corresponds to the maximum billable amount of 60 hours with a penalty of 30%, since it should have been answered at the eights workday and was only answered in the tenth workday. In cases the supplier did not agree with classifying a new functionality as critical, the customer had to explain how the new functionality would improve business results (e.g., avoiding losses or enabling higher gains).

On the other hand, if a critical correction with estimated effort of 40 hours is fully answered on the tenth working day after the request and with a total effort of 80 hours, then 18 billable hours would be deduced from the total monthly billable hours. In this case, corresponding to a 30% penalty for the delay over the 60 maximum billable hours.

Given this scenario, in which delays have direct financial impact, monitoring the request against the SLA becomes of critical importance. Therefore, to monitor compliance with the SLA, requests were recorded on a spreadsheet, one of the internal managerial controls used to facilitate management of services. More information concerning managerial controls is provided in subsection Supplier-side managerial controls.

Service level agreement and penalties

This service level agreement is valid for corrections, as well as for changes and new developments, requested from the entry date of this agreement.

Agreement

The requests will have the following deadlines to be fully met (with no defects)

- *Critical Requests*
  Deadline in hours = (1.5 x estimated effort) Hours.
  Deadline in days = (Deadline in hours/8) Working Days.
- *High Priority Requests*
  Deadline in hours = (1.5 x estimated effort) Hours.
  Deadline in days = (Deadline in hours/8) + 1 Working Days.
- *Medium Priority Requests*
  Deadline in hours = (1.5 x estimated effort) Hours.
  Deadline in days = (Deadline in hours/8) + 2 Working Days.
- *Low Priority Requests*
  Deadline in hours = (1.5 x estimated effort) Hours.
  Deadline in days = (Deadline in hours/8) + 4 Working Days.

The deadline in hours will be used as a limit on the number of billable hours. The deadline in days will be used for penalties related to the deadline. Whenever this number is odd it should be rounded up, i.e., a period of 8.32 days should be met within the ninth day.

Penalties

Change requests or new developments that are not answered within the service level agreement will automatically be penalized by 30%.

Correction requests, included in the monthly amount, that are not answered within the service level agreement, will be automatically converted into a penalty of 30% of the deadline in hours, taking into account the hourly cost established in this agreement. This amount will be deduced from the variable cost to be billed monthly.

Supplier-side managerial controls

The following three internal managerial controls were used for supporting service management at the software supplier:

- a *request-tracking spreadsheet* for monitoring the requests and their conformance to the SLA;
- an *issue-tracking system* (integrated with the version control), in which a ticket is registered for each service request; and
- a *Kanban chart* to show the service status at any time to the whole team involved in providing the overall continuous development service.

Kanban charts have been used in agile development approaches such as Lean and SCRUM, for more information on the use of Kanban charts in the technology business refer to (Anderson 2010). Figure 2 shows the sequence in which these controls are applied for handling service requests according to the precepts of the MPS-SV Service Level Management and Incident Management processes. This figure also highlights the purpose and facilities offered by each of these controls.

Initially, a new service request is recorded in the request-tracking spreadsheet. The spreadsheet containing the requests made between 01/16/2013 and 01/31/2013 is shown in Figure 3. The columns for the developer and the cost have been deliberately modified to avoid revealing individual performance and cost information. The cost is represented by the number of billable hours rather than the expected cash value of the services. This spreadsheet allows incident management and monitoring the conformance of the provided services to the SLA, as required for compliance with the MPS-SV Incident Management and Service Level Management processes. This enables services delivery according to their business value and priority. It is important to state that this spreadsheet was also shared with the customer for billing purposes, thus communicating the status to

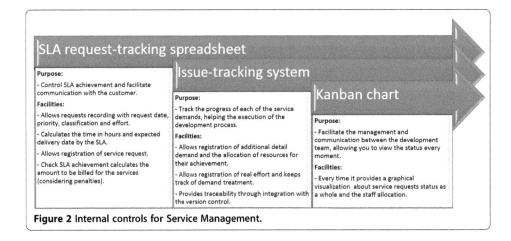

Figure 2 Internal controls for Service Management.

Legend: Critical · High Priority · Medium Priority · Low Priority · Approved/Met · Not Approved/Met

SLA REQUEST TRACKING SPREADSHEET																
REQUEST DATA											SERVICE DATA					
STATUS	PRIORITY	REQUEST DATE	REQUEST TYPE	TICKET OPENING DATE	TICKET NUMBER	MODULE	USE CASE / DESCRIPTION	ESTIMATED EFFORT	DEADLINE IN HOURS	DELIVERY DEADLINE	DEVELOPER	REAL EFFORT	DELIVERY DATE	APPROVED	SLA	COST
Delivered		1/16/2013	Change	1/16/2013	560	MFI	Lançar Despesa	8	12	1/21/2013	A	8	1/20/2013			8
Delivered		1/16/2013	Change	1/16/2013	561	MFI	Lançar Despesa	8	12	1/21/2013	A	16	1/21/2013			12
Delivered		1/17/2013	Correction	1/17/2013	563	MFI	Lançar Despesa	8	12	1/21/2013	B	10	1/21/2013			0
Delivered		1/17/2013	Change	1/18/2013	564	SGI	Todos que cada:	8	12	1/24/2013	C	16	2/1/2013			8,4
Delivered		1/17/2013	Change	1/18/2013	565	SGI	Todas que utiliz:	16	24	1/28/2013	B	20	1/24/2013			20
Delivered		1/18/2013	Change	1/18/2013	566	SGI	Todas que utiliz:	16	24	1/29/2013	D	24	1/30/2013			16,8
Delivered		1/18/2013	Correction	1/18/2013	567	MFI	Imprimir Chequ	4	6	1/21/2013	C	6	1/21/2013			0
Delivered		1/18/2013	Correction	1/18/2013	568	MOP	Manter Serviços	16	24	1/29/2013	C	16	1/28/2013			0
Delivered		1/18/2013	Change	1/18/2013	569	MFI	Importar Despe:	16	24	1/29/2013	E	8	1/28/2013			8
Cancelled		1/23/2013	Correction	1/23/2013	570	MOP	Manter Serviços	6	9	1/24/2013	E	8	Not Delivered			
Delivered		1/23/2013	Correction	1/25/2013	571	MFI	Lançar Despesa	8	12	1/28/2013	A	8	2/4/2013			-2,4
Delivered		1/24/2013	Change	1/25/2013	572	SGI	Banco de Dados	16	24	2/4/2013	B	16	1/30/2013			16
Delivered		1/24/2013	Change	1/25/2013	573	MALO	Relatório de Alo	16	24	1/31/2013	F	20	1/29/2013			20
Delivered		1/25/2013	Change	1/25/2013	574	MFI	Lançar Despesa	24	36	2/6/2013	A	32	1/31/2013			32
Delivered		1/28/2013	Correction	1/28/2013	575	MOP	Manter Serviços	2	3	2/1/2013	C	2	2/4/2013			-0,6
Delivered		1/28/2013	Change	1/28/2013	576	MADM	Manter Clientes	8	12	1/29/2013	D	8	1/29/2013			8
Delivered		1/28/2013	Change	1/30/2013	577	MFI	Consultar Despe	6	9	2/4/2013	F	8	2/1/2013			8
0		1/29/2013	Change	1/29/2013	579	MFI	Importar Despe:	16	24	2/5/2013	A					
1		1/29/2013	Correction	1/30/2013	578	MOP	Cadastrar C.T	12	18	2/6/2013	D					
Delivered		1/31/2013	Change	1/31/2013	580	MFI	Lançar Despesa	8	12	2/1/2013	E	8	2/1/2013			8
3		1/31/2013	Change	1/31/2013	581	SGI	Telas do SGI	12	18	2/8/2013	E					
																162,2

Figure 3 Spreadsheet for controlling SLA.

the interested stakeholders, as also required by the MPS-SV Service Level Management process, is also achieved. Figures 4 and 5 present a zoomed view of the parts containing data related to registering and processing the new service request.

Figure 4 shows the data registered for each request: (i) the date of the request, (ii) the request type ("correction" or "change" – in this case "change" also includes new development requests), (iii) the opening date of the ticket, (iv) the ticket number (to enable monitoring in the issue-tracking system), (v) the system module (e.g., administrative, financial), (vi) the related use case, and (vii) the estimated effort. Using this information, the deadline in work hours is calculated and the intended delivery date is set in accordance with the SLA. The first column highlights the overall managerial status, showing whether each request has been delivered, cancelled or how many days are left before delivery ought to be accomplished.

Figure 5 shows the data registered in the spreadsheet for the service being processed for each request, including the chosen developer, real development effort (obtained from the issue-tracking system), actual delivery date and customer approval (validation). With this information, the spreadsheet calculates the extent of compliance of the work performance with the SLA and the amount to be billed for the service, taking into account contractual SLA penalties for late delivery, when applicable. In the fifteen day period shown in Figure 3, for instance, besides the fixed cost (regarding the internalized requirements analyst and the corrections), there are 162.2 billable hours concerning the provided services of implementing changes and eventual penalties.

The issue-tracking system used was *Assembla* (Assembla 2013), a cloud-based service system, already including the integration of tickets (requests) with version control. The integration with version control provides traceability on how the tickets were handled.

REQUEST DATA										
STATUS	PRIORITY	REQUEST DATE	REQUEST TYPE	TICKET OPENING DATE	TICKET NUMBER	MODULE	USE CASE / DESCRIPTION	ESTIMATED EFFORT	DEADLINE IN HOURS	DELIVERY DEADLINE
Delivered		1/16/2013	Change	1/16/2013	560	MFI	Lançar Despesa	8	12	1/21/2013
Delivered		1/16/2013	Change	1/16/2013	561	MFI	Lançar Despesa	8	12	1/21/2013
Delivered		1/17/2013	Correction	1/17/2013	563	MFI	Lançar Despesa	8	12	1/21/2013

Figure 4 Part of the spreadsheet used for registering new requests.

SERVICE DATA					
DEVELOPER	REAL EFFORT	DELIVERY DATE	APPROVED	SLA	COST
A	8	1/20/2013	✓	✓	8
A	16	1/21/2013	✓	✓	12
B	10	1/21/2013	✓	✓	0

Figure 5 Part of the spreadsheet used for registering the treatment of the requests.

For each ticket all the files added or changed for providing the technical solution can be explicitly identified, as well as the modifications done in each file. Therefore, if a change request on a given ticket is received, the files to be modified can be traced, supporting the involved impact analysis and effort estimation.

This system was also used for allocating the developers and registering the real effort. As soon as a developer concludes the technical solution of a request, he registers the effort and passes corresponding ticket to be tested by an independent team. If the ticket passes testing then its status is changed and it is considered ready to be deployed for customer validation, with the support from the internalized requirements analyst at the customer side.

Finally, monitoring the service status for each request was facilitated by the Kanban chart, which was physically displayed in the room where the development team was located. Figures 6 and 7 show a real example of a request in Assembla and a Kanban chart with the progress status of service requests, respectively. In this Kanban chart the status of each ticket can be easily identified. Each ticket becomes a separate post-it, using different colors reflecting the SLA priorities. To illustrate the use of the Kanban chart, Figure 7 highlights the status of ticket #560, shown in Figure 6, as being in the queue for supplier side testing.

The importance of tests in this context is obvious, since a service request is only accepted for billing if it does not show any failures during validation. Moreover, if an

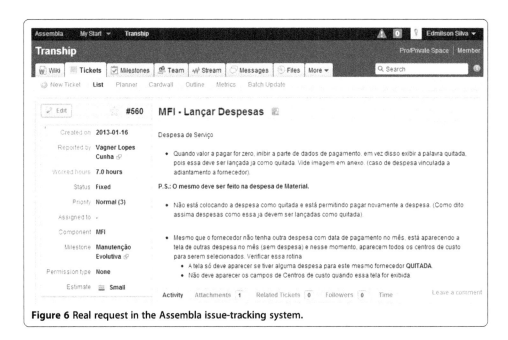

Figure 6 Real request in the Assembla issue-tracking system.

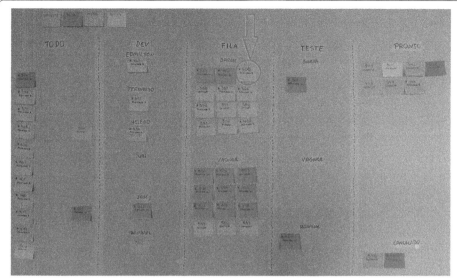

Figure 7 Kanban chart showing the status of requests.

acceptance test fails, the delivery data remains unchanged and the SLA will probably not be met, resulting in penalties. Considering this critical quality issue, requirements inspections (Kalinowski *et al.* 2007) and code peer reviews (Kemerer and Paulk 2009) were also adopted.

Having presented the contractual aspects and the internal managerial controls defined in this industrial experience, based on the guidelines of the MPS-SV service reference model, to allow switching from a project-oriented to a service-oriented software development approach, the next section presents the discussion and evaluation of the overall experience.

Discussion and evaluation

Aiming at understanding the feasibility and effects of restructuring software development from a project-oriented to a service-oriented approach guided by a service reference model, two research issues were identified in the Background Section. RI-1, related to the perceived utility, was investigated through a survey reported in detail in (Jordão and Kalinowski 2013).

Results indicated that the MPS-SW software engineering consultants consider service reference models, such as the MPS-SV, useful for providing continuous delivery capabilities to their software industry customers (93% totally or partially agreed). The consultants also indicated an expected ease of use (76% totally or partially agreed) and intention to adopt (63% totally or partially agreed). The survey's overall confidence level was of 78.5%.

These survey results can be seen as an additional motivation for investigating the second identified research issue, RI-2, which is the main contribution of this article and concerns the feasibility and results or restructuring software development guided by a service reference model. The discussion and evaluation of questions that provide further insights into RI-2, based on the reported experience, follows.

What are typical stakeholder needs that trigger the restructuring from a project-oriented approach to a service-oriented approach?

Table 2 provides an overview on the main stakeholders and their interests. From the customer's point of view, the main interests on software development were facilitating contract negotiations and integrating value considerations into the development process. Therefore, allowing faster deployment of new system capabilities prioritized according to the added business value. From the supplier's point of view, on the other hand, the main interests were related to simple contract negotiation, a steady (or growing) inflow of development requests, and translating productivity directly into higher monthly net gains. It is noteworthy that there were no specific expectations regarding changes in the cost of developing individual functionalities. Actually, given the need to comply with the SLA (and potential penalties) the customer and supplier agreed to increase the hourly cost rate.

We assume that the restructuring allowed properly addressing the stakeholder's main interests, by (i) providing a contractual framework that avoids excessive negotiation effort for new development requests, and (ii) allowing the new service requests to be directly addressed according to the added business value, as defined in the SLA. From the supplier's point of view, the variable monthly net gain also accounted for the direct return of investment of efforts to improve productivity.

The general perception from the customer and the supplier was that a more flexible model had been adopted to meet the customer's business needs and to live up to his expectations in terms of supply, as expressed in the SLA. In fact, the contract model considers the business priority of individual requests and does not have to be reconsidered due to a variation in the volume of requests, for instance.

Can a service reference model be helpful to meet those needs?

In this experience, the Brazilian MPS-SV service reference model, which is representative for similar international standards, directly supported the restructuring to the service-oriented approach. The resulting process implementation followed the guidelines of MPS-SV maturity level G (SOFTEX 2012b). The Service Delivery, Service Level Management, and Incident Management reference processes, directly related to providing services, were considered helpful to structure basic service delivery capabilities in order to meet the identified stakeholder needs and to increase the confidence in the provided solutions. The main purpose of each of those processes, their expected results according to the MPS-SV reference model, and how they were implemented during this experience are shown in Table 3. This implementation does also meet (SOFTEX 2012b) the specific goals of the CMMI-SVC (SEI 2010) Service Delivery process area (maturity level 2), and of the related ISO/IEC 20000 processes (ISO/IEC 2011).

What is the effort to be expected?

The restructuring took 160 person hours and happened within the timeframe of one month. As the restructuring included aspects of all processes at Level G of the MPS-SV model, we assert that implementing this model for software development requires only moderate effort, when compared for instance to the average duration of over 12 month for implementing MPS-SW maturity levels (Travassos and Kalinowski 2013). Especially if work management and requirements management capabilities, including requirements

Table 3 MPS-SV level G processes and how they were implemented

MPS-SV process purpose and expected results	How the expected results were implemented
Service Delivery (SD)	
Purpose:	
The purpose of this process is defining the strategy and establishing the service system to deliver services in conformance with the service agreements.	
Required Results:	
SD 1. A service delivery and operation strategy is established and maintained;	SD 1. The defined service delivery and operation strategy is shown in Figure 1.
SD 2. The availability of the needed elements for providing the service is confirmed;	SD 2. The availability of needed elements was assured by the contractual framework, which included an internalized requirements analyst at the customer side.
SD 3. The service system is put into operation to deliver the agreed services;	SD 3. The service system was put into operation.
SD 4. The service system is maintained to assure continuous service delivery.	SD 4. The service system was maintained operating.
Service Level Management (SLM)	
Purpose:	
The purpose of this process is to assure that the SLA goals for each customer are met.	
Required Results:	
SLM 1. Services and their dependencies are identified;	SLM 1. The identified service was software development, including corrective and evolutionary (new functionalities) maintenance.
SLM 2. Service level goals are defined in an SLA;	SLM 2. The defined SLA is shown in subsection 'Service Level Agreement and Penalties'.
SLM 3. Services are monitored against the SLA;	SLM 3. Monitoring was achieved by defining the service management controls depicted in Figure 2.
SLM 4. Service level performance is communicated to relevant stakeholders;	SLM 4. The request-tracking spreadsheet (Figure 3) was shared with the customer and sent monthly for billing purposes. It provides an overview of the service performance against the SLA.
SLM 5. Changes in service requirements reflect in the SLA.	SLM 5. Those changes did not happen in the context of this experience, but would imply in changing the SLA appendix of the contractual framework and both sides, supplier and customer) were open to discuss such changes.
Incident Management (IM)	
Purpose:	
The purpose of this process is to handle individual incidents and service requests within a SLA.	
Required Results:	
IM 1. A strategy for incident and service request management is established and maintained;	IM 1. The defined strategy involved fine-grained request monitoring by using the internal managerial controls shown in Figure 2.
IM 2. An incident and service request management system is established and maintained;	IM 2. The internal managerial controls were established and maintained.
IM 3. Incidents and service requests are registered and classified;	IM 3. Each request was registered into the request-tracking spreadsheet (Figure 3) and classified as an incident (correction) or a new service request (change or new functionality).
IM 4. Incidents and service requests are prioritized and analyzed;	IM 4. Each request had its priority defined and impact analysis performed, using the traceability provided by the issue-tracking system, to estimate the required effort.

Table 3 MPS-SV level G processes and how they were implemented *(Continued)*

IM 5. Incidents and service requests are resolved and concluded;	IM 5. The request-tracking spreadsheet shows the managerial status of each request, allowing managing them until conclusion.
IM 6. Incidents and service requests that did not progress according the SLA are communicated to higher level management;	IM 6. The request-tracking spreadsheet was shared and monthly sent to directors of both companies. It explicitly identifies the request that did not meet the SLA.
IM 7. Status information on incidents or service requests is communicated to relevant stakeholders.	IM 7. Status communication to higher management and customer stakeholders was achieved through the spreadsheet. Communication to the internal development team by using the Kanban chart.

traceability, are previously installed, as in the experience here described. Besides the moderate effort, interesting results were obtained, including increases in the productive capacity, as pointed out in the answer to the next question.

What are the potential effects on quality and productivity?

Quantitative data concerning this question was obtained by comparing the deliveries in the new service format to the most recent delivery in the previously established project format. For this comparison, only new use case developments of comparable medium complexity (according to the criteria for counting use case points: from 4 to 7 transactions including alternative steps) were considered. Table 4 summarizes these quantitative results.

Regarding quality, during customer acceptance tests of medium complexity cases, the number of failures was notably lower, falling from 0.33 failures per use case to 0.18 failures per use case. Concerning productivity, the real development effort spent per use case was also slightly lower, falling from 24 person hours per use case to 21 person hours per use case. Note that these productivity improvements directly translate into saved costs as the supplier pays for the overall development effort in person hours.

Of course, these differences are not statistically significant since only 23 medium complex use cases served as the basis for the comparison (12 implemented in the project format and 11 implemented in the IT service format). Moreover, there are several factors that can influence these results (e.g., low precision in measuring use case complexity, inherent variations of individual productivity, learning factor). However, feedback from the customer also allowed observing a perceived improvement in quality (fewer problems during acceptance tests) and productivity, especially regarding the fact that the new service-oriented value-based approach resulted in faster delivery of demands of higher added business value.

An informal causal analysis session (Kalinowski *et al.* 2008b) (Kalinowski *et al.* 2012), aiming at investigating the causes of these changes in quality and productivity, was conducted with the suppliers development team and showed that the existence of the SLA and closer management resulted in greater commitment on the part of the developers.

Table 4 Comparison of the project and IT service delivery approaches

Approach	# of use cases	# Failures (Acceptance)	Effort (Person-hours)
Project	12	4	284
IT Service	11	2	232

Some developers mentioned that, knowing of the individual penalties that the company would be liable to pay in each request, they saw that it was much more important to meet deadlines than they did when the project format was in use, in which the tasks were scheduled but the overall deadline was scoped to the entire project. Indeed, closer management and finer granularity are suggestions included in Humphrey's reflections on efficient team management (Humphrey 2010).

What are the main lessons learned?

In the reported experience, applying practices of service management to software development resulted in a flexible contractual framework, allowing addressing the customer's business needs according to their priorities without additional contract negotiation delays. New requests could be directly Among the lessons learned, that could be passed on to international SME companies that seek to supply development as an IT service guided by a service reference model, the following stand out:

- **Contractual framework.** In this supply model, it is important to have some headroom in the budget for the fixed monthly part of the contractual framework, compensating for possible variations in the volume of delivered requests to be billed in the variable part. Otherwise, financial constraints may lead to excessive pressure, on management and development levels, at the supplier's side. After all, the development team has to be paid by the supplier anyway, although if the supplier has different customers following similar contractual service frameworks he might be able to allocate developers to his project portfolio according to the individual project's volume of received demands.
- **Prioritization criteria.** The priority criteria for customer requests should be very clear, as it might be applied when it comes to avoiding undue financial penalties, as specified in the SLA. After all, ambiguities involving financial aspects may lead to potential relationship problems between the contractor and the supplier.
- **SLA and team capacity.** It is important to assess the SLA carefully, checking whether the company has the installed productive capacity of actually satisfying the requested service level. If not, this would result in deliveries not meeting the SLA and the application of penalties with direct impact on the monthly net gain.
- **Managerial controls.** The managerial controls were fundamental to allow handling the demands as separate service requests, by facilitate monitoring the compliance with the SLA. Not having such controls established may imply in several request passing the SLA's deadline and, as a consequence, in penalties.
- **Traceability.** Traceability plays a key role when handling request as separate services to be provided, by supporting effective impact analysis, effort estimation and risk assessments for handling each new request.
- **Build, Test and Deployment Automation.** Aiming at continuous delivery, efficient build, test and deployment automation is strongly desired (Humble and Farley 2010). In the case of our experience the build and deployment were fully automated. Test automation however could be improved to reduce regression testing effort. So far, only superficial smoke tests had been recorded to allow identifying major side effects of new handled request, by using the Selenium IDE plugin (Selenium 2013).

- **Team and individual benefits.** Some employees felt pressured by the SLA and the close and quantitative monitoring. Therefore, it might be interesting to establish a complementary policy for awarding employees with bonuses for improved productivity. Note that this is feasible, since an improvement in productivity also implies in a higher monthly net gain.
- **Overall restructuring effort and benefits.** Around one person month effort was required for the restructuring and benefits were perceived in terms of improved quality, productivity, and customer satisfaction. We take it that the increased customer satisfaction was mainly related to meeting their main interests by considering the integration of added business value into the software engineering practices.

What are the involved success and risk factors?

Another fruitful consequence of the experience was the opportunity to identify success (and risk) factors related to restructuring software development in the format of service delivery. Based on the lessons learned from the experience report, the main success factors were:

- **Success factor service reference model.** The adoption of a service reference model allowed benchmarking the new service format against IT service delivery best practices and improved the confidence in the solutions provided by the restructuring approach. These solutions include the internal managerial controls to facilitate monitoring the compliance with the SLA.
- **Success factor senior management support.** The idea of the restructuring addressed specific interests of stakeholders including the directors of both companies. Therefore, direct support from senior management was obtained for the process improvement initiative. We saw on several occasions that this support has considerably facilitated and accelerated the restructuring.
- **Success factor relationship of trust.** The previous period of over one year providing development services successfully allowed establishing a relationship of trust between the contractor and the supplier. This relationship provided the basis to discuss the new contractual framework for continuous delivery with varying monthly net payments and gains.
- **Success factor previously established capabilities.** Some previously established software engineering capabilities were crucial in the successful transition. Concrete requirement traceability capacity, for instance, helps to handle request separately by allowing effective impact analysis, effort estimation and risk assessments for handling each new request. Moreover, build, test and deployment automation was also extremely helpful for implementing the continuous delivery strategy.

Concerning the risk factors, we see a direct mapping, in the sense that the absence of any of the success factors represents a significant risk. Additional risks can also be identified from not addressing major issues in the the lessons learned.

Conclusions

This article reported on an experience of restructuring software development in the form of providing IT services in the context of an SME software supplier. The restructuring involved, in addition to the technical changes, important management changes, i.e., establishing a contractual framework and capacities for managing service requests in order to comply with a Service Level Agreement (SLA) made between the supplier and the customer to satisfy the business needs of the latter.

The restructuring project was guided by the MPS-SV service reference model, which is compatible to the CMMI-SVC reference model, complementing already established software engineering practices for the provision of development as a continuous IT service. The contractual aspects and internal managerial controls employed to facilitate the compliance with the SLA were described. Those controls included the integrated use of a managerial spreadsheet, an issue-tracking system, and a Kanban chart to monitor how demands were prioritized to be met.

Further insight into the feasibility and results on such structuring were provided by discussing valuable and experience-grounded answers to the following core questions: What are typical stakeholder needs that trigger such a restructuring? Can a service reference model be helpful to meet those needs? What effort is to be expected? What are the potential effects on development quality and productivity? What are the main lessons learned? What are the involved success and risk factors?

The overall analysis of the experience showed that only moderate effort, around one person month, was required for structuring software development as a service guided by a reference model and that perceived benefits were obtained in terms of quality, productivity, and customer satisfaction. The increased customer satisfaction was mainly related to meeting the customer's business needs by integrating value considerations into software engineering practices. Therefore, using a service reference model for restructuring software development can represent an alternative path towards value-based software engineering. Nevertheless, we would like to reinforce that, as expected in an experience report, the obtained results relate to a specific scenario and industrial environment. However, those results provide preliminary indications into feasibility and potential benefits, further motivating the conduct of more rigorous studies (e.g., case studies or controlled experiments) on the impact of applying service reference models to re-structure software development from a project-oriented to a service-oriented management format.

A key benefit of the Brazilian standards is the provision of smaller steps in the lower range of the process maturity levels, which allows, in particular, small companies with limited resources to systematically define and achieve software and service maturity levels that suit their needs and means. This report and the identified lessons learned can serve as a reference for SME companies that operate in the context of an international software maturity reference model and wish to restructure in order to supply software development in the format of an IT service. These companies can benefit from adopting a service reference model, such as the MPS-SV or CMMI-SVC models, in synergy with their already established software engineering practices.

Competing interests
The authors declare that they have no competing interests.

Authors' contributions
MK was the executive director of the supplier company and worked directly with the customer on establishing the contractual framework and the service level agreement. He also worked with the supplier team to enable the restructuring in the format of the service-oriented approach. He was the lead author of the initial report and of this extended paper. SB helped to extend the initial report, discussing the overall solution and argumentation line and

enriching it with his strong scientific stakeholder analysis and value-based software engineering background. ROS was the operations director of the supplier and helped extending the report with additional details of the overall experience. SR is the main responsible person for the MPS-SV reference model and used her service quality background to help writing the initial report and to support the extension with the argumentation on the international standards and reference models. All authors read and approved the final manuscript.

Authors' information

MK holds a MS and PhD in Computer and Systems Engineering from the Federal University of Rio de Janeiro (UFRJ) and is currently professor of Software Engineering at the Federal University of Juiz de Fora (UFJF) in transference to Fluminense Federal University (UFF). He is part of the MPS.BR project team and a certified MPS.BR lead appraiser and process implementation consultant.

SB holds a MS and PhD in Computer Science from the Vienna University of Technology (TUW) and a MS in Social and Economic Sciences from the University of Vienna. He also received a Habilitation degree (Venia Docendi) in "Praktische Informatik" for his contributions on empirical software engineering. Currently he is professor of Software Engineering at TUW and the head of the Christian Doppler research laboratory – Software Engineering Integration for Flexible Automation Systems. He was lead editor for the book "Value-Based Software Engineering" in collaboration with co-editors A. Aurum, B.W. Boehm, H. Erdogmus, and P. Grünbacher.

ROS holds a MS and PhD in Computer and Systems Engineering from the Federal University of Rio de Janeiro (UFRJ) and is currently professor of Software Engineering at the University of Salvador (UNIFACS). He is a certified MPS.BR process implementation consultant.

SR holds a MS in Informatics from the Catholic University of the State of Paraná (PUCPR) and a PhD in Production Engineering from the University of São Paulo (USP) and is currently professor of Software Engineering at PUCPR. She is the coordinator of the service area of the MPS.BR project team and a certified MPS.BR lead appraiser and process implementation consultant.

Acknowledgements

We would like to thank CNPq (Brazilian Research Council) for financial support. Thanks also to everyone at Tranship Transportes Marítimos and Kali Software directly involved in the experience reported in this article, especially Rosiene Dilly (the project manager) and Vagner Lopes (the internalized requirements analyst). This research was in part supported by the Christian Doppler Forschungsgesellschaft and the BMWFJ, Austria.

Author details

[1]Federal University of Juiz de Fora, Rua José Kelmer s/n, Juiz de Fora 36.036-330, Brazil. [2]Institute of Software Technology and Interactive Systems, CDL-Flex-, Vienna University of Technology, Favoritenstr. 9/188, Vienna 1040, Austria. [3]University of Salvador, Rua Doutor José Peroba 251, Salvador 41.770-235, Brazil. [4]Catholic University of the State of Paraná, Rua Imaculada Conceição 1155, Curitiba 80.215-901, Brazil.

References

Anderson DJ (2010) Kanban: successful evolutionary change for your technology business. Blue Hole Press, Sequim, WA

Assembla (2013) Assembla task & issue management., http://www.assembla.com. Accessed 29 Sep 2013

Barney S, Aurum A, Wohlin C (2008) A product management challenge: creating software product value through requirements selection. J Syst Architecture 54(6):576–593

Biffl S, Aurum A, Boehm B, Erdogmus H, Grünbacher P (eds) (2006) Value-based software engineering. Springer, Heidelberg

Boehm B (2006) Value-based software engineering: overview and agenda. In: Biffl S, Aurum A, Boehm B, Erdogmus H, Grünbacher P (eds) Value-based software engineering. Springer, Heidelberg

Boehm B, Turner R (2003) Balancing agility and discipline: a guide for the perplexed. Wesley, Addison

Davis F (1989) Perceived usefulness, perceived ease of use, and user acceptance of information technology. MIS Quarterly 13(3):319–340

Humble J, Farley D (2010) Continuous delivery: reliable software releases through build, test, and deployment automation. Addison-Wesley, Boston, MA

Humphrey WS (2010) Reflections on management: How to manage your software projects, your teams, your boss, and yourself. Addison-Wesley, Boston, MA

ISO/IEC (2004) ISO/IEC 15504-1: information technology - process assessment – part 1 - concepts and vocabulary. ISO, Geneve

ISO/IEC (2011) ISO/IEC 20000-1:2011 – information technology service management. ISO, Geneve

Jordão L, Kalinowski M (2013) Investigando a Aplicabilidade do MPS-SV na Melhoria de Serviços de Desenvolvimento e Manutenção de Software. In: IX Workshop Anual do MPS.BR (WAMPS). Brazilian Computer Society (in Portuguese), Campinas, Brazil

Kalinowski M, Reinehr S (2013) Estruturando Desenvolvimento de Software como um Serviço de TI: Uma Experiência Prática. In: XII Simpósio Brasileiro de Qualidade Software (SBQS). Brazilian Computer Society (in Portuguese), Salvador, Brazil

Kalinowski M, Spínola RO, Dias-Neto AC, Bott A, Travassos GH (2007) Inspeções de requisitos de software em desenvolvimento incremental: Uma experiência prática. In: VI simpósio brasileiro de qualidade software (SBQS). Brazilian Computer Society (in Portuguese), Porto de Galinhas, Brazil

Kalinowski M, Weber KC, Travassos GH (2008a) IMPS: an experimentation based investigation of a nationwide software development reference model. In: International symposium on empirical software engineering and measurement (ESEM). ACM and IEEE, Kaiserslautern, Germany

Kalinowski M, Travassos GH, Card DN (2008b) Guidance for efficiently implementing defect causal analysis. In: VII Brazilian symposium on software quality (SBQS). Brazilian Computer Society (in Portuguese), Florianópolis, Brazil

Kalinowski M, Santos G, Reinehr S, Montoni M, Rocha AR, Weber KC, Travassos GH (2010) MPS.BR: Promovendo a Adoção de Boas Práticas de Engenharia de Software pela Indústria Brasileira. In: XIII Congreso Iberoamericano en "Software Engineering" (CIBSE). Universidad del Azuay (in Portuguese), Cuenca, Equador, ISBN 978-9978-325-10-0

Kalinowski M, Card DN, Travassos GH (2012) Evidence-based guidelines to defect causal analysis. IEEE Software 29(4):16–18, doi:10.1109/MS.2012.72

Kemerer CF, Paulk MC (2009) The impact of design and code reviews on software quality: an empirical study based on PSP data. IEEE Trans Softw Eng 35(4):534–550

Khan SU, Niazi M, Ahmad R (2011) Factors influencing clients in the selection of offshore software outsourcing vendors: an exploratory study using a systematic literature review. J Syst Softw 84(4):686–699

Lehman TJ, Sharma A (2011) Software development as a service: agile experiences. In: Annual SRII global conference (SRII). IEEE, San Diego, USA

MCTI (2013) Brazilian ministry of science, technology and innovation., http://www.mcti.gov.br. Accessed 29 Sep 2013

Penn ML (2011) Applying CMMI-SVC process areas to CMMI-DEV projects. Presentation at SEPG North America 2011, available via CMMI Institute., http://cmmiinstitute.com/resources. Accessed 29 Sep 2013

Penn ML (2013) Harmonization of CMMI-SVC and CMMI-DEV, Presentation at SEPG North America 2013, available via SEPG., http://sepgconference.org/harmonization-of-cmmi-svc-and-cmmi-dev. Accessed 29 Sep 2013

PMI (2013) A guide to the project management body of knowledge, 5th edn. Project Management Institute, Newtown Square, PA

Santos G, Kalinowski M, Rocha AR, Travassos GH, Weber KC, Antonioni JA (2012) MPS.BR program and MPS model: main results, benefits and beneficiaries of software process improvement in Brazil. In: International Conference on the Quality in Information and Communications Technology (QUATIC). IEEE, Lisbon, Portugal

SEI (2010) CMMI for services, version 1.3 (CMU/SEI-2010-TR-034), available via Software Engineering Institute, Carnegie Mellon University., http://www.sei.cmu.edu/library/abstracts/reports/10tr034.cfm. Accessed 29 Sep 2013

Selenium (2013) Selenium IDE., http://docs.seleniumhq.org/projects/ide. Accessed 29 Sep 2013

SOFTEX (2012a) MR-MPS-SW – guia geral MPS de software., Available via SOFTEX. http://www.softex.br/mpsbr. Accessed 29 Sep 2013

SOFTEX (2012b) MR-MPS-SV – guia geral MPS de serviços., Available via SOFTEX. http://www.softex.br/mpsbr. Accessed 29 Sep 2013

SOFTEX (2014) SOFTEX MPS.BR program website., http://www.softex.br/mpsbr. Accessed 06 May 2014

Travassos GH, Kalinowski M (2013) IMPS 2012: evidências sobre o desempenho das empresas que adotaram o modelo MPS-SW desde 2008. SOFTEX, Campinas, English edition: Travassos GH, Kalinowski M (2013) iMPS 2012: Evidence on Performance of Organizations that Adopted the MPS-SW Model since 2008 (trans: Kalinowski M). SOFTEX, Campinas

TSO (2011) ITIL – information technology infrastructure library v2011, Available via TSO – the stationery office., http://www.itil.org.uk. Accessed 29 Sep 2013

Turner M, Kitchenham B, Brereton P, Charters S, Budgen D (2010) Does the technology acceptance model predict actual use? a systematic literature review. Inf Softw Technol 52:463–479

4

NextBug: a Bugzilla extension for recommending similar bugs

Henrique Rocha[1][*], Guilherme de Oliveira[2], Humberto Marques-Neto[2] and Marco Tulio Valente[1]

*Correspondence:
henrique.rocha@dcc.ufmg.br
[1] Department of Computer Science, UFMG, 31.270-901 Belo Horizonte, Brazil
Full list of author information is available at the end of the article

Abstract

Background: Due to the characteristics of the maintenance process followed in open source systems, developers are usually overwhelmed with a great amount of bugs. For instance, in 2012, approximately 7,600 bugs/month were reported for Mozilla systems. Improving developers' productivity in this context is a challenging task. In this paper, we describe and evaluate the new version of NextBug, a tool for recommending similar bugs in open source systems. NextBug is implemented as a Bugzilla plug-in and it was design to help maintainers to select the next bug he/she would fix.

Results: We evaluated the new version of NextBug using a quantitative and a qualitative study. In the quantitative study, we applied our tool to 130,495 bugs reported for Mozilla products, and we consider as similar bugs that were handled by the same developer. The qualitative study reports the main results we received from a survey conducted with Mozilla developers and contributors. Most surveyed developers stated their interest in working with a tool like NextBug.

Conclusion: We achieved the following results in our evaluation: (i) NextBug was able to provide at least one recommendation to 65% of the bugs in the quantitative study, (ii) in 54% of the cases there was at least one recommendation among the top-3 that was later handled by the same developer; (iii) 85% of Mozilla developers stated that NextBug would be useful to the Mozilla community.

Keywords: Bugs; Recommendation systems; Bug mining techniques

Background

Software maintenance requests can be grouped and implemented as part of large software projects (Aziz et al. 2009; Marques-Neto et al. 2013; Junio et al. 2011; Tan and Mookerjee 2005). open source projects typically adopt continuous maintenance policies where the maintenance requests are addressed by maintainers with different skills and commitment levels, as soon as possible, after being registered in an issue tracking platform, such as Bugzilla and Jira (Tan and Mookerjee 2005; Mockus et al. 2002; Liu et al. 2012).

This process is usually uncoordinated, which results in a high number of issues from which many are invalid or duplicated (Liu et al. 2012). In 2005, a certified maintainer from the Mozilla Software Foundation made the following comment on this situation: "Everyday, almost 300 bugs appear that need triaging. This is far too much for only the Mozilla programmers to handle" (Anvik et al. 2006). The dataset with bugs reported for the Mozilla projects indicates that, in 2011, the number of issues reported per year increased approximately 75% when compared to 2005. In this context, tools to assist in the issue processing would be very helpful and can contribute to increase the productivity of open source systems development.

Furthermore, software developers are often involved in situations of changes of context in a typical workday. These changes normally happen due to meetings, mails, instant messaging, etc., or when a given task is concluded and developers need to choose a new task to work on. Regardless the reasons, the negative effect of context changes on developers' productivity are well-known and studied. For example, in a recent survey with developers of the industry, more than 50% of the participants answered that a productive workday is one that flows without context-switches and having no or few interruptions (Meyer et al. 2014). Another study shows that developers spent at least two thirds of their time in activities related to task context, i.e., searching, navigating, and understanding the code relevant to the current task at hand (Ko et al. 2005). We argue that this time can be reduced if developers consistently decide to work on new tasks similar to the one previously concluded.

More specifically, context switches can be reduced by guiding developers to work on a set of bugs $B_0, B_1, \ldots, B_n$, where B_i requires changes on parts of the system related to a previous bug B_{i-1}, for $i > 0$. By following this workflow, context changes could be mitigated because the order of handled bugs naturally fosters a kind of periodic maintenance policy, i.e., a bug that is selected, comprehended, and changed at a given time helps other bug corrections in a near future.

In this paper, we claim that a simple form of periodic maintenance policy can be promoted in open source systems by recommending similar maintenance requests to maintainers whenever they manifest interest in handling a given request. Suppose that a developer has manifested interest in a bug with a textual description d_i. In this case, we rely on text mining techniques to retrieve open bugs with descriptions d_j similar to d_i and we recommend such bugs to this maintainer.

More specifically, we present *NextBug*, a tool to recommend similar bugs to maintainers based on the textual description of each bug stored in Bugzilla, an issue tracking system widely used by open source projects. The proposed tool is compatible with the software development process followed by open source systems for the following reasons: (a) it is based on recommendations and, therefore, maintainers are not required to accept extra bugs to fix; (b) it is a fully automatic and unsupervised approach which does not depend on human intervention; and (c) it relies on information readily available in Bugzilla. Assuming the recommendations effectively denote similar bugs and supposing that the maintainers would accept the recommendations pointed out by NextBug, the tool can contribute to introduce gains of scale in the maintenance of open source systems similar to the ones achieved with periodic policies (Banker and Slaughter 1997). We also report a quantitative and qualitative study focusing on the Mozilla ecosystem. In the quantitative study, we applied NextBug to a dataset of 130,495 bugs reported for Mozilla systems. In the qualitative study, we performed a survey asking Mozilla developers if they would use a tool to recommend similar bugs to work on.

We also present in this paper the following improvements over our first work on NextBug (Rocha et al. 2014): (a) new features introduced in NextBug version 0.9, including recommendation filters and logging files; (b) an extended section presenting the tool and its architecture in more detail; (c) more tools presented and analysed in the related tools section; (d) a new quantitative study using the full dataset of 130,495 bugs (the previous conference paper used a subset of this dataset); (e) a new section describing the qualitative study.

The remainder of this paper is organized as follows. Section 2 discusses related tools, including tools for finding duplicated issue reports in bug tracking systems and also tools proposed to assign bugs to developers. The architecture, the central features, and an example of usage of NextBug are described in Section 2. We present the dataset and the evaluation of the tool in Section 2. Conclusions and future work are offered in Section 2. Finally, the availability and requirements for NextBug are presented in Section 2.

Related tools

Most open source systems adopt an Issue Tracking System (ITS) to support their maintenance process. Normally, in such systems both users and testers can report modification requests (Liu et al. 2012). This practice usually results in a continuous maintenance process where maintainers address the change requests as soon as possible. The ITS provides a central knowledge repository which also serves as a communication channel for geographically distributed developers and users (Anvik et al. 2006; Ihara et al. 2009).

Recent studies focused on finding duplicated issue reports in bug tracking systems. Duplicated reports can hamper the bug triaging process and may drain maintenance resources (Cavalcanti et al. 2013). Typically, tools for finding duplicated issues rely on traditional information retrieval techniques such as natural language processing, vector space model, and cosine similarity (Alipour et al. 2013; Sun et al. 2011; Wang et al. 2008). One of such approaches, called REP, analyzes both the textual information (using traditional techniques) along such with categorical information available in bug reports to improve the accuracy when finding duplicated reports (Sun et al. 2011).

When we compare techniques to find duplicated reports (Alipour et al. 2013; Sun et al. 2011; Wang et al. 2008) with NextBug, some differences emerge. First, duplicated bug techniques exclude bugs before they become available for developers to work on, i.e., duplicated techniques are applied in earlier stages of the maintenance process. On the other hand, NextBug is applied at later stages in the maintenance process, i.e., it shows bug recommendations when the developer is selecting bugs to work on. Second, NextBug only executes if the developer actively clicks on it. Therefore, NextBug causes no additional overhead unless the user wants to see its recommendations. The duplicate bug techniques do not specify whether their approach will be always executed and the overhead costs for such techniques. The third difference is the design objective; techniques to detect duplicated bugs need to be very precise to sort out duplicated bugs and not similar ones. NextBug aims to do the opposite and therefore needs to be precise to find similar bugs and not duplicated ones.

Tools to recommend the most suitable developer to handle a software issue are also reported in the literature (Anvik and Murphy 2011; Tamrawi et al. 2011; Kagdi et al. 2012). Most of them can be viewed as recommendation systems that suggest developers to handle a reported bug. For instance, Anvik and Murphy (2011) proposed an approach based on supervised machine learning that requires training to create a classifier. This classifier assigns the data (bug reports) to the closest developer.

Tools to recommend developers are usually applied at the same stages of the maintenance process as NextBug. However, these tools are more appropriate to organizations where most of the maintenance work is assigned to developers by their manager. NextBug is design to help in open source projects, where most developers usually have the liberty to chose what to work on.

We found in the literature few studies dealing with similar issue reports. There is one approach that suggests the fixing effort (in person-hours) required to correct an issue by using similar issues already fixed as training data (Weiss et al. 2007). Another approach also tries to predict the fixing time of bugs but to classify them as fast or slow fixing (Giger et al. 2010). These approaches could also improve maintenance productivity like NextBug, particularly if developers decide to work on fast fixing bugs. However, unlike NextBug, they do not help to reduce context switches which may reduce their productivity gains. Another study that deals with similar issue reports relies on similarity to extract terms and locate source code methods that may cause defects based on polymorphism (Wang et al. 2010). This is a completely different application domain than NextBug, as this study tries to predict defects, while NextBug aims to help developers address bugs in a more productive manner.

BugMaps is a tool that extracts information about bugs from bug tracking systems, link this information to other software artifacts, and provides many interactive visualizations of bugs, which are called bug maps (Hora et al. 2012). BugMaps-Granges extends BugMaps with visualizations for causal analysis of bugs (Couto et al. 2014b; Couto et al. 2014a).

To conclude, to the best of our knowledge, no available tools are capable of recommending similar bugs to help maintainers of open source systems.

Implementation

In this section, we present NextBug version 0.9, an open source tool available under the Mozilla Public License (MPL). In Section 2, we describe the main features. We present the tool's architecture and its main components in Section 2. Finally, in Section 2, we present an example of NextBug recommendation.

Main features

Currently, there are several ITSs that are used in software maintenance such as Bugzilla, Jira, Mantis, and RedMine. NextBug is implemented as a Bugzilla plug-in because this ITS is used by the Mozilla project, which was used to validate our tool. However, NextBug could be extended and applied to other ITS.

When a developer is analysing or browsing an issue, NextBug can recommend similar bugs in the usual Bugzilla web interface. NextBug uses a textual similarity algorithm to verify the similarity among bug reports registered in Bugzilla. This algorithm is described in Section 2.

Figure 1 shows an usage example of our tool. This figure shows a real bug from the Mozilla project, which refers to a FirefoxOS application issue related to a mobile device camera (Bug 937928). As we can observe, Bugzilla shows detailed information about this bug, such as a summary description, creation date, product, component, operational system, and hardware information. NextBug extends this original interface by showing a list of bugs similar to the browsed one. This list is shown on the lower right corner. Another important feature is that NextBug is only executed if its Ajax link is clicked and, thus, it

Figure 1 NextBug Screenshot. A screenshot showing the original Bugzilla interface for browsing a bug enhanced with the NextBug plug-in. Similar bugs are shown in the lower right corner.

does not cause additional overhead or hinder performance to developers who do not wish to follow similar bug recommendations.

In Figure 1, NextBug suggested three similar bugs to the one which is presented on the screenshot.

As we can note, NextBug not only detects similar bugs but it also reports an index to express this similarity.

By proposing NextBug, our final goal is to guide the developer's workflow by suggesting similar bugs to the one he/she is currently browsing. If a developer chooses to handle one of the recommended bugs, we claim he/she can minimize the context change inherent to the task of handling different bugs and, consequently, improve his/her productivity.

An important new feature of NextBug regarding its first released version (Rocha et al. 2014) is the support of filters to configure the provided recommendations. We implemented this feature after conducting a survey with Mozilla developers. Many developers said the previous version of our tool is indeed useful but we should provide a feature to customize the search results. The following comments show a sample feedback received from 66 Mozilla developers:

"It would not be bad, as long as it could be configured to do the recommendations according to a set of parameters." – R.C. * (We show only the initials from survey subjects to preserve their anonymity).

"If it presented similar bugs that I did not file, and which were not assigned to anyone, that might be useful." – B.B.

"It would probably need to be able to at least check if a bug is already assigned to the current user (or to another user, which probably makes them ineligible, too)." – T.S.

The recommendations produced by NextBug follow the established criteria set up by the filters. By clicking on the gear icon next to the NextBug label, a dialog popup shows the configuration options for the filters (Figure 2). These filters include the following options: (a) similarity threshold, i.e, the minimum similarity index required for a recommendation to be considered valid, (b) maximum number of recommendations given by NextBug, (c) maximum and minimum bug severities considered valid for the recommendations, (d)

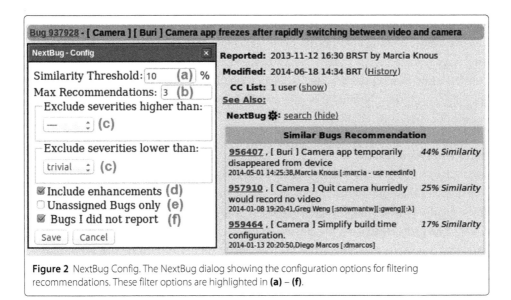

Figure 2 NextBug Config. The NextBug dialog showing the configuration options for filtering recommendations. These filter options are highlighted in **(a)** – **(f)**.

option to consider enhancements requests along with with bugs when presenting the recommendations for similar bugs, (e) searching only for unassigned bugs, i.e., recommend only bugs that no one is currently working on, and (f) shows only bugs that have not been reported by the current user; this filter might be useful because the current user is probably aware of the bugs he/she reported and he/she may not want them to be recommended back to him/her. Except for the first and second filters, all other filters are optional, e.g., the user is not required to check for unassigned bugs if he/she doesn't want to.

Moreover, the similarity threshold (i.e., the first filter) needs some experimentation from the user to fit his preferences. We suggest an initial value of 10%, which usually results in a good number of relevant recommendations. As the user increases this value, NextBug gives less recommendations but more precise ones as the tool becomes more strict. The decision is up to the user, who can decide if he/she wants fewer but more precise recommendations, or more recommendations but not as precise.

Figure 3 shows NextBug's architecture, including the system main components and the interaction among them. As described in Section 2, NextBug is a plug-in for Bugzilla.

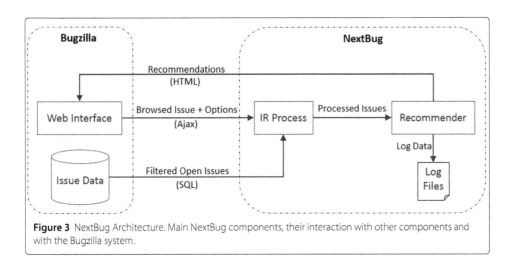

Figure 3 NextBug Architecture. Main NextBug components, their interaction with other components and with the Bugzilla system.

Therefore, it is implemented in Perl, the same language used in the implementation of Bugzilla. Basically, NextBug instruments the Bugzilla interface used for browsing and for selecting bugs reported for a system. NextBug registers an Ajax event in this interface that calls NextBug passing the browsed issue and the filter options as input parameters. We opt for an Ajax event because it is executed only if it is called by the developer and therefore it does not cause additional overhead.

Architecture and Algorithms

Algorithm 1 summarizes the processing of a NextBug Ajax event. It selects the filtered open issues that follows the criteria defined by the filter options (line 3), and then performs standard IR techniques on these open issues along with the browsed issue (lines 4-9). The processed issues are passed to the recommender system which selects the ones that are more relevant to the browsed issue (line 10). Finally, the produced recommendations are returned to the Bugzilla interface (line 14).

Algorithm 1 Recommendation Algorithm

 1: **function** NEXTBUG-EVENT(*BrowsedIssue, Options*)

 2:     *StartTime* = get-System-Time-Milisecs( );

 3:     *FilteredOpenIssues* = get-Open-Issues(*Options*);

 4:     q = IR-Processing(*BrowsedIssue*);

 5:     $D = \emptyset$;

 6:     **for each** issue $d' \in$ *FilteredOpenIssues* **do**

 7:         d_j = IR-Processing(d');

 8:         $D = D \cup d_j$;

 9:     **end for**

10:     *Recommendations* = recommender(q, D, *Options*);

11:     *EndTime* = get-System-Time-Milisecs( );

12:     *ExecutionTime* = *EndTime* − *StartTime*;

13:     log(q, *Recommendations, ExecutionTime*);

14:     **return** *Recommendations* ;

15: **end function**

Figure 3 shows that NextBug architecture has two central components: *Information Retrieval (IR) Process* and *Recommender*. We discuss these two components in the following subsections.

Information retrieval process component

The *IR Process* component obtains the filtered open issues currently available on the Bugzilla system along with the browsed bug. Then it relies on the following standard IR techniques for natural language processing: tokenization, stemming, and stop-words removal (Wang et al. 2008; Runeson et al. 2007). We implemented all such techniques in Perl. After this initial processing, the issues are transformed into vectors using the Vector Space Model (VSM) (Runeson et al. 2007; Baeza-Yates and Ribeiro-Neto 1999). VSM is a classical information retrieval model to process documents and to quantify their similarities. The usage of VSM is accomplished by decomposing the data (available bug reports and queries) into t-dimensional vectors, assigning weights to each indexed term. The weights w_i are positive real numbers that represent the i-th index term in the vector. To calculate w_i we used the following equation, which is called a *tf-idf* weighted formula:

$$w_i = (1 + \log_2 f_i) \times \log_2 \frac{N}{n_i}$$

where f_i is the frequency of the i-th term in the document, N is the total number of documents, and n_i is the number of documents in which the i-th term occurs.

Recommender component

The *Recommender* component receives the processed issues and verifies the ones similar to the browsed one. The similarity is computed using the cosine similarity measure (Baeza-Yates and Ribeiro-Neto 1999; Runeson et al. 2007). More specifically, the similarity between the vectors of a document d_j and a query q is described by the following equation, which is called the cosine similarity because it measures the cosine of the angle between the two vectors:

$$Sim(d_j, q) = \cos(\Theta) = \frac{\vec{d_j} \bullet \vec{q}}{||\vec{d_j}|| \times ||\vec{q}||} = \frac{\sum_{i=1}^{t} w_{i,d} \times w_{i,q}}{\sqrt{\sum_{i=1}^{t} (w_{i,d})^2} \times \sqrt{\sum_{i=1}^{t} (w_{i,q})^2}}$$

Since all the weights are greater or equal to zero, we have $0 \leq Sim(d_j, q) \leq 1$, where zero indicates that there is no relation between the two vectors, and one indicates the highest possible similarity, i.e., both vectors are actually the same.

The issues are then ordered according to their similarity before being returned to Bugzilla. Since NextBug executes as an Ajax event, the recommendations are showed in the same Bugzilla interface used by developers when browsing and selecting bugs to fix.

Logging files are also updated with anonymous information about the process before the recommendations return to Bugzilla interface. The anonymity is important to preserve the user's privacy and to prevent NextBug being perceived as a spyware program. The logging files register execution time data, the browsed issue, and the recommendations given. Therefore, it is possible to monitor how long it takes for NextBug event to execute. The anonymous data collected can also be used in future studies to support further analysis and evaluation on NextBug.

Example of recommendation

Table 1 presents an example of a bug opened for the component `DOM:Device Interfaces` of the `Core` Mozilla product and the first three recommendations (top-3) suggested by NextBug for this bug. As we can observe in the summary description, both the query and the recommendations require maintenance in the `Device Storage` API,

Table 1 Example of Recommendation

	Sim	Bug ID	Summary	Creation	Fixed
Bug	–	788588	Device Storage - Default location for device storage on windows should be NS_WIN_PERSONAL_DIR	2012-09-05	2012-09-06
Top-1	56%	754350	Device Storage - Clean up error strings	2012-05-11	2012-10-17
Top-2	47%	788268	Device Storage - Convert tests to use public types	2012-09-04	2012-09-06
Top-3	42%	786922	Device Storage - use a properties file instead of the mime service	2012-08-29	2012-09-06

used by Web apps to access local file systems. Moreover, all four issues were handled by the same developer (Dev ID 302291).

We can also observe that the three recommended issues were created before the original query. In fact, the developer fixed the bugs associated to the second and the third recommendations in the same date on which he/she fixed the original query, i.e., on 2012-09-06. However, he/she only resolved the first recommended bug (ID 754350) 41 days latter, i.e., on 2012-10-17. Therefore, NextBug could have helped this maintainer to discover quickly the related issues, which probably demanded more effort without a recommendation tool.

Results and discussion

In this section, we initially describe the dataset used to evaluate NextBug in quantitative terms (Section 2). Section 2 presents the main results from this quantitative study. Finally, Section 2 shows the main findings of a qualitative study with Mozilla developers.

Dataset

We used a dataset with bugs from the Mozilla project to evaluate NextBug. Mozilla is composed of 69 products from different domains which are implemented in different programming languages. The Mozilla project includes some popular systems such as Firefox, Thunderbird, SeaMonkey, and Bugzilla. We considered only issues that were actually fixed from January 2009 to October 2012, in a total of 130,495 issues. More specifically, we ignored issue types such as "duplicated", "incomplete", and "invalid". Figure 4 shows the monthly number of issues fixed in this time frame.

Mozilla issues are also classified according to their severity in the following scale: *blocker, critical, major, normal, minor,* and *trivial.* Table 2 shows the number and the percentage of each of these categories in our dataset. This scale also includes enhancements as a particular severity category.

Table 2 also shows the number of days required to fix the issues in each category. We can observe that *blocker* bugs are quickly corrected by developers, showing the lowest values for maximum, average, standard deviation, and median measures among the considered categories. The presented lifetimes also indicate that issues with *critical* and *major* severity are closer to each other. Finally, *enhancements* are very different from the others, showing the highest values for average, standard deviation, and median.

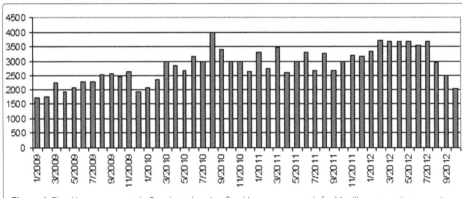

Figure 4 Fixed issues per month. Bar chart showing fixed issues per month for Mozilla systems between jan 2009 to oct 2012.

Table 2 Issues per severity

Severity	Issues		Days to resolve				
	Number	%	Min	Max	Avg	Dev	Med
blocker	2,720	2.08	0	814	15.44	52.25	1
critical	7,513	5.76	0	1258	37.87	99.52	6
major	7,508	5.75	0	1275	41.59	109.83	5
normal	103,385	79.23	0	1373	46.27	108.84	8
minor	3,660	2.80	0	1355	77.05	161.72	11
trivial	2,109	1.62	0	1288	80.84	164.74	11
enhancement	3,600	2.76	0	1285	126.14	195.25	40
Total	130,495	100	–	–	–	–	–

Quantitative study

For the quantitative part of our study, we simulated the use of NextBug for each bug in the dataset, i.e., all bugs were processed as if they were the *browsed issue* selected by a developer and processed by Algorithm 1 (described in Section 2). We considered bugs that were open when the *browsed issue* was created for the *filtered open issues* used by the Algorithm 1. For this study, we configured NextBug with a similarity threshold of 10%.

In this evaluation, we defined a relevant recommendation as one that shares the same developer with the browsed issue. More specifically, we consider that a recently created issue is related to a second opened issue when they are handled by the same developer. The assumption in this case is that NextBug fosters gains of productivity whenever it recommends issues that are later fixed anyway by the same developer.

We used three metrics in our evaluation: Feedback, Precision, and Likelihood. These metrics are inspired by the evaluation followed by the ROSE recommendation system (Zimmermann et al. 2004). Although, ROSE targets a different context, their metrics are appropriate to evaluate any kind of recommendation system.

Before we present the equations to calculate the metrics, we must first define the following sets:

- A_q: the set of recommendations provided by NextBug.
- $A_q(k)$: top-k issues in A_q ordered by textual similarity (only defined for $|A_q| \geq k$).
- R_q: the set of open issues when the query (or browsed issue) is processed, ordered by textual similarity. These open issues must also share the same developer as the query. This is the formal definition of relevant recommendations used in our evaluation.
- Z: the set of all processed queries. For our evaluation, the Z set is composed by 130,495 queries (i.e., the same size as our dataset).
- Z_k: a subset of Z with the queries that returned at least k recommendations.

Feedback: measures the number of recommendations provided to a given query. Formally, the feedback $Fb(k)$ is the percentage of queries with at least k recommendations, as follows:

$$Fb(k) = \frac{|Z_k|}{|Z|}$$

For example, suppose a recommendation system that executed 100 queries ($|Z| = 100$). If all those queries returned at least 1 recommendation each, then Feedback for $k = 1$, i.e., Fb(1) would be 100%. On the other hand, if only 40 of those queries returned at lest 3 recommendations, then $Fb(3) = 40\%$.

Precision: measures the ratio of relevant recommendations. More specifically, we define the precision of the first k recommendations provided by NextBug as follows:

$$P_q(k) = \frac{|A_q(k) \cap R_q|}{|A_q(k)|}$$

Moreover, the overall precision in our dataset is defined as the average of the precisions achieved for each query, as follows:

$$P(k) = \frac{1}{|Z_k|} \sum_{q \in Z_k} P_q(k)$$

Suppose that a query returned 4 recommendations. If the first recommendation is a relevant one, then $P_q(1) = 100\%$. Otherwise, if the first recommendation is not relevant, then $P_q(1) = 0\%$. Moreover, if among all 4 recommendations only the second one is relevant, then the precision values would be $P_q(2) = 50\%$, $P_q(3) = 33\%$, and $P_q(4) = 25\%$.

Likelihood: is a common measure to assess the usefulness of recommendations. In our particular approach, it checks whether there is a relevant recommendation among the top-k suggested issues. Formally, we define the likelihood of the top-k recommendations provided by our approach as follows:

$$L_q(k) = \begin{cases} 1 & \text{if } A_q(k) \cap R_q \neq \emptyset \\ 0 & \text{otherwise} \end{cases}$$

Therefore, $L_q(k)$ is a binary measure. If there is at least a relevant recommendation among the top-k recommendations, it returns one; otherwise, it returns zero.

The overall likelihood in our dataset is defined as the average of the likelihood measured for each query, as follows:

$$L(k) = \frac{1}{|Z_k|} \sum_{q \in Z_k} L_q(k)$$

Suppose that a query returned 4 recommendations but only the third one is relevant. Then the likelihood values would be $L_q(1) = 0\%$, $L_q(2) = 0\%$, $L_q(3) = 100\%$, and $L_q(4) = 100\%$.

Summary: Feedback is the ratio of queries where NextBug makes at least k recommendations. Precision is the ratio of relevant recommendations among the top-k recommendations provided by NextBug. Finally, Likelihood indicates whether at least one relevant recommendation is included among NextBug's top-k suggestions.

Results: Figure 5 shows the average feedback (left chart), precision (central chart) and likelihood (right chart) up to $k = 5$. The results presented in this figure are summarized as follows:

- NextBug achieves a feedback of 0.65 for $k = 1$. Therefore, on average, NextBug makes at least one suggestion for 65% of the bugs, i.e., for every five bugs NextBug provides at least one similar recommendation for three of them. Moreover, NextBug shows on average 3.2 recommendations per query.
- NextBug achieves a precision of at least 0.31 for all values of k. In other words, 31% of NextBug recommendations are on average relevant (i.e., further handled by the same developer), no matter how many suggestions are given.

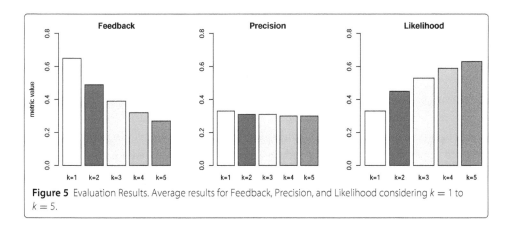

Figure 5 Evaluation Results. Average results for Feedback, Precision, and Likelihood considering $k = 1$ to $k = 5$.

- NextBug achieves a likelihood of 0.54 for $k = 3$. Therefore, in about 54% of the cases, there is a top-3 recommendation that is later handled by the same developer responsible for the original bug.

Since we are not aware of other next bug recommendation tool, we compared our results with a recommender system targeting other software engineering tasks. For example, ROSE (Zimmermann et al. 2004) achieved the following results for recommending co-change relations in the Eclipse system: feedback 64% ($k = 1$), precision 30% ($k = 1$), and likelihood 57% ($k = 3$). Therefore, we believe our results are good enough to encourage developers to adopt NextBug in their maintenance tasks.

Qualitative study

For the qualitative part of our study, we conducted a survey with Mozilla developers. During one week, we analysed bugs that were fixed for Mozilla systems on their official Bugzilla website (<https://bugzilla.mozilla.org/>, verified 2014-11-01). For each fixed bug, we used NextBug to give recommendations based on the bugs that were still open at each day.

We sent by e-mail the top-3 recommendations suggested by NextBug to Mozilla maintainers with two questions. The first question asked whether the recommendations given were relevant, i.e., if the recommendations were similar bugs that could be fixed next. The second question asked if they thought a tool like NextBug to recommend similar bugs would be useful for developers from their community. A total of 66 maintainers (from 176) answered our survey. The following comments show a sample of the feedback we received from those developers:

"(...) this would help contributors to discover and be active on the code." – N.P.

"(...) anything that would make parsing and organising bugs easier would be amazing – they're currently very hard for some of the staff to keep track of!" – K.B.

Our results in this survey are summarized as follows: (i) 77% of the developers found our recommendations relevant, i.e., they answered yes for our first question; (ii) 85% of the developers confirmed that a tool to recommend similar bugs would be useful to the Mozilla community, i.e., they answered yes for the second question.

Conclusion

This paper presented NextBug version 0.9, a tool for recommending similar bugs. NextBug is implemented in Perl as a plug-in for Bugzilla, a widely used Issue Tracking

Systems (ITS), specially popular in open source systems. NextBug relies on information retrieval techniques to extract semantic information from issue reports in order to identify the similarity of open bugs with the one that is being handled by a developer.

We evaluate NextBug with a dataset of 130,495 Mozilla bugs, achieving feedback results of 65%, precision results around 31%, and likelihood results greater than 54% (considering top-3 recommendations for likelihood). We also conducted a survey with Mozilla developers using recommendations provided by NextBug. From such developers, 77% of them ranked our recommendations as relevant and 85% confirmed that NextBug would be useful to the Mozilla community.

Future work

First, we plan to make NextBug an official Bugzilla extension. We believe that once NextBug becomes an official plug-in, real open source projects will install the tool in their Issue Tracking System (ITS). Second, we want to acquire log data from real working projects using our tool. We plan to use this data to better analyse the tool's usage by developers, and thus, propose future improvements for NextBug. Third, we want to apply our tool algorithm in a slightly different context, creating another tool called PreviousBug. Instead of looking for similar open issues, PreviousBug would look for similar resolved bugs. Thus, PreviousBug would help developers implement a given task by looking at similar tasks already resolved in the past. PreviousBug would require an integration with Version Control System to retrieve the parts of code related to resolved tasks.

Availability and requirements

Availability information and requirements are as follows:

- **Project name:** NextBug
- **Project home page:** <http://aserg.labsoft.dcc.ufmg.br/nextbug/>
- **Operating system(s):** NextBug is a plugin for Bugzilla, and as such it executes in the same operating systems as Bugzilla.
- **Programming language:** Perl
- **License:** Mozilla Public License.
- **Other requirements:** Bugzilla 3.6 or higher.
- **Any restrictions to use by non-academics:** no additional restrictions as described in the license.

Competing interests
The authors declare that they have no competing interests.

Authors' contributions
HR and GO worked on the implementation of the tool. HR and MTV worked on the conception and design of the tool. HR, HMN, and MTV wrote and revised this manuscript. All authors read and approved the final manuscript.

Acknowledgements
This work is supported by CNPq, CAPES, and FAPEMIG.

Author details
[1]Department of Computer Science, UFMG, 31.270-901 Belo Horizonte, Brazil. [2]Department of Computer Science, PUC Minas, 30.535-901 Belo Horizonte, Brazil.

References

Alipour A, Hindle A, Stroulia E (2013) A contextual approach towards more accurate duplicate bug report detection. In: 10th Working Conference on Mining Software Repositories (MSR). IEEE Press, Piscataway, NJ, USA. p 183

Anvik J, Hiew L, Murphy GC (2006) Who should fix this bug?. In: 28th International Conference on Software Engineering (ICSE). ACM, New York, NY, USA. pp 361–370

Anvik J, Murphy GC (2011) Reducing the effort of bug report triage: recommenders for development-oriented decisions. ACM Trans Softw Eng Methodol (TOSEM) 20(3):10–11035

Aziz J, Ahmed F, Laghari MS (2009) Empirical analysis of team and application size on software maintenance and support activities. In: 1st International Conference on Information Management and Engineering (ICIME). IEEE Computer Society, Washington, DC, USA. pp 47–51

Banker RD, Slaughter SA (1997) A field study of scale economies in software maintenance. Manage Sci 43:1709–1725

Baeza-Yates RA, Ribeiro-Neto B (1999) Modern Information Retrieval. 2nd edn. Addison-Wesley, Boston, MA, USA

Cavalcanti YC, Mota Silveira Neto PA, Lucredio D, Vale T, Almeida ES, Lemos Meira SR (2013) The bug report duplication problem: an exploratory study. Softw Qual J 21(1):39–66

Couto C, Pires P, Valente MT, Bigonha R, Anquetil N (2014a) Predicting software defects with causality tests. J Syst Softw 93:24–41

Couto C, Valente MT, Pires P, Hora A, Anquetil N, Bigonha R (2014b) Bugmaps-granger: A tool for visualizing and predicting bugs using granger causality tests. J Softw Eng Res Dev 1(2):1–12

Giger E, Pinzger M, Gall H (2010) Predicting the fix time of bugs. In: 2nd International Workshop on Recommendation Systems for Software Engineering (RSSE). ACM, New York, NY, USA. pp 52–56

Hora A, Couto C, Anquetil N, Ducasse S, Bhatti M, Valente MT, Martins J (2012) BugMaps: A tool for the visual exploration and analysis of bugs. In: 16th European Conference on Software Maintenance and Reengineering (CSMR), Tool Demonstration Track. IEEE Computer Society, Washington, DC, USA. pp 523–526

Ihara A, Ohira M, Matsumoto K (2009) An analysis method for improving a bug modification process in open source software development. In: 7th International Workshop Principles of Software Evolution and Software Evolution (IWPSE-Evol). ACM, New York, NY, USA. pp 135–144

Junio GA, Malta MN, de Almeida Mossri H, Marques-Neto HT, Valente MT (2011) On the benefits of planning and grouping software maintenance requests. In: 15th European Conference on Software Maintenance and Reengineering (CSMR). IEEE Computer Society, Washington, DC, USA. pp 55–64

Kagdi H, Gethers M, Poshyvanyk D, Hammad M (2012) Assigning change requests to software developers. J Softw: Evol Process 24(1):3–33

Ko AJ, Aung H, Myers BA (2005) Eliciting design requirements for maintenance-oriented IDEs: A detailed study of corrective and perfective maintenance tasks. In: 27th International Conference on Software Engineering (ICSE). ACM, New York, NY, USA. pp 126–135

Liu K, Tan HBK, Chandramohan M (2012) Has this bug been reported?. In: 20th ACM SIGSOFT International Symposium on the Foundations of Software Engineering (FSE). pp 28–1284

Marques-Neto H, Aparecido GJ, Valente MT (2013) A quantitative approach for evaluating software maintenance services. In: 28th ACM Symposium on Applied Computing (SAC). pp 1068–1073

Meyer AN, Fritz T, Murphy GC, Zimmermann T (2014) Software developers' perceptions of productivity. In: 22th International Symposium on Foundations of Software Engineering (FSE). pp 26–36

Mockus A, Fielding RT, Herbsleb JD (2002) Two case studies of open source software development: Apache and Mozilla. ACM Trans Softw Eng Methodol 11(3):309–346

Rocha H, Oliveira G, Maques-Neto H, Valente MT (2014) NextBug: A Tool for Recommending Similar Bugs in Open-Source Systems. In: V Brazilian Conference on Software: Theory and Practice – Tools Track (CBSoft Tools). SBC, Maceio, AL, Brazil, Vol. 2. pp 53–60

Runeson P, Alexandersson M, Nyholm O (2007) Detection of duplicate defect reports using natural language processing. In: 29th International Conference on Software Engineering (ICSE). IEEE Computer Society, Washington, DC, USA. pp 499–510

Sun C, Lo D, Khoo S-C, Jiang J (2011) Towards more accurate retrieval of duplicate bug reports. In: 26th IEEE/ACM International Conference on Automated Software Engineering (ASE). IEEE Computer Society. pp 253–262

Tamrawi A, Nguyen TT, Al-Kofahi JM, Nguyen TN (2011) Fuzzy set and cache-based approach for bug triaging. In: 19th ACM SIGSOFT Symposium and the 13th European Conference on Foundations of Software Engineering (ESEC/FSE). ACM, New York, NY, USA. pp 365–375

Tan Y, Mookerjee VS (2005) Comparing uniform and flexible policies for software maintenance and replacement. IEEE Trans Softw Eng 31(3):238–255

Wang X, Zhang L, Xie T, Anvik J, Sun J (2008) An approach to detecting duplicate bug reports using natural language and execution information. In: 30th International Conference on Software Engineering (ICSE). ACM, New York, NY, USA. pp 461–470

Wang D, Lin M, Zhang H, Hu H (2010) Detect related bugs from source code using bug information. In: 34th IEEE Computer Software and Applications Conference (COMPSAC). IEEE Computer Society, Washington, DC, USA. pp 228–237

Weiss C, Premraj R, Zimmermann T, Zeller A (2007) How long will it take to fix this bug? In: 4th International Workshop on Mining Software Repositories (MSR). IEEE Computer Society, Washington, DC, USA

Zimmermann T, Weisgerber P, Diehl S, Zeller A (2004) Mining version histories to guide software changes. In: 26th International Conference on Software Engineering (ICSE). IEEE Computer Society, Washington, DC, USA. pp 563–572

5

Applying statistical process control in small sized evolutionary projects: results and lessons learned in the implementation of CMMI-DEV maturity level 5 in Synapsis Brazil

Carlos Simões[1] and Mariano Montoni[2*]

* Correspondence:
mmontoni@promovesolucoes.com
[2]ProMove – Business Intelligence
Solutions, Rua da Assembleia, No
10, Sala 2805, CEP 22.011-000
Centro, Rio de Janeiro, RJ, Brasil
Full list of author information is
available at the end of the article

Abstract

This paper presents the roadmap adopted by Synapsis Brazil to implement the process areas of CMMI-DEV Maturity Level 5 in small sized evolutionary projects. We also discuss the results of applying statistical process control in more than 20 projects, and the lessons learned in conducting successfully a SCAMPI A assessment of CMMI-DEV Maturity Level 5.

Background

Process maturity models like CMMI-DEV and Brazilian model MPS.BR are adopted by organizations as a reference for software process improvement. Many benefits are observed by organizations that adopted such models, for instance, increase in software development team productivity, reduction of projects schedule and costs, and increase in software product quality (Travassos and Kalinowski 2012).

Nonetheless, CMMI-DEV and MPS.BR assessments concentrate on the lower maturity levels, making more difficult to obtain benefits with implementation of higher maturity level best practices. According to (SOFTEX 2013), less than 2% (8 out of 440) of all MPS.BR assessments conducted in Brazil were on the higher maturity level (level A), and 88% of the assessments concentrated on the first two maturity levels (G and F). According to (SEI 2012), only 6% (11 out of 174) of the official valid assessments of SCAMPI A of CMMI-DEV model in Brazil were on the highest maturity level (level 5), while 50% of these assessments concentrated on the lowest two maturity levels (1 and 2).

Many factors difficult the successful execution of software process improvement initiatives. According to (Montoni and Rocha 2011), many of these factors are related to software organization members (for instance, easy to accept changes and higher management support), and also to factors related to consultancy organization members (for instance, knowledge, experience and skills of members of the consultancy) and factors related to organizational strategy and policies (for instance, inexistence of conflict interest in the software process implementation initiative), among others. Therefore, it is likely that many of these factors may also difficult the conduction of software process initiatives in higher maturity levels, like CMMI level 5 and MPS level A.

This paper presents the roadmap adopted by Synapsis Brazil to overcome critical success barriers of the implementation of process areas of level 5 of CMMI-DEV in small sized evolutionary projects. The paper also discusses the results of the application of statistical process control in more than 20 projects, and the lessons learned in the successful conduction of a SCAMPI A assessment of CMMI-DEV maturity level 5 after only 12 months of process implementation with the support of ProMove, a consultancy specialized in software process improvement.

In the CMMI maturity levels 2 and 3 and MPS.BR maturity levels G to C the control of the software process is reactive. In higher maturity levels (CMMI levels 4 and 5, for instance) software process control shall be proactive, based on its performance (Luo et al. 2008; Florac et al. 2000). In this context, traditional software measurement methods and techniques such as comparing planned versus actual data are not sufficient to predict process performance.

One of the mayor difficulties to achieve higher maturity levels in software development is the lack of adequacy of the collected measures and measurement database available in software organizations to apply statistical process control, and the difficulty to access project data (Kitchenham et al. 2006). Therefore, organizations seeking to achieve high maturity in their process shall measure software process efficiently since the early stages of a process improvement program.

Some organizations get frustrated with the assessment of process performance by using statistical process control mainly because they start using these powerful techniques to measure large processes, composed of a great variety of subprocesses (Florac et al. 2000). Statistical process control do not need to be applied in all processes or process components that compose the organization software development process, but it shall be applied only to critical process and not all statistical process control techniques are applicable to all software processes (Sargut and Demirors 2006).

Statistical process control focus in controlling key processes and process components. Moreover, in order to be effective certain requirements must be satisfied, such as reasonable amount of observations, existence of controlled processes and performance objectives aligned to business strategy, definition of measures associated to activities that produce tangible products, and product quality characteristics defined by the clients should be used to select and define measures. Moreover, a process or process component should be easy to control, i.e., should be defined appropriately and of short duration (Sargut and Demirors 2006; Weller et al. 2008).

Case description

Synapsis Brazil is one of the most relevant Latin America IT services and technology integration organization, with a wide portfolio of IT services that include IT outsourcing, cloud computing services, IT consultancy and SAP, software factory, technical and business solutions, smart grid solutions and development/implementation of customized solutions. Synapsis Brazil is also leader in specific segments as utilities, oil and gas, and Brazilian govern sectors. The company is also aggressively expanding in other vertical industries with significant presence in Argentina, Brazil, Chile, Colombia and Peru.

In order to demonstrate excellence in software development, Synapsis Brazil invested highly in the last years in the improvement of its processes. The organization was successfully assessed in CMMI maturity levels 2 and 3 in August 2006 and July 2009, respectively. In December 2011, Synapsis Brazil higher management established as a process objective to achieve in December 2012, the official assessment of CMMI maturity level 5. This objective was considered ambitious since the average of the organizations take 2 years to move from CMMI level 3 to 5 (SEI – Software Engineering Institute 2012) (double of the time established by Synapsis Brazil higher management). Even though the objective was ambitious, Synapsis Brazil conducted successfully an official SCAMPI A appraisal on CMMI maturity level 5 in December 2012, after 12 month of process improvement implementation.

One of the factors that most contributed to the success of the initiative was the higher management support. Since the beginning of the implementation, Synapsis Brazil higher management dedicated sufficient human and financial resources to successfully implement CMMI level 5 process areas. Moreover, they participated actively of all meetings to analyze the situation of organization process performance. The support of higher management was also essential in the establishment of quality and process performance objectives. After many meeting with the process group, it was established as performance objective that the project real productivity should be equal or higher than 90% of the expected productivity, whilst the quality objective were that the client acceptance test approval should be equal or higher than 95%. Table 1 presents the evolution of Synapsis Brazil processes to achieve these objectives.

Table 1 Evolution of Synapsis Brazil processes to high maturity

Baseline number	Publication date	Project name	Process improvement objective	Results achieved	CMMI level
14 - 19	May to December 2011	Input Carga de Vendas Input Outros Lançamentos Caixa Input Projeto de Investimento Exportação de Investimento Input Carga de Depreciação Input faturamento entre Empresas DRE Input Cálculos de Pessoal Input Dados de Pessoal Manter Parametrização de DRE Fluxo de Caixa	To assess implemented improvements and identify new process and templates improvement opportunities focused on the adequacy to changes in strategic objectives.	Process and templates improved.	3
20 – 24	January to July 2012	POAB_Fase_2_Incremento_1 POAB_Fase_2_Incremento_2 POAB_Fase_2_Incremento_3 POAB_Fase_2_Incremento_4	To pilot incremental improvements (process and templates) and innovations (adaptation to small sized projects, code inspection, peer review of technical specification).	Quality and productivity improvement tendency. Process and templates adjusted to new objectives.	3 -> 4
25 - 26	October 2012	SCEBR-1754 SCEBR-1760 SCEBR-3024 SCEBR-4947 SCEBR-4949	To analyze subprocesses performance aiming to achieve subprocesses stabilization.	Quality and productivity improvement. Process and templates adjusted to new objectives.	4 -> 5
27 (Actual)	December 2012	SCEBR_1621 SCEBR_6811	To verify quality and productivity improvement. To pilot innovative improvement (peer programming and test coverage analysis).	Process analysis confirmed significant quality and productivity improvement were achieved in the projects.	5

In order to achieve quality and performance objectives established by Synapsis Brazil, first we conducted an analysis of the organizational process baselines that were adherent to CMMI level 3 practices adopted in the projects in the period of May to December 2011 (baselines 14 to 19 of Table 1). The analyses demonstrated that the quality and performance objectives were not being achieved and that several process improvements were necessary to achieve the goal. One of the main improvements conducted were the process optimization. This optimization was executed by automating process activities, and by eliminating redundant standard process activities that do not aggregate direct value to the software product. As a result, we obtained an optimized process with a minimum set of activities easy to understand, plan, monitor, measure and execute. After implementing the process optimization, 77% of the process activities were eliminated (104 out of 135 activities) without losing adherence to CMMI level 3 practices. This reduction were critical to allow the adoption of CMMI level 5 practices not only in small sized evolutionary projects, but also in large software development projects.

In the period of January to July 2012, were published baselines with not only the purpose of piloting incremental improvements in processes and templates, but also aiming to implement innovative improvements such as adaptation of the standard process to small sized evolutionary projects (less than 200 man-hour), and adoption of code inspection and peer review of technical specifications (baselines 20 to 24 of Table 1). The process adaptation strategy to small projects, and the adoption of practices to increase the quality of intermediate software development products (software architecture, test plans, requirement and technical specifications etc.) were considered critical success factors, because help to achieve the organizational quality and performance objectives (assertiveness of estimated productivity and reduction of defects detected by the client). Measurement analysis demonstrated that small projects were easier to be estimated, monitored and controlled, since corrective actions to manage deviations from project plans have more effect on the project than on large projects. Moreover, the anticipation of defects detection helped to improve product quality, and consequently, to reduce the amount of defects detected by the client in the acceptance testes. As a result of the pilot of these improvements, we could observe a tendency in the improvement of quality and productivity.

The next step was the stabilization of the processes by conducting performance analysis of selected subprocesses. The following subprocesses were selected for statistical process control since they are in the critical path of the projects: Specify product requirements, Elaborate technical specification and effort estimates, Code and integrate units, Conduct product tests and Conduct product acceptance tests. Improvements in processes and templates were adopted in new projects (baselines 25 and 26 of Table 1). The specialized knowledge of the consultancy team in high maturity practices, mainly knowledge about statistical process control were considered a critical success factor to conduct performance analysis and to evolve the process baselines. The knowledge acquired by taking specialized courses in the field helped to understand potential problems that affect process performance, and to suggest incremental and innovative improvements that could help to achieve organizational quality and performance objectives. Nevertheless, performance analysis of baseline data demonstrated that although the performance objective were achieved, it was not possible to achieve the quality objective, since many defects continued to be detected by the client in the acceptance tests.

The final step was to pilot innovative improvements like the adoption of peer programming and test coverage analysis in the projects (baseline 27). The performance analysis of the processes executed in the pilot projects confirmed the improvement in the quality and process performance. Consequently, we could successfully achieve the objectives established by the organization. The easy of process change acceptance and the tool support for statistical process control were considered critical success factors in this phase. During the conduction of the pilots, many improvements were implemented in the projects, including during projects execution, requiring some rework by the project managers and the development team. All project members were open to process changes, helping the organization to achieve its objectives. The adopted tools for statistical process control such as MiniTab™ and Oracle Crystall Ball™ reduced considerably the effort to perform data analysis; helping to rapidly verify if subprocesses attributes relations were statistically relevant.

Discussion and evaluation

In the last section, the knowledge about statistical process control, and the use of support tools to statistical process control were considered critical success factors in the implementation of high maturity practices in Synapsis Brazil. In order to manage those factors effectively, the process and templates of Synapsis Brazil were adjusted so that the application of statistical process control knowledge and techniques could be easily adopted by project managers during quantitative management of small sized evolutionary projects. This section presents some of the results obtained with the implementation of these improvements.

The lack of an adequate measurement repository in the market to support statistical process control was a problem for the implementation of statistical software process control. In order to minimize this problem, Synapsis Brazil implemented a specific measurement repository to support adoption of statistical software process control techniques. The adopted strategy in the implementation of the repository and in loading the necessary data was the following: (i) Defect information originated in Excel spreadsheets in which we implemented specific entries to facilitate collection of measures and to load data in the measurement repository; (ii) Information of estimated man-power effort, activities, process, size, complexity, productivity are loaded in the planning and monitoring tool used by project managers from size and effort data extracted of the estimation tool; (iii) Information of actual effort are loaded in the planning and monitoring tool used by project managers from data extracted of the Jira™ workflow tool; and (iv) Information about activities executed, estimated man-power effort, actual effort, activities schedule, productivity, product size, team, profile, technology etc., are loaded from measurement data extracted from the planning and monitoring tool. The processing of data stored in the repository, and two tools supported the visualization and generation of control graphics: Oracle Crystal Ball™ e Minitab™.

The lack of adequate tools to support quantitative management motivated the elaboration of a spreadsheet to support project managers in storing baseline and prediction models data. Figure 1 presents an example of the support tool to quantitative management. The tool presented in Figure 1 supports two statistical process control mechanisms. The top of the figure presents a control graphic automatically generated from

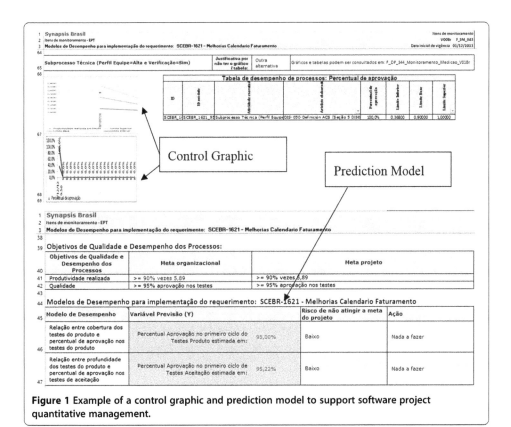

Figure 1 Example of a control graphic and prediction model to support software project quantitative management.

project data. The bottom part of Figure 1 presents the probability analysis of not achieving the project quality and performance objectives based on the prediction models developed. By using the spreadsheet, statistical knowledge becomes transparent, thus facilitating its use and diminishing resistance by the project team.

It was observed that one of the most complex activities to be executed involved the selection of which subprocesses attributes should be controlled to address the established quality and performance objectives. The analysis of existence measurement data in the repository indicated that some of the characteristics of the subprocesses have greater influence in achieving the quality and performance indexes established by the organization. The combination of information about the characteristics of the subprocesses and other project information, such as characteristics of the team allocated in the project, allowed the project managers to verify the probability of achieving the quality and performance objectives every time the data were updated, thus providing the means to manage action plans to minimize associated risks of not achieving the objectives. This mechanism of subprocesses and its attributes selection not only simplified the implementation of a complex high maturity practice, but also facilitated the understanding of the process selection concept by the project managers.

Synapsis Brazil process group identified that the Minitab™ tool to support data regression analysis helps not only in the early stages of performance analysis, for instance, to verify correlation of subprocesses attributes selected for statistical process control, but also supports the calculation of prediction models adopted in the quantitative management of Synapsis Brazil projects. For instance, the following performance model was developed by the application of regression analysis technique supported by MiniTab™:

Percentage of Approved = 0,818 + 0,0717 * Amount of Criteria by Function Point. This model indicates that exists a positive correlation among the amount of criteria by function point in the product tests and the percentage of test cases approved in the product acceptance tests by the client. One of the problems of application of regression analysis is the identification of outliers, i.e., specific data points that do not represent a common behavior in the project. MiniTab™ helped to automatically identify the outliers, thus facilitating the elimination of anomalies in the data that hindered the development of trustful models.

We also noticed that the sensitivity analysis technique of Monte Carlo simulation using Oracle Crystal Ball™ tool helped to identify critical subprocesses that affected the achievement of quality and process performance objectives of Synapsis Brazil, such as Product Tests subprocesses. After the implementation of incremental and innovative improvements in those subprocesses, we could verify a significant change in the processes performance, helping the organization to achieve its objectives. One of the problems in the application of Monte Carlo simulation was the lack of past project data necessary for conduction of simulations. As the understanding of critical subprocesses and its relationships increase, new measures are necessary for performing the analysis. Nevertheless, many times these measures are not found in the repository. This problem forced the elimination of several projects in the early stages of baselines data analysis due to lack of data that could be used in the simulation analysis.

The implementation of software process improvement is a complex activity that requires significant amount of human and financial resources. Moreover, the return of investment is observed in a long-term period. Nevertheless, software process improvement is likely to pay-off when the improvements are adopted across the organization and software development maturity is consistently observed during projects execution. We could observe some significant results after successfully conducting software process improvement initiatives in Synapsis Brazil. Table 2 presents some of the direct results in defect density, productivity and schedule observed after implement CMMI maturity levels 2, 3 and 5.

Table 2 shows that there was a significant reduction of defect density from level 2 to level 3 (42%). This was considered a good result since the focus of CMMI level 3 process areas is product engineering and verification and validation practices. Although the reduction of defect density from CMMI level 3 to level 5 were smaller (16%), Synapsis Brazil higher management was satisfied with the result since it was possible to achieve the business objectives concerning product quality.

With respect to productivity, we could observe a continuous improvement from level 2 to 3 (19%) and from level 3 to 5 (15%) in Table 2. One of the causes of this result was

Table 2 Defect density, productivity and schedule improvement results in Synapsis Brazil after implementing CMMI levels 2, 3 and 5

	Defect density		Productivity		Schedule	
	Defects/ function point	% reduction	Man-hours/ function Point	Improvement	% projects delayed	Improvement
CMMI 2	0,65	-	13,5	-	45%	-
CMMI 3	0,38	42%	10,9	19%	20%	56%
CMMI 5	0,32	16%	9,3	15%	4%	80%

the process optimization performed during CMMI level 3 and 5 implementation thus reducing the overall effort to develop software.

The best results were observed in the percentage of delayed projects in Table 2. This percentage dropped from 45% of delayed projects to 20% after implementing CMMI level 3 and continued to drop to 4% of delayed projects after implementing CMMI level 5. The reduction of project size can be one of the causes of this significant improvement. Moreover, the implementation of quantitative project management practices and statistical process control techniques helped to prevent future process performance and to take more effective corrective actions during projects execution.

The Synapsis Brazil process group observed as a lesson learned the fact that the process implementation aiming high maturity levels do not represent greater effort related to CMMI level 3 implementation. The project team is not significantly affected by the implementation, since the new process areas to be implemented in the standard processes do not affect directly the team. The measurement group is the most affected group by high maturity implementation since they have to assist project managers, some members of the project team and the higher management with control information so that improvement actions can be planned and executed in time to correct deviations before concluding projects activities. Another issue that the process group considered as a differential was the facility that the project manager had to initiative the project planning concerning subprocesses definition that compose the adapted process to the project. The activity of subprocesses selection is fundamental to assess achievement of quality and performance objectives with the composition of the project process. This activity was facilitated by the automated support in the selection of subprocesses based on project characteristics and organizational performance baselines.

Project managers observed that the available tools and process and quality groups were the main structure to support quantitative management, providing the mechanisms for planning and controlling projects activities, i.e., those groups not only supported project managers in the effective planning, but also supported the project team to solve problems during projects execution. Risks planning and monitoring helped to increase the understanding of factors that may jeopardize projects execution concerning achievement of quality and performance objectives. A continuous monitoring minimizes the occurrence of problems during projects execution, since it is fundamental to be aware of the situation of projects products, team and client commitments and accomplishment of established milestones and budget. The project managers also noted that the process efficacy is important but the team involvement and commitment to work have also great influence in projects success. People continue to be the essential part of the process and project managers should always keep that in mind. In this work, the great differential was the use of statistical data. Project managers noted that using these data in an adequate manner increases the chances of predicting future process performance aiming to facilitate achievement of project objectives.

The consultancy observed that the lack of data jeopardizes the assessment of process performance. A way to overcome this problem is to focus the analysis in evolutionary projects of small size, because they allow rapid data generation. The development of initial prediction models with few independent variables (one to two at most), also helps to obtain more trustful models when few data is available.

Conclusion

This paper presented the experience of Synapsis Brazil in the evolution of its processes to achieve high maturity. We presented the main critical success factors, such as easy to accept changes by project teams, support and commitment of higher management, adequate supporting tools for statistical process control, incremental and innovative improvements and the specialized knowledge of the consultancy in statistical process control. The paper also discussed the results of adopting statistical process control in small sized evolutionary projects. Lessons learned by the teams were also discussed.

Considering that the purpose of CMMI level 5 is continuous optimization, the next steps for Synapsis Brazil process improvement is to analyze performance of the actual baseline aiming to identify the subprocesses that affect the achievement of quality process performance objectives reviewed by the higher management aiming a more competitive position both in the national and international software market.

Competing interests
The authors declare that they have no competing interests.

Authors' contribution
MM identified common problems of similar cases, elicited some critical barriers for conducting the reported experience and drafted the manuscript. CS documented the case results and lessons learned. Both authors read and approved the final manuscript.

Author details
[1]Synapsis Brasil, S.A., Rua São Pedro n 181, CEP 24.020-054 Centro, Niterói, RJ, Brasil. [2]ProMove – Business Intelligence Solutions, Rua da Assembleia, No 10, Sala 2805, CEP 22.011-000 Centro, Rio de Janeiro, RJ, Brasil.

References
Florac WA, Carleton AD, Barnard JR (2000) Statistical process control: analyzing a space shuttle onboard software process. IEEE Software 17:97–106. n 4, July/August. IEEE Computer Society Press Los Alamitos, CA, USA
Kitchenham B, Kutay C, Jeffery R, Connaughton C (2006) Lessons learnt from the analysis of large-scale corporate databases. ICSE '06 Proceedings of the 28th international conference on Software engineering. ACM New York, NY, USA, pp 439–444
Luo W, Wang M, Zhou B, Liu P (2008) Research on CMMI-based project management environment, 2008 International Conference on Wireless Communications, Networking and Mobile Computing. WiCOM 2008, Dalian, China
Montoni MA, Rocha AR (2011) Using grounded theory to acquire knowledge about critical success factors for conducting software process improvement implementation initiatives. Int J Knowl Manag (IJKM) 7(3):43–60
Sargut KU, Demirors O (2006) Utilization of statistical process control (SPC) in emergent software organizations: pitfalls and suggestions. Software Quality Journal. Kluwer Academic Publishers 14(2):135–157
SEI – Software Engineering Institute (2012) CMMI for SCAMPI class a appraisal results 2012 Mid-year. Update, http://cmmiinstitute.com/assets/presentations/2012 SepCMMI.pdf, accessed in April/2013
SOFTEX (2013) Total number of organizations with MPS Assessment (valid or not valid) (in Portuguese). http://www.softex.br/mpsbr/_avaliacoes/avaliacoes_mpsbr_total.pdf, accessed in April/2013
Travassos GH, Kalinowski M (2012) iMPS 2011 Performance Results of Organizations that Adopted the MPS Model from 2008 to 2011 (in Portuguese). SOFTEX, Campinas/SP, p 36. http://www.softex.br/wp-content/uploads/2013/08/iMPS-2011-Resultados-de-Desempenho-das-Empresas-que-Adotaram-o-Modelo-MPS-de-2008-a-2011.pdf, accessed in April/2013 (2012). ISBN 978-85-99334-33-1
Weller E, Card D, Curtis B, Raczynski B (2008) Point/counterpoint applying SPC to software development: where and Why, software. IEEE Software 25(3):48–51. May-June. IEEE Computer Society Press Los Alamitos, CA, USA

6

Revealing influence of model structure and test case profile on the prioritization of test cases in the context of model-based testing

João Felipe Silva Ouriques[*], Emanuela Gadelha Cartaxo[†] and Patrícia Duarte Lima Machado[†]

*Correspondence:
jfelipe@copin.ufcg.edu.br
[†]Equal Contributors
Federal University of Campina
Grande, Aprigio Veloso 882,
58429-900 Campina Grande, Brazil

Abstract

Background: Test case prioritization techniques aim at defining an order of test cases that favor the achievement of a goal during test execution, such as revealing failures as earlier as possible. A number of techniques have already been proposed and investigated in the literature and experimental results have discussed whether a technique is more successful than others. However, in the context of model-based testing, only a few attempts have been made towards either proposing or experimenting test case prioritization techniques. Moreover, a number of factors that may influence on the results obtained still need to be investigated before more general conclusions can be reached.

Methods: In order to evaluate factors that potentially affect the performance of test case prioritization techniques, we perform three empirical studies, an exploratory one and two experiments. The first study focus on expose the techniques to a common and fair environment, since the investigated techniques have never been studied together, and observe their behavior. The following two experiments aim at observing the effects of two factors: the structure of the model and the profile of the test cases that fail. We designed the experiments using the one-factor-at-a-time strategy.

Results: The first study suggests that the investigated techniques performs differently, however other factors, aside from the test suites and number of failures, affect the techniques, motivating further investigation. As results from the two experiments, on one hand, the model structure do not affect significantly the investigated techniques. On the other hand, we are able to state that the profile of the test case that fails may have a definite influence on the performance of the techniques investigated.

Conclusions: Through these studies, we conclude that, a fair evaluation involving test case prioritization techniques must take into account, in addition to the techniques and the test suites, different characteristics of the test cases that fail as variable.

Keywords: Experimental software engineering; Software testing; Model-based testing; Test case prioritization

1   Introduction

The artifacts produced and the modifications applied during software development and evolution are usually validated by executing test cases. Often, the produced test suites are also subject to extensions and modifications, making management a difficult task. Moreover, their use may become increasingly less effective due to the difficulty to abstract and obtain information from test execution. For instance, if test cases that fail are either run too late or are difficult to locate due to the size and complexity of the suite.

To cope with this problem, a number of techniques have been proposed in the literature; they may be classified as test case selection, test suite reduction and test case prioritization. The general test case selection problem is concerned with selecting a subset of the test cases according to a specific (stop) criterion, whereas test suite reduction techniques focus on selecting a subset of the test cases, but the selected subset must provide the same requirement coverage as the original suite (Harrold et al. 1993). While the goal of selection and reduction is to produce a more cost-effective test suite, studies presented in the literature show that the techniques may not work effectively, since they discard test cases and consequently, some failures may not be revealed (Jeffrey and Gupta 2007).

On the other hand, test case prioritization techniques have been investigated in order to address the problem of defining an execution order of the test cases according with a given testing goal, particularly, detecting failures as early as possible (Rothermel et al. 1999). These techniques are suitable for general development context or in a more specific context, such as regression testing, depending on the information considered by the techniques (Rothermel et al. 2001). Moreover, both code-based and specification-based test suites may be handled, although, most techniques presented in the literature have been defined and evaluated for code-based suites in the context of regression testing (Elbaum et al. 2002) (Jiang et al. 2009).

Model-based Testing (MBT) is an approach to automate the design and generation of black-box test cases from specification models with all oracle information needed (Utting and Legeard 2007). MBT may operate with any model with different purposes and at different testing levels. As usually, automatic generation produces a huge amount of test cases that may also have a considerable degree of redundancy (Cartaxo et al. 2008, 2011).

Techniques for ordering the test cases may be required to support test case selection, for instance, to address constrained costs of running and analyzing the complete test suite and to improve the rate of failure detection. However, to the best of our knowledge, there are only few attempts presented in the literature to define test case prioritization techniques based on model information (Korel et al. 2008) (Gopinathan and Mohanty 2009). Generally, empirical studies are preliminary, making it difficult to assess current limitations and applicability of the techniques in the MBT context.

To provide useful information for the development of prioritization techniques, empirical studies must focus on controlling and/or observing factors that may determine the success of a given technique. Considering the goals of prioritization in the context of MBT, a number of factors can be determinant such as the size and the coverage of the suite, the structure of the model (that may determine the size and structure of test cases), the amount and distribution of failures and the degree of redundancy of test cases.

In this paper, we investigate the influence of two factors: the structure of the model and the profile of the test cases that fail. For this, we conduct three empirical studies, where real application models, as well as automatically generated ones, are considered. The focus is on general prioritization techniques suitable to MBT test suites. We represent the system level behavior through Labeled Transition Systems - LTS.

The purpose of the first study is to acquire preliminary observations by considering real application models. From this study, we conclude that a number of different factors might influence on the performance of the techniques. Therefore, the purpose of the second and third studies, the main contribution of this paper, is to investigate specific factors by controlling them through synthetic models.

In the studies, we considered four prioritization techniques: Adaptive Random Testing (ART) (Chen et al. 2004) with two different distance functions, producing two variant techniques named **ART_Jac** (Jaccard distance) and **ART_Man** (Manhattan distance); **Fixed Weights** (Gopinathan and Mohanty 2009) and **STOOP** (Gopinathan and Mohanty 2009).

This paper is an extension of the work presented by Ouriques *et al.* (2013). We extend it by: i) providing an example to illustrate the impacts of external factors over the techniques; ii) considering two more techniques in the second and third performed experiments (in the original paper, only **ART_Jac** and **STOOP** are considered); and iii) replicating the second and the third experiments, using new samples, better explained in the correspondent sections.

The conclusions of the replication of the experiments discussed in this paper, point to the same direction of the results already presented in the previous work. Despite the fact that the structure of the models may present or not certain constructions (for instance the presence of loops[a]), it is not possible to differentiate the performance of the techniques when focusing on the presence of the construction investigated. On the other hand, depending on the profile of the test cases that fail (longest, shortest, essential, and so on), one technique may perform better than the other one, leading to some influence of this factor.

The studies presented in this paper focus on system level models, represented as activity diagrams and/or LTS with inputs and outputs as transitions. We generate synthetic models according to the strategy presented by Oliveira Neto *et al.* (2013). Test cases are sequences of transitions extracted from a model by a depth-search algorithm as presented by Cartaxo *et al.* (2011) and Sapna and Mohanty (2009). Prioritization techniques receive as input a test suite and produce as output an ordering for the test cases.

The paper presents the following structure. Section 2 exposes fundamental concepts, along with a quick definition of the prioritization techniques considered in this paper and discusses the related works. Section 3 presents a motivating example, showing the performance of three test case prioritization strategies. Section 4.1 shows a preliminary study where techniques are investigated in the context of two real applications, varying the amount of failures. Sections 4.2 and 4.3 present the main empirical studies conducted: the former reports a study with automatically generated models, in which we control the presence of certain structural constructions, whereas the latter depicts a study that we investigated different profiles of the test case that fails, also using synthetic models. Section 6 presents concluding remarks about the results obtained and pointers for further research. Details about the input models and data collected in the studies are available at the project site (Ouriques et al. 2015). We defined and planned the empirical studies according to the general framework proposed by Wohlin et al. (2000) and used the R tool (Gentleman and Ihaka 2015) to support data analysis.

2 Background

This section presents the test case prioritization concept (Subsection 2.1), details about the techniques considered in this paper (Subsection 2.2) and the related work (Subsection 2.3).

2.1 Test case prioritization

Test Case Prioritization (TCP) is a technique that orders test cases in an attempt to maximize an objective function. Elbaum *et al.* (2000) formally define the problem as follows:

Given: *TS*, a test suite; *PTS*, a set of permutations of *TS*; and, *f*, a function that maps *PTS* to real numbers $(f : PTS \rightarrow \mathbb{R})$.

Problem: Find a $TS\prime \in PTS \mid \forall\ TS\prime\prime \in PTS$ with $TS\prime\prime \neq TS\prime, f(TS\prime) \geq f(TS\prime\prime)$

In other words, a prioritization algorithm must define the set of every permutation *PTS* of the test cases in order to choose the element *TS'* that maximizes *f*. The analysis of every permutation is infeasible, mainly in a big test suite (de Lima 2009) with *n* test cases, because the high number of elements in the permutation set, which are *n*! elements. The prioritization problem might be represented as an instance of the Traveling Salesman Problem and it is computationally NP-complete (Aho et al. 1974) (Cormen et al. 2009). Therefore, the prioritized test case sequence is iteratively built, mainly through heuristics and functions for test cases evaluation.

The objective function is defined according with the goal of the test case prioritization. For instance, the manager may need to increase the rate of failure detection or coverage of requirements by scheduling execution of test cases in an order in which the first test cases reveal as more failures as possible or cover as more requirements as possible. Realize that failure detection capability and requirements coverage of the suite are not affected because test cases are only reordered. Depending on the goal of the prioritization, the required information is not available. One of the main goals considered in the TCP research is the fault/failure detection, and it is the goal considered in this research. The required information to prioritize the test cases with this goal is not available before the execution of the test cases. Thus, the techniques propose surrogates to the desired goal (Yoo et al. 2009).

When the goal is to increase failure detection, the *Average Percentage of Fault Detection* (APFD) metric has been largely applied in order to evaluate prioritization techniques. APFD is a weighted average of the percentage of faults detected, over the life of the test suite (Elbaum et al. 2000). The APFD values range from 0 to 100 and the higher APFD numbers, the faster fault detection rates. For a test suite *T* with *n* test cases, and TF_i the index of the first test case that detects the $i - th$ fault, with $i \leq m$:

$$APFD = 1 - \frac{TF_1 + TF_2 + \ldots + TF_m}{nm} + \frac{1}{2n}$$

Test case prioritization is suitable for code-based and specification-based contexts, but it has been more applied in the code-based context, moreover it is often related to regression testing. Therefore, Rothermel *et al.* (2001) propose the following classification:

- General test case prioritization - test case prioritization is applied any time in the software development process, even in the initial testing activities;

- Regression testing prioritization - test case prioritization techniques execute after a set of changes in the SUT. Therefore, test case prioritization can use information gathered in previous runs of existing test cases to help the action of prioritize the test cases for subsequent runs.

In this paper, we focus on general test case prioritization. Therefore, we are not considering that any other information is available, besides the behavioral model and the application. Regression testing approaches may also consider test case execution history and/or applied modifications.

Since the context is the specification-based, more specifically model-based testing, we model the applications used in this work as Labeled Transition Systems (LTS). LTS is a directed graph in which vertexes are states, and edges are transitions. Formally, it is a 4-tuple $S = \{Q, A, T, q_0\}$, where (de Vries and Tretmans 2000):

- Q is a finite, nonempty set of states;
- A is a finite, nonempty set of labels;
- T is a subset of $QxAxQ$ named transition relation;
- q_0 is the initial state.

In our experiments, the LTS model represents the behavior of an application where the transitions represent either input or output actions, triggered by actors or systems, and test cases are able to be generated from them.

2.2 Techniques

Following the classification provided by Rothermel *et al.* (2001), this subsection presents general test case prioritization techniques that we approach in this paper. Our choice excludes regression testing techniques and includes the ones that may be applied to system level models represented as activity diagrams and/or as labeled transition systems.

Optimal. Empirical evaluations frequently include this technique as upper bound on the effectiveness of the other techniques. It presents the best result that a technique is able to achieve. To obtain the best result, for example, for failure detection purposes, the failure record must be available. Since the target information may not be available in practice, the technique is not feasible. Thus, we can only use applications with known failures. Therefore, we can determine the order of test cases that maximizes the rate of failure detection of a test suite.

Random. This technique consists in defining the order of test cases by random choice. Despite the fact that, random choices can lead to optimal results by chance, experiments with test case prioritization techniques have applied it as a lower bound control technique (Jiang et al. 2009).

Adaptive Random Testing (ART). This strategy distributes the selected test case as spaced out as possible based on a distance function (Chen et al. 2004). To apply this strategy, two sets of test cases are required: the prioritized sequence (the sequence of distinct test cases already in order) and the candidate set (the set of test cases randomly selected without replacement). Initially, the prioritized sequence is empty and the algorithm selects the first test case randomly from the input domain. Then, it selects the next test case among the candidates and adds in the prioritized sequence. This selected test case is the **farthest away** from all the already prioritized test cases. There are several ways to implement the concept of **farthest away**. In this paper, we will consider:

- **Jaccard distance**: Jiang *et al.* (2009) propose the use of this function in the prioritization context. The function calculates the distance between two sets, taking into account the size of intersection and union of their elements. In our context, we consider a test case as an ordered set of edges (that represent transitions). Considering p and c as test cases and $B(p)$ and $B(c)$ as a set of branches covered by the test cases p and c respectively, the distance between them is defined as follows:

$$J(p, c) = 1 - \frac{|B(p) \cap B(c)|}{|B(p) \cup B(c)|}$$

- **Manhattan distance**: This function measures the distance between two sets based on their elements. According to Zhou et al. (2010), consider two test cases a and b, with $a = (b_{11}, b_{12}, \cdots, b_{1i})$ and $b = (b_{21}, b_{22}, \cdots, b_{2i})$ representing which branches are covered by the two test cases respectively. The sequences a and b have the same length i, which is the total number of branches in the application model. Moreover, each $b_{xy} \in \{0, 1\}$, where 1 indicates that the test case x covers the branch y, 0 indicates otherwise. Thus, the function is defined as follows:

$$Man(a, b) = \sum_{x=1}^{N} |b_{1x} - b_{2x}|$$

Fixed Weights. Sapna and Mohanty (2009) propose this prioritization technique based on UML activity diagrams. It uses the activity diagram structures in order to prioritize the test cases. First, the algorithm converts the activity diagram into a tree structure, where each loop is traversed twice at most.

Then, it assigns weights to the structural elements of the activity diagram (3 for fork-join nodes, 2 for branch-merge nodes, 1 for action/activity nodes). Lately, the algorithm calculates the weight for each path (sum of the weights assigned to nodes and edges) and sorts the test cases according to the weight sums obtained.

STOOP. Kundu *et al.* (2009) proposed this technique, which receives sequence diagrams as input. The algorithm converts the input diagrams into a graph representation called as Sequence Graph (SG) and then merges them into a single SG. After that, it generates the test cases, traversing the SG that represent the system. Lastly, the test cases are sorted into descending order taking into account the *average weighted path length* (AWPL) metric, defined as:

$$AWPL(p_k) = \frac{\sum_{i=1}^{m} eWeight(e_i)}{m}$$

where $p_k = \{e_1, e_2, \ldots, e_m\}$ is a test case and *eWeight* is the amount of test cases that contains the edge e_i.

2.3   Related work

Several test case prioritization techniques have been proposed and investigated in the literature. Most of them focus on code-based test suites and the regression testing context (Elbaum et al. 2004) (Korel et al. 2005). The experimental studies already presented have discussed whether a technique is more effective than others, comparing them mainly by the APFD metric. Moreover, so far, there is no experiment that presented general results. This evidences the need for further investigation and empirical studies that can contribute to advances in the state-of-the-art.

Regarding code-based prioritization, Zhou *et al.* (2012) compare failure-detection capabilities of the Jaccard-distance-based ART and Manhattan-distance-based ART. The authors use branch coverage information and the results showed that, for code-based test suites, Manhattan distance is more effective than Jaccard (2012). Jeffrey and Gupta (2006) propose an algorithm that prioritizes test cases based on coverage of statements in relevant slices and discuss insights from an experimental study that considers also total coverage. Moreover, Do *et al.* (2010) present a series of controlled experiments evaluating the effects of time constraints and faultiness levels on the costs and benefits of test case prioritization techniques. They define faultiness level as a variable that manipulates the numbers of faults (mutants) randomly placed in applications. They consider three faultiness levels: FL1 involves cases in which mutant groups contain from 1 to 5 faults; the second level, FL2, involves cases in which mutant groups contain from 6 to 10 faults; and FL3, involves cases in which mutant groups contain from 11 to 15 faults. The results show that time constraints can significantly influence both the cost and effectiveness. Moreover, when there are time constraints, the effects of increased faultiness are stronger.

Furthermore, Elbaum *et al.* (2002) compare the performance of 5 prioritization techniques in terms of effectiveness, and show how the results of the comparison can be used to select a technique (regression testing) (Elbaum et al. 2004). The compared techniques consider the coverage of functions in the source code, modifications between two versions and feedback of functions already covered as guide to prioritize test cases. They apply the prioritization techniques to 8 programs and their characteristics (such as number of versions, KLOC, number and size of the test suites, and average number of faults) are taken into account.

By considering the use of models in the regression testing context, Korel *et al.* (2007; 2008; 2005) present two model-based test prioritization methods: selective test prioritization and model dependence-based test prioritization. Both techniques focus on modifications made to the system and models. The inputs are the original EFSM system model and the modified EFSM. On the other hand, our focus is on general prioritization techniques, as defined by Rothermel *et al.* (2001), where modifications are not considered.

Generally, in the MBT context, we can find proposals to apply general test case prioritization from UML diagrams, such as: i) the technique proposed by Kundu *et al.* (2009) where sequence diagrams are used as input; and ii) the technique proposed by Sapna and Mohanty (2009) where activity diagrams are used as input. We investigate both techniques in this paper.

In summary, the original contribution of this paper is to present empirical studies in the context of MBT that consider different techniques and factors that may influence on their performance such as the structure of the model and the profile of the test case that fails.

3   Motivating example

The effectiveness of a prioritized test suite is often evaluated by the ability of revealing failures as fast as possible. Ideally, a technique for test case prioritization should put all test cases that will unveil failures in the first positions of the prioritized test suite. However, this may require key information that is not usually available such as historical data and experts' knowledge of what test cases will fail.

Disregarding whatever previous knowledge about failures of the system may be available, most of the prioritization techniques are based on structural aspects and also make some assumptions for ordering the test cases. For example, the longer, the more branches it covers or the more different the test case is, the higher the probability of revealing failures is.

Let us consider the model presented in Figure 1, and seven test cases obtained from that model (Table 1) by performing a generation algorithm, instrumented with a coverage criterion that traverses a loop twice at most. Moreover, consider that when the test cases are executed, only the scenario that represents the successful login failed, in another words, TC1 failed.

Suppose the application of three basic prioritization strategies: 1) greedy, choosing test cases with higher number of branches, 2) greedy, choosing test cases with lower number of branches and 3) random choice. By applying these strategies, the obtained orders are available in Table 2. Note that Strategy 1 places the failure represented by TC1 near to the end of the sequence – a poor result for a prioritization technique. Likewise, Strategy 3 places the failure in the middle of the sequence – another case that a prioritization technique must avoid. On the other hand, Strategy 2 places the failure in the first position – a desirable behavior for a prioritization technique. TC1 has the fewest number of branches along with TC7.

Despite the absolute results, in order to make these strategies applicable in practice, it is important to understand why one strategy was more successful than the other. Why did TC1 appear in the first position when running Strategy 2? Due to the low amount of branches in the model? Or due to the amount of the branches in the test case that fails? The conducted experiments reported in this paper address this question.

After performing experiments with different techniques (Ouriques et al. 2010), we have identified some factors that probably impact on the performance of the techniques: i) the

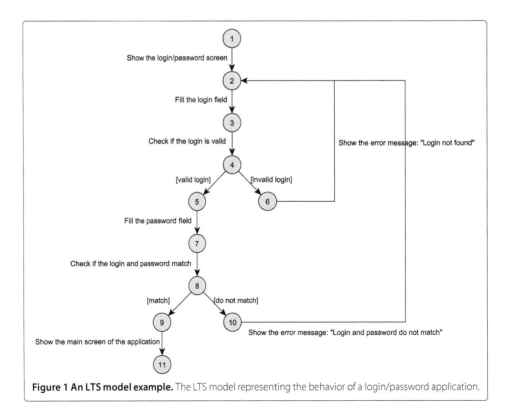

Figure 1 An LTS model example. The LTS model representing the behavior of a login/password application.

Table 1 Test cases generated from the model in Figure 1

Label	Steps
TC1	- Show the login/password screen - Fill the login field - Check if the login is valid - [valid login] - Fill the password field - Check if the login and password match - [match] - Show the main screen of the application
TC2	- Show the login/password screen - Fill the login field - Check if the login is valid - [valid login] - Fill the password field - Check if the login and password match - [do not match] - Show error message: "Login and password do not match" - Fill the login field - Check if the login is valid - [valid login] - Fill the password field - Check if the login and password match - [match] - Show the main screen of the application
TC3	- Show the login/password screen - Fill the login field - Check if the login is valid - [valid login] - Fill the password field - Check if the login and password match - [do not match] - Show error message: "Login and password do not match" - Fill the login field - Check if the login is valid - [valid login] - Fill the password field - Check if the login and password match - [do not match] - Show error message: "Login and password do not match"
TC4	- Show the login/password screen - Fill the login field - Check if the login is valid - [valid login] - Fill the password field - Check if the login and password match - [do not match] - Show error message: "Login and password do not match" - Fill the login field - Check if the login is valid - [invalid login] - Show error message: "Login not found"
TC5	- Show the login/password screen - Fill the login field - Check if the login is valid - [invalid login] - Show error message: "Login not found" - Fill the login field - Check if the login is valid - [valid login] - Fill the password field - Check if the login and password match - [match] - Show the main screen of the application
TC6	- Show the login/password screen - Fill the login field - Check if the login is valid - [invalid login] - Show error message: "Login not found" - Fill the login field - Check if the login is valid - [valid login] - Fill the password field - Check if the login and password match - [do not match] - Show error message: "Login and password do not match"
TC7	- Show the login/password screen - Fill the login field - Check if the login is valid - [invalid login] - Show error message: "Login not found" - Fill the login field - Check if the login is valid - [invalid login] - Show error message: "Login not found"

number of test cases of the test suite that fail when executed, ii) the characteristics of a test case (long, medium, short) and iii) the model structure (number of branches, joins and loops). Aiming to investigate those factors, we performed three experimental studies and discuss their details in the following sections.

4   Methods

In order to investigate the influence of the already mentioned factors, we performed three empirical studies, an exploratory study (discussed in Section 4.1), an experiment evaluating the impact of the model structure on the performance of the investigated techniques (reported in Section 4.2) and an experiment evaluating the impact of the characteristics of the test cases that fail (detailed in Section 4.3).

4.1   Experiment 1: the number of test cases that fail in the test suite

The main **goal** of this study is to "analyze general prioritization techniques for the purpose of comparing their performances, **observing** the impact of the number of test cases that fail, **with respect to** their ability to reveal failures earlier, from the **point of view of**

Table 2 Prioritized test suites

Strategy	Test cases sequence
Strategy 1	TC2, TC4, TC6, TC3, TC5, TC1, TC7
Strategy 2	TC1, TC7, TC4, TC7, TC3, TC6, TC2
Strategy 3	TC5, TC6, TC2, TC1, TC7, TC4, TC3

The sequence of test cases proposed by the strategies.

the tester and in the **context of** MBT". We worked with the following research hypothesis: "The general test case prioritization techniques present different abilities of revealing failures, considering different amount of failing test cases in the test suite". In the next subsections, we present the planning of the study and the data analysis.

4.1.1 Planning

We conducted this experiment in a research laboratory – a controlled environment. This characteristic leads to an *offline* study. Moreover, all the techniques involved in the study only require the set of test cases with the mapping between them and the branches that they cover (satisfiability relation). Thus, no human intervention is required, eliminating the "expertise" influence.

The objects of our experiments are LTS models. Despite the fact that the applications are real ones, this experiment deals with a *specific context*.

In order to analyze the performance of the techniques, observing the influence of the number of test cases that fail, we define the following variables:

Independent variables and factors

- **General prioritization techniques**: Techniques defined in Section 2. We will consider the following short-names for the sake of simplicity: **Optimal**, **Random**, **ART_Jac** (Adaptive Random Testing with Jaccard distance), **ART_Man** (Adaptive Random Testing with Manhattan distance), **Fixed_Weights**, and **Stoop**;
- **Number of test cases that fail**: low (lower than 5% of the total), medium (between 5% and 15% of the total), high (higher than 15% of the total). This choice of levels is related to the actual distribution of real failures detected when testing the applications – these distribution allow us to examine different settings from few failures from a single fault to more than one fault and more failures;

Dependent variable

- Average Percentage of Fault Detection - APFD

In this study, we use two LTS models representing two real-world applications: i) Labeled Transition System-Based Tool – LTS-BT (Cartaxo et al. 2008) – a MBT activities supporting tool, developed in the context of our research group and ii) PDF Split and Merge - PDFsam (Vacondio et al. 2015) – a tool for PDF files manipulation.

These two applications are modeled through UML Activity Diagram, using the provided use cases documents and the applications themselves. From this diagram a graph model was obtained for each application, from which test cases were generated by using a depth search-based algorithm proposed by Sapna and Mohanty (2009) where each loop is considered two times at most. The Table 3 shows some structural properties from the models and the test cases that were generated from them to be used as input to the techniques.

All test cases for all techniques are obtained from the same model using a single algorithm. In addition, even though the STOOP technique has been generally proposed to be applied from sequence diagrams, the technique itself works on an internal model that combines the diagrams. Therefore, it is reasonable to apply STOOP in the context of this experiment.

We define the 'number of test cases that fail' variable considering real and known defects in the models and allocated as shown in Table 4.

Table 3 Structural properties of the models in the experiment

Property	LTS-BT	PDFSam
Branching nodes	26	11
Loops	0	5
Join nodes	7	6
Test cases	53	87
Shortest test case	10	17
Longest test case	34	43
Defects	4	5
TC reveal failures	14	32

This table contains some properties of the models used in the Experiment 1.

For the applications considered in this study, we could observe that the relationship between a defect (associated with a specific edge in the model) and a failure (a test case that fails) is that when a test case exercises the edge, it reveals the failure. For each different level, we consider a different set of defects of each model, and in the high level, two defects originate the failures. Moreover, these test cases do not reveal the two defects at the same time for the two models.

By using the defined variables and detailing the informal hypothesis, we postulate eight pairs of statistical hypotheses (null and alternative): three pairs evaluating the techniques at each level of number of test cases that fail (e.g. $H_0 : APFD_{(low,i)} = APFD_{(low,j)}$ and $H_1 : APFD_{(low,i)} \neq APFD_{(low,j)}$, for techniques i and j, with $i \neq j$) and five pairs evaluating the levels for each technique (e.g. $H_0 : APFD_{(Random,k)} = APFD_{(Random,l)}$ and $H_1 : APFD_{(Random,k)} \neq APFD_{(Random,l)}$, for levels k and l, with $k \neq l$), excluding the **Optimal** technique.

Based on the elements already detailed, the experimental design for this study is **One-factor-at-a-time** (Wu and Hamada 2009). The data analysis for the hypotheses pairs is based on 2-Way ANOVA (Montgomery and Runger 2003) (Jain 1991), after check the assumptions of normality of residuals and equality of variances. Whether any assumption is not satisfied, we must perform a non-parametric analysis.

We calculated the number of repetitions based on a pilot sample, using the following formula proposed by Jain (1991). We obtained 815 as result, for a precision (r) of 2% of the sample mean and significance (α) of 5%.

$$repli = \left(\frac{100 \cdot Z_{\frac{\alpha}{2}} \cdot s}{r \cdot \bar{x}} \right)^2 \tag{1}$$

We performed the following steps in order to perform the experiment: 1) Instantiate lists for data collection for each repetition needed; 2) Instantiate the failure models to be considered; 3) Generate test cases; 4) Map branches to test cases; 5) Execute each technique for each object (LTS model) considering the repetitions needed; 6) Collect data

Table 4 Failures of the models in Experiment 1

Level	Failures in LTS-BT	Failures in PDFSam
Low	2 test cases → 3,77%	4 test cases → 4,59%
Medium	4 test cases → 7,54%	7 test cases → 8,04%
High	8 test cases → 15,09%	16 test cases → 18,39%

Definition of the Test Cases that Fail variable.

and compute dependent variable; 7) Record and analyze results. All the techniques were executed automatically.

4.1.2 *Data analysis*

When analyzing data collected, we must verify the ANOVA assumptions. Figure 2 assures that the residuals are not normally distributed, because the black solid line should be near of the straight continuous line of the normal distribution. Thus, we proceed a non-parametric analysis.

A confidence interval analysis, as seen in Table 5 of the 95% confidence intervals of the pseudomedians[b] of APFD values collected might give a first insight about some null hypotheses rejection.

The set of hypothesis defined for this experiment compares the techniques under two points of view: i) the set of techniques at each single level, and ii) each technique isolated in the different levels.

For the first set of hypothesis, considering the levels of number of test cases that fail separately (set of two columns for each level), some confidence intervals do not overlap, and therefore the null hypotheses of equality must be rejected. However, in the three levels, there is an overlap between **Random** and **ART_Man**, and the *p*-values of Mann-Whitney tests between the two techniques are 0.9516, 0.9399 and 0.4476 for low, medium and high, respectively. These *p*-values are greater than the significance of 5%, thus the performance of these techniques are statistically similar at this significance.

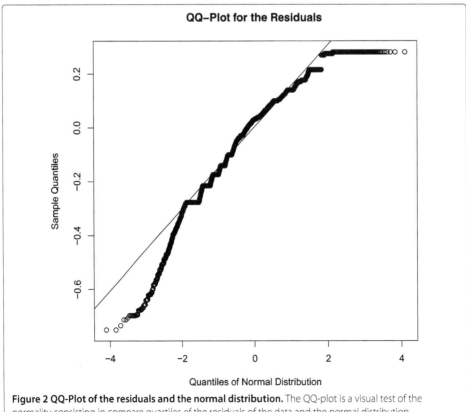

Figure 2 QQ-Plot of the residuals and the normal distribution. The QQ-plot is a visual test of the normality consisting in compare quartiles of the residuals of the data and the normal distribution.

Table 5 Confidence interval of the pseudomedians

–	Low		Medium		High	
Optimal	0.992	0.992	0.992	0.992	0.992	0.992
Random	0.807	0.829	0.864	0.876	0.834	0.847
ART_Jac	0.902	0.906	0.888	0.900	0.877	0.885
ART_Man	0.808	0.830	0.863	0.876	0.839	0.850
Fixed_Weights	0.540	0.543	0.436	0.439	0.679	0.679
Stoop	0.244	0.244	0.319	0.319	0.560	0.560

The low, medium and high values of the confidence intervals of the samples.

For the second set of hypothesis, by analyzing each technique separately (lines of Table 5), every null hypothesis of equality must be rejected, since every technique present no overlap between the confidence intervals at each level. This means that the performance of the techniques may vary when more or less test cases fail.

As general observations, **ART_Jac** presents the best performance for the three levels. Moreover, the techniques present slightly variations when considering the three levels (by increasing or decreasing), except from **Fixed_Weights** and **Stoop** that increase more than other techniques. These techniques that are mostly based on structural elements of the test cases, may be more affected by the number of test cases that fail than the random based ones.

Furthermore, by increasing the level of the number of test cases that fail, different evolution patterns in the performance of the techniques arise, *e.g.* **Stoop** increases its performance with the growth of the level, while **Fixed_Weights** decreases its performance when the level goes from low to medium and increase when the level goes from medium to high. These different patterns compose an evidence of influence of other factors over the researched techniques that motivated the execution of the experiments presented in Sections 4.2 and 4.3. It is also important to remark that, analyzing separately the results for the systems leads to similar observations.

4.1.3 Threats to validity

As a controlled experiment with statistical analysis, we have taken rigorous measures to address **conclusion validity** regarding data treatment and assumptions, number of repetitions and tests needed. For the **internal validity** of this experiment, it is often difficult to represent a defect at a high abstract level since a code defect may refer to detailed contents. Therefore, an abstract defect may correspond to one or more defects at code level and so on. To mitigate this threat, we considered test cases that fail as measure instead of counting defects (even though we had data on the real defects). This decision suits our experiment perfectly, since the APFD metric focus on failure rather than defects.

The **construct validity** regarding the set of techniques and evaluation metric chosen to compose the study was supported by a systematic review (Ouriques January 2012), which reveals suitable techniques and evaluation metrics, representing properly the research context. The low number of LTS models used in this experiment threatens its **external validity**, since two models do not represent the whole universe of applications. However, as preliminary study, we aims at a specific context observation only.

4.2 Experiment 2: the model structure

Motivated by the first study reported in this paper, this section contains a report of an empirical study that aims at "analyzing general prioritization techniques **for the purpose**

of observing the model structure influence over the studied techniques, **with respect to** their ability to reveal failures earlier, from the **point of view of** the tester and in the **context of** Model-Based Testing". Complementing the definition, we postulated the following research hypothesis: "The general test case prioritization techniques present different abilities to reveal failures, considering models with different structures".

4.2.1 Planning

We also conduct this experiment in a controlled environment and the techniques involved in the study require the same artifacts from the first experiment – the test suite generated through a MBT test case generation algorithm. Moreover, the execution of the techniques does not need human intervention, what eliminates the factor "experience level" from the experiment.

We generate the synthetic models that originate the test suites processed in this experiment using a parameterized graph generator, detailed in a subsequent section. For this, we configure the generator with values obtained from the real applications investigated in the first experiment (Section 4.1) so that the generated models would have a similar size and complexity to real application models. Moreover, when the study requires the focus on a specific structure, we fixed the correspondent argument to n in order to make sure that all generated models present the structure n times. Therefore, the generated models considered in this experiment: i) resemble the structure of models of real applications; ii) present a similar size and complexity; and iii) have a comparable structure with fixed parameters when required.

For this study, we define the following variables:

Independent variables

- **General prioritization techniques** (factor): **ART_Jac**, **ART_Man**, **Fixed_Weights** and **Stoop**;
- **Number of branch constructions to be generated in the input models** (factor): 10, 30, 80;
- **Number of join constructions to be generate in the input models** (factor): 10, 20, 50;
- **Number of loop constructions to be generate in the input models** (factor): 1, 3, 9;
- Maximum depth of the generated models (fixed value equals to 25);
- Rate of test cases that fail (fixed value equals to 10%);

Dependent variable

- Average Percentage of Fault Detection - APFD.

We define the values for the variables that shape the models based on the structural properties from the models considered in the first experiment reported in this paper.

In this experiment, we do not desire to observe the effect of the failures location over the techniques, thus we select failures randomly. To mitigate the effect of the number of test cases that fail, we assign a constant rate of 10% of the test cases to reveal failure based on the profile of the applications considered in the first experiment. Likewise, the fixed value of depth of generated models is chosen according to the general depth of the models of the first experiment.

In order to evaluate the model structure, we define three different experimental designs and according to Wu and Hamada (2009), each one is a **one-factor-at-a-time**. We describe the designs in the next subsections.

Branches evaluation In order to evaluate the impact of the number of branches in the capacity of revealing failures, we define three levels for this factor and fix the number of joins and loops in zero. For each considered level of number of branches with the other parameters fixed, we generated 31 models through the parameterized generator. For each model, the techniques execute with 31 different random failure attributions and we collected the APFD value of each execution.

We formulate seven pairs of statistical hypotheses: i) three of them analyzing each level of the branches with the null hypothesis of equality between the techniques and the alternative indicating they have a different performance (e.g. Considering $T = \{ART\_Jac, ART\_Man, Fixed\_Weights, Stoop\}$, $H_0 : APFD_{(t_1, 10\_branch)} = APFD_{(t_2, 10\_branch)}, \forall t_1, t_2 \in T$ and $H_1 : APFD_{(t_1, 10\_branch)} \neq APFD_{(t_2, 10\_branch)}, \exists t_1, t_2 \in T)$ and ii) four pairs related to each technique isolatedly, comparing the performance in the three levels with the null hypotheses of equality and alternative indicating some difference (e.g. $\forall t_1 \in T$, $H_0 : APFD_{(t_1, 10\_branch)} = APFD_{(t_1, 30\_branch)} = APFD_{(t_1, 80\_branch)}$ and $H_1 : APFD_{(t_1, 10\_branch)} \neq APFD_{(t_1, 30\_branch)} \neq APFD_{(t_1, 80\_branch)})$.

Joins evaluation In the number of joins evaluation, we propose a similar design, but just varying the number of joins and fixing the other variables. We fix the number of branches in 50, loops in zero and every detail that were exposed in the branch evaluation are applied for this design. The reason for allowing 50 branches is that branches may be part of a join, therefore, we cannot consider zero branches. The corresponding set of hypotheses follows the same structure of the branch evaluation, but considering the number of joins.

Loops evaluation In the number of loops evaluation, once again, we propose a similar design, but varying only the number of loops and fixing the number of branches in 30 and the joins in 15 (again, this structures are commonly part of a loop, so it is not reasonable to consider zero branches and joins). We structure a similar set of hypotheses as in the branch evaluation, but considering the three levels of the number of loops variable.

We executed the following steps to perform the experiment: 1) Generate test models as described in the next section; 2) Instantiate lists for data collection for each repetition needed; 3) Instantiate the failure models to be considered; 4) Generate test cases; 5) Map branches to test cases; 6) Execute each technique for each object considering the repetitions needed; 7) Collect data and compute dependent variable; 8) Record and analyze results.

4.2.2 Model generation

The considered objects for this study are the randomly generated models. The generator receives five parameters:

1. Number of branch constructions;
2. Number of join constructions;
3. Number of loop constructions;
4. The maximum depth of the graphs;
5. The number of graphs to generate.

The generator creates a graph by executing operations to include the constructions in sequences of transitions (edges). The first step is to create an initial sequence using the fourth parameter, *e.g.* let a maximum depth be equal to five, so a sequence with five edges is created, as in Figure 3.

Over this initial configuration, the generator executes the operations. To increase the probability of generating structurally different graphs, the generator executes operations randomly, but respecting the amounts passed as parameters. Therefore, the generator performs the operations of adding branches, joins, and loops (illustrated in Figure 4) as follows:

- Branching: from a non-leaf random node x, create two more new nodes y and z and create two new edges (x, y) and (x, z);
- Joining: from two non-leaf different random nodes x and y, create a new node z and create two new edges (x, z) and (y, z));
- Looping: from two non-leaf different random nodes x and y, with $depth(x) > depth(y)$, create a new edge (x, y)).

The generator executes the same process as many times as the **number of graphs to generate** parameter indicates.

4.2.3 Data analysis

Since we divide the whole experiment into three similar experimental designs, the data analysis will respect this division and we follow the same chain of tests for the designs. Firstly, we test the normality assumptions over the samples using the Anderson-Darling and visual QQ-Plot tests and the equality of variances through Bartlett test. Depending on the result of these tests, we choose the next one, which evaluate the equality of the samples, Kruskal-Wallis or ANOVA. After evaluate the levels separately, we test the techniques isolatedly through the three levels. We consider for every test the significance level of 5%.

The objective in this work is to expose influences of the studied structural aspects of the models on the performance of the techniques, thus if the p-value analysis in a hypothesis testing suggests that the null hypothesis of equality may not be rejected, this is an evidence that the variable considered alone does not affect the performance of the techniques. On the other hand, if the null hypothesis must be rejected, it represents an evidence of some influence.

Branches analysis The first activity for the analysis is the normality test and Table 6 summarizes this step. Among the samples, just the three with p-values in boldface have their null hypotheses of normality not rejected, which implies that a minor part of the samples was considered normal.

Figure 3 Initial configuration of a graph with maximum depth equals to 5. The parameterized graph generator, as the first step of the generation process, create a chain of edges with the size of the given maximum depth parameter.

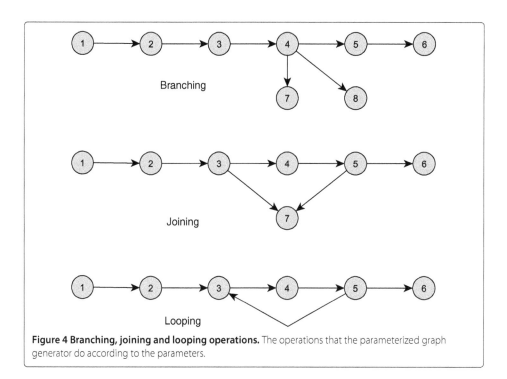

Figure 4 Branching, joining and looping operations. The operations that the parameterized graph generator do according to the parameters.

Following the analysis, we perform three tests, as summarized in the Table 7. We select the test according to the normality from the samples: for normal samples, we verify the variances of the samples, and perform the Analysis of Variance (ANOVA) and for non-normal samples, the Kruskal-Wallis test. All the p-values are greater than the defined significance of 5%, so the null hypothesis of equality of the techniques cannot be rejected, at the defined significance level, in other words, the four techniques presented similar performance at each level separately.

The next step of the analysis is to evaluate each technique separately through the levels and we proceed a non-parametric test of Kruskal-Wallis to test their correspondent hypothesis. The tests calculate for **ART_Jac**, **ART_Man**, **Fixed_Weights** and **Stoop** the p-values 0.2687, 0.848, 0.856 and 0.5289 respectively. Comparing them against the significance level of 5%, we cannot reject the null hypothesis of equality between the levels for each technique, so the performance is similar, at this significance level.

Joins analysis Following the same approach from the first experimental design, we can see on Table 8 the p-values of the normality tests. The bold face p-values indicate the samples normally distributed, at the considered significance.

Table 6 Normality test of the branches variation

	10 Branches	30 Branches	80 Branches
ART_Jaccard	$1.638 \cdot 10^{-15}$	0.02166	0.001239
ART_Manhattan	$9.94 \cdot 10^{-14}$	0.03604	**0.3784**
Fixed_Weights	$1.087 \cdot 10^{-12}$	0.02633	**0.335**
Stoop	$7.473 \cdot 10^{-11}$	**0.07524**	0.0002715

p-values for the Anderson-Darling normality tests with 5% of significance from the first experimental design samples. Normal samples are in bold face.

Table 7 p-values for tests in the branches variation

10 Branches	30 Branches	80 Branches
0.8658	0.4064	0.2217

p-values for the samples equality Kruskal-Wallis tests with 5% of significance from the first experimental design samples.

Based on these normality tests, we test the equality of the performance of the techniques at each level and, according to Table 9, the techniques perform statistically in a similar way at all levels.

The next step is to assess each technique separately. The samples for ART_Jac, ART_Man, Fixed_Weights were considered normal, according Table 8, but presented different variances, violating an ANOVA assumption. Therefore, we executed Kruskal-Wallis tests comparing the three samples for ART_Jac, ART_Man, Fixed_Weights and Stoop and the p-value obtained was 0.2235, 0.7611, 0.6441 and 0.3936, respectively. Comparing with the significance level considered of 5%, the null hypotheses of equality were not rejected, what means the techniques behave similarly through the levels.

Loops analysis Following the same line of argumentation, the first step is to evaluate the normality of the measured data and Table 10 summarizes these tests.

According to the results of the normality tests, we test the equality of the techniques at each level of this experimental design. As we can see on Table 11, the null hypotheses for 1 Loop, 3 Loops and 9 loops cannot be rejected because they have p-value greater than 5%, thus the techniques present similar behavior for all levels of the factor.

Analyzing the four techniques separately through the levels, we performed the non-parametric Kruskal-Wallis test, because the variances were not similar according to a Bertlett-Test. The p-values of the Kruskal-Wallis tests are 0.883, 0.9255, 0.3834 and 0.05507 for **ART_Jac**, **ART_Man**, **Fixed_Weights** and **Stoop**, respectively. These p-values, compared with the significance level of 5%, indicate that the null hypotheses of the considered pairs cannot be rejected, in other words, the techniques perform statistically similar through the different levels of the number of looping operations.

4.2.4   Threats to validity

About the validity of the experiment, we can point some threats. To the **internal validity**, we define different designs to evaluate separately the factors, therefore, it is not possible analyze the interaction between the number of joins and branches, for example. We do it because some of the combinations between the three variables might be infeasible, *e.g.* a model with many joins and without any branch.

Moreover, we do not calculate the number of repetitions in order to achieve a defined precision, because the execution would be infeasible (**conclusion validity**). The executed

Table 8 Normality test of the joins variation

	10 Joins	20 Joins	50 Joins
ART_Jaccard	**0.1163**	**0.8237**	**0.5517**
ART_Manhattan	**0.5849**	**0.5674**	**0.5136**
Fixed_Weights	**0.7522**	**0.4447**	**0.9402**
Stoop	**0.1482**	0.01024	**0.7262**

p-values for the Anderson-Darling normality tests with 5% of significance from the second experimental design samples. Normal samples are in bold face.

Table 9 p-values for tests in the joins variation

10 Joins	20 Joins	50 Joins
0.2269	0.6796	0.2409

p-values for the samples equality tests with 5% of significance from the second experimental design samples. For the 10 Joins and 50 Joins samples were performed an ANOVA and for the 20 Joins, Kruskal-Wallis test.

configuration took several days because some test suites were huge. To deal with this limitation, we limit the generation to 31 graphs for each experimental design and 31 failure attributions for each graph, keeping the balancing principle (Wohlin et al. 2000) and samples with size greater than, or equal to, 31 are wide enough to test for normality with confidence (Jain 1991) (Montgomery and Runger 2003).

Furthermore, we generate synthetic application models to deal with the problem of lack of applications, but, at the same time, this reduces the capability of representing the reality, threatening the **external validity**. To deal with this, we used structural properties, *e.g.* depth and number of branches, from existent models.

4.3 Experiment 3: the failure profile

This section contains a report of an experiment that aims at "analyzing general prioritization techniques for the purpose **of observing** the failure profile influence over the studied techniques, **with respect to** their ability to reveal failures earlier, from the **point of view of** the tester and in the **context of** Model-Based Testing".

Complementing the definition, we postulate the following research hypothesis: "The general test case prioritization techniques present different abilities to reveal failures, considering that the test cases that fail have different profiles". We are considering profiles as structural characteristics of the test cases that reveal failures.

4.3.1 Planning

We perform the current experiment in the same environment of the previous ones and the application models used in this experiment are a subset of the used in the second study. Since we do not aim at observing variations of model structure, we consider the 31 models that we generated in the second experiment, with 30 branches, 15 joins, 1 loop and maximum depth 25.

For this experiment, we define these variables:

Independent variables

- General prioritization techniques (factor): **ART_Jac**, **ART_Man**, **Fixed_Weights**, and **Stoop**;

Table 10 Normality test of the loops variation

	1 Loop	3 Loops	9 Loops
ART_Jaccard	**0.8769**	**0.4739**	0.006094
ART_Manhattan	**0.08255**	**0.8771**	0.001863
Fixed_Weights	**0.1785**	**0.7189**	**0.09979**
Stoop	**0.786**	**0.8434**	**0.1808**

p-values for the Anderson-Darling normality tests with 5% of significance from the third experimental design samples. Normal samples are in bold face.

Table 11 *p*-values for tests in the loops variation

1 Loop	3 Loops	9 Loops
0.09984	0.9722	0.8342

p-values for the samples equality tests with 5% of significance from the third experimental design samples. The samples for 1 and 3 Loops we performed an ANOVA and the 9 Loops sample, the Kruskal-Wallis test.

- Failure profiles, i.e., characteristics of the test cases that fail (factor);

    - Long test cases – with many steps (longTC);
    - Short test cases – with few steps (shortTC);
    - Test cases that contains many branches (manyBR);
    - Test cases that contains few branches (fewBR);
    - Test cases that contains many joins (manyJOIN);
    - Test cases that contains few joins (fewJOIN);
    - Essential test cases (ESSENTIAL) (the ones that uniquely covers a given edge in the model);

- Number of test cases that fail: fixed value equals to 1;

Dependent variable

- Average Percentage of Fault Detection - APFD.

A special step is the failure assignment, according to the profile. As the first step, the algorithm sorts the test cases according to the profile. For instance, for the **longTC** profile, the test cases are sorted decreasingly by the length or number of steps. If there are more than one with the biggest length (same profile), one of them is chosen randomly. For example, if the maximum size of the test cases is 15, the algorithm selects randomly one of the test cases with size equals to 15.

Considering the factors, this experiment is a **one-factor-at-a-time**, and we may proceed the analysis between the techniques at each failure profile and between the levels at each technique. In the execution of the experiment, each one of the 31 models were executed with 31 different and random failure assigned to each profile, with just one failure at once (a total of 961 executions for each technique). This number of repetitions keeps the design balanced and gives confidence for testing normality (Jain 1991).

Based on these variables and in the design, we define the correspondent pairs of statistical hypotheses: i) to analyze each profile with the null hypothesis of equality between the techniques and the alternative indicating they have a different performance (e.g. Considering $T = \{ART\_Jac, ART\_Man, Fixed\_Weights, Stoop\}$, $H_0 : APFD_{(t_1,longTC)} = APFD_{(t_2,longTC)}, \forall t_1, t_2 \in T$ and $H_1 : APFD_{(t_1,longTC)} \neq APFD_{(t_2,longTC)}, \exists t_1, t_2 \in T$), and also ii) to analyze each technique with the null hypothesis of equality between the profiles (e.g. Considering $P = \{longTC, shortTC, manyBR, fewBR, manyJOIN, fewJOIN, ESSENTIAL\}$, $H_0 : APFD_{(ARTJac,p_1)} = APFD_{(ARTJac,p_2)}, \forall p_1, p_2 \in P$ and $H_1 : APFD_{(ARTJac,p_1)} \neq APFD_{(ARTJac,p_2)}, \exists p_1, p_2 \in P$). Whether the tests reject null hypotheses, we will consider it as an evidence of the influence of the failure profile over the techniques.

The experiment execution follows the same steps defined to the model structure experiment. However, as mentioned before, each technique runs by considering one failure profile at a time.

4.3.2 Data analysis

By analyzing the profiles separately to test the first set of hypotheses, it is possible to visualize in the boxplots from Figures 5 and 6, significant differences among the techniques, represented by some lack of overlap among the notches in the boxplots. The notches in the boxplots are a graphical representation of a confidence interval calculated by the R software. When these notches overlap, it suggests a better and deeper investigation of the statistical similarity of the samples. Thereby, the boxplots in the figures already mentioned are enough to reject every null hypotheses of the first set, in another words, the techniques perform different at each failure profile isolatedly.

For testing the second set of hypotheses, from a visual analysis of the boxplots of the samples in Figure 7, we can see that there are profiles that do not overlap for each technique, thus the null hypotheses of equality must be rejected. In other words, at 5% of significance, **ART_Jac**, **ART_Man**, **Fixed_Weights** and **Stoop** perform statistically different for every researched profile.

As a secondary analysis, by observing the profiles *longTC* and *manyBR*, in Figure 5, they incur in similar performances for the techniques, because frequently a test case among the longest ones are also among the ones with the biggest number of branches. The same happens with the profiles *ShortTC* and *FewBR*, by the same reason.

In summary, the rejection of every null hypothesis of equality is a strong evidence of the influence of the failure profiles over the performance of the general prioritization

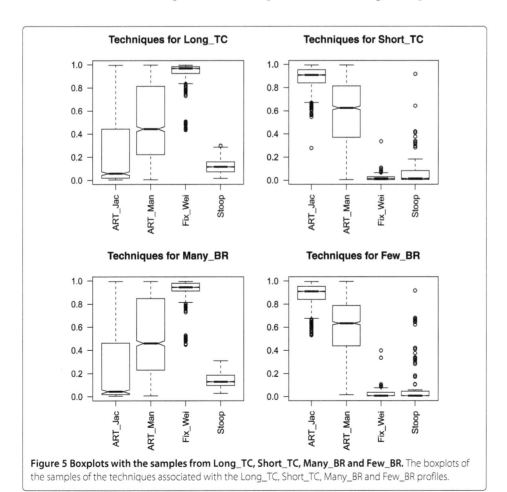

Figure 5 Boxplots with the samples from Long_TC, Short_TC, Many_BR and Few_BR. The boxplots of the samples of the techniques associated with the Long_TC, Short_TC, Many_BR and Few_BR profiles.

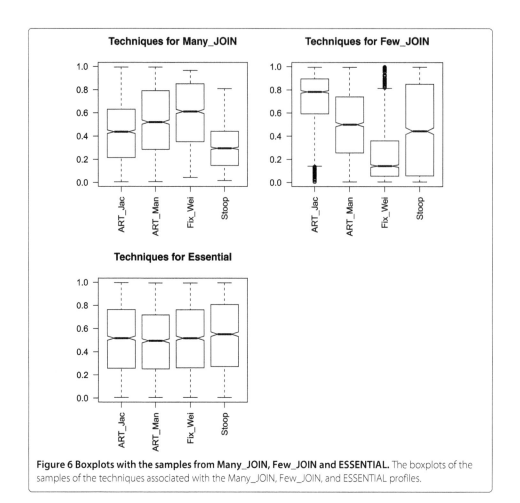

Figure 6 Boxplots with the samples from Many_JOIN, Few_JOIN and ESSENTIAL. The boxplots of the samples of the techniques associated with the Many_JOIN, Few_JOIN, and ESSENTIAL profiles.

techniques. Furthermore, data suggests that the techniques may present better and worse performances with different failure profiles.

4.3.3 Threats to validity

Regarding **conclusion validity**, we do not calculate the number of repetitions needed to achieve a defined precision, we limited the random failure attributions at each profile for each graph in 31, keeping the balancing principle (Wohlin et al. 2000) and samples with size greater than, or equal to, 31 are wide enough to test for normality with confidence (Jain 1991) (Montgomery and Runger 2003).

Construct validity is threatened by the definition of the failure profiles. We choose the profiles based on data and observations from previous studies, not necessarily the specific results. Thus, we define them according to our experience and there might be other profiles not investigated yet. This threat is reduced by the experiment's objective, which is just to expose the influence of different profiles on the prioritization techniques performance, and not to show all possible profiles.

5   Results and Discussion

Analyzing the first study (refer to Section 4.1), even though we cannot expect to know precisely the rate of failure of a system before test execution, it is worthy investigating how techniques perform when more or less failures occur. It is often possible to predict

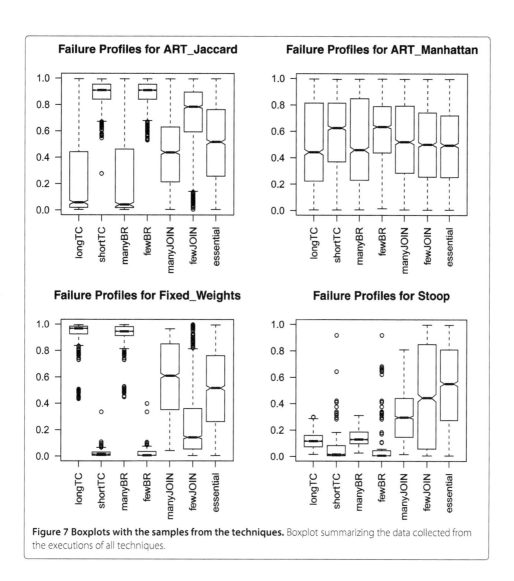

Figure 7 Boxplots with the samples from the techniques. Boxplot summarizing the data collected from the executions of all techniques.

failure rate by analyzing the application history or even similar applications. Based on prediction, a tester can choose the technique that presents the best behavior.

By varying the number of test cases that fail, we can observe differences on the performance of the techniques. However, we may not be confident to use only this information when choosing a technique. On one hand, from the results of the motivational study, techniques based on random choice have a best performance when the rate of failure is low, whereas **Stoop** increases performance as the rate of failures increase and **Fixed_Weights** increases performance when the level goes from medium to high. On the other hand, growth rates do not follow a pattern as well as they are not regular. Furthermore, Stoop and Fixed Weights are mostly based on structural elements of the test cases and their performance present different patterns. Thus, these results are consonant with our research hypothesis, which stated that prioritization techniques present different abilities of revealing failures, varying the amount test cases that fail in the test suite, motivating the investigation of the influence of the structure of the model.

For the first experiment, considering models with different structures such as branches, joins and loops (refer to Section 4.2), we expect that algorithms generate test cases with different lengths. For instance, cascade branches (or branches distributed at different levels of the model structure) may lead to a variety of short to long test cases. Moreover, we expect that test cases may be more or less redundant with respect to covering common transitions, particularly the more branches, joins and loops the model has, more redundancy the test cases have since they might cover common prefix of the branches and joins as well as repetitive sequences of loops. Since the techniques investigated either focus on the use of distance functions or on the presence of certain structures explicitly, we expect that by focusing on certain structure patterns, we could observe related behavior from the techniques.

Nevertheless, the configurations of structures we considered for each treatment of the independent variables do not show statistical difference on the behavior of the studied techniques, leading us to reject our initial research hypothesis, which stated that the prioritization techniques present different performances considering models with specific structures.

It is important to remark that each configuration considered may represent specific kinds of applications. For example, at system level: i) more branches may indicate the prevalence of alternate and exception flows that do not join with the main flow of the application; ii) more joins may indicate the prevalence of alternate and exception flows that join with the main flow; and iii) more loops may indicate the prevalence of repetitive cycles of execution. In practice, the distribution of these structural elements in the model depends on the system behavior as well as on the level of modeling. Overall, results show that from a practical point of view, only based on the structure of the model, we are unable to define what is the most effective technique to execute.

By closely analyzing the model for each configuration, we realize that results are influenced only if the test cases that fail cover the structure. This observation motivates the execution of the experiment presented in Section 4.3.

However, in the second experiment (refer to Section 4.3), we already had some intuition about techniques being more successful in determined situations, through less controlled studies, but now we have evidence supporting it. These techniques are sensitive to test cases that fail with different characteristics, as proposed by the data analysis, since techniques may perform well with failures with a characteristic and bad with another scenario.

As an example of how the profile of the test case that fail may influence on the performance of the technique, consider one of the models from our study as presented in Figure 8. From this model, consider a short test case $T_1 = (AW)$.

For this test case, for example, the APFD values obtained in the first trial by the **ART_Jac** and **Stoop** techniques are 0.8373 and 0.0060 respectively. This is because **ART_Jac** selects, among the candidates, the test case with the highest minimum distance to the already prioritized ones and, as soon as T_1 appear in the candidate set, it is chosen. On the other hand, the **Stoop** technique focus on test cases with more common steps and, since T_1 has just one step and it is unique, this test case is placed in the end of the sequence.

Now, consider the following long test case: $T_2 = (A, B, C, D, E, F, G, H, I, J, K, L, M, N, O, P, Q, R, S, T, U, V, W, X, Y)$. For this test case, the APFD values obtained in the eighth trial for **ART_Jac** and **Stoop** techniques are 0.0662 and 0.1144 respectively. This is because **ART_Jac** takes into account the number of branches in common in order to

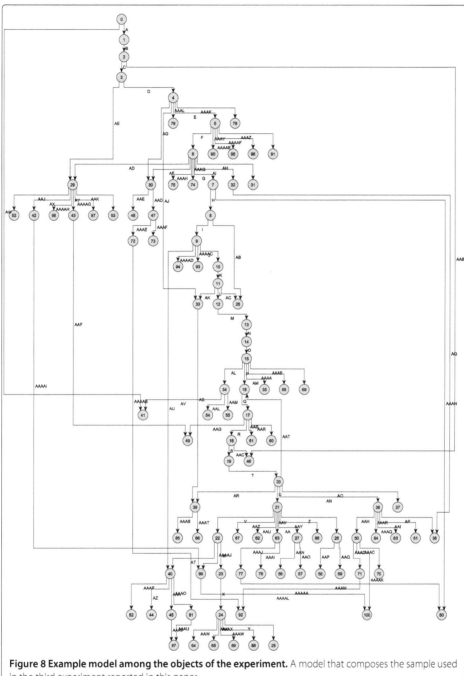

Figure 8 Example model among the objects of the experiment. A model that composes the sample used in the third experiment reported in this paper.

select the next test case, through the Jaccard function, and, since T_2 has more chance to have more branches in common with other already prioritized test case, it will appear just in the end of the sequence. On the other hand, the Stoop technique quickly returns it since it has many common steps with the other test cases.

After this study, the factor "failure profile" must be considered into any further evaluation of prioritization techniques, since it is an important factor for explaining the performance of prioritization techniques. Its importance corroborates our initial research hypothesis, which stated that prioritization techniques present different abilities of reveal failures, varying the characteristics of the test cases that fail.

6 Conclusions

This paper presents and discusses the results obtained from empirical studies about test case prioritization techniques in the context of MBT. Furthermore, this paper is an extension of the study presented in (Ouriques et al. 2013) and gives more evidences favoring the proposed results, since the conclusions are the same. It is widely accepted that a number of factors may influence on the performance of the techniques, particularly because the techniques can be based on different aspects and strategies, including or not random choice.

In this sense, the main contribution of this paper is to investigate the influence of two factors: the structure of the model and the profile of the test case that fails. The intuition behind this choice is that the structure of the model may determine the size of the generated test suites and the redundancy degree among their test cases.

Therefore, this factor may affect all of the techniques involved in the experiment due to either the use of distance functions or the fact that the techniques consider certain structures explicitly. On the other hand, depending on the selection strategy, the techniques may favor the selection of given profiles of test cases despite others. Thereby, whether the test cases that fail have a certain structural property may also determine the success of a technique. To the best of our knowledge, there are no similar studies presented in the literature.

In summary, in the first study, since we perform the experiment with real applications in a specific context, different growth patterns of APFD for the techniques compose an evidence of influence of more factors in the performance of the general prioritization techniques other than the number of test cases that fail. This result motivated the execution of the other studies.

On one hand, the second study, which aims at investigating the influence of the number of occurrences of branches, joins, and loops over the performance of the techniques, shows that there is no statistical difference on these performances, considering a significance of 5%. On the other hand, in the third study, based on the profile of the test case that fail, the fact that all of the null hypotheses must be rejected may indicate a high influence of the failure profile on the performance of the general prioritization techniques.

Moreover, from the perspective of the techniques, this study exposed weaknesses associated with the profiles. For instance, **ART_Jac** presented low performance when long test cases (and/or with many branches) reveal failures and high when short test cases (and/or with few branches) reveal failures. On the other hand, **Stoop** showed low performance with almost all profiles.

Overall, the results may contribute the improvement of prioritization techniques by addressing the weaknesses exposed. However, from a practitioner point of view, we do not have enough data to provide guidelines to apply the techniques yet. Generally, the results obtained point to a tendency that knowledge of which technique performs better for a given profile can be worthy if the team have some assumption about the characteristics of the test cases that fail. For example: if they have the assumption that test cases that cover more branches are more likely to fail because they go through many conditions, then it can be better to use **Fixed Weights**.

As future work, we will perform a more complex factorial experiment, calculating the interaction between the factors analyzed separately in the experiments reported in this paper. Moreover, we plan an extension of the third experiment to consider other profiles of test cases that may be of interest. From the analysis of the results obtained, a new (possibly hybrid) technique may emerge.

Endnotes

[a] A number of loops distributed in a model may lead to huge test suites with a certain degree of redundancy between the test cases even if they are traversed only once for each test case.

[b] The pseudomedian is a non-parametric estimator for the median of a population (Lehmann 1975).

Competing interests
The authors declare that they have no competing interests.

Authors' contributions
JF idealized the studies, implemented the techniques and the scripts for data analysis. EG helped in the project of the experiments and reviewed the paper. PD reviewed the initial draft and the final version of the paper. All authors read and approved the final manuscript.

Acknowledgements
This work was supported by CNPq grants 484643/2011-8 and 560014/2010-4. Also, this work was partially supported by the National Institute of Science and Technology for Software Engineering (2015), funded by CNPq/Brasil, grant 573964/2008-4. First author was also supported by CNPq.

References
Aho AV, Hopcroft JE, Ullman JD (1974) The Design and Analysis of Computer Algorithms. Addison-Wesley, Massachusetts, USA

Cartaxo EG, Andrade WL, Neto FGO, Machado PDL (2008) LTS-BT: a tool to generate and select functional test cases for embedded systems. In: SAC '08: Proc. of the 2008 ACM Symposium on Applied Computing, ACM, New York, NY, USA Vol. 2. pp 1540–1544

Cartaxo EG, Machado PDL, Neto FGO (2008) Seleção automática de casos de teste baseada em funções de similaridade. In: XXIII Simpósio Brasileiro de Engenharia de Software, pp 1–16

Cartaxo EG, Machado PDL, Oliveira FG (2011) On the use of a similarity function for test case selection in the context of model-based testing. Software Test Verification Reliability 21(2):75–100

Chen TY, Leung H, Mak IK (2004) Adaptive random testing. In: Advances in Computer Science - ASIAN 2004. Lecture Notes in Computer Science, Springer, Auckland, New Zealand Vol. 3321/2005. pp 320–329

Cormen TH, Leiserson CE, Rivest RL, Stein C (2009) Introduction of Algorithms, 3rd edn. MIT Press, Massachusetts, USA

de Lima LA (2009) Test case prioritization based on data reuse for black-box environments. Master's thesis, Universidade Federal de Pernambuco

de Vries RG, Tretmans J (2000) On-the-fly conformance testing using spin. International Journal on Software Tools for Technology Transfer 2(4):382–393

Do H, Mirarab S, Tahvildari L, Rothermel G (2010) The effects of time constraints on test case prioritization: A series of controlled experiments. IEEE Trans Software Eng 36(5):593–617

Elbaum S, Malishevsky AG, Rothermel G (2000) Prioritizing test cases for regression testing. In: Proceedings of the 2000 ACM SIGSOFT International Symposium on Software Testing and Analysis. ISSTA '00, ACM, New York, NY, USA, pp 102–112

Elbaum SG, Malishevsky AG, Rothermel G (2002) Test case prioritization: A family of empirical studies. IEEE Transactions in Software Engineering 26(2):159–182

Elbaum Sebastian, Rothermel Gregg, Kaduri Satya, Malishevsky Alexey G (2004) Selecting a cost-effective test case prioritization technique. Software Qual J 12:2004

Gopinathan Sapna Ponaraseri, Mohanty H (2009) Prioritization of scenarios based on uml activity diagrams. In: CICSyN, pp 271–276

Gomes de OliveiraNeto, F, Feldt R, Torkar R, Machado PDL (2013) Searching for models to evaluate software technology. In: Combining Modelling and Search-Based Software Engineering (CMSBSE), 2013 1st International Workshop On. IEEE, San Francisco, pp 12–15

Harrold MJ, Gupta R, Soffa ML (1993) A methodology for controlling the size of a test suite. ACM Trans Softw Eng Methodol 2(3):270–285

Ouriques JFS, Cartaxo EG, Machado PDL (2015) Empirical Studies on Model-Based Testing Prioritization. https://sites.google.com/a/computacao.ufcg.edu.br/mb-tcp/. Acessed in 21 Jan 2015

Gentleman R, Ihaka R (2015) The R Project for Statistical Computing. http://www.r-project.org/. Acessed in 21 Jan 2015

Vacondio A, Bortolotti E, Benblidia H (2015) PDF Split and Merge. http://www.pdfsam.org. Acessed in 21 Jan 2015

National Institute of Software Engineering (2015). www.ines.org.br. Acessed in 21 Jan 2015

Jain RK (1991) The Art of Computer Systems Performance Analysis: Techniques for Experimental Design, Measurement, Simulation, and Modeling. Wiley, New York, NY, USA

Jeffrey D (2006) Test case prioritization using relevant slices. In: In the Intl. Computer Software and Applications Conf. IEEE, Chicago, pp 411–418

Jeffrey D, Gupta R (2007) Improving fault detection capability by selectively retaining test cases during test suite reduction. Software Eng IEEE Trans 33(2):108–123

Jiang B, Zhang Z, Chan WK, Tse TH (2009) Adaptive random test case prioritization. In: Automated Software Engineering. IEEE, Auckland, pp 233–244

Korel B, Koutsogiannakis G, Tahat LH (2007) Model-based test prioritization heuristic methods and their evaluation. In: Proceedings of the 3rd International Workshop on Advances in Model-based Testing A-MOST '07. ACM, New York, NY, USA, pp 34–43

Korel, B, Koutsogiannakis G, Tahat LH (2008) Application of system models in regression test suite prioritization. In: IEEE International Conference on Software Maintenance. IEEE, Beijing, pp 247–256

Korel B, Tahat LH, Harman M (2005) Test prioritization using system models. In: Software Maintenance, 2005. ICSM'05. Proceedings of the 21st IEEE International Conference On. IEEE, Budapest, pp 559–568

Kundu D, Sarma M, Samanta D, Mall R (2009) System testing for object-oriented systems with test case prioritization. Softw Test Verif Reliab 19(4):297–333

Lehmann E (1975) Nonparametrics: Statistical Methods Based on Ranks. Holden-Day series in probability and statistics. Holden-Day, San Francisco

Montgomery DC, Runger GC (2003) Applied Statistics and Probability for Engineers. John Wiley and Sons, New York, NY, USA

Ouriques JFS (January 2012) Análise comparativa entre técnicas de priorização geral de casos de teste no contexto do teste baseado em especificação. Master's thesis, UFCG

Ouriques JFS, Cartaxo E, Machado PDL (2010) Comparando técnicas de priorização de casos de teste no contexto de teste baseado em modelos. In: Proceedings of the IV Brazilian Workshop on Systematic and Automatic Software Testing (SAST 2010). UFRN, Natal

Ouriques JFS, Cartaxo EG, Machado PDL (2013) On the influence of model structure and test case profile on the prioritization of test cases in the context of model-based testing. In: Proceedings of XXVII Brazilian Symposium on Software Engineering, UnB, Brasilia, Vol. 1. pp 134–143

Rothermel G, Untch RH, Chu C, Harrold MJ (1999) Test case prioritization: an empirical study. In: Software Maintenance, 1999. (ICSM '99) Proceedings. IEEE International Conference On. IEEE, Oxford, pp 179–188

Rothermel, G, Untch RH, Chu C, Harrold MJ (2001) Prioritizing test cases for regression testing. IEEE Trans Software Eng 27:929–948

Utting M, Legeard B (2007) Practical Model-Based Testing - A Tools Approach. Morgan Kaufmann, San Francisco, CA, USA

Wohlin C, Runeson P, Host M, Ohlsson MC, Regnell B, Wesslen A (2000) Experimentation in Software Engineering: an Introduction. Kluwer Academic Publishers, Norwell, MA, USA

Wu CFJ, Hamada MS (2009) Experiments: Planning, Analysis, and Optimization. 2nd edn. John Wiley and Sons, New York, NY, USA

Yoo S, Harman M, Tonella P, Susi A (2009) Clustering test cases to achieve effective and scalable prioritisation incorporating expert knowledge. In: Proceedings of the Eighteenth International Symposium on Software Testing and Analysis. ISSTA '09, New York, NY, USA, pp 201–212

Zhou ZQ (2010) Using coverage information to guide test case selection in adaptive random testing. In: IEEE 34th Annual COMPSACW. IEEE, Seoul. pp 208–213

Zhou ZQ, Sinaga A, Susilo W (2012) On the fault-detection capabilities of adaptive random test case prioritization: Case studies with large test suites. In: HICSS, IEEE, Maui, pp 5584–5593

7

A metrics suite for JUnit test code: a multiple case study on open source software

Fadel Toure[1,2*], Mourad Badri[1] and Luc Lamontagne[2]

* Correspondence:
Fadel.Toure@uqtr.ca
[1]Software Engineering Research
Laboratory, Department of
Mathematics and Computer
Science, University of Quebec,
Trois-Rivières, Quebec, Canada
[2]Department of Computer Science
and Software Engineering, Laval
University, Quebec, Canada

Abstract

Background: The code of JUnit test cases is commonly used to characterize software testing effort. Different metrics have been proposed in literature to measure various perspectives of the size of JUnit test cases. Unfortunately, there is little understanding of the empirical application of these metrics, particularly which metrics are more useful in terms of provided information.

Methods: This paper aims at proposing a unified metrics suite that can be used to quantify the unit testing effort. We addressed the unit testing effort from the perspective of unit test case construction, and particularly the effort involved in writing the code of JUnit test cases. We used in our study five unit test case metrics, two of which were introduced in a previous work. We conducted an empirical study in three main stages. We collected data from six open source Java software systems, of different sizes and from different domains, for which JUnit test cases exist. We performed in a first stage a Principal Component Analysis to find whether the analyzed unit test case metrics are independent or are measuring similar structural aspects of the code of JUnit test cases. We used in a second stage clustering techniques to determine the unit test case metrics that are the less volatile, i.e. the least affected by the style adopted by developers while writing the code of test cases. We used in a third stage correlation and linear regression analysis to evaluate the relationships between the internal software class attributes and the test case metrics.

Results and Conclusions: The main goal of this study was to identify a subset of unit test case metrics: (1) providing useful information on the effort involved to write the code of JUnit test cases, (2) that are independent from each other, and (3) that are the less volatile. Results confirm the conclusions of our previous work and show, in addition, that: (1) the set of analyzed unit test case metrics could be reduced to a subset of two independent metrics maximizing the whole set of provided information, (2) these metrics are the less volatile, and (3) are also the most correlated to the internal software class attributes.

Keywords: Software testing; Unit testing; Testing effort; JUnit code; Metrics; Principal components analysis; Clustering techniques; Correlation analysis and linear regression analysis

1 Background

Software testing plays a crucial role in software quality assurance. It is an important part of the software development lifecycle. Software testing is, however, a time and resource consuming process. The overall effort spent on testing depends on many different factors, including human factors, testing techniques, used tools, characteristics of the software development artifacts, and so forth. We focus, in this paper, on unit test case construction, and particularly on the effort required to write unit test cases. Software metrics can be used to quantify different perspectives related to unit test case construction. Different metrics have, in fact, been proposed in literature in order to quantify various perspectives related to the size of JUnit test cases. Unfortunately, there is little understanding of the empirical application of these metrics, particularly which metrics provide more useful information on the effort involved to write the code of JUnit test cases.

In a previous work (Toure et al. 2014), we extended existing JUnit test case metrics by introducing two new metrics. We analyzed the code of the JUnit test cases of two open source Java software systems. We used in total five unit test case metrics. We investigated, using the Principal Component Analysis technique, the orthogonal dimensions captured by the studied suite of unit test case metrics. We wanted, in fact, to better understand the structural aspects of the code of JUnit test cases measured by the metrics and particularly determine which metrics are more useful for quantifying the JUnit test code. Results show that, overall: (1) the new introduced unit test case metrics are relevant in the sense that they provide useful information related to the code of unit test cases, (2) the studied unit test case metrics are not independent (overlapping information), and (3) the best subset of independent unit test case metrics providing the best independent information (maximizing the variance) varies from one system to the other. As the number of analyzed system was limited to two, we could not reasonably draw final conclusions about the best subset of metrics. Furthermore, this preliminary study leads us to suspect that some of the unit test case metrics are more volatile than others, in the sense that they are more influenced by the style adopted by developers while writing the code of unit test cases.

The empirical study presented in this paper extends our previous work and aims at analyzing more deeply the suite of unit test case metrics. The study was conducted in three main stages. We used the same five unit test case metrics. This time, we collected data from six open source Java software systems for which JUnit test cases exist. The analyzed case studies are of different sizes and from different domains. In a first stage, we replicated the study performed in our previous work on the data we collected from the six selected systems. We performed a Principal Component Analysis (PCA). We used this technique to find whether the analyzed unit test case metrics are independent or are measuring similar structural aspects of the code of JUnit test cases. We used in a second stage clustering techniques, particularly K-Means and Univariate clustering, to determine the unit test case metrics that are the less volatile, i.e. the less influenced by the style adopted by developers while writing the code of unit test cases. We investigated the distribution and the variance of the unit test case metrics based on three important internal software class attributes. We focused on size, complexity and coupling. We used in a third stage correlation and linear regression analysis to evaluate the relationships between the internal software class attributes and the suite of unit test case metrics, and particularly to determine what are the unit test case metrics that are the most related to the internal software class attributes. Results confirm two observations made in our previous work: (1) the studied unit test case metrics are not independent, i.e. they capture overlapping information, and (2) the new introduced unit test case metrics provide useful information related to the code of JUnit test cases. Results also show three new findings: (3) there is a couple of independent unit test case metrics that maximizes the information, (4) these two metrics are the less affected by the style adopted by developers while writing the code of unit test cases, and (5) these metrics are also the most related to the internal software class attributes.

The rest of this paper is organized as follows: Section 2 gives a brief survey of related work. The studied unit test case metrics are presented in Section 3. Section 4 presents the different stages of the empirical study we conducted. Finally, Section 5 concludes the paper and outlines some future work directions.

2 Related work

Several studies in literature have addressed the estimation (prediction) of the testing effort by considering various factors such as use case points, number of test cases, test case execution, defects, cost, and so forth. Unfortunately, only few studies have focused on the analysis (quantification) of different aspects related to the test code. Unit test code has, however, been used in different studies addressing for example the testing coverage (Mockus et al. 2009) or the relationships (links) between the units under test and corresponding test code (Rompaey and Demeyer 2009, Qusef et al. 2011).

Bruntink and Van Deursen (2004, 2006) investigated factors of testability of object-oriented software systems. The authors studied five open source Java software systems in order to explore the relationships between object-oriented design metrics and some characteristics of the code of JUnit test cases. Testability was measured inversely by the *number of lines of test code* and the *number of assert statements* in the test code. Results show that there is a significant relationship between the used object-oriented design metrics and the measured characteristics of JUnit test classes. The two unit test case metrics (the *number of lines of test code* and the *number of assert statements* in the test code) used by Bruntink and Van Deursen were, in fact, intended to measure two perspectives related to the size of the JUnit test cases. The authors used an adapted version of the fish bone diagram developed by Binder in (1994) to identify testability factors. Bruntink and Van Deursen argued that the used test case metrics reflect, in fact, different source code factors Bruntink and Van Deursen (2004, 2006): factors that influence the *number of required test cases* and factors that influence the *effort involved to develop each individual test case*. These two categories have been referred as *test case generation* and *test case construction* factors.

Singh et al. (2008) used object-oriented metrics and neural networks to predict the testing effort. The testing effort was measured in terms of *lines of code added or changed* during the lifecycle of a defect. Singh and Saha (2010) focused on the prediction of the testability of Eclipse at the package level. Testability was measured using several metrics including the *number of lines of test code*, the *number of assert statements* in the test code, the *number of test methods* and the *number of test classes*. Results show that there is a significant relationship between the used object-oriented metrics and test metrics.

Badri et al. (2010) explored the relationship between lack of cohesion metrics and unit testability in object-oriented software systems. Badri et al. (2011) investigated the capability of lack of cohesion metrics to predict testability of classes using logistic regression methods. In these studies also, testability was measured inversely by the *number of lines of test code* and the *number of assert statements* in the test code. Results show that lack of cohesion is a significant predictor of unit testability of classes. Badri and Toure (2012) explored the capacity of object-oriented metrics to predict the unit testing effort of classes using logistic regression analysis. Results indicate, among others, that multivariate regression models based on object-oriented design metrics are able to accurately predict the unit testing effort of classes. The same unit test case metrics have been used in this study.

Zhou et al. (2012) investigated the relationship between the object-oriented metrics measuring structural properties and unit testability of a class. The investigated structural metrics cover in fact five property dimensions including size, cohesion, coupling, inheritance, and complexity. In this study, the *size of a test class* is used to indicate the effort involved in unit testing.

We can intuitively expect that all the metrics mentioned above are related to the size of test suites. However, there is little understanding of the empirical application of these metrics, particularly which metrics provide more useful information on the effort involved to write the code of JUnit test cases. To the best of our knowledge, there is no empirical evidence on the underlying orthogonal dimensions captured by these metrics. Also, is that these metrics are independent or are measuring similar structural aspects of the code of JUnit test cases (overlapping information). In addition, is that the distribution of these metrics is influenced by the systems design and the style adopted by the developers while writing the code of unit test cases? In others words, do the distribution of these metrics varies significantly from one developer to another for similar classes (test case metrics information could be strongly biased)? In the case where the unit test case metrics vary significantly, what is the subset of metrics that are the less sensitive to the development style variations? Furthermore, are there others structural aspects that these metrics do not capture? Indeed, some classes, depending on the design and particularly on the collaboration between classes, will require drivers and/or monitors to achieve unit testing. We believe that this will also affect the effort involved in the construction of test cases. The metrics mentioned above do not seem to capture these dimensions. This issue needs, however, to be investigated.

3 Unit test case metrics

We used in our study the following unit test case metrics:

TLOC: This metric counts the *number of lines of code* of a test class (Bruntink and Van Deursen 2004). It is used to indicate the size of the test class.

TASSERT: This metric counts the *number of assert statements* that occur in the code of a test class (Bruntink and Van Deursen 2004). In JUnit, assert statements are used by the testers to compare the expected behavior of the class under test to its current behavior. This metric is used to indicate another perspective of the size of a test class. It is directly related to the construction of test cases.

TNOO: This metric counts the *number of methods* in a test class (Singh and Saha 2010). It reflects another perspective of the size of a test class.

The metrics TLOC, TASSERT and TNOO, were chosen in our study because they were used in many (related) empirical studies in literature. Size is an attribute that strongly characterizes the effort involved in writing the code of test cases. TLOC and TNOO are size related metrics. TNOO is, however, a little bit different from TLOC in the way that it captures a different perspective of the size by counting the number of methods in a test class. Furthermore, even if intuitively we can expect that the TASSERT metric is correlated with the size of a test class, it is a little bit different from the others size related metrics. It is rather related to the effort involved in the verification between the expected behavior and the actual behavior of the class under test.

We also used in our study the two unit test case metrics that we introduced in our previous work (Toure et al. 2014):

TINVOK: This metric counts the *number of direct method invocations* in a test class. It captures the dependencies needed to run the test class.

TDATA: This metric gives the *number of new Java objects* created in a test class. These data are required to initialize the test.

We assume that the effort necessary to write the code of a test class is proportional to the characteristics measured by the selected unit test case metrics.

4 Empirical study

4.1 Selected case studies

Six open source Java software systems were selected for the study: (1) ANT[a]: is a Java library and command-line tool that drives processes described in build files as targets and extension points dependent upon each other. (2) JFREECHART (JFC)[b]: is a free chart library for Java platform. (3) JODA-Time (JODA)[c]: is the de facto standard library for advanced date and time in Java. It provides a quality replacement for the Java date and time classes. The design supports multiple calendar systems, while still providing a simple API. (4) Apache Lucene Core (LUCENE)[d]: is a high-performance, full-featured text search engine library. It is a technology suitable for nearly any application that requires full-text search, especially cross-platform. (5) POI[e]: is a Java APIs for manipulating various file formats based upon the Office Open XML standards (OOXML) and Microsoft's OLE 2 Compound Document format (OLE2). It can read and write MS Excel files using Java. (6) IVY[f]: is a popular dependency manager. It is characterized by flexibility, simplicity and tight integration with Apache ANT.

These systems have been selected based on different requirements, such as: (1) the source code (and test code) archives of the subject systems must be available and important enough to provide a significant data set on the systems and corresponding JUnit test cases, (2) the subject systems must be of different overall size and from different domains, in order to see if our results will differ from one system to another, (3) the subject systems must be developed in Java. Table 1 summarizes some of the characteristics of the analyzed systems. It gives, for each system: (1) the total number of source code classes, (2) the total number of lines of code of source code classes, (3) the number of classes for which JUnit test cases have been developed, (4) the total number of lines of code of JUnit test cases, (5) the percentage of source code classes for which JUnit test cases have been developed, (6) the percentage of tested lines of

Table 1 Some statistics on the selected systems

Systems	(1)	(2)	(3)	(4)	(5)	(6)	(7)
ANT	713	64062	111	8121	15.60%	27.50%	46.12%
JFC	496	68312	226	20657	45.60%	77.80%	38.89%
JODA	225	31591	77	46702	34.22%	55.80%	264.17%
LUCENE	659	56902	114	21997	17.30%	38.80%	99.54%
POI	1539	136005	404	41610	26.25%	43.20%	70.82%
IVY	610	50080	95	12531	15.57%	36.00%	69.44%

code (source code classes for which JUnit test cases have been developed), and (7) the ratio of the number of lines of test code per number of tested lines of source code.

From Table 1, it can be seen that the analyzed systems present effectively different characteristics. We can make several observations:

- POI is the largest of the systems analyzed in terms of number of classes (with 1539 classes), and JODA is the smallest one (with 225 classes). Moreover, systems with a relatively smaller number of classes may be large in terms of number of lines of code. For example, JFC has a smaller number of classes compared to ANT, LUCENE and IVY. However, in terms of number of lines of source code, JFC is the largest one. This suggests that classes in JFC are larger, in terms of lines of code, than those in ANT, LUCENE or IVY.
- For all systems, it can be seen that JUnit test classes have not been developed for all source code classes. We have calculated for each system the percentage of classes for which JUnit test classes have been developed (Table 1, column 5). From Table 1, it can be seen that JFC is the most covered system (45.60%) followed by JODA (34.22%). ANT and IVY present the weakest coverage rates (respectively 15.60% and 15.57%).
- From Table 1 (column 6), it can be seen that for systems JFC and JODA the value of the percentage of tested lines of code (source code classes for which JUnit test cases have been developed), respectively 77.80% and 55.80%, is greater than 50%. Moreover, it can also be seen that for systems ANT and IVY, for which the values of the percentage of source code classes for which JUnit test cases have been developed are comparable (Table 1 – column 5: respectively 15.60% and 15.57%), the values of the percentage of tested lines of code (source code classes for which JUnit test cases have been developed) are significantly different (Table 1 – column 6: respectively 27.50% and 36.00%).
- The values of the ratio of the number of lines of test code per number of tested lines of source code (Table 1 – column 7) show two particular systems: JODA and JFC. In the case of JODA, the value of the ratio is greater than 1, which means that there are more lines of test code for a given line of source code. In the case of JFC, the value of the ratio is the lowest compared to the values of the other systems.

4.2 Research methodology and data collection

We conducted an empirical analysis organized into three main stages. We used the five unit test case metrics to collect data on the JUnit test cases of the six selected systems.

In order to better understand the underlying orthogonal dimensions captured by the suite of unit test case metrics, we performed in a first stage a Principal Component Analysis (PCA). PCA is a technique that has been widely used in software engineering to identify important underlying dimensions captured by a set of software metrics. We used this technique to find whether the analyzed unit test case metrics are independent or are measuring similar structural aspects of the code of JUnit test cases. Furthermore, we used in a second stage clustering techniques, particularly K-Means and Univariate clustering, to determine the unit test case metrics that are the less volatile, i.e. the least affected by the style adopted by developers while writing the code of unit test cases. We investigated the distribution and the variance of the unit test case metrics based on three important internal software class attributes. We focused on size, complexity and coupling. In addition, we evaluated in a third stage the relationships between the considered internal software class attributes and the suite of unit test case metrics. We used correlation and linear regression analysis.

We selected for our study, from each of the investigated systems, only the classes for which JUnit test cases have been developed. The same approach has been used in others previous empirical studies that addressed the testing effort prediction problem (e.g., Bruntink and Van Deursen (2004, 2006), Singh and Saha (2010), Zhou et al. (2012)). JUnit[g] is a simple Framework for writing and running automated unit tests for Java classes. Test cases in JUnit are written by testers in Java. JUnit gives testers some support so that they can write those test cases more conveniently. A typical usage of JUnit is to test each class C_s of the program by means of a dedicated test class C_t. To actually test a class C_s, we need to execute its test class C_t. This is done by calling JUnit's test runner tool. JUnit will report how many of the test methods in C_t succeed, and how many fail.

We noticed that developers usually name the JUnit test classes by adding the prefix (suffix) "Test" ("TestCase") into the name of the classes for which JUnit test cases were developed. Only classes that have such name-matching mechanism with the test class name are included in the analysis. This approach has already been adopted in others studies (e.g., Mockus et al. 2009). However, we observed by analyzing the JUnit test classes of the subject systems that in some cases there is no one-to-one relationship between JUnit classes and tested classes. This has also been noted in other previous studies (e.g., Rompaey and Demeyer 2009, Qusef et al. 2011). In these cases, several JUnit test cases have been related to a same tested class. The matching procedure has been performed on the subject systems by three research assistants separately (a Ph.D. student (first author of this paper) and two Master students, both in computer science). We compared the obtained results and noticed only a few differences. We rechecked the few results in which we observed differences and chose the correct ones based on our experience and a deep analysis of the code. For each class C_s selected, we used the suite of unit test case metrics to quantify the corresponding JUnit test class (classes) C_t. We used a tool that we developed (JUnit code analyzer).

4.3 Understanding the underlying dimensions captured by the unit test case metrics

Principal Component Analysis (PCA) is a statistical technique that has been widely used in software engineering to identify important underlying dimensions captured by a set of software metrics (variables). It is a useful technique that aims to reduce variables. We used this technique to find whether the unit test case metrics are independent or are measuring (capturing) similar underlying dimensions (structural aspects) of the code of JUnit test cases. PCA is a standard technique to identify the underlying, independent/orthogonal dimensions that explain relationships between variables in a data set (Quah and Thwin 2003).

From M_1, M_2, M_3,... M_n metrics, PCA creates new artificial components P_1, P_2, P_3, ..., P_m such as: P_i are independent, P_i are linear combinations of M_i, and each P_i maximizes the total variance. The linear factors are called loadings and the variables with high loadings require some degree of interpretation. In order to find out these variables and interpret the new components, we focussed on rotated component. Orthogonal rotation is performed to improve the interpretation of results. There are various strategies to perform such rotation. According to literature, Varimax is the most frequently used strategy (Dash and Dubey 2012, Aggarwal and Singh 2006). The sum of squared values of loadings that describe the dimension is referred to as eigenvalue. Since PCA is a projection method in a smaller dimension space, projected variables may seem close in the small dimension space but far from each other in the real space, according to the projection direction. In order to avoid misinterpretation of the new components, the square cosines are computed. A value closed to zero indicates that the point is far from the projection axe. A large proportion of the total variance (information captured by the unit test case metrics) is usually explained by the first few PCs. We reduce the metrics without a substantial loss of the explained information by selecting the first PCs. Three criteria are generally used to determine the factors to retain for interpretation: (1) The Scree test (Cattell 1966) is based on the decreasing curve of eigenvalues analysis. Only the factors that appear before the first inflection point detected on the curve are considered. (2) The cumulative amount of variance criterion considers only the first components that cumulative amount of variance is greater than a given value (in most cases: 80%). (3) The eigenvalue criterion considers only factors with associated eigenvalue greater than 1 (Quah and Thwin 2003). We used in our study criterion (2) which ensures us to consider at least 80% of variance captured by the unit test case metrics. We used the XLSTAT[h] tool to perform the analysis. We present in what follows the application of the PCA technique on the data collected from each of the selected systems and discuss the obtained results.

4.3.1 ANT

Table 2 presents the results of the application of the PCA technique on the data collected from ANT. It gives the variability of new components, their correlation with unit test case metrics, and the square cosine of the projection (metrics) in the new components. From Table 2, it can be seen that the components F1 and F2 cumulate more than 80% of total variance (exactly 80.337%), which leads us to interpret only the two first components F1 and F2.

As it can be seen from Table 2, component F1 is represented by the metrics TASSERT (0.934), TDATA (0.899) and TLOC (0.775). Component F2 is represented by the metrics TINVOK (0.843) and TNOO (0.837). The two first components oppose the group of relatively large test classes (high values of TLOC) having high verification effort and data creation (high values of TASSERT and TDATA) to the group of test classes that contain many method invocations (high values of TINVOK) with high number of operations

Table 2 PCA results – ANT

	F1	F2	F3	F4	F5
Variability (%)	46.6	33.737	12.049	4.235	3.379
% Cumulated	46.6	80.337	92.386	96.621	100
	ANT (Correlation)			ANT (Square-cosine)	
	F1	F2		F1	F2
TINVOK	0.013	0.843		0	0.71
TDATA	0.899	−0.002		0.809	0
TASSERT	0.934	0.102		0.873	0.01
TLOC	0.775	0.515		0.601	0.265
TNOO	0.217	0.837		0.047	0.701

(TNOO). High contribution of the metrics TDATA, TASSERT and TLOC in the first component indicates that, in large majority of test classes, data creation and number of assertions increase with the size of test classes (lines of code).

The independence between F1 and F2 indicates that, in some test classes, the number of methods and invocations increase together independently of the metrics TDATA, TLOC, and TASSERT. The overall information (related to unit testing effort implementation) captured by the suite of unit test case metrics is distributed in the two dimensions F1 and F2, which can be represented by one of the couples of {TASSERT, TDATA, TLOC} × {TINVOK, TNOO}. The couple of metrics (TASSERT, TINVOK) represents the best subset of independent unit test case metrics providing the best independent information (maximizing the variance).

4.3.2 JFC

The results of the application of the PCA technique on the data collected from JFC are given in Table 3. It can be seen that the cumulated variance of the two first components F1 and F2 (89.28%) suggests to limit the interpretation to these two components. As it can be seen, component F1 regroups the metrics TNOO (0.887), TINVOK (0.837) and TLOC (0.746). Component F2 is represented by the metric TDATA (0.951). TASSERT, in spite of its relative high correlation with component F2 (0.694), is far from the projection axe as shown by its low square cosine (0.481 < 0.5). TASSERT provides, in fact, insignificant information in the considered set of unit test case metrics.

Table 3 PCA results – JFC

	F1	F2	F3	F4	F5
Variability (%)	50.152	39.124	6.923	2.771	1.029
% Cumulated	50.15	89.28	96.2	98.97	100
	JFC (Correlation)			JFC (Square cosine)	
	F1	F2		F1	F2
TINVOK	0.837	0.358		0.701	0.129
TDATA	0.209	0.951		0.044	0.905
TASSERT	0.647	0.694		0.419	0.481
TLOC	0.746	0.634		0.556	0.402
TNOO	0.887	0.197		0.787	0.039

For JFC, the two first components oppose the most important set of test classes containing a relative high number of methods, having many invocations and large number of lines of code, to the set of test classes with many data creation. One of the couples of {TNOO, TINOK, TLOC} × {TDATA} could represent the set of unit test case metrics for JFC. The couple of metrics (TNOO, TDATA) is, however, the best representative sub set of the suite of unit test case metrics.

4.3.3 JODA

For JODA (see Table 4), the first component F1 that cumulates 93.36% of total variance is sufficient to interpret the whole set of unit test case metrics. As it can be seen from Table 4, the component F1 regroups all the unit test case metrics. So, the first component captures all dimensions measured by the unit test case metrics. The effort involved in writing, verifying and creating data are equally distributed. From Table 1, it can be seen that the value of the ratio of the number of lines of test code per number of tested lines of source code corresponding to JODA system (264.17%) shows that there are two times more lines of test code than lines of source code. It is the highest value of the column 7 of Table 1. This may suggest that the verification effort is more important for JODA relatively to the others systems. In fact, by investigating this issue, we observed that the average number of assertions is of 223 assertions per tested class for JODA against 12 for ANT, 18 for JFC, 31 for LUCENE, 22 for POI, and 30 for IVY.

For JODA, according to the results, we can say that each test case metric is a good representative of the whole set of unit test case metrics. However, TLOC provides the maximum information.

4.3.4 LUCENE

Table 5 gives the results of the application of the PCA technique on the data collected from LUCENE. It can be seen that the first component F1 is, here also, sufficient (88.965% of variance) for interpretation. Moreover, all the unit test case metrics are closed and highly correlated to component F1. Here also the first component captures all dimensions measured by the unit test case metrics.

From Table 5, we can also observe that the effort involved in writing, verifying and creating data are equally distributed as in the case of JODA. In this case also, we can observe the same trend in terms of the value of the ratio of the number of lines of test code per number of tested lines of source code (Table 1 – column 7: 99.54%). Indeed,

Table 4 PCA results – JODA

	F1	F2	F3	F4	F5
Variability (%)	93.366	2.949	2.454	0.996	0.235
% Cumulated	93.366	96.315	98.769	99.765	100
	JODA (Correlation)			JODA (Square cosine)	
	F1			F1	
TINVOK	0.952			0.906	
TDATA	0.953			0.908	
TASSERT	0.955			0.911	
TLOC	0.99			0.98	
TNOO	0.982			0.964	

Table 5 PCA results - LUCENE

	F1	F2	F3	F4	F5
Variabilité (%)	88.965	6.462	2.144	1.429	1
% Cumulated	88.965	95.427	97.571	99	100
	LUCENE (Correlation)			LUCENE (Square Cosine)	
	F1			F1	
TINVOK	0.972			0.945	
TDATA	0.95			0.903	
TASSERT	0.86			0.936	
TLOC	0.967			0.739	
TNOO	0.962			0.925	

this value indicates that there are as many lines of test code as lines of source code. This suggests that the same effort of writing was spent for all tested classes. TINVOK is the best representative of the suite of unit test case metric for LUCENE.

4.3.5 POI

In the case of POI, it can be seen from Table 6 that to aggregate more than 80% of variance, we have to consider the two first components F1 and F2 (84.214%) in our interpretation. As we can see from Table 1, POI is the largest of the analyzed systems (with 1539 source code classes). Moreover, POI has the largest number of classes for which JUnit test classes have been developed (403). The first component F1 is highly correlated with the metrics TDATA (0.896) and TLOC (0.887) compared to the others unit test case metrics. The second component F2 is more correlated with the metrics TINVOK (0.912) and TNOO (0.758). The square cosine values of the two metrics (0.832 and 0.574) are all greater than 0.5, which indicates that the metrics are close enough to the projection axe to allow correct interpretation. The metric TASSERT provides here also insignificant information in the considered set of unit test case metrics. The components F1 and F2 oppose the set of large test classes having many data creation to the set of classes having many methods and invocations. The first two components could be represented by each couple in {TDATA, TLOC} × {TINVOK, TNOO}. The couple of metrics (TDATA, TINVOK) is, however, the best representative sub set of the suite of unit test case metrics.

Table 6 PCA results – POI

	F1	F2	F3	F4	F5
Variability (%)	47.43	36.784	8.409	5.713	1.664
% Cumulated	47.43	84.214	92.623	98.336	100
	POI (Correlation)			POI (Square cosine)	
	F1	F2		F1	F2
TINVOK	0.264	0.912		0.069	0.832
TDATA	0.896	0.237		0.802	0.056
TASSERT	0.697	0.467		0.486	0.218
TLOC	0.887	0.399		0.787	0.159
TNOO	0.476	0.758		0.227	0.574

4.3.6 IVY

Table 7 gives the results of the application of the PCA technique on the data collected from IVY. The two first components F1 and F2 (89.323% of total variance) are considered for interpretation. As it can be seen from Table 7, component F1 regroups the metrics TASSERT (0.923), TNOO (0.792), and TLOC (0.780). Component F2 is highly correlated to the metrics TDATA (0.921) and TINVOK (0.748). Square cosine value greater than 0.5 shows that the metrics TDATA (with 0.851) and TINVOK (with 0.559) are close to the component F2. For IVY, the two first components oppose the group of large test classes containing a relatively high number of methods with many assertions to the group of test classes with many data creation and method invocations. Any couple of metrics selected from {TASSERT, TLOC, TNOO} × {TDATA, TINVOK} could represent the information captured by all the unit test case metrics. The couple of metrics (TASSERT, TDATA) is, however, the best representative subset of the suite of unit test case metrics.

4.3.7 Summary

Table 8 gives a summary of the PCA analysis. It shows, for each system, the possible couples of unit test case metrics that could represent the set of unit test case metrics for capturing information (first and second columns), and the best representative couple of independent unit test case metrics providing the maximum of information (third column). From Table 8, it can be seen that the optimum subset (maximizing variance and not linearly related) of unit test case metrics varies from one system to another. Some metrics are, however, more common than others (e.g., TINVOK, TDATA). Moreover, we can also reasonably say that TLOC could also represent the first component in the case of all systems since it has the most constant impact on the first factor F1 (significantly correlated to the first component in the case of all considered systems). In the same vein, TINVOK tends to represent the second component F2, since the metric appears three times on four cases as second member of the best couples. The metrics TLOC and TINVOK could be considered as the most independent unit test case metrics maximizing information.

Overall, we can observe from Table 8 that the two metrics TDATA and TINVOK, which we introduced in our previous work, always appear in either of the two columns (F1, F2). Moreover, the variations that we can observe from one system to another concerning the best subset of metrics may be due to the sensitivity of (some) unit test case metrics to the differences in the styles adopted by the developers while writing the code of JUnit test cases.

Table 7 PCA results – IVY

	F1	F2	F3	F4	F5
Variability (%)	48.525	40.798	6.483	3.782	0.412
% Cumulated	48.525	89.323	95.806	99.588	100

	IVY (Correlation)			IVY (Square Cosine)	
	F1	F2		F1	F2
TINVOK	0.529	0.748		0.280	0.559
TDATA	0.240	0.923		0.058	0.851
TASSERT	0.923	0.201		0.853	0.041
TLOC	0.780	0.613		0.609	0.375
TNOO	0.792	0.462		0.627	0.214

Table 8 Summary of the PCA results

	F1	F2	Best subset
ANT	TASSERT,TDATA, TLOC	TINVOK, TNOO	TASSERT, TINVOK
JFC	TNOO, TINVOK, TLOC	TDATA	TNOO, TDATA
JODA	Each metric		TLOC
LUCENE	Each metric		TINVOK
POI	TDATA, TLOC	TINVOK, TNOO	TDATA, TINVOK
IVY	TASSERT, TLOC, TNOO	TDATA, TINVOK	TASSERT, TDATA

In fact, we suspect that the style adopted by the developers while writing the code of JUnit test cases can have a significant impact on the distribution of the values of the selected unit test case metrics. The selected systems as mentioned above are from different domains, of different sizes and complexities, and developed by different teams. By analyzing the code of the unit test cases of the different systems, we observed that the test development style, in general, differs from one system to another (which is reflected somewhere in Table 1). For example, the number of assert statements in the code of a test class, given by the metric TASSERT, could change according to the adopted style. Indeed, while analyzing the code of some test classes of the selected systems, we observed in some cases that developers, for a given test class, group all assertTrue (…) calls in a single utile method that is invoked in different places in the code instead of invoking assertTrue (…) in those places. So, before investigating this question more deeply in the following section, we decided to group the data collected from all systems studied to have a single set of data on which we wanted to apply the PCA technique. By doing this, we wanted to group all styles (systems design and test code) in a single sample of data and observe how the unit test case metrics behave. Results are given in Table 9. As we can see, the first two components capture more than 80% of total information (exactly 91.361%). Based on the analysis of the coefficients associated with each unit test case metric within each of the components, the principal components are interpreted as follows: (1) F1: the first component is characterized by size. Each of the metrics TLOC, TASSERT, TDATA and TNOO could represent this component. (2) F2: the second component is rather characterized by invocations. It is clear that the best representative metric is TINVOK with the highest values of correlation and square-cosine (respectively 0.917 and 0.842). According to results, any couple of

Table 9 PCA results – all systems

All Systems	F1	F2	F3	F4	F5
Variability (%)	58.040	33.321	4.968	2.048	1.623
% Cumulated	58.040	91.361	96.329	98.377	100.000
	Correlation			Square-cosine	
	F1	F2		F1	F2
TLOC	0.825	0.498	TLOC	0.680	0.248
TASSERT	0.848	0.398	TASSERT	0.718	0.159
TDATA	0.831	0.400	TDATA	0.691	0.160
TINVOK	0.395	0.917	TINVOK	0.156	0.842
TNOO	0.810	0.507	TNOO	0.656	0.257

metrics selected from {TLOC, TASSERT, TDATA, TNOO} × {TINVOK} could represent the information captured by all unit test case metrics.

4.4 Investigating the distribution and the variance of the unit test case metrics

The previous section shows that the couple of unit test case metrics TLOC and TINVOK is overall the best representative subset of the initial suite of unit test case metrics in the sense that these metrics are the most independent unit test case metrics maximizing information.

In this section, we focus on the sensitivity of the unit test case metrics when the writing style of test classes changes. In others words, we wanted to determine what are the unit test case metrics that are the less volatile, i.e. the least affected by the style adopted by developers while writing the code of test cases. In fact, a unit test case metric that is strongly influenced by the style adopted by developers while writing the code of test cases may not adequately reflect the real effort required for test cases construction. The high variance (from one style to another) of such a metric may strongly impact its value (distribution) and limit its applicability and its interpretation for different systems. In order to investigate this issue, we used clustering techniques: (1) to investigate and better understand the distribution and the variance of unit test case metrics based on different categories of classes, and (2) to determine what are the less volatile unit test case metrics, which are the less influenced by the style adopted by the developers while writing the code of unit test cases.

4.4.1 K-Means clustering

In a first step, we used *K*-Means clustering to classify the tested classes (source code classes) in various categories based on three internal software class attributes: size, complexity and coupling. *K*-means clustering is a method of cluster analysis that aims to partition *n* observations (classes for which JUnit test cases have been developed in our study) into *k* clusters (five in our study) in which each observation belongs to the cluster with the nearest mean. We wanted, in fact, to reflect in the analysis five different categories of the effort involved in writing the code of test cases: very low, low, medium, high and very high. We used here also the XLSTAT tool, which implements many statistic and data mining algorithms. We used this technique to partition the tested classes in five clusters (categories) based on the three internal class attributes taken together. Clustering provides, indeed, a natural way for identifying clusters of related objects (classes for which JUnit test cases have been developed in our study) based on their similarity (the three internal software class attributes in our case). The resulting clusters are to be built so that tested classes within each cluster are more comparable in terms of size, complexity and coupling than tested classes assigned to different clusters (minimizing intra-cluster variance and maximizing inter-cluster variance).

We used in this step of our study the group of data collected from all systems. In total, we have 1027 observations (Java classes and corresponding JUnit test cases). To measure the selected internal software class attributes, we used the following metrics: LOC (size), WMC (complexity) and CBO (coupling). The LOC (*Lines of Code per class*) metric counts for a class its number of lines of code. The WMC (*Weighted Methods per Class*) metric gives the sum of complexities of the methods of a given class, where each method is weighted by its cyclomatic complexity. The CBO (*Coupling between*

Objects) metric counts for a class the number of other classes to which it is coupled (and vice versa). The object-oriented metrics WMC and CBO have been proposed by Chidamber and Kemerer (1994) and Chidamber et al. (1998). The three metrics have been used in many empirical software engineering studies. We computed the values of the three metrics using the Borland Together Tool[i]. The values of the unit test case metrics have been computed using the tool we developed. Table 10 gives the descriptive statistics (total of observations) of the internal class attribute metrics we used in our study. Table 11 gives the descriptive statistics (total of observations) of the unit test case metrics. Table 12 gives the descriptive statistics of the internal software class attribute metrics and the unit test case metrics for each system separately. As we can see in Table 12, the selected systems vary in terms of size, complexity and coupling.

We used the XLSTAT tool to perform the clustering analysis. Moreover, in order to assess the representativeness of the different styles of design and test code (different systems used: source code classes and corresponding JUnit test cases) in the different clusters, we computed the IQV (index of qualitative variance) for each cluster as follows (Mueller and Schuessler 1961):

$$IQV = \frac{k\left(n^2 - \sum_{i=0}^{n}\left(f_i^2\right)\right)}{n^2(k-1)}.$$

Where: n indicates the cluster size, k indicates modalities (number of systems), and f_i indicates the frequency of modality i (number of classes in cluster i). The index of qualitative variance can vary from 0 to 1. When all of the cases of the distribution are in one category, there is no diversity (or variation) and the IQV is equal to 0. The IQV reflects the percentage of differences relative to the maximum possible differences in each distribution. As it can be seen from Table 13, the IQV values obtained are quite high (close to 1). The relatively lowest value is observed for cluster 5, which may be explained by the size of the cluster (17 observations – see Table 14 and Table 15) compared to the others clusters. This index reflects the good representativeness of the different styles (different systems) in the different clusters (different systems are represented in clusters).

Table 14 gives the descriptive statistics of the three internal software class attribute metrics LOC, WMC and CBO corresponding to the five clusters (1–5). As we can see from Table 14, the mean values of the three internal software class attribute metrics, overall, increase from the first cluster (1 – relatively simple classes) to the last one (5 – relatively most complex classes). This is also true for the standard deviation of the three internal software class attribute metrics. It can also be seen from Table 14 that the distribution of the internal software class attribute metrics reflects properly the classification of tested classes: the mean values of the metrics LOC, WMC and CBO increase from cluster 1 to

Table 10 Descriptive statistics of the internal class attribute metrics

	CBO	LOC	WMC
Nb. Obs.	1027	1027	1027
Min	0	2	0
Max	111	2644	557
Mean (μ)	12.36	182.38	35.42
St. Dev. (σ)	13.45	241.36	45.82

Table 11 Descriptive statistics of the unit test case metrics

	TLOC	TASSERT	TDATA	TINVOK	TNOO
Nb. Obs.	1027	1027	1027	1027	1027
Min	6	0	0	0	0
Max	4063	1156	758	516	242
Mean (μ)	147.63	36.77	21.20	35.06	10.26
St. Dev. (σ)	288.87	96.36	51.08	42.44	22.19

cluster 5 (most complex classes). We can also observe from Table 14 (standard deviation) that the internal software class attribute metric that varies the least is CBO, followed by the WMC metric.

Table 15 gives the descriptive statistics of the five unit test case metrics corresponding to the five clusters (1–5). As we can see from Table 15 and Figure 1, the mean values of the five unit test case metrics, overall, increase from the first cluster (1) to the last one (5). This is also true, overall, for the standard deviation of the five unit test case metrics. The only exceptions that we can observe from Table 15 are for the unit test case metrics TASSERT and TNOO between clusters 4 and 5, where the standard deviation of the two metrics decreases.

Table 12 Descriptive statistics of the metrics for each system

	Statistics	CBO	LOC	WMC	TLOC	TASSERT	TDATA	TINVOK	TNOO
ANT	Nb. Obs.	111	111	111	111	111	111	111	111
	Min	0	5	1	8	0	0	20	1
	Max	39	846	178	493	165	47	118	40
	Mean	10.49	158.64	31.31	73.16	12.03	4.56	83.72	6.43
JFC	Nb. Obs.	226	226	226	226	226	226	226	226
	Min	0	7	1	18	1	4	5	2
	Max	67	2041	470	635	143	265	118	45
	Mean	16.19	235.02	46.89	91.40	17.96	23.93	22.15	5.77
JODA	Nb. Obs.	77	77	77	77	77	77	77	77
	Min	0	14	1	27	6	1	3	5
	Max	29	1760	176	2624	1156	482	401	242
	Mean	10.55	229.60	44.81	606.52	220.95	88.69	92.97	56.60
LUCENE	Nb. Obs.	114	114	114	114	114	114	114	114
	Min	0	8	1	8	0	0	0	0
	Max	55	2644	557	4063	329	758	516	148
	Mean	9.90	193.84	35.89	192.96	30.66	31.28	32.48	9.68
POI	Nb. Obs.	404	404	404	404	404	404	404	404
	Min	0	2	0	6	0	0	0	1
	Max	111	1427	374	2379	396	188	138	72
	Mean	10.39	145.42	28.42	103.00	22.36	8.44	20.94	5.42
IVY	Nb. Obs.	95	95	95	95	95	95	95	95
	Min	0	5	1	10	0	0	1	1
	Max	92	1039	231	1019	528	191	92	41
	Mean	18.23	189.97	34.47	131.91	29.75	21.64	25.07	9.10

Table 13 IQV rate for each cluster

Clustering	All systems	Cluster 1	Cluster 2	Cluster 3	Cluster 4	Cluster 5
K-means (5)	0.910	0.867	0.923	0.968	0.886	0.839

Overall, the distribution of the unit test case metrics reflects properly the classification of tested classes and corresponding JUnit test cases: the values of the metrics TLOC, TASSERT, TDATA, TINVOK and TNOO increase from cluster 1 to cluster 5 (most complex classes). Also, Table 15 gives the distribution of the C_V (coefficient of variation) of each unit test case metric, based on the five clusters. We compared test cluster variance by using C_V to limit the variable scale effects. As we can see, the metric TINVOK has the lowest coefficient of variation values, except for the last cluster (5), followed by the metric TLOC. Results suggest therefore that the TINVOK metric is the test case metric that varies the least followed by TLOC. So, we can conclude that for comparable classes in terms of size, complexity and coupling (based on the performed clustering), the metric TINVOK is the less volatile. Two main factors may explain the low value of C_V for TINVOK: (1) the possible lack of relationship between TINVOK and the internal software class attributes, and/or (2) the impact of the variation of the test code writing style in the different systems. The increasing mean value of TLOC and TINVOK observed in Figure 1 with respect of clusters (from relatively simple to relatively high), suggests that there is a relationship between internal software class attribute metrics and unit test case metrics TLOC and TINVOK. Then, the low value of C_V does not appear to be due to the lack of correlation. This question will be investigated in the following section (4.5).

From Table 15, Figure 2 and Figure 3, we can also observe that the unit test case metrics which vary the most are TASSERT and TDATA (respectively for the three first clusters and for the two last clusters).

4.4.2 Univariate clustering

We used, in a second step, the univariate clustering technique to optimally cluster in k (5 here also) homogeneous groups the source code classes of the analyzed systems

Table 14 Descriptive statistics of the internal class attribute metrics (K-means clustering)

		Cluster 1	Cluster 2	Cluster 3	Cluster 4	Cluster 5
Nb. Obs.		587	267	118	38	17
CBO	Min	0	0	0	4	3
	Max	44	68	57	92	111
	Mean (μ)	6.06	14.461	24.56	43.03	43.71
	Std. Dev (σ)	5.42	10.03	12.33	19.90	28.83
LOC	Min	2	124	292	592	1134
	Max	128	288	562	1039	2644
	Mean (μ)	61.57	192.56	387.11	770.45	1458.24
	Std. Dev (σ)	33.27	48.30	77.07	134.68	406.54
WMC	Min	0	3	16	10	10
	Max	86	98	157	231	557
	Mean (μ)	13.33	38.69	77.86	137.34	224.29
	Std. Dev (σ)	8.68	13.99	22.52	48.71	154.63

Table 15 Descriptive statistics of the unit test case metrics (K-means clustering)

		Cluster 1	Cluster 2	Cluster 3	Cluster 4	Cluster 5
Nb. Obs.		587	267	118	38	17
TLOC	Min	6	8	10	16	18
	Max	1280	2035	2236	2624	4063
	Mean (μ)	84.78	146.99	289.71	399.08	779.59
	Std. Dev (σ)	110.60	208.20	434.08	605.59	996.46
	Coef. of var ($C_v = \sigma/\mu$)	1.304	1.416	1.498	1.517	1.278
TASSERT	Min	0	0	0	1	2
	Max	329	1058	1014	1156	396
	Mean (μ)	17.76	36.88	84.70	130.40	149.35
	Std. Dev (σ)	34.36	86.89	165.35	243.50	136.26
	Coef. of var ($C_v = \sigma/\mu$)	1.935	2.356	1.952	1.867	0.912
TDATA	Min	0	0	0	0	0
	Max	324	482	393	482	758
	Mean (μ)	11.64	22.31	43.62	56.79	98.94
	Std. Dev (σ)	21.62	44.61	75.64	106.23	172.48
	Coef. of var ($C_v = \sigma/\mu$)	1.857	2	1.734	1.871	1.743
TINVOK	Min	0	2	1	6	2
	Max	175	192	401	399	516
	Mean (μ)	26.28	34.34	60.75	72.87	86.29
	Std. Dev (σ)	27.04	31.10	61.49	84.23	114.92
	Coef. of var ($C_v = \sigma/\mu$)	1.029	0.906	1.012	1.156	1.332
TNOO	Min	0	1	1	1	3
	Max	153	164	242	238	148
	Mean (μ)	6.19	10.27	21.09	30.74	29.65
	Std. Dev (σ)	10.38	17.74	39.20	53.56	35.95
	Coef. of var ($C_v = \sigma/\mu$)	1.678	1.728	1.859	1.743	1.213

based this time on a single variable (an internal class attribute in our case). We wanted to investigate here also how the unit test case metrics vary according to the different clusters obtained using separately the three different internal software class attributes: size, complexity and coupling. Here also, we grouped the data collected from all systems studied to have a single set of data.

The univariate clustering clusters *n* one-dimensional observations (tested classes in our case), described by a single quantitative variable (an internal software class attribute

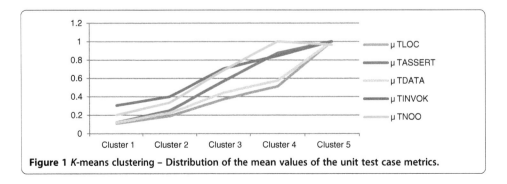

Figure 1 *K*-means clustering – Distribution of the mean values of the unit test case metrics.

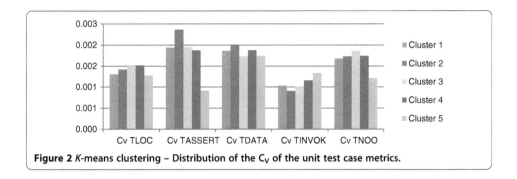

Figure 2 *K*-means clustering – Distribution of the C$_V$ of the unit test case metrics.

in our case), into *k* homogeneous clusters (five in our case, indicating different levels of size, complexity and coupling). Homogeneity is measured here using the sum of the within-cluster variances. To maximize the homogeneity of clusters, we therefore try to minimize the sum of the within-cluster variances. This method can be seen as a process of turning a quantitative variable (one internal software class attribute in our case) into a discrete ordinal variable.

We used the univariate clustering algorithm of the XLSTAT tool[h]. Here also, we computed the IQV (index of qualitative variance) for each cluster as previously. As it can be seen from Table 16, the values obtained are in most cases quite high (close to 1), and this for each univariate clustering. This reflects the good representation of different styles of writing test code in different clusters. The lowest values for the IQV are observed for cluster 5. This may be explained by the size of this cluster (5 elements only – see Tables 17, 18 and 19) compared to the others clusters. Tables 17, 18 and 19 give the descriptive statistics of the unit test case metrics corresponding to the five clusters obtained respectively for the variables *size* (LOC), *complexity* (WMC) and *coupling* (CBO).

The first univariate clustering we performed was based on the variable *size* (LOC). As we can see from Table 17 and Figure 4, the mean values of the unit test case metrics, overall, increase from the first cluster (1) to the last one (5), except for cluster 4 and this for unit test case metrics TASSERT, TDATA, TINVOK and TLOC. This is also true for the standard deviation of the unit test case metrics, here also except for cluster 4 and this, for all unit test case metrics. Overall, results suggest that the TINVOK metric is the test case metric that varies the least, followed by TLOC. Results suggest therefore that the TINVOK metric, for classes comparable in terms of size (based on the performed univariate clustering), is the least volatile. From Table 17 and Figure 4, we can also observe that the unit test case metrics which vary most are TASSERT and TDATA.

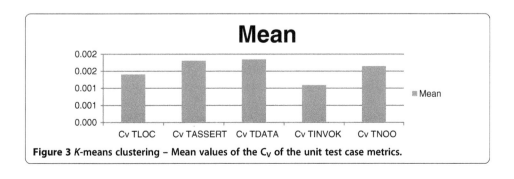

Figure 3 *K*-means clustering – Mean values of the C$_V$ of the unit test case metrics.

Table 16 IQV rate for each cluster

Clustering	All systems	Cluster 1	Cluster 2	Cluster 3	Cluster 4	Cluster 5
WMC	0.910	0.869	0.941	0.957	0.889	0.672
LOC		0.877	0.943	0.912	0.895	0.768
CBO		0.842	0.946	0.952	0.806	0.762

The second univariate clustering we performed was based on the variable *complexity* (WMC). As we can see from Table 18 and Figure 5, the mean values of the unit test case metrics, overall, increase from the first cluster (1) to the last one (5). Unlike the first univariate clustering, in this case the growth of the mean values of the unit test case metric is continuous, from the first cluster to the fifth one. This is also true for the standard deviation of the unit test case metrics, here also except for cluster 4 and this for all the unit test case metrics. Overall, results suggest here also that the TINVOK metric is the test case metric that varies the least, followed by the TLOC metric. Results suggest therefore that the TINVOK metric, for classes comparable in terms of complexity (based on the performed univariate clustering), is the least volatile. From Table 18 and Figure 5, we can also observe that the unit test case metrics which vary most are TASSERT and TDATA.

Table 17 Descriptive statistics of the unit test case metrics (Univariate clustering - LOC)

LOC		Cluster 1	Cluster 2	Cluster 3	Cluster 4	Cluster 5
Nb. Obs.		707	236	53	26	5
TLOC	Min	6	8	23	16	323
	Max	1620	2035	2624	2379	4063
	Mean (μ)	93.92	193.04	406.76	437.58	1344.8
	Std. Dev (σ))	124.39	287.19	658.85	516.76	1407.67
	Coef. of var ($C_v = \sigma/\mu$)	1.324	1.488	1.62	1.181	1.047
TASSERT	Min	0	0	1	1	79
	Max	615	1058	1156	528	329
	Mean (μ)	20.45	49.39	142.28	129.73	146.8
	Std. Dev (σ)	40.98	107.48	269.95	153.84	92.81
	Coef. of var ($C_v = \sigma/\mu$)	2.004	2.176	1.897	1.186	0.632
TDATA	Min	0	0	0	0	9
	Max	482	326	482	323	758
	Mean (μ)	13.11	30.42	56.93	47.65	214.8
	Std. Dev (σ)	27.33	53.84	108.95	68.07	275.09
	Coef. of var ($C_v = \sigma/\mu$)	2.085	1.77	1.914	1.428	1.281
TINVOK	Min	0	2	1	2	17
	Max	175	327	401	138	516
	Mean (μ)	27.08	44.64	75.60	58.85	157
	Std. Dev (σ)	26.94	42.80	92.46	40.06	182.80
	Coef. of var ($C_v = \sigma/\mu$)	0.995	0.959	1.223	0.681	1.164
TNOO	Min	0	1	1	1	3
	Max	164	156	242	94	148
	Mean (μ)	6.86	13.19	33.40	22.69	42.6
	Std. Dev (σ)	11.68	23.99	60.92	23.50	53.45
	Coef. of var ($C_v = \sigma/\mu$)	1.704	1.82	1.824	1.035	1.255

Table 18 Descriptive statistics of the unit test case metrics (Univariate clustering - WMC)

WMC		Cluster 1	Cluster 2	Cluster 3	Cluster 4	Cluster 5
Nb. Obs.		632	279	93	18	5
TLOC	Min	6	8	20	16	408
	Max	1358	1745	2624	2280	4063
	Mean (μ)	83.97	175.68	375.18	473.28	1224.6
	Std. Dev (σ)	109.76	234.83	585.26	548.94	1422.32
	Coef. of var ($C_v = \sigma/\mu$)	1.307	1.337	1.56	1.16	1.161
TASSERT	Min	0	0	0	1	104
	Max	528	615	1156	832	391
	Mean (μ)	17.57	42.33	120.12	143.67	217.4
	Std. Dev (σ)	36.70	76.55	232.38	197.31	118.50
	Coef. of var ($C_v = \sigma/\mu$)	2.089	1.808	1.935	1.373	0.545
TDATA	Min	0	0	0	1	19
	Max	161	482	482	323	758
	Mean (μ)	10.90	27.34	54.66	59	223.2
	Std. Dev (σ)	16.16	52.08	94.16	93.15	270.37
	Coef. of var ($C_v = \sigma/\mu$)	1.483	1.905	1.723	1.579	1.211
TINVOK	Min	0	1	1	6	82
	Max	154	216	401	323	516
	Mean (μ)	25.67	39.88	66.95	82.39	188.4
	Std. Dev (σ)	25.55	35.83	75.98	71.34	165.06
	Coef. of var ($C_v = \sigma/\mu$)	0.995	0.898	1.135	0.866	0.876
TNOO	Min	0	1	1	1	11
	Max	82	164	242	188	148
	Mean (μ)	5.76	12.92	26.55	33.5	44
	Std. Dev (σ)	7.64	21.94	49.65	45.04	52.21
	Coef. of var ($C_v = \sigma/\mu$)	1.328	1.698	1.87	1.345	1.187

The third univariate clustering we performed was based on the variable *coupling* (CBO). As we can see from Table 19 and Figure 6, the mean values of the unit test case metrics, overall, increase from the first cluster (1) to the last one (5), except for cluster 4 and this for all the unit test case metrics. The same observation was made in the case of the first clustering. This is also true for the standard deviation of the unit test case metrics, here also except for cluster 4 and this for all unit test case metrics. The same trend is also observed for the coefficient of variation of the unit test case metrics. Overall, results suggest here also that the TINVOK metric is the unit test case metric that varies the least, followed by the TLOC metric. Results suggest therefore that the TINVOK metric, for classes comparable in terms of coupling (based on the performed univariate clustering), is the least volatile. From Table 19 and Figure 6, we can also observe that here also (overall) the unit test case metrics which vary most are TASSERT and TDATA.

4.4.3 Summary

Figure 7 summarizes the distribution of the coefficient of variation of the five unit test case metrics studied according to the three variables (internal software class attributes)

Table 19 Descriptive statistics of the unit test case metrics (Univariate clustering - CBO)

	CBO	Cluster 1	Cluster 2	Cluster 3	Cluster 4	Cluster 5
	Nb. Obs.	506	284	153	64	20
TLOC	Min	6	9	12	18	16
	Max	1620	2379	2624	1353	4063
	Mean (μ)	91.81	175.62	236.54	149	477.85
	Std. Dev (σ)	144.91	298.76	421.83	206.07	854.09
	Coef. of var ($C_v = \sigma/\mu$)	1.578	1.701	1.783	1.383	1.787
TASSERT	Min	0	0	0	1	1
	Max	615	1058	1156	305	391
	Mean (μ)	20.32	46.26	65.52	38.31	93.3
	Std. Dev (σ)	42.41	116.36	161.77	58.25	101.53
	Coef. of var ($C_v = \sigma/\mu$)	2.087	2.515	2.469	1.52	1.088
TDATA	Min	0	0	0	0	0
	Max	482	393	482	223	758
	Mean (μ)	12.84	25.68	33.76	22.05	70.35
	Std. Dev (σ)	31.17	52.80	67.72	30.42	161.49
	Coef. of var ($C_v = \sigma/\mu$)	2.427	2.056	2.006	1.38	2.295
TINVOK	Min	0	0	3	1	6
	Max	175	401	399	190	516
	Mean (μ)	25.22	38.76	54.06	35.69	84.05
	Std. Dev (σ)	26.18	42.52	59.67	30.24	107.34
	Coef. of var ($C_v = \sigma/\mu$)	1.038	1.097	1.104	0.847	1.277
TNOO	Min	0	1	1	1	1
	Max	164	242	238	54	148
	Mean (μ)	6.76	11.05	19.46	8.66	21.85
	Std. Dev (σ)	13.15	22.79	37.89	10.39	33.04
	Coef. of var ($C_v = \sigma/\mu$)	1.941	2.063	1.947	1.2	1.512

used in the univariate clustering. It can be seen that the coefficient of variation of the unit test case metrics varies according to the used variable. It can also be seen that the coefficients of variation of the unit test case metrics for the clustering based on WMC are smaller compared to the coefficients of variation obtained for the other two classifications. This suggests that the internal software class attribute WMC is the most determining (compared to the others internal class attributes LOC and CBO) in the sense that it impacts the most the distribution (values) of the unit test case metrics. In others words, we can expect that source code classes having comparable values of WMC will likely have test classes that are comparable. Here also, we can observe that the TINVOK metric varies less than the others test case metrics (followed by the TLOC metric), which seems suggesting that this metric is the least affected by the development style used by the developers while writing the code of unit test cases.

Overall, as we have seen in this section, results of both *K*-Means and Univariate clustering show clearly that the TINVOK metric is the unit test case metric that varies the least followed by TLOC. As in the previous step, two main factors may explain the low values of Cv for the two unit test case metrics TINVOK and TLOC: (1) The two unit test case metrics TINVOK and TLOC are weakly or not correlated to the internal

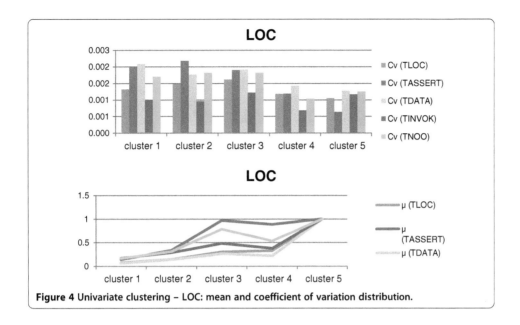

Figure 4 Univariate clustering – LOC: mean and coefficient of variation distribution.

software class attribute metrics, and/or (2) The two unit test case metrics TINVOK and TLOC are the less affected by the styles adopted by developers while writing the code of unit test cases. Here also, the increasing mean values of TINVOK and TLOC observed in Tables 17, 18 and 19, tends to exclude the lack of correlation as an explaining factor of low variance of TINVOK and TLOC metrics.

Moreover, in order to better understand the decrease in the mean values of the unit test case metrics for cluster 4, and particularly why the cluster 4 is an exception compared to the four others clusters, we decided to investigate the ratio (RT) of the number of lines of test code per number of tested lines of source code (as in Table 1, column 7) for all the clusters, according to each univariate clustering variable (internal

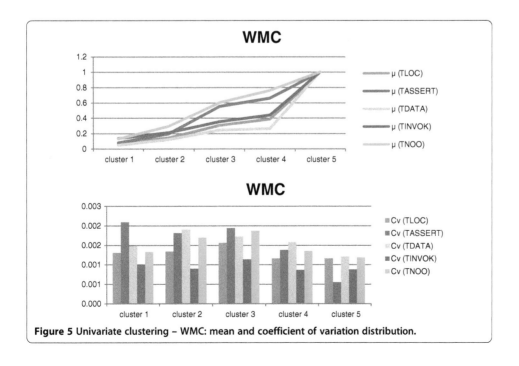

Figure 5 Univariate clustering – WMC: mean and coefficient of variation distribution.

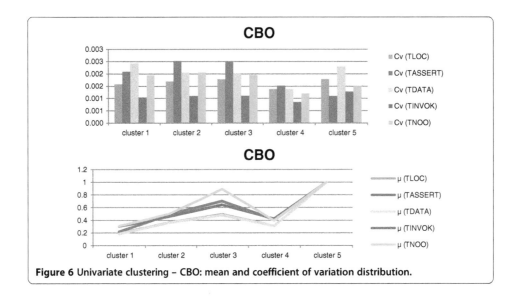

Figure 6 Univariate clustering – CBO: mean and coefficient of variation distribution.

software class attribute). We found, as it can be seen from Table 20 that this ratio is particularly low for cluster 4 and this for the three univariate clustering (based separately on LOC, CBO and WMC). This suggests that partial tests were conducted (corresponding JUnit test code) on some large classes of cluster 4. We analyzed the source code of the classes of cluster 4. We found that 5 of the 18 classes that contains cluster 4, which are large and containing many methods, have only one complex method for which JUnit test code has been developed. As a consequence, the values of the unit test case metrics of the JUnit test cases corresponding to cluster 4 are relatively low, knowing that corresponding Java classes are relatively large. The measures of these five classes have an impact on the mean values of the unit test case metrics of cluster 4.

4.5 Exploring the relationships between the internal software class attributes and the unit test case metrics

4.5.1 Correlation between metrics

In this section, we investigate the relationships between the three internal software class attributes used in the clustering analysis and the unit test case metrics. We tested the following hypothesis:

Hypothesis: There is a significant relationship between an internal software class attribute and the unit test case metrics.

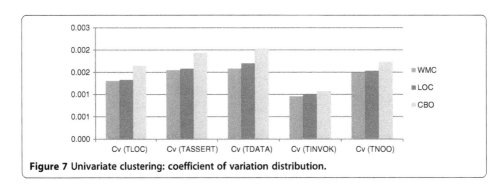

Figure 7 Univariate clustering: coefficient of variation distribution.

Table 20 RT ratio for each cluster

Clustering	All systems	1	2	3	4	5
LOC	0.809	1.235	0.703	0.699	0.409	0.673
CBO		1.072	1.032	0.855	0.292	0.462
WMC		1.097	0.755	0.730	0.493	0.684

In order to validate the hypothesis, we analyzed the correlations between each internal class attribute (LOC, WMC and CBO) and the unit test case metrics. We performed statistical tests using correlation. We used both Spearman's and Pearson's correlation coefficients in our study. These techniques are widely used for measuring the degree of relationship between two variables. Correlation coefficients will take a value between −1 and +1. A positive correlation is one in which the variables increase (or decrease) together. A negative correlation is one in which one variable increases as the other variable decreases. A correlation of +1 or −1 will arise if the relationship between the variables is exactly linear. A correlation close to zero means that there is no linear relationship between the variables.

We used the XLSTAT tool to perform the analysis. We applied the typical significance threshold ($\alpha = 0.05$) to decide whether the correlations were significant. Tables 21 and 22 give the results of the correlation analysis respectively for Spearman and Pearson techniques. The obtained correlation values between each internal software class attribute and the suite of unit test case metrics are all significant (according to the used significance threshold), and this between all pairs of metrics (internal software class attribute metric, unit test case metric). Moreover, this is also true for the correlation values between the internal software class attribute metrics, and between the unit test case metrics. Overall, we can also observe from Table 21 and Table 22 that the internal software class attributes WMC and LOC are better correlated to the unit test case metrics than CBO. Furthermore, as we can see, the correlation values between particularly the three internal software class attribute metrics and the unit test case metrics TLOC and TASSERT are all significant, which confirms the results of many previous studies that addressed the relationship between object-oriented metrics (including the three used metrics LOC, WMC and CBO) and unit test case metrics (e.g., Bruntink and Van Deursen (2004, 2006), Singh and Saha (2010), Badri et Toure (2012)). We can also see that the correlation values between the three internal software class attributes and the unit test case metrics that we introduced in our previous work, TDATA and TINVOK,

Table 21 Correlations between metrics (Spearman)

Metrics	TLOC	TASSERT	TDATA	TINVOK	TNOO	LOC	WMC	CBO
TLOC	1	0.786	0.716	0.581	0.794	0.429	0.439	0.321
TASSERT	0.786	1	0.581	0.471	0.611	0.393	0.420	0.236
TDATA	0.716	0.581	1	0.417	0.561	0.339	0.366	0.305
TINVOK	0.581	0.471	0.417	1	0.588	0.355	0.369	0.342
TNOO	0.794	0.611	0.561	0.588	1	0.365	0.389	0.296
LOC	0.429	0.393	0.339	0.355	0.365	1	0.936	0.710
WMC	0.439	0.420	0.366	0.369	0.389	0.936	1	0.655
CBO	0.321	0.236	0.305	0.342	0.296	0.710	0.655	1

Table 22 Correlations between metrics (Pearson)

Metrics	TLOC	ASSERT	TDATA	TINVOK	TNOO	LOC	WMC	CBO
TLOC	1	0.866	0.881	0.778	0.887	0.449	0.459	0.180
TASSERT	0.866	1	0.765	0.706	0.891	0.312	0.343	0.149
TDATA	0.881	0.765	1	0.703	0.828	0.364	0.420	0.148
TINVOK	0.778	0.706	0.703	1	0.776	0.360	0.436	0.224
TNOO	0.887	0.891	0.828	0.776	1	0.284	0.326	0.127
LOC	0.449	0.312	0.364	0.360	0.284	1	0.885	0.684
WMC	0.459	0.343	0.420	0.436	0.326	0.885	1	0.715
CBO	0.180	0.149	0.148	0.224	0.127	0.684	0.715	1

are also all significant. In some case, the unit test case metrics TDATA and TINVOK are better correlated to the internal software class attributes than the metric TASSERT.

Moreover, the correlation values between the three internal software class attributes and the suite of unit test case metrics are positive. A positive correlation, as mentioned previously, is one in which both variables (internal software class attribute, unit test case metric) increase together. These results are plausible and not surprising. In fact, a class with a high value of LOC (WMC and CBO) is more likely to require a high testing effort (in terms of test case construction) than a class with a low value of LOC (WMC and CBO).

Also, it can be seen from Table 21 and Table 22, that overall WMC and LOC metrics are relatively better correlated to the unit test case metrics than CBO metric. As stated in the previous section, the unit test case metrics are less volatile in the clustering based on the WMC and LOC metrics compared to the clustering based on CBO (Figure 7). These results support therefore our hypothesis.

The unit test case metrics TLOC and TINVOK, which emerged from our previous analyses (as the most independent and the less volatile unit test case metrics) have in most cases (Table 21 and Table 22) the highest or comparable (to the others unit test case metrics) correlation values with the internal software class attribute metrics. The high correlation values of the unit test case metrics TLOC and TINVOK confirm that their low volatility observed previously is not due to their lack of correlation with the software attributes (LOC, WMC and CBO). We can then reasonably conclude that the unit test case metrics TINVOK and TLOC are the unit test case metrics that are the least sensitive to the changes in the style of test code writing.

Table 23 SLR analysis - results

SLR		TLOC	TASSERT	TDATA	TINVOK	TNOO
LOC	R^2	0.201	0.096	0.132	0.129	0.080
	beta	0.449	0.312	0.364	0.360	0.284
	pvalue	<0.0001	<0.0001	<0.0001	<0.0001	<0.0001
WMC	R^2	0.210	0.117	0.176	0.189	0.106
	beta	0.459	0.343	0.420	0.436	0.326
	pvalue	<0.0001	<0.0001	<0.0001	<0.0001	<0.0001
CBO	R^2	0.031	0.021	0.021	0.049	0.015
	beta	0.180	0.149	0.148	0.224	0.127
	pvalue	<0.0001	<0.0001	<0.0001	<0.0001	<0.0001

4.5.2 Linear regression analysis

Linear regression is a commonly used statistical technique. It is used to modeling the relationship between a dependent variable y and one or more explanatory variables denoted X. Linear regression analysis is of two types: The case of one explanatory variable is called *simple linear regression* (SLR). For more than one explanatory variable, it is called *multiple linear regression* (MLR). In this study, we used the SLR analysis, which is based on: $Y = \beta 0 + \beta_1 X$, where Y is the dependent variable (unit test case metric) and X is the independent variable (internal software class attribute metric).

We used the SLR technique to explore the capacity of each internal software class attribute metric to predict the unit test case metrics and quantify the strength of the relationship between each pair of metrics (internal software class attribute metric and unit test case metric). Table 23 gives the results of the SLR analysis. Moreover, the linear regression analysis here is not intended to be used to determine or to build the best prediction model, based on one internal software class attribute or combining the internal software class attribute metrics. Such a model, and multiple linear regression analysis, is out of the scope of this paper. Instead, our analysis intends only to investigate (and compare) the effect of each internal software class attribute metric on the unit test case metrics.

From Table 23, it can be seen that, overall, all the linear regression models based on the internal software class attribute metrics are significant (p-value < 0.0001). We can also see that the linear regression model based on WMC has the highest R^2, followed by the linear regression model based on LOC. The R^2 value is the coefficient of determination of the model. It varies from 0 to 1. It is interpreted as the proportion of the variability of the dependent variable explained by the model. The more the R^2 value is close to 1, better is the model. Moreover, it can be seen that, overall, the unit test case metrics TLOC, TDATA and TINVOK are better predicted by the three linear regression models based respectively on WMC, LOC and CBO than the unit test case metrics TASSERT and TNOO.

Furthermore, the issue of training and testing data sets is very important during the construction and evaluation of prediction models. If a prediction model is built on one data set (used as training set) and evaluated on the same data set (used as testing set), as was done in the previous step, then the accuracy of the model may be artificially inflated. A common way to obtain a more realistic assessment of the predictive ability of the model is to use cross validation (k-fold cross-validation), which is a procedure in which the data set is partitioned in k subsamples (groups of observations). The regression model is built using $k - 1$ groups and its predictions evaluated on the last group. This process is repeated k times. Each time, a different subsample is used to evaluate the model, and the remaining subsamples are used as training data to build the model.

We used the validation option of the XLSTAT tool to validate the linear regression models. We used the option that consists of choosing randomly a subset of the data (10% of the observations) as a testing set, and the rest of the data (90% of the observations) as a training set. As mentioned previously, the total number of observations in our study is 1027, which corresponds to the total number of classes for which JUnit test classes have been developed. We repeated this process 10 times. Table 24 gives the mean values of the R^2 and coefficient of each internal software class attribute metric. All the predictions are significant ($p$value < 0.0001). Again, we can observe that the results follow the same trend as before.

Table 24 SLR analysis – models validation

Mean 10 cross-validation		TLOC	TASSERT	TDATA	TINVOK	TNOO
LOC	R^2	0.193	0.096	0.124	0.124	0.078
	beta	0.438	0.311	0.350	0.351	0.280
WMC	R^2	0.213	0.115	0.178	0.194	0.107
	beta	0.463	0.341	0.423	0.442	0.328
CBO	R^2	0.032	0.021	0.022	0.049	0.016
	beta	0.182	0.149	0.150	0.223	0.129

Furthermore, according to results (particularly in Section 4.5.1 and Section 4.5.2), WMC is better correlated to the unit test case metrics TLOC and TINVOK. Furthermore, results of Section 4.4 showed particularly that: (1) the unit test case metrics, overall, are less volatile in the clustering based on WMC compared to the two others clustering based respectively on LOC and CBO, (2) the TINVOK metric, followed by the TLOC metric, are the least affected by the development style used by the developers while writing the code of unit test cases, and (3) WMC is the most determining (compared to the others internal software class attribute metrics LOC and CBO) in the sense that it impacts the most the distribution (values) of the unit test case metrics. So, according to all these results, we can reasonably conclude that the couple of unit test case metrics (TLOC, TINVOK) is the best subset of unit test case metrics which are the most impacted by the systems design (characterized by the internal software class attributes), the least affected by the style adopted by developers while writing the code of unit test cases, and providing the best independent information that maximizes the variance.

4.6 Threats to validity

The study has been performed on open source systems, which may not be representative of all industrial domains. However, the use of open-source systems in empirical studies is a common practice in the software engineering research community. We analyzed more than 1 000 Java classes and corresponding JUnit test cases. Even if we believe that the analyzed data set is large enough to allow obtaining significant results, we do not claim that our results can be generalized to all systems. The study presented in this paper should be replicated on a large number of OO software systems to increase the generality of our findings. The findings in this paper should be viewed as exploratory and indicative rather than conclusive. Moreover, there are a number of factors that may affect the results of the study and limit their interpretation and their generalization.

4.6.1 Internal validity threats

An important internal threat to validity is from the identification of the links between Java classes and corresponding JUnit test cases. As mentioned in the paper (Section 4.2), we noticed by analyzing the code of the JUnit test cases of the investigated systems that, in some cases, there is no one-to-one relationship between JUnit test cases and corresponding Java classes. In these cases, several JUnit test cases have been related to a same Java class. Even if we followed a systematic approach for associating the JUnit test cases to the corresponding Java classes, which was not an easy task, unfortunately we were not able to match all test classes. The loss of this part of the information on the effort involved in writing the test code of the analyzed systems, due to the few test classes that we were not able to match with Java classes, may affect the results of our analysis.

Moreover, the used matching procedure, which has also been adopted in other related studies in literature as mentioned in the paper, is based on a static analysis of the code of test cases. In some cases, test classes are reused using the inheritance mechanism. This may also bias the results. Adopting an approach based on dynamic analysis could reduce this bias. Dynamics analysis is out of the scope of this paper and could be considered in our future work.

For our study, and particularly in the second stage, we have deliberately chosen five clusters. We wanted, in fact, to reflect in the analysis five different categories of the effort involved in writing the code of test cases: very low, low, medium, high and very high. When changing the number of clusters, the distribution of classes in the different categories will probably differ. This may affect our results. In our future work, we plan to select different number of clusters (for example, three for reflecting low, medium and high testing effort) in order to investigate the impact of changes in the number of clusters on the volatility of analysis.

4.6.2 External validity threats

The JUnit test cases used in our study were developed only for a part of classes of each analyzed system (Table 1, columns 3 and 5). The testing coverage, in terms of Java classes for which JUnit test cases have been explicitly developed, differs from one system to another. In addition, the classes for which JUnit test cases have been developed were generally relatively large and complex. This is true for the six subject systems. It is often due to the adopted testing strategy and/or the criteria used by the developers while selecting the software classes for which they developed test cases (randomly or depending on their size or complexity e.g., or on other criteria). It would be interesting to replicate this study using systems for which JUnit test cases have been developed for a maximum number of classes, for example, in a controlled environment. This threat could limit the applicability of the study to other systems.

Furthermore, we observed by analyzing the code of test classes that in some cases, the developed JUnit classes do not cover all the methods of the corresponding software classes but only one or two complex methods. Since the internal software class attribute metrics are computed using the whole class source code, the potential testing effort predicted by the internal software class attribute metrics in these cases will not match the actual effort spent for writing these partial tests. Since this observation depends on the testing strategy adopted by developers, it could limit the applicability of the study to other systems. Here also, using a controlled environment, in which JUnit test cases cover all the methods of each tested Java class (or at least a large number of methods), could help to eliminate (or reduce) the effect of this bias.

Finally, the study has been performed using only case studies for which JUnit test classes have been developed by programmers. It would be interesting to replicate the study on systems for which JUnit test cases have been generated automatically using tools such as Codepro. We expect that this will reduce the impact on the distribution of the unit test case metrics and produce more generalizable results.

4.6.3 Construct threats

In Section 4.4, we wanted to investigate the effect of the test code writing style on the distribution of the unit test case metrics, and to determine which metrics are the less affected by the writing style variations. This goal leads us to group the classes of the six open source systems used in our study, with different development styles, and cluster them in five subgroups of comparable classes (in terms of size, complexity and coupling). We ensured of the good representativeness of each development style in the different clusters, by computing and analyzing the index of qualitative variance (IQV) of each cluster. The variances of unit test case metrics (standard deviation σ, coefficient of variance σ/μ) were analyzed to determine those that undergo the least of variations. Results show that two of the analyzed unit test case metrics (TLOC, TINVOK) vary the less in the subgroups. Pearson, Spearman and linear regression analyzes show that those metrics are also the most correlated to the considered internal software class attribute metrics (LOC, WMC, and CBO). The tight relationship between the unit test case metrics (TLOC and TINVOK) and internal software class attribute metrics confirms that their little variance observed in the five clusters is not due to their insensitivity to the internal software class attributes, but to the test code writing style. Since we fixed the number of categories to five, one of major construct threats of validity coming from this constraint could be the relative high intra-cluster variances (high variance of internal software class attributes) obtained with the K-Means or Univariate clustering. To reduce the effect of this threat we could, in a controlled environment, and for the same software, use different test suites developed by different groups of testers. We could analyse, for each software class, the variances of the different unit test class attributes produced by different groups of testers.

5 Conclusions and future work

We analyzed, in this paper, the JUnit test cases of six open source Java software systems. We used five metrics to quantify different perspectives related to their code. We conducted an empirical analysis organized into three main stages. The main goal of the study was to identify a subset of independent unit test case metrics: (1) providing useful information reflecting the effort involved in writing the code of unit test cases, and (2) that are the less volatile, i.e. the least affected by the style adopted by developers while writing the code of test cases.

In order to find whether the analyzed unit test case metrics are independent or are measuring similar structural aspects of the code of JUnit test cases, we performed in a first stage a Principal Component Analysis (PCA). We used in a second stage clustering techniques to determine the unit test case metrics that are the less volatile by investigating the distribution and the variance of the unit test case metrics based on three important internal software class attributes (size, complexity and coupling). We evaluated in a third stage the relationships between the internal software class attribute metrics and the suite of unit test case metrics. We used correlation and linear regression analyzes.

While confirming the results of our previous work, our current results show that: (1) the metrics TLOC and TINVOK maximize the independent information captured by all the unit test case metrics, and (2) these metrics are the less affected by changes in the test code writing style and the most correlated with internal software class attributes.

The performed study should, however, be replicated using many other case studies in order to draw more general conclusions. The findings in this paper should be viewed as exploratory and indicative rather than conclusive. As future work, we plan to replicate the present study using case studies for which JUnit test cases have been generated automatically using tools such as Codepro.

Endnotes

[a]The Apache Ant Project [http://ant.apache.org].

[b]JFreeChart [http://www.jfree.org/jfreechart].

[c]Joda-Time Java date and time API [http://www.joda.org/joda-time].

[d]Apache Lucene Core [http://lucene.apache.org].

[e]Java API for Microsoft Documents [http://poi.apache.org].

[f]The agile dependency manager [http://ant.apache.org/ivy].

[g]A programmer-oriented testing framework for Java [http://www.junit.org].

[h]XLSTAT [www.xlstat.com].

[i]Borland Solutions [http://www.borland.com].

Competing interests
Authors in this paper have no potential conflict of interests.

Authors' contributions
All authors have contributed to the different conceptual and experimental aspects of the approach presented in this paper. They read and approved the final manuscript.

Acknowledgments
This work was supported by NSERC (Natural Sciences and Engineering Research Council of Canada) grant.

References
Aggarwal KK, Singh Y, Kaur A, Malhotra R (2006) Empirical study of object-oriented metrics. In: Journal of Object Technology, vol 5., p 8, November-December 2006
Badri M, Toure F (2012) Empirical analysis of object-oriented design metrics for predicting unit testing effort of classes. J Software Eng Appl (JSEA) 5:7
Badri L, Badri M, Toure F (2010) Exploring empirically the relationship between lack of cohesion and testability in object-oriented systems. In: Th K, Kim HK, Khan MK et al (eds) Advances in Software Engineering, vol 117 of Communications in Computer and Information Science. Springer, Berlin, Germany
Badri L, Badri M, Toure F (2011) An empirical analysis of lack of cohesion metrics for predicting testability of classes. Int J Software Eng Appl 5(2):2011
Binder RV (1994) Design for testability in object-oriented systems. Commun ACM 37:1994
Bruntink M, Van Deursen A (2004) Predicting class testability using object-oriented metrics. In: Proceedings of the 4th IEEE International Workshop on Source Code Analysis and Manipulation (SCAM'04)., pp 136–145
Bruntink M, Van Deursen A (2006) An empirical study into class testability. J Syst Softw 79:1219–1232
Cattell RB (1966) The scree test for the number of factors. Multivar Behav Res 1(2):1966
Chidamber SR, Kemerer CF (1994) A metrics suite for OO design. IEEE Trans Softw Eng 20(6):476–493
Chidamber RB, Darcy DP, Kemerer CF (1998) Managerial use of metrics for object-oriented software: an exploratory analysis. IEEE Trans Softw Eng 24(8):629–637
Dash Y, Dubey SK (2012) Application of Principal Component Analysis in Software Quality Improvement. In: International Journal of Advanced Research in Computer Science and Software, Engineering Vol. 2, Issue 4, April 2012
Mockus A, Nagappan N, Dinh-Trong TT (2009) Test coverage and post-verification defects: a multiple case study. In: Proceedings of the 3rd International Symposium on Empirical Software Engineering and Measurement (ESEM'09)., pp 291–301
Mueller JH, Schuessler KF (1961) Statistical Reasoning. In Sociology. Boston: Houghton Mifflin Company.
Quah JTS, Thwin MTT (2003) Application of Neural Networks for Software Quality Prediction Using Object-Oriented Metrics. In: Proceedings of the International Conference on Software Maintenance (ICSM'03), IEEE Computer Society
Qusef A, Bavota G, Oliveto R, De Lucia A, Binkley D (2011) SCOTCH: test-to-code traceability using slicing and conceptual coupling. In: Proceedings of the International Conference on Software Maintenance (ICSM'11)
Rompaey BV, Demeyer S (2009) Establishing traceability links between unit test cases and units under test. In: Proceedings of the 13th European Conference on Software Maintenance and Reengineering (CSMR'09)., pp 209–218
Singh A, Saha A (2010) Predicting testability of eclipse: a case study. J Software Eng 4(2):2010

Singh Y, Kaur A, Malhotra R (2008) Predicting Testing Effort Using Artificial Neural Network. In Proceedings of the World Congress on Engineering and Computer Science (WCECS 2008) San Francisco, USA. Newswood Limited, pp 1012–1017

Toure F, Badri M, Lamontagne L (2014) Towards a metrics suite for JUnit Test Cases. In Proceedings of the Twenty-Sixth International Conference on Software Engineering and Knowledge Engineering (SEKE 2014) Vancouver, Canada. Knowledge Systems Institute Graduate School, USA pp 115–120

Zhou Y, Leung H, Song Q, Zhao J, Lu H, Chen L, Xu B (2012) An in-depth investigation into the relationships between structural metrics and unit testability in object-oriented systems. In: SCIENCE CHINA, Information Sciences, Vol. 55, No. 12

8

The problem of conceptualization in god class detection: agreement, strategies and decision drivers

José Amancio M Santos[1][*][†], Manoel Gomes de Mendonça[2,3][†], Cleber Pereira dos Santos[4][†] and Renato Lima Novais[4][†]

*Correspondence:
zeamancio@ecomp.uefs.br
[†]Equal contributors
[1]Department of Technology, State University of Feira de Santana, Transnordestina avenue S/N - Feira de Santana - Bahia, Feira de Santana, Brazil
Full list of author information is available at the end of the article

Abstract

Background: The concept of code smells is widespread in Software Engineering. Despite the empirical studies addressing the topic, the set of context-dependent issues that impacts the human perception of what is a code smell has not been studied in depth. We call this the code smell *conceptualization problem*. To discuss the problem, empirical studies are necessary. In this work, we focused on conceptualization of god class. God class is a code smell characterized by classes that tend to centralize the intelligence of the system. It is one of the most studied smells in software engineering literature.

Method: A controlled experiment that extends and builds upon a previous empirical study about how humans detect god classes, their decision drivers, and agreement rate. Our study delves into research questions of the previous study, adding visualization to the smell detection process, and analyzing strategies of detection.

Result: Our findings show that agreement among participants is low, which corroborates previous studies. We show that this is mainly related to agreeing on what a god class is and which thresholds should be adopted, and not related to comprehension of the programs. The use of visualization did not improve the agreement among the participants. However, it did affect the choice of detection drivers.

Conclusion: This study contributes to expand empirical evidences on the impact of human perception on detecting code smells. It shows that studies about the human role in smell detection are relevant and they should consider the conceptualization problem of code smells.

Keywords: Code smell; God class; Controlled experiment; Code visualization

Background

Challenges in object-oriented (OO) software design have been historically addressed from different perspectives. Riel (1996) wrote one of the first books on the subject in 1996. This book presents insights into OO design improvements and introduces the now well-known term "design flaws". In 1999, Fowler (1999) came up with the concept of refactoring and coined the term "smell" to represent bad characteristics observable in the code. In 2005, Lanza and Marinescu (2005) focused on OO metrics to characterize what they called "disharmonies". All these terms are used to define potential design problems. In this paper, we adopt the term *code smell*, or simply *smell*, to refer to such design problems.

The works of (Riel 1996; Fowler 1999 and Lanza and Marinescu 2005) discuss code smells from the principles of the OO paradigm, such as information hiding or polymorphism (Meyer 1988). However, there is a set of context-dependent issues that impacts how one considers the concept of smell. These include: developers' experience, the software process, software domain, and others. The extensive number of context-dependent issues make it difficult to express even simple tasks rigorously, such as smell detection. Fontana et al. (2011) claim that smell detection "can provide uncertain and unsafe results". This is because most smells are subjectively defined and their identification is human-dependent.

Fowler (1999) does not define smell formally. He says that one needs to develop one's own sense of observation of attributes that could characterize pieces of code as a smell. For example, one has to develop one's own sense of how many lines of code define a long method. This is because smell detection is a subjective task by nature. In contrast, Lanza and Marinescu (2005) use a formal definition for smells based on metrics and thresholds. However, Rapu et al. (2004) state that the thresholds are mainly chosen based on the experience of the analysts. These indicate that smell detection remains an ill-defined task. In addition, as cited by Parnin et al. (2008), "metrics produce voluminous and imprecise results". Given these pitfalls, alternatives have emerged to address smell detection. One of them is the use of software visualization (Murphy-Hill and Black 2010; Parnin et al. 2008; Simon et al. 2001; Van Emden and Moonen 2002). Software visualization tools combined with metrics may help humans to identify design problems.

Understanding which, and how, subjective aspects affect smell detection demands empirical evaluation. According to Mäntylä, "we need more empirical research aiming at critically evaluating, validating and improving our understanding of subjective indicators of design quality" (Mäntylä et al. 2004). Recent empirical studies carried out to better understand this scenario, can be classified into three categories. The first type is correlation studies. They evaluate the impact of smells based on data extracted from software repositories (Li and Shatnawi 2007; Olbrich et al. 2009, 2010), establishing a correlation between a smell and some attribute of the software, such as bugs or the number of modifications on classes. The second type is related to tool assessment, such as automatic detection (Moha et al. 2010; Mäntylä and Lassenius 2006a; Schumacher et al. 2010) or software visualization (Carneiro et al. 2010; Murphy-Hill and Black 2010; Parnin et al. 2008; Simon et al. 2001). Finally, the third type investigates the role of humans in smell detection (Mäntylä 2005; Mäntylä and Lassenius 2006b; Santos et al. 2013; Schumacher et al. 2010). Although the number of studies on this topic is increasing, they are considered insufficient (Schumacher et al. 2010; Sjøberg et al. 2013; Zhang et al. 2011). In particular, the role of humans has not been studied in depth (Mäntylä and Lassenius 2006a).

The role of humans is one of the most important and one of the most open and broad topics in this area. Several uncontrollable variables affect the smell conceptualization. Examples include experience, personal differences in cognition, level of knowledge on the subject, and the environment. In this context, this work aims to understand how some aspects of the human conceptualization impact smells detection. In particular, this exploratory study investigates how personal comprehension of the smell concept affects the detection of god classes. God class is a term proposed by Riel (1996) to refer to classes that tend to centralize the intelligence of the system. Fowler (1999) defined it as a class that tries to do too much, and adopted the term large class. Lanza and Marinescu (2005) proposed a heuristic based on metrics to identify god class. The definition of god class has been addressed in several empirical studies (Abbes et al. 2011; Li and Shatnawi 2007; Olbrich et al. 2010; Padilha et al. 2013).

Our exploratory study was based on a controlled experiment carried out in an in-vitro setting. The experiment extended an empirical study presented by Schumacher et al. in (Schumacher et al. 2010). While Schumacher et al. presented a wide discussion about both human and automatic detection of god classes, our work focused on questions related to the human perception. We considered two factors, the use or non use of software visualization to achieve the study goal. The use of visualization made it possible to evaluate the impact of the overall comprehension of the design on human aspects, increasing the evidences of the relevance of conceptualization in the detection of god class. It is important to note that we did not adopt a visualization tool to support smell detection, instead, we adopted a tool focused on enhancing the comprehension of the code design. The tool helps developers to perceive of coupling, size, complexity, and hierarchical relations among classes from the use of visual resources. We evaluated the effect of these facilities on human aspects, such as decision drivers, agreement and strategies adopted by the participants detecting god classes. To the best of our knowledge, this is the first study that analyses smell conceptualization using all of these variables. We have already featured this experiment partially (Santos et al. 2013), addressing effort, decision drivers, and agreement on smell detection, but disregarding the use of visualization.

The structure of this paper is as follows. Section 'Method' presents the planning and execution of the experiment. Section 'Results' and 'Discussion' present the results and a discussion about them. Section 'Threats to validity' discusses the threats to the validity of the study. Section 'Context and related works' summarizes prior empirical studies that address aspects which are context-related to smells. Lastly, Section 'Conclusions' presents our conclusions and proposes future works.

Method

In this section, we present the experimental planning and execution of the experiment.

In order to attend ethical issues on Empirical Software Engineering, we followed principles proposed by (Vinson 2008).

Research question

Our work aims to investigate the impact of conceptualization on god class detection. The research questions (RQ) are:

1. *How well do humans agree on identifying god classes?*
2. *How well do humans and an oracle agree on identifying god classes?*
3. *Which strategies are used to identify god classes?*
4. *What issues in code lead humans to identify a class as a god class?*

All questions help us to observe the differences in perception among the participants during the detection of god classes. They were used to observe how conceptualization affects the identification of god classes in our experiment. Research questions one and four were first proposed by Schumacher et al. (2010). In this paper, we analyzed them using a different approach: by the use of both code review and visualization. We have introduced question two and three. Question two addresses agreement between participants and an oracle, defined in a controlled process. Question three addresses the strategies adopted by participants when detecting god classes.

Experimental units

The experiment involved 11 undergraduate Computer Science students from the Federal University of Bahia (UFBA), in Brazil. All students were enrolled in the Software Quality course offered in the first semester of 2012. This is an optional subject of the Computer Science program, in which design quality and smells are addressed. The course was considered appropriate for the experiment, both because it was focused and was not mandatory, which means that most students enrolled on it were interested in the subject. Furthermore, participation in the experiment was a voluntary activity.

Experimental material
Tools

We adopted four software tools in the experiment[a]: (i) The Eclipse Indigo IDE; (ii) Usage Data Collector (UDC), an Eclipse plug-in for collecting IDE usage data information (interactions between participants and Eclipse can be accessed by the log of UDC). This tool is embedded in the Eclipse Indigo IDE; (iii) Task Register plug-in, a tool we developed to enable participants to indicate what task was being done at any given moment. This information was also registered in the UDC log. All the participants had to do was to click on a "Task Register" view on Eclipse (Figure 1-F) to indicate when they were starting or finishing a task; and (iv) SourceMiner, an Eclipse plug-in that provides visual resources to enhance software comprehension activities (Carneiro and Mendonça 2013; Carneiro et al. 2010).

SourceMiner has five views, divided into two groups. The first group is made up of three coupling views. These views show different types of dependencies among entities, like direct access to attributes or method calling, for instance. Moreover, they show the

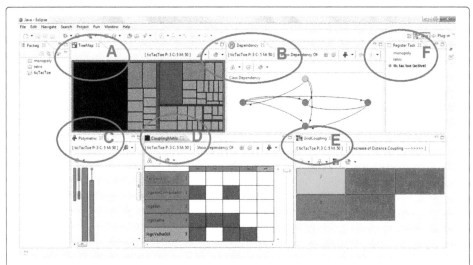

Figure 1 Eclipse IDE showing the Task Register (F) plug-in and SourceMiner views: hierarchical views (A and C) and coupling views (B, D and E).

direction of the coupling. The coupling views are based on radial graphs (Figure 1-B), matrix of relationships (Figure 1-D), and tabular view (Figure 1-E). The second group is made up of two hierarchical views. These views associate the number of lines of code, complexity and number of methods of classes to the area and colors of the rectangles. The Treemap view (Figure 1-A) shows the hierarchy of package-class-method of the software. A Treemap is a hierarchical 2D visualization that maps a tree structure into a set of nested rectangles (Johnson and Shneiderman 1991). In SourceMiner, the nested rectangles represent software entities, like packages, classes and methods. Rectangles representing methods of the same class are drawn together inside the rectangle of the class. Likewise, the rectangles of the classes that belong to the same package are drawn together inside the rectangle of the package. The Polimetric view (Figure 1-C) shows the hierarchy between classes and interfaces. A polymetric view uses a forest of rectangles to represent the inheritance trees formed by classes and interfaces in a software system (Lanza and Ducasse 2003). Rectangles are linked by edges representing the inheritance relationship between them. The length and width of the rectangles can be used to represent software attributes such as the size and number of methods of a class.

Forms

We used five forms and two guides during the experiment. During the training, which we will present thereafter, the participants filled in a Consent and a Participant Characterization form, and received a SourceMiner exercise guide. During the experiment itself, participants received a Support Question guide to steer them in search for god classes. The questions are the same ones used by Schumacher et al. (2010):

- Does the class have more than one responsibility?
- Does the class have functionality that would fit better into other classes?

    – By looking at the methods, could one ask: "Is this the class' job?"

- Do you have problems summarizing the class' responsibility in one sentence?
- Would splitting up the class improve the overall design?

Another document used during the experiment was the Step-by-Step guide used to assure consistency during the data collection process. This document prompts the participants to open and close the projects on Eclipse and to select the task under execution in the Task Register view. It is important to note that this guide did not define how participants should do the task of identifying god classes. It defined some activities that participants had to do before and after the identification of god classes. Each participant defined their own strategy to identify god classes.

The Answer form was one of the most important forms used during the experiment. On this form, participants had to fill in: i) one or more candidate(s) god class(es), ii) their level of certainty, i.e., fill in the "yes" or "maybe" option for each candidate class, iii) the decision driver(s) which helped her/him to select the class, and iv) the start and end time of the task, which we used to evaluate effort in (Santos et al. 2013) (this topic is out of the scope of this paper).

We considered the items i) the candidate god classes and ii) level of certainty, which is self-explanatory. Here, we will explain item iii) decision drivers: the form listed nine drivers as predefined options for the participants, but it was also possible to write down a new one. The drivers listed in the form are the ones identified by Schumacher et al. (2010) during their think-aloud data collection. Some examples are "method is misplaced" and "class is highly complex".

The last form of FinG was the Feedback form. At the end of the experiment the participants filled in a Feedback form. On it, we asked the participants to classify the training and the level of difficulty performing the task. It was also possible to write down suggestions and observations about the experiment.

Software artifacts

Six programs were used in the experiment. All of them implement familiar applications or games in Java e.g. Chess, Tic Tac Toe, Monopoly and Tetris. Solitaire-Freecell (Solitaire) is a framework for card games with Solitaire and Freecell. Jackut implements a simple social network application, such as Facebook and Orkut.

During our selection, we looked for familiar applications to minimize the effort of participants during the task of identifying god classes. However, we also looked for programs with different characteristics: some without god classes, others which perhaps had god classes and others with, at least, one god class. An oracle was used to identify god classes in each of the selected programs. This oracle is presented later. Table 1 characterizes the programs we used in terms of the number of packages, number of classes and number of lines of code (LOC).

Task

While Schumacher et al. (2010) designed a mini-process for participants to detect god classes, we gave only support questions as a guide. Each participant was free to use her/his own strategy to do the task. Furthermore, they could choose the order of the tasks. The Step-by-Step guide only indicated the activities to be done before and after the god class detection for each program, such as filling in the start and finish time on the answer form.

Design

The experiment was carried out in a laboratory at UFBA. Participants had 2 hours to carry out the task. Each participant worked at a separate workstation. At each workstation, we set up two Eclipses IDEs. One contained the SourceMiner plug-in, and the other did not. Both Eclipses were fitted with a Task Register and UDC plug-ins. Each Eclipse had three of the six programs in their workspace. The workstations were divided into two groups. After analysis of the characterization form, participants were randomly allocated to groups, because they had similar profiles: years of programming and knowledge on the topic were used. There were six participants in group 1 and five participants in group 2. We present the distribution of participants by group in Table 2. The ID of the participants was formed by the position of the workstation in the lab where the task was performed.

Table 1 Software objects

Software	Chess	Jackut	Tic Tac Toe	Monopoly	Solitaire	Tetris
Packages	5	8	2	3	6	4
Classes	15	19	5	10	23	16
LOC	1426	978	616	2682	1758	993

Table 2 Set of Eclipses installations at the workstations and allocation of participants

Group	With SourceMiner	Without SourceMiner	Participants' ID
1	Chess, Jackut and Solitaire	Monopoly, Tetris and Tic Tac Toe	F14, F21, F32, F35, F42 and F44
2	Monopoly, Tetris and Tic Tac Toe	Chess, Jackut and Solitaire	F13, F15, F25, F31 and F41

Execution

The experiment took four days. Two days were allocated to training, one day for a pilot and one day to perform the experiment. There were three small presentations on the first day of training. As the experiment was a voluntary activity and students had little experience with experimental software engineering, we decided to do a motivational presentation. In this presentation, we discussed the experimental software engineering scene, tying it with discussions about smell effects. The second presentation focused on smells and god class concepts. The third presentation showed the design of the experiment: we just talked about the lab, the individual use of a workstation with two different set ups of the IDE, and the time.

On the second day of training, we did an activity in the lab focusing on the SourceMiner tool (explanation and exercise).

On the third day, we ran a pilot experiment with two students who were also enrolled in the same course of the participants. These two students were out of the 11 we presented in the Table 2. The pilot helped us to evaluate the use of the answer form in paper or electronic format. In the pilot, we presented the Step-by-Step guide in paper format. We did this because we thought that it would not be useful to use electronic format forms because the experiment ran with two opened Eclipses installations. However, after the pilot, we noted that paper forms were less convenient. Therefore, in the final experiment, we kept only the answer sheet form and Support Questions in paper format. The pilot also helped us to validate the inspection time. We confirmed that 1.5 - 2.0 hours was enough time to analyze the six programs.

On the final day we ran the experiment. Table 3 shows the complete schedule. The column Day gives an idea of the time between the activities. For example, the second training (Day 8) was seven days after the first training (Day 1).

Table 3 Experiment schedule

Day	Activity	Presentation	Local	Time (Hour)
1	Training	Motivational + Concepts + Experiment design	Classroom	2,0
8	Training	SourceMiner + Exercise	Lab Lab	2,0
18	Pilot	-	Lab	1,5
20	Experiment	-	Lab	2,0

Deviations

We ran the experiment with 17 students, but only 11 completed the experiment. Four students missed at least one presentation and were excluded. Two students participated in the pilot experiment. We also had an unexpected problem with the schedule. The original schedule was changed and there was a holiday between the SourceMiner presentation and experiment. Due to this, there were only 2 days between the pilot and the experiment. Despite this, the pilot still helped us, as previously discussed.

Data

We collected and analyzed two types of data. The first was the answers on the answer form, as explained in the Section 'Forms': i) the selected god class candidates; ii) the level of certainty, i.e. "yes" or "maybe" option for each candidate class; and iii) decision drivers that helped participants to indicate the candidate god classes.

The other type of data was the UDC Log. We used the UDC plug-in to log participants' actions while the experiment was running. UDC is a framework for collecting usage data on various aspects of the Eclipse workbench. It gathers information about the kinds of activities that the user does in the IDE (i.e. activating views, editors, etc.). The Task Register (Figure 1-F) was used to enrich the UDC log with the name of the program on which the participant was performing the task. Figure 2 shows a clipping of the UDC log annotated by the Task Register plug-in. The first column ("task") does not exist in the original UDC log. It was added by the Task Register. We highlighted columns that we were interested in. The first column ("task") indicates the program for which the participant was doing the god class detection task. Columns "what", "kind" and "description" describe the actions. For example, the first line represents: user activated the Package Explorer view.

Each line represents one user action. As a result, we have sequences of actions for each participant and for each program.

Results

This section presents the results of the experiment. We created one subsection to present the results for each research question.

RQ1: How well do the participants agree on identifying god classes?

To evaluate this research question we considered the agreement on the candidate god classes for both cases, with and without visualization. For the case without visualization, there were six participants in group 1 (Monopoly, Tetris and Tic Tac Toe) and five in group 2 (Chess, Jackut and Solitaire). In the case of with visualization, there were six participants in group 1 (Chess, Jackut and Solitaire) and five participants in group 2 (Monopoly, Tetris and Tic Tac Toe). We tabulated god class candidates into the "yes" and "maybe" category

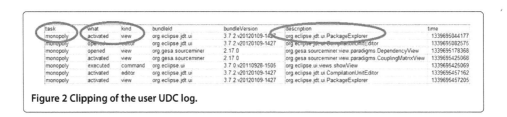

Figure 2 Clipping of the user UDC log.

for each participant. Table 4 summarizes the results for the Solitaire program. The F13 participant, for example, marked one class as a "yes" and one class as a "maybe" god class. To analyze the results, we consider both to be god class candidates.

Out of all of the data sets, there were ten cases in which participants filled in the class name and the drivers, but did not mark the option "yes" or "maybe". In these cases, we considered the weakest option, i.e., "maybe". There were also two cases in which the participants did not fill in the name of the class. In this case, we excluded the data entry from the analysis.

We used two approaches to address the research question. The first considered the percentage of candidate classes. The second was an agreement test.

The percentage of god class candidates

To analyze and compare cases with and without visualization, we generated bar chart diagrams (Figure 3). The diagrams show the percentage of candidate god classes with respect to the number of classes for each program. We show the number of classes for each program under the name of the programs. Considering "yes" or "maybe" options, the percentage of god class candidates tends to be higher for programs with a fewer number of classes. In the case of without visualization, the blue bars, there is a small difference for the Tetris program. However the tendency is the same: the percentage of god class candidates tends to be higher for programs with a fewer number of classes. In the case of with visualization, the gray bars, the difference is for the Solitaire program.

Considering only the "yes" option, the difference in the percentage of god class candidates is very small among the programs. Despite this, in the case without visualization, the percentage of god class candidates tends to be higher for programs with a fewer number of classes, once again. For the case with visualization, we noted that the values are very similar, excepted for the Monopoly program, which had the lowest percentage of god class candidates.

Finn agreement test

To evaluate the level of agreement among participants, we adopted the Finn coefficient (Finn 1970) as opposed to the Kappa coefficient (Fleiss 1971), adopted by Schumacher et al. (2010). We did this because of the problems identified in the Kappa coefficient by other authors (Feinstein and Cicchetti 1990; Gwet 2002; Powers 2012; Whitehurst 1984). The Kappa test is done in two phases. First an agreement rate is calculated, and, then this value is used to calculate the coefficient. Feinstein (1990) shows that one can have high

Table 4 God classes for participants working on the Solitaire-Freecell program (task carried out without visualization)

God Class	Solitaire-Freecell (23 classes)				
	Participant				
	F13	F15	F25	F31	F41
ControladorGlobal	Yes		Yes	Maybe	Yes
FrameFreecell	Maybe	Yes	Yes		Maybe
InterfacePaciencia		Maybe	Maybe		Maybe
Estoque		Maybe			

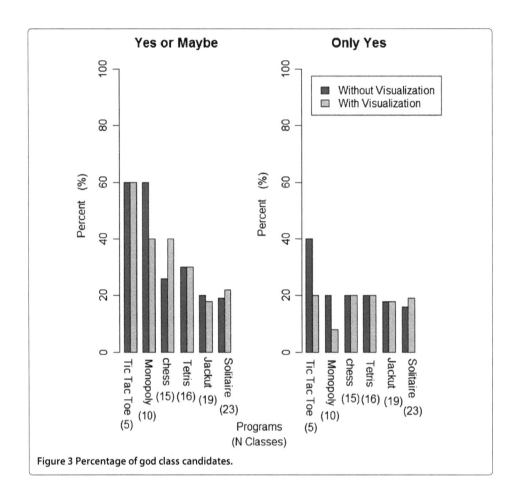

Figure 3 Percentage of god class candidates.

agreement rate and low values of the Kappa coefficient, when the variance on values of raters is low. We noted this situation in the work of Schumacher et al. The Finn coefficient is recommended when variance between raters is low (Finn 1970). Whitehurst (1984) proposes Finn as an alternative to problems with Kappa, and affirms that it is the most reasonable index for agreement.

To make the comparison of agreement values for the cases with and without visualization easier, we adopted classification levels. We used the same defined by Landis and Koch (1977), such as Schumacher et al. (2010) had done. Landis and Koch proposed the following classification: slight, for values between 0.00 and 0.20; fair (between 0.21 and 0.40); moderate (between 0.41 and 0.60); substantial (between 0.61 and 0.80); and almost perfect (between 0.81 and 1.00) agreement.

Table 5 presents Finn values for the programs considering "yes" or "maybe" options. On the left, we present values for the case of without visualization. On the right, we present values for the case with visualization. There were two cases where the agreement level was higher with visualization: Monopoly (from moderate to substantial) and Jackut (from substantial to almost perfect). There was a reduction in agreement for Tic Tac Toe (from moderate to slight), but it is the only change without significance (p-value = 0.283), therefore we did not consider it in the agreement analysis. Table 6 considers only cases where participants were sure about the god classes. There were two cases where the level of agreement was higher with visualization (Tic Tac Toe and Chess, changing from

Table 5 Agreement among participants, considering "yes" or "maybe" marked

Program	Without visualization				With visualization			
	Number of classes	Raters (participants)	Finn coefficient	p-value	Agreement	Number of classes	Raters (participants)	Finn coefficient	p-value	Agreement
Monopoly	10	6	0.507	0.000996	Moderate	10	4	0.7	7.37e-05	Substantial
Tetris	16	6	0.733	5.09e-12	Substantial	16	5	0.8	4.91e-13	Substantial
Tic Tac Toe	5	6	0.6	0.00335	Moderate	5	5	0.2	0.283	Slight
Chess	15	5	0.787	1.21e-11	Substantial	15	6	0.664	4.46e-08	Substantial
Jackut	19	4	0.772	1.73e-10	Substantial	19	6	0.881	1.33e-27	Almost perpect
Solitaire	23	5	0.843	4.38e-22	Almost perfect	23	5	0.843	4.38e-22	Almost perpect

Table 6 Agreement among participants, considering only "yes" marked

Program	Without visualization					With visualization				
	Number of classes	Raters (participants)	Finn coefficient	p-value	Agreement	Number of classes	Raters (participants)	Finn coefficient	p-value	Agreement
Monopoly	10	6	0.827	8.44e-12	Almost perpect	10	4	0.867	3.87e-09	Almost perpect
Tetris	16	6	0.892	5.34e-25	Almost perpect	16	5	0.675	5.89e-08	Substantial
Tic Tac Toe	5	6	0.653	0.00102	Substantial	5	5	0.84	7.14e-06	Almost perpect
Chess	15	5	0.787	1.21e-11	Substantial	15	6	0.84	5.26e-18	Almost perpect
Jackut	19	4	0.842	3.31e-14	Almost perfect	19	6	0.895	6.683-30	Almost perpect
Solitaire	23	5	0.896	3.62e-29	Almost perfect	23	5	0.843	4.38e-22	Almost perpect

substantial to almost perfect agreement). There was one case where the level of agreement was lower with visualization (Tetris changing from almost perfect to substantial).

RQ2: How well do humans and an oracle agree on identifying god classes?

To deepen the analysis of the impact of conceptualization on god class identification, we extended the human performance questions in Schumacher et al. (2010) using an oracle and comparing the answers of the oracle and participants. The oracle was made up of two experienced researchers in academia and industry. Each of the researchers did the task independently and without any contact with the participants' answers. We show their answers in Table 7.

We used the Finn coefficient (1970), the same as the previous RQ, to test the agreement. Table 8 shows the results. Tic Tac Toe, Tetris and Solitaire all had an agreement. The Chess and Jackut programs had one disagreement. The Monopoly program had two disagreements.

After these observations, the researchers met to discuss the differences and to define the oracle. An interesting observation is that the researchers noted that they were very strict in their analysis. Due to this, for some cases (two classes for Monopoly, one class for Chess, one class for Solitaire and one class for Jackut), classes were deleted from the list. We highlight the class FrameFreeFreecell in the Solitaire program. In this case, both researchers found that the class was a candidate to be god class. However, during the meeting, the researchers were more flexible about the size and the few methods out of scope, because the class represents the graphical user interface of the program. After the meeting, the oracles reached the agreement presented in Table 9.

Figure 4 shows the distribution of the Finn coefficient, comparing the agreement among the participants and the oracle. Let us initially focus on Figure 4(A) and (B), confirmed and possible god classes. It is possible to note that the average agreement with visualization

Table 7 Oracle answers

Program	God class	Oracle	
		Or1	Or2
Ti Tac Toe (5 classes)			
	-	-	-
Monopoly (10 classes)			
	Jogo	Yes	Yes
	Tabuleiro	Maybe	Yes
	UserStoriesFacade	-	Maybe
	Jogador	-	Maybe
Chess (15 classes)			
	Chess	Yes	Yes
	BoardGUI	-	Yes
Tetris (16 classes)			
	Tetris	Maybe	Maybe
Jackut (19 classes)			
	Usuario	-	Maybe
Solitaire (23 classes)			
	FrameFreeFreecell	Maybe	Yes

Table 8 Finn coefficient among the researches considering "yes" marked and "yes" or "maybe"

Program	Subjects (Nclasses)	Raters (oracle)	Finn coefficiente	
			Yes or maybe	Only yes
Ti Tac Toe (5 classes)	5	2	1	1
Monopoly	10	2	0.6	0.8
Chess	15	2	0.867	0.867
Tetris	16	2	1	1
Jakut	19	2	0.895	1
Solitaire	23	2	1	0.913

is higher only for the Monoploy program, is the same for Tic Tac Toe, and is lower for the other four cases. Figure 4(C) and (D) focus on confirmed god classes. First, one should notice that, as expected, the average is higher and the variances are smaller than in Figure 4(A) and (B). Comparing Figure 4(C) and (D), the values are higher for cases with visualization for three cases (Chess, Solitaire and Tic Tac Toe), and lower for the other three cases (Jackut, Monopoly and Tetris).

RQ3: Which strategies are used to identify god classes?

We used the logged actions to investigate the strategy adopted by the participants to detect god classes. We analyzed two aspects. The first one was the differences between relevant actions for the cases, with and without visualization. The second were the preferences of the participants. We grouped participants with similar preferences and evaluated if there was a "better" strategy.

Relevant actions

Table 10 shows the number of actions performed during the experiment by all participants. We grouped the columns "what", "kind" and "description" from the log and shortened the terms presented in Figure 2. The first action represents the activation of the Package Explorer view. The Package Explorer shows the Java element hierarchy of Java projects. It is a tree view that shows Eclipse projects on the first level, folders on the

Table 9 Final oracle answers

Program	God class	Oracle
Ti Tac Toe (5 classes)		
	-	-
Monopoly (10 classes)		
	Jogo	Yes
	Tabuleiro	Maybe
Chess (15 classes)		
	Chess	Yes
Tetris (16 classes)		
	Tetris	Maybe
Jackut (19 classes)		
	-	-
Solitaire (23 classes)		
	-	-

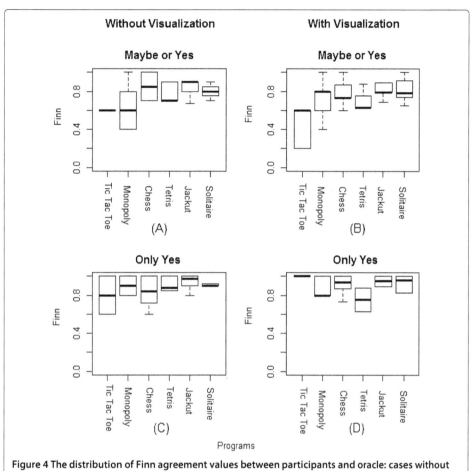

Figure 4 The distribution of Finn agreement values between participants and oracle: cases without visualization in (A) and (C); cases with visualization in (B) and (D).

second level, packages on the third level, classes on the fourth level, and methods and attributes on the fifth level. It is used to navigate in the original Eclipse's set up.

The second relevant action represents the activation of the Compilation Unit Editor, which is commonly used for code reading/writing. The actions numbered three to seven represent the activation of views of the visualization tool. For example, action three represents the activation of the Polimetric view, presented in Section 'Tools'. Actions four

Table 10 Actions performed with and without the visualization tool

No	Actions	Visualization	
		With	Without
1	activated_view_PackageExplorer	311	806
2	activated_editor_CompilationUniEditor	263	1240
3	activated_view_PolymetricView	135	
4	activated_view_DependencyView	117	
5	activated_view_TreeMapView	114	
6	activated_view_CouplingMatrixView	70	
7	activated_view_GridMatrixView	59	
8	Others: 10 with SourceMiner and 23 without SourceMiner	47	71
	Total	1116	2117

to seven represent the activation of the Dependency, Tree Map, Coupling Matrix and Grid Coupling views. The other actions were not shown because they did not occur very often.

It is possible to note the difference in the total. For the case with visualization, the total number of actions was 1116. Without visualization the total number was 2117. The views of the visualization tool were used frequently, when permitted: Polymetric (135), Dependency (117), Tree Map (114), Coupling Matrix (70) and Grid Coupling (59).

Strategies of god class detection

To evaluate the strategies we only observed cases with visualization because, in the case without visualization, the main action was related to activation of the Compilation Unit Editor, i.e. reading source code, and Eclipse does not log its use in detail.

As discussed in Section 'Data', we defined a sequence as all actions performed by the participant for a program.

In this experiment, there were three sequences of actions for each participant using the visualization tool, one for each program. There were 11 participants, but we deleted three of the sequences because we found problems in these sequences. The problems were caused by misuse of the Task Register plug-in. Therefore, 30 sequences were evaluated.

Our first analysis was related to individual sequences. We searched for common patterns. To do this, we used the LTL Checker of the ProM[b], a support tool for techniques of process mining (van der Aalst 2011). With the LTL Checker it is possible to check a property of the set of sequences expressed in terms of Linear Temporal Logic (LTL).

Consider the following three sequences, as a simple example. The sequences one and two have three actions, and the third sequence has two actions:

1. *activate_view_Polimetric, activate_view_TreeMap, open_CompilationUnitEditor*
2. *activate_view_Polimetric, open_CompilationUnitEditor, activate_view_TreeMap*
3. *activate_view_Polimetric, activate_view_TreeMap*

The LTL Checker allows checking, for example, that the action *activate_view_ TreeMap* always occurs some time after *activate_view_Polimetric*. It is also possible to check that the action *open_CompilationUnitEditor* occurs in two out three sequences. Or that the action *activate_view_TreeMap* occurs next to *activate_view_Polimetric* in two out three sequences. Table 11 shows the main results and interpretations for the sequences of the experiment.

We also investigated preferences grouped by participants. Some participants read more and used fewer views, whereas others did the opposite. To evaluate these aspects, we calculated the ratio between the number of classes investigated for each program and the use of views and readings. We counted the number of actions related to reading (activation of Compilation Unit Editor), activation of hierarchical views (Polymetric or Tree Map), and activation of coupling views (Dependency, GridCoupling or CouplingMatrix). For example, there were 12, two and four (18 in total) "activated_editor_CompilationUnitEditor" for the sequences of the F13 participant, for the programs Monopoly, Tetris and Tic Tac Toe, respectively. The total number of classes for these three programs is 31. We defined the ratio of using the CompilationUnitEditor, for F13 participant, as 18/31. He/she activated Coupling views 31 times for the three programs. In this case, the ratio is 31/31. Note that, if the participant activated the views more than the total number of classes of the

Table 11 Main results of the evaluation of sequences with LTL checker

Formula eventually_activity...	Action (activity) Activitation of ...	Number of cases (in 30)	Interpretation
A	Compilation Unit Editor	20	There were 20 cases where the participants read source code to identify god classes
A, B, C, D and E	Polimetric, TreeMap, Grid Coupling, Coupling Matrix, Dependency	11	Despite hierarchical views ad coupling views show the same attributes, there were 11 cases where the participants adopted all views of the visualization tool to identity god classes
A and B	Hierarchical views and Coupling views	27	There were 27 cases where the participants combine the use, at least, one of the hierarchical views and one of the coupling views to identify god classes
A, B and C	Hierarchical views and Coupling views and Compilation Unit Editor	17	There were 17 cases where the participants combined reading source code with one of the hierarchical (at least) and one of the coupling views (at least)

investigated programs, the ratio will be greater than 1. The complete results are presented in Figure 5.

From the figure, we identified six different profiles. We present them in Table 12. The first profile is composed of participants F14, F21 and F42. They used very little or no reading, and had a slight preference for coupling views. In profile 2, the two participants (F31 and F41) also did little reading in comparison to the usage of coupling views. In profile 3, participants F15 and F25 had preferences for coupling views, but they focused on reading unlike the previous group. For the other cases we found only one participant.

To investigate the "quality" of profiles we evaluated the agreement between each participant and the oracle. We plotted the Finn coefficient in Figure 6. From the graphs, it can be seen that no participants strongly agreed with the oracle. For example, participant F21 (Figure 6(A) and (C)) had the highest agreement for the program Chess and the worst agreement for Jackut. This was the general pattern.

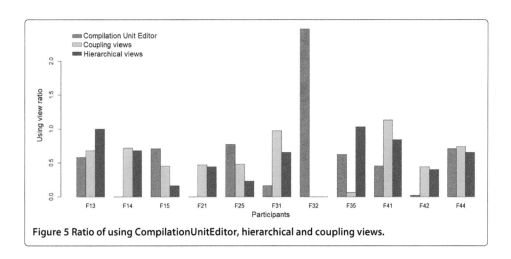

Figure 5 Ratio of using CompilationUnitEditor, hierarchical and coupling views.

Table 12 Profiles of participants related to the use of reading, hierarchical and coupling views

No	Profile	Participants
1	No reading and slight preference by coupling views	F14, F12 and F42
2	Few reading and strong preference by coupling views	F31 and F41
3	Focus on reading and preference by coupling views	F15 and F25
4	Preference by hierarchical views	F35
5	Slight preference by hierarchical views	F13
6	Similar using of all views and reading	F44
7	None using the visualization tool	F32

RQ4: What issues in code lead humans to identify a class as a god class?

To address this question we collected data related to drivers used by participants on the identification of god classes. The answer form provided a multiple choice list of nine drivers extracted from the work of Schumacher et al. (2010) (see Section 'Forms'). It also allowed the participants to write down new drivers.

For cases where visualization was not used, the participants wrote down 19 short descriptions of new drivers. The coding process on these 19 new drivers' descriptions was simple. For example, some participants wrote down "class has many lines of code", others wrote down "class has big size". In these cases, we defined "class has high LOC" as the driver. After this process, we narrowed the descriptions down to six actually new drivers. Table 13 shows all the drivers. The most common drivers were "class is highly complex" (48 times) and "method is highly complex" (31 times). An intermediate group included drivers like "class is special/framework" (12 times), "class represents a global function" (8 times) and "lack of comments" (7 times). The other drivers had low marks (≤ 5 times).

We also analyzed the distribution of drivers by participants. The drivers "class is highly complex" and "method is highly complex" were filled by all and almost all participants, respectively. The other 13 drivers were used by no more than four participants,

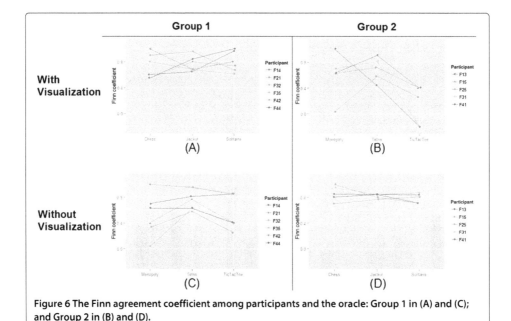

Figure 6 The Finn agreement coefficient among participants and the oracle: Group 1 in (A) and (C); and Group 2 in (B) and (D).

Table 13 Drivers by participants (Schumacher et al. and new drivers) without visualization

| Participant | Based on Schumacher et al. coding | | | | | | | | | Coding on comments | | | | | |
| | Class | | | Special/ framework | Method | | | Attribute | Method/class | High LOC | Many dependencies | Class | | Method | |
	Not used	Highly complex	Misplaced		Wrong named	High complex	Misplaced	Not used	Lacks comments			Many methods	Global functions	Can be split	High LOC
F13	0	6	0	3	0	6	2	0	3	0	0	0	0	1	1
F14	0	3	0	0	1	1	1	0	0	1	0	0	0	0	0
F15	0	4	0	0	1	3	0	0	0	0	0	0	0	0	0
F21	0	4	0	4	0	0	0	1	0	0	0	0	0	0	0
F25	0	9	0	0	0	6	0	3	1	0	0	0	0	0	0
F31	0	1	0	0	0	1	0	0	0	0	0	0	1	0	0
F32	0	4	0	0	0	0	0	0	0	0	0	0	7	0	0
F35	0	5	0	0	0	2	1	0	0	0	0	0	0	0	0
F41	0	5	0	2	0	7	0	1	0	3	0	2	0	0	2
F42	0	3	0	3	0	1	0	0	0	0	4	0	0	0	0
F44	0	4	1	0	0	4	0	0	3	0	0	0	0	0	0
Totals	0	48	1	12	2	31	4	5	7	4	4	2	8	1	3

even the drivers in the intermediate group. This indicates that drivers like "class is special/framework" were consistently adopted by some, but this was not a consensus among the participants.

For cases where visualization was used, the participants wrote down 27 short descriptions of "new drivers". Like before, these descriptions were reduced to a group of six actually new drivers. This group was almost the same as before. As shown in Table 14, it excludes/includes just one driver ("method can be split" is substituted by "problem with hierarchy"). The most common drivers were "class is highly complex" (46 times), "method is highly complex" (21 times) and "class has many dependencies" (20 times). The intermediate drivers were "class is special/framework" (11 times), "class/method lack comments" (8 times) and "class has high LOC" (7 times). The others had low marks ($\leq$ 3 times).

Like before, "class is highly complex" and "method is highly complex" were chosen by all or almost all participants. "class has many dependencies" was also chosen by most (seven) participants. "class is special/framework" was chosen by five. The other 11 drivers were chosen by less than three participants, following the same pattern previously described.

Finally, we analyzed the differences by cases with and without visualization. The coding we performed produced practically the same new drivers and the distribution of the total marks was also quite similar. The most common drivers were the same: "class is highly complex" and "method is highly complex". The notable difference was the "class has many dependencies" driver. It was common in the visualization-based analysis and uncommon in the code-based analysis (without visualization).

Discussion

This section presents the discussion of the results of the experiment. Following the same logic of the previous section, we created one subsection to present the discussion for each question.

RQ1: How well do the participants agree on identifying god classes?

We addressed this question from two perspectives: i) number of candidate classes and ii) agreement test.

Number of candidate god classes

Comparison with Schumacher et al. (2010)'s work. Schumacher et al. (2010) found a very small number of god class candidates: only two in 52 inspected for one of the projects and three in 51 for the other project (3.8% and 5.8%, respectively). The numbers were much higher in our case: the average number of candidate classes were 34.8% and 35.8% for cases with and without visualization, respectively. One possibility is that the difference was related to the type of programs. Because the programs used in our experiment have a smaller number of classes, one god class candidate represents a high percentage.

On the other hand, it is possible to conjecture about the difference on the number and experience of the participants. In both studies, the number of participants is small: 11 in our case, and only four in the Schumacher et al. work. Our participants were undergraduates and Schumacher et al. ran the study with professionals. However, despite experience, three of their participants were unfamiliar with the concept of smell and god class in the experiment. The other participant had only heard about god classes before. Therefore, for both studies the participants had little knowledge about the concepts. We consider this

Table 14 Drivers by participants (Schumacher et al. and new drivers) with visualization

| Subject | Based on Schumacher et al. coding | | | | | | | | | Coding on comments | | | | | |
| | Class | | | | Method | | | Attribute | Method/class | | | Class | | | Method |
	Not used	Highly complex	Misplaced	Special/framework	Wrong named	High complex	Misplaced	Not used	Lacks comments	High LOC	Many dependencies	Many methods	Global functions	Hierarchy structure	High LOC
F13	0	4	0	1	0	4	0	0	2	3	4	1	0	0	1
F14	0	5	0	0	1	1	0	0	0	1	3	0	0	0	1
F15	0	3	0	0	0	1	0	0	0	0	0	0	0	0	0
F21	0	4	0	5	0	0	0	1	0	0	0	0	0	0	0
F25	0	8	0	0	0	3	0	1	2	0	0	0	0	0	0
F31	0	1	0	0	0	1	0	0	0	0	1	0	0	0	0
F32	0	2	0	3	0	0	0	0	0	0	0	0	2	0	0
F35	0	6	0	0	0	3	2	0	0	0	0	0	0	0	0
F41	0	3	0	1	0	3	0	1	0	3	2	0	0	1	0
F42	0	6	0	1	0	3	0	0	0	0	5	0	0	0	0
F44	0	4	0	0	0	2	0	0	4	0	1	0	0	0	0
Totais	0	46	0	11	1	21	2	3	8	7	20	1	2	1	2

aspect empirical evidence that the knowledge related to reading or having heard about the concept of smell or god class is weaker than the experience related to work in a development environment. We usually believe in that, but we do not have much empirical evidence. To us, this makes the importance of expanding the discussion on the context of software engineering experiments evident. This problem has been rarely addressed in Experimental Software Engineering (Dybå et al. 2012; Höst et al. 2000, 2005).

Comparison between cases with and without visualization. There was no significant difference between the number of god class candidates with and without visualization (Figure 3). Considering the "yes" or "maybe" marks, values for cases with visualization are higher for the two programs, and lower for two other programs. Considering only "yes" marks, values for cases with visualization are higher only for one program and lower for two programs. The main finding is that the use of visualization does not impact the number of candidate god classes, i.e. people do not identify more or fewer god classes because of a better comprehension of the design of the program (obtained via the visualization tool). For us, this is evidence that people have their own conceptualization of what a god class is, and the visualization tool does not affect this.

This finding appears to run contrary to the one presented by Murphy et al. 2010. In this work, the first hypothesis is "Programmers identify more smells using the tool than not using the tool". However, their tool uses visual aids based on detection mechanisms. These mechanisms use metrics to visually highlight certain smells related to attributes. This contributes to harmonize (for better or worse) the conceptualization of what a smell is.

Agreement test

Comparison with Schumacher et al. (2010)'s work. We could not compare both works in terms of numbers because Schumacher et al. used Cohen's Kappa and we adopted the Finn coefficient. In Shcumacher's et al. work, the agreement for the one project was -2%. Based on Landis's and Koch's (1977) interpretation of Kappa, this indicates no agreement among the two participants. In the other project, the calculated Kappa was 48% (suggesting moderate agreement). Their conclusion was that there was not a high level of agreement. The work of Mäntylä (2005), in a similar study about agreement, found a similar result. For comparative purposes, we tested agreement with the Fleiss Kappa coefficient[c] and Landis's and Koch's interpretation. Our results showed only a slightly higher agreement than Schumacher's et al. work.

The values of the Finn coefficient were significantly higher as we can see in Tables 5 and 6. However, it is important to note that the Finn and Kappa tests measure agreement using both god and non-god classes. Consequently, we were cautious about finding high levels of agreement (almost perfect), because many classes are clearly not god classes. Participants were expected to agree on this. The same situation might have happened in the Scumacher's et al. work. We believe that their values were affected by the problem of the Kappa coefficient, which we discussed in the Subsection 'Finn agreement test'. Despite this, the results considering just the "yes" mark were convincing. Almost perfect agreement occurred for four of the six cases without visualization, and five of the six cases with visualization. The results were not as convincing when some level of doubt was allowed. For the "maybe" and "yes" marks, almost perfect agreement occurred in only one of the six cases without visualization, and two of the six with visualization. Based on these analyses, we consider our results aligned with previous studies: we did not find a high level of agreement.

The main finding here is that the participants have different conceptualizations of what makes a god class. This may happen in two dimensions. First, participants may have different classification thresholds in their evaluation of candidates. For example, participants may have different perceptions of how many roles a class can assume before it becomes a god class. Another possibility is that participants simply have different views of the god class concept. We consider this to be the weaker possibility because they had the same training and they had a similar level of knowledge before the experiment. Furthermore, the difference in the classification threshold was observed first hand when the oracle was being defined by more experienced professionals.

Comparison between cases with and without visualization. Another important dimension is the impact of visualization. We can not affirm that the use of visualization leads to "big" improvements. We can see in Tables 5 and 6 that there were four in 11 cases where the level of agreement was higher and there was one case where the level of agreement was lower with visualization. As a result, the agreement was slightly better for cases with visualization. We use the next research question to further investigate the impact of visualization.

RQ2: How well do humans and an oracle agree on identifying god classes?

We addressed this question from two perspectives: i) the oracle definition process; and ii) the agreement between the oracle and participants.

The oracle definition process

An important aspect in the agreement analysis between participants and the oracle is that we can not claim that the discrepancies between the participants and the oracle are errors, but we can claim that the oracle definition process was more rigorous. During the oracle meeting, both oracle researchers noted that the choice of a god class was associated with their personal perception about "how many roles the class needs to be considered god class" or "how much LOC the class needs to be considered a large class", or other subjective thresholds related to the characteristics of classes. This can be an explanation for the lack of agreement found among the participants of our study, as well as in (Mäntylä's 2006a and Schumacher's et al. 2010) studies.

The agreement between the oracle and participants

We analyzed this from two perspectives: level of certainty or doubts ("yes" or "maybe" marks) , and the use of visualization (Figure 4).

Comparison between cases with and without doubts. From Figure 4, we can see that when certainty – "yes" mark – is involved, the agreement between the participants and the oracle is generally high, while the variation in these agreements – see the box sizes – is usually small. These values are significantly reduced for the "yes or maybe" marks. The agreement average and variation between the oracle and the participants are much lower. If we consider the discussion on the high level values naturally produced by the Finn coefficient, this reinforces the thesis that agreement is low when doubt is involved. This also reinforces the evidence that participants have a personal conceptualization of what is a god class. As discussed previously, the likely causes for this is the different classification thresholds, or the different views of the god class concept. Like before, we consider the former more probable.

Comparison between cases with and without visualization. Considering the averages and the "yes or maybe" options in Figure 4(A) and (B), one can observe that there was only one case where the visualization improved agreement. Considering only the "yes" option (Figure 4(C) and (D)), there were three out of six cases where the visualization improved agreement. We conclude that the visualization does not affect the agreement values. This weakens the argument made in the discussion of RQ2, where we stated that visualization slightly improves the agreement among the participants. It might be the case that visualization slightly improves the precision among the participants, but it does not improve the accuracy of their detection against an oracle reference.

RQ3: Which strategies are used to identify god classes?
Relevant actions

First we addressed differences in the amount of reading for the cases with and without visualization. Comparing both cases, the reduction in the activation of the Compilation Unit Editor, or the reading of source code, was significant: from 1240 (without visualization) to 263 (with visualization). On the other hand, actions related to the activation of the views of the visualization tool emerged. We concluded that participants exchanged reading for the observation of views, i.e., they used visualization to search for attributes that indicate god classes. Based on the use of the views and tacit knowledge, we suggest that, to identify god classes, participants compared LOC, complexity or number of methods; observed coupling attributes and read code to understand the context of the class in the program.

Strategies of god class detection

Evaluating sequences. We analyzed each case presented in Section 'Strategies of god class detection'. The first case was related to reading. It was found in 20 of the 30 sequences. We believe that it was adopted by the participants to comprehend the role of the class in the program. Considering the concepts presented by (Fowler 1999 and Lanza and Marinescu 2005), some reading is necessary. In the definition of a Large Class, Fowler says that "...*it often shows up as too many instance variables*". In the God Class and Brain Class definitions, Lanza and Marinescu adopt metrics that involve a number of branches, deep nesting and a number of variables. In the experiment, it was not possible to see these characteristics with the visualization tool. However, despite the expected behavior, 10 sequences did not contain actions related to reading code. We analyze these aspects in the evaluation of participants hereafter.

In the other formula, we detected that in 11 sequences participants activated all five views of the visualization tool. As discussed in Section 'Tools', the two hierarchical views present similar attributes, like the other three coupling views. This indicates that in some cases participants worked more than necessary. Our conjecture is that they wanted to increase their level of certainty. It is important to note that, for most sequences (19), the participants did not use all the views, which we consider more efficient. Despite this, the need to confirm ideas is a behavior that must be considered in the analysis.

Another analysis that we performed was related to the combination of views and reading. The combination of hierarchical and coupling views occurred in 27 of the 30 sequences. This was the main strategy used to detect god classes.

Evaluating participants' strategies. We identified three participants who combined structural, coupling views, and used very little or no reading. It is profile 1 in Table 12. In profile 2, the two participants also used little reading in comparison with their preference for coupling views. From these two profiles, we suggest that the preference for coupling indicates that this attribute is the strongest, and that reading source code was not considered so relevant in god class detection. Another interesting profile is the number 3. In this case, the participants focused on reading and had a preference for coupling. In comparison with the other two profiles, this agrees with our previous discussion that participants exchanged reading for observation of specific attributes in the views of the visualization tool. In some cases, participants seem to be more confident reading than using the visualization tool. The other profiles indicate different preferences. For example, profile 4 shows a strong preference for structural views and profile 6 shows the similar use of all types of views and reading.

An interesting observation is related to the absence of a "better" strategy, or even a "better" participant, considering the agreement with the oracle (Figure 6). This reinforces our idea that god class detection is strongly affected by personal conceptualizations. If this was not true, a participant with a similar approach to the oracle would produce high levels of agreement with it for most programs. This was not what happened in our experiment.

RQ4: What issues in code lead humans to identify a class as a god class?

Some drivers were chosen by participants, independent of visualization. "Class is highly complex" (chosen by all participants) and "Method is highly complex" (chosen by nine out eleven participants), two of the strongest drivers, are examples of that. The only, and very interesting exception to the rule, is the "class has many dependencies" driver. Only one participant chose this driver for the case without visualization, and seven participants chose the driver for the case with visualization. While the visualization tool provides several views which showed signs of dependency, the current IDEs and the source code do not help in the identification of dependency. This case is evidence that the use of a visualization tool can indeed help, because some detection drivers are poorly supported by the current state of the practice. This, however, does not solve the conceptualization problem.

It is also worthwhile to observe that, although participants did not always use the same drivers, they were very consistent in using their drivers of choice. For "Method is highly complex", for example, the two participants who did not choose the driver are the same (F21 and F32) with and without visualization. Other cases where the same participants chose the same drivers were: "attribute is not used", "methods or class lack comments". For other cases, the difference between the choices of the participants is very small; at most one participant. That suggests that in some cases the choice of drivers is a personal issue. This idea reinforces our conjecture about the importance of the community discussing the problem of conceptualization on smells in depth.

Summary of findings and insights

In this work, we addressed the problem of conceptualization in the god class detection, from different perspectives. In this section, we gather the findings and present our conclusions. We also present peripheral, but not less important findings:

- Agreement

  - *Related to the conceptualization problem*: The low agreement rate showed us that the problem exists. However, we consider the question related to visualization more interesting, because it showed us where the problem is, or at least where it is not. The problem of conceptualization is that it is not related to the comprehension of design, as we had expected. We argue this because visualization did not increase agreement. The finding is that the problem is related to personal understanding of the smell concepts or of personal thresholds adopted.

  - *Peripheral findings*: We found evidence that experience affects the degree of agreement. Our evidence was: i) the comparison of the number of candidate god classes in our and Shumacher's et al. work; and ii) low agreement among the participants and our oracle (made up of more experienced researchers). Another interesting peripheral finding is related to the using of the Kappa coefficient for agreement analysis. We noted that, for the Kappa coefficient, in some cases, the agreement value is high and the coefficient is low. Based on our research, we suggest the adoption of the Finn coefficient (see discussion in the Section 'Finn agreement test').

- Strategies

  - *Related to conceptualization problem*: The absence of a "better" strategy reinforced our finding that each participant has his/her own idea about how and what he/she has to do to identify god classes.

  - *Peripheral findings*: We proposed an approach to identify strategies: the identification of used views from the logs. We grouped participants according to their strategies. The main profile identified focused on coupling attributes, and little reading.

- Decision drivers

  - *Related to the conceptualization problem*: As mentioned under "strategies of god class detection", some decision drivers are also personal choices. In a consistent way, participants had different preferences for characteristics they used to identify god classes. This also reinforced our previous findings.

  - *Peripheral findings*: The main decision driver was "class is highly complex".

The results discussed here strengthen the idea that the problem in god class detection is more related to conceptualization than to making the comprehension of the code design easier by facilitating the (visual) observation of certain attributes of the code. Note that this type of problem is not solved by using other observation approaches, such as proposing a new metric. The key problem is to identify concrete "good" examples of smells, providing standard definitions of them, teaching people about their conceptualization, and only then providing the tools and methods (using metrics, thresholds or visualizations) to aid their identification.

Threats to validity

Our analysis of threats was based on Wohlin et al. (2012).

External validity. Our first threat fits in the "interaction of selection and treatment" sub-category and is related to the fact that the participants in our experiment were undergraduates and had little experience in a real software development environment. Moreover, the experiment was run with 11 participants. Although the aspects related to the participants could be considered a problem for generalization, we have strong evidence that the existence of the problem discussed in this work is intrinsic to smell detection and also happens with experienced developers. The evidence is: i) smell concepts are presented subjectively Fowler (1999) or are dependent on thresholds Lanza et al. (2005); ii) findings show low agreement in other works with more experienced participants Schumacher et al. (2010); and iii) the initial lack of agreement among the experienced researchers who created the oracle in this work. We believe that experience affects our results only in terms of intensity, but the problem of conceptualization exists for all cases. We are planning to replicate this experiment with more experienced participants to evaluate the impact of experience.

Other threats to external validity fit in the "interaction of setting and treatment" subcategory. In this case, the threat is the type of program. We adopted simple programs. Another point is the domain: they are familiar software, and in most of the cases, games. Software of a different domain might present different characteristics. However, we argue that the same, previous reasoning is valid here, weakening the threat: the phenomenon can be studied in any type of software. In fact, because we used simple and familiar software, the problem should be minimized, which was not the case. Moreover, we did not address the difficulty of god class identification, but how conceptualization affects smell detection.

Internal validity. The study has threats in two subcategories related to internal validity. The first one is "ambiguity about direction of causal influence". We highlight the fact that the training about god classes reflects the view of the experimenter. The view of the experimenter could affect the participants' conceptualization and their ideas about what they had to look for to identify a god class. To minimize this effect, we limited the time of the training in the god class concept and adopted the support questions from Schumacher's experiment to guide participants in god class detection during our experiment. These actions also mitigate the same threat in the opposite way: participants could not have a general idea of what to search for. We consider that the training and the support questions steered the participants to search for classes that represent the god class concept adopted.

Another threat is the training in the visualization tool. In our feedback form, participants indicated that the quality of training was good, in general. However, we can not confirm that it was sufficient to prepare participants in the use of visualization. Another subcategory of the internal validity is "maturation". Participants could be affected because they do the same task over six programs, so they may learn as they go and work faster. On the other hand, they could be affected negatively because of boredom. We consider maturation a weak threat because the experiment was performed in 1.5 hours, on average. We consider this a reasonable period of time to do a task in a balanced way.

Conclusion validity. In the "reliability of measures" category, we should report that the logged information represents the actions of the participants only indirectly. They actions of the Eclipse IDE. For example, if a developer changes the perspective in the Eclipse, some views are activated by the tool and these actions are registered in the log. To mitigate this aspect, we investigated the logging to evaluate actions in detail and eliminated lines clearly related to Eclipse actions. Moreover, these registers occurred for all participants and did not affect the general conclusion. In the "reliability of treatment implementation", we have to consider that a participant who could have used visualization may have completely disregarded the views of the visualization tool. However, we checked the UDC logging and only one participant did not use the visualization resources. Because this occurred in one case, the results were not affected. Lastly, due to the number of data points, some of our findings were based on the analysis of graphs and tables, and inferential testing was done in a few cases.

Context and related works

As the use of the concept of smells has become widespread, empirical studies have been presented to help understand their effects. As discussed in Section 'Background', we identified three types of empirical work in the area. In this section we present them. We provide more details of papers related to human aspects, which are closer to our work. However, we present correlation studies because they provide evidence that the use of code smells as an indicator of a problem in the design has been inconsistent, which we believe might be caused by the problem of conceptualization. We also present some works related to the use of support tools, because our work is focused on the use of a visualization tool.

Correlation studies

This type of work usually focuses on analyzing software evolution and tries to link smells with some characteristic of code. Normally, they investigate data in software repositories. Olbrich et al. (2010), for example, investigated the influence of two smells ("God Class" and "Brain Class") on the frequency of defects. In order to do this, they analyzed historical data from three open-source software systems. They found that, in specific cases, the presence of these smells might be beneficial to a software system. In another study, Olbrich et al. (2009) investigated the evolution of two other smells ("God Class" and "Shotgun Surgery") for these same systems. Li and Shatnawi (2007) studied the relationship between smells and error probability. They investigated three error-severity levels in an industrial-strength open source system. Their findings indicate that some bad smells are positively associated with the probability of errors.

Sjoberg et al. (2013) presented a controlled study where six professionals were hired to maintain four systems for 14 days. Their aim was to quantify the relationship between code smells and maintenance effort. One of the main findings was that "the ... smells appear to be superfluous for explaining maintenance effort". Abbes et al. (2011) adopted the concept of anti-pattern, which, like the concept of code smell, presents "poor" solutions to recurring design problems. They performed an empirical study to investigate whether the occurrence of anti-patterns does indeed affect the understandability of systems by developers during comprehension and maintenance tasks. They found that the occurrence of one anti-pattern does not significantly decrease developers' performance while the combination of two anti-patterns significantly impedes developers.

Smells and support tools

Some works evaluated smell detection using automatic detection tools (Moha et al. 2010; Mäntylä and Lassenius 2006a; Schumacher et al. 2010). Other works addressed smell detection with visualization tools (Carneiro et al. 2010; Murphy-Hill and Black 2010; Parnin et al. 2008; Simon et al. 2001). From the former, we discuss the first tool, because it was developed to mitigate subjectiveness. The authors propose DECOR. It is a method/tool "that embodies and defines all the steps necessary for the specification and detection of code and design smells". Despite the tool mitigating some subjectiveness, the focus of the work was on the method, not on the aspect that affects (or does not affect) the conceptualization.

Here, we also discuss here the two most recent tools related smell detection and software visualization. In (Murphy-Hill and Black 2010), Murphy-Hill and Black presented a visualization implemented as an Eclipse plug-in. The tool is composed of sectors in a semicircle on the right-hand side of the editor pane, called petals: each petal corresponds to a smell. They performed a controlled experiment with 12 participants (6 programmers and 6 students) to evaluate the tool. Their main findings were: i) programmers identify more smells using the tool than not using the tool ii) smells are subjective and iii) the tool helps in deciding. Carneiro et al. (2010) presented the SourceMiner tool; a multi-perspective environment Eclipse based plug-in. SourceMiner has visualizations that address inheritance and coupling characteristics of a program. The visualizations also portray the previously mapped concerns of the analyzed software. The authors performed an exploratory study with five developers, using a concern mapping multi-perspective approach to identify code smells. Two main findings were presented. First, the concern visualizations provided useful support to identify God Class and Divergent Change smells. Second, strategies for smell detection supported by the multiple concern views were revealed.

Smells and human aspects

Mäntylä (2005) presents results of two experiments addressing agreement in smell detection and factors to explain it. A small application in Java with nine classes and 1000 LOC was created and used in both experiments. In the first experiment, there were three questions about "Long Method", "Long parameter List" and "Feature Envy" smells, and one question asked if the method should be refactored to remove the detected smells. In the second experiment, participants were only asked if some specific methods should be refactored. He found high rates of agreement for simple smells: long method and long parameter list. He found weaker agreement levels, however, concerning the feature envy smell and the decisions regarding refactoring. Mäntylä then tried to identify factors that influenced agreement in smell detection. He investigated both the influence of software metrics and demographic data as factors for smell detection agreement. His findings point to the influence of metrics.

Mäntylä and Lassenius (2006a) investigated why and when people think a code needs refactoring. They analyzed one of the experiments presented in (Mäntylä 2005) to investigate what drivers define the refactoring decisions. They applied a questionnaire to understand refactoring decisions. A taxonomy was defined after a qualitative analysis (coding process) of the textual answers. The authors also compared the results with an automatic detection tool. The most important driver was the size of a method. One of their important findings was that there was a conflict of opinions between the participants. The conflict was related to the assessed internal quality of the methods and the need to refactor them. Regarding the automatic detection, they found that some drivers are difficult or impossible to detect automatically, and some smells are better detected by experienced participants than by automatic means.

Schumacher et al. (2010) build on and extend Mäntylä and Lassenius's (2006a) work. They investigated the way professional software developers detect god class smells, and then compared these results to automatic classification. The study was done in a professional environment, with two real projects and two participants in each project. The research questions focused on "Evaluation of Human Performance" and "Evaluation of Automatic Classifiers". Participants were introduced to the god class smell in a short presentation and were asked to detect them in specific code pieces. During this task, they received a list of questions to help with the identification of god classes (the support questions adopted by us in this work), questions such as: "Does the class have more than one responsibility?". A process was designed to ensure that all participants performed the inspection of classes in a similar fashion. To evaluate the participant performance in the task, they used a "think-aloud" protocol (recorded as audio) and data collection forms. Coding was carried out to identify drivers and answers from the data collection form were used to evaluate time and agreement. Their main findings were: (1) there was low agreement among participants and (2) "misplaced method" was the strongest driver for god class detection. Related to the evaluation of automatic detection, their main findings were: (1) an automated metric-based pre-selection decreases the effort needed for manual code inspections and (2) automatic detection followed by manual review increases the overall confidence.

A study with aims similar to Schumacher's was presented by (Mäntylä et al. in 2004 and Mäntylä and Lassenius 2006b). Through a survey, they asked participants about 23 smells and used a scale from 1 (lack) to 7 (large presence) to evaluate the presence of smells in a piece of code. They received 12 completed questionnaires from 18 sent, all being sent to developers in a small software company. In one of the findings the authors declare: *"the use of smells for code evaluation purposes is hard due to conflicting perceptions of different evaluators"*.

It is important to note that these studies focused on specific human aspects. Basically, they investigated agreement and decision drivers adopted by participants. We built on the discussions considering two important aspects: the strategies adopted and the impact of visualization on each investigated aspect. Moreover, we proposed a discussion about how each of these aspects reflects the problem of conceptualization. We consider this our main contribution.

Conclusions

The purpose of this work was to find empirical evidence to evaluate the impact of personal conceptualization in god class detection. We were interested in understanding how differences in the perception of the concept affect identification. To do this, we performed a controlled experiment that extended another study focusing on investigating how developers detect god classes. Our experiment deepened and detailed some research questions previously presented and added new research questions. We addressed agreement among participants, and also among participants and an oracle, decision drivers, the impact of using a visualization tool, and strategies adopted by participants in god class detection. Our analysis considered how these elements are more related to personal choice than to the conceptual aspects in god class detection.

Our main finding is that the problem of god class detection is mainly related to conceptualization, i.e., agreeing on what a god class is, and which thresholds should be adopted. We believe that this type of problem is not solved by using other observation approaches, such as proposing a new metric or a new visual resource. We also believe this issue is transversal to other code smells. The smell detection problem would be better addressed if the community identifies concrete "good" examples of smells, providing standard definitions of them, teaching people about their conceptualization, and only then providing tools and methods (using metrics, thresholds or visualizations) to aid in their identification. Another important finding was that our work produced low agreement rates in code smell detection among the experiment participants, which is in accordance with other works.

To address the limitations of this study and to further develop it in this area, we are planning to replicate the experiment with more experienced participants to evaluate the impact of experience on the process. Other aspects that we may replicate as well is the evaluation of other software and other smells. To support replication we provide the experimental package[d]. The package contains forms, data and software.

Endnotes

[a] Eclipse IDE - http://www.eclipse.org/downloads/; Usage Data Collector (UDC) plug-in - http://www.eclipse.org/epp/usagedata/; Task Register - private; SourceMiner - visual support http://www.sourceminer.org/

[b] Web address of ProM tool: www.processmining.org

[c] Fleiss Kappa is a Cohen's Kappa variation that permits test with more than two raters

[d] Experimental package: http://wiki.dcc.ufba.br/LES/FindingGdoClassExperiment2012

Competing interests
The authors declare that they have no competing interests.

Authors' contributions
JAMS and MGM planned, performed and analyzed the experiment and drafted the manuscript. CPS supported some specific analysis. RLN also supported some analysis and drafted the manuscript. All authors read and approved the final manuscript.

Acknowledgements
We would like to thanks: Claudio Sant'Anna for allowing execution of the experiment in the Software Quality course; Bruno Carneiro for valuable participation in definition of oracle; and to participants for their availability and effort.

Author details
[1] Department of Technology, State University of Feira de Santana, Transnordestina avenue S/N - Feira de Santana - Bahia, Feira de Santana, Brazil. [2] Mathematics Institute, Federal University of Bahia, Ademar de Barros Avenue, S/N, Salvador - Bahia, Salvador, Brazil. [3] Fraunhofer Project Center for Software & Systems Eng., Ademar de Barros Avenue, S/N, Salvador - Bahia, Salvador, Brazil. [4] Information Technology Department, Federal Institute of Bahia, Araujo Pinho Avenue, 39, Salvador - Bahia, Salvador, Brazil.

References

Abbes M, Khomh F, Guéhéneuc Y-G, Antoniol G (2011) An empirical study of the impact of two antipatterns, blob and spaghetti code, on program comprehension. In: Proc. of 15th European Conference on Software Maintenance and Reengineering (CSMR). IEEE, Oldenburg, Germany, pp 181–190

Carneiro GF, Mendonça MG (2013) Sourceminer: A multi-perspective software visualization environment. In: Proceedings of 15th International Conference on Interprise Information Systems. ICEIS. SciTePress, Angers, France

Carneiro G, Silva M, Maia L, Figueiredo E, Sant'Anna C, Garcia A, Mendonça M (2010) Identifying code smells with multiple concern views. In: Proc. of 1th Brazilian Conference on Software: Theory and Practice, CBSOFT. IEEE, Salvador, Bahia, Brazil

Dybå T, Sjøberg DIK, Cruzes DS (2012) What works for whom, where, when, and why?: On the role of context in empirical software engineering. In: Proceedings of the ACM-IEEE International Symposium on Empirical Software Engineering and Measurement. ESEM '12. ACM, New York, NY, USA, pp 19–28

Feinstein AR, Cicchetti DV (1990) High agreement but low kappa: I. the problems of two paradoxes. J Clin Epidemiol 43(6):543–549

Finn RH (1970) A note on estimating the reliability of categorical data. Educ Psychol Meas 30:71–76

Fleiss JL (1971) Measuring nominal scale agreement among many raters. Psychol Bull 76(5):378–382

Fowler M (1999) Refactoring: Improving the Design of Existing Code. Addison-Wesley Longman Publishing Co., Inc., Boston, MA, USA

Fontana FA, Mariani E, Morniroli A, Sormani R, Tonello A (2011) An experience report on using code smells detection tools. In: Proc. of 4th Software Testing, Verification and Validation Workshops, ICSTW. IEEE, Berlin, Germany

Gwet K (2002) Kappa statistic is not satisfactory for assessing the extent of agreement between raters. Stat Methods Inter-rater Reliability Assess 1:1–5

Höst M, Regnell B, Wohlin C (2000) Using students as subjects— a comparative study of students and professionals in lead-time impact assessment. Empirical Softw Eng 5(3):201–214

Höst M, Wohlin C, Thelin T (2005) Experimental context classification: incentives and experience of subjects. In: Software Engineering, 2005. ICSE 2005. Proceedings. 27th International Conference On. IEEE, St Louis, Missouri, USA, pp 470–478

Johnson B, Shneiderman B (1991) Tree-maps: a space-filling approach to the visualization of hierarchical information structures. In: Visualization, 1991. Visualization '91, Proceedings., IEEE Conference On. IEEE, San Diego, CA, USA, pp 284–291

Landis JR, Koch GG (1977) The measurement of observer agreement for categorical data. Biometrics 33(1):159–174

Lanza M, Ducasse S (2003) Polymetric views - a lightweight visual approach to reverse engineering. Softw Eng IEEE Trans 29(9):782–795

Lanza M, Marinescu R, Ducasse S (2005) Object-Oriented Metrics in Practice. Springer, Secaucus, NJ, USA

Li W, Shatnawi R (2007) An empirical study of the bad smells and class error probability in the post-release object-oriented system evolution. J Syst Softw 80(7):1120–1128

Meyer B (1988) Object-Oriented Software Construction, 1st edn. Prentice-Hall, Inc., Upper Saddle River, NJ, USA

Moha N, Gueheneuc Y-G, Duchien L, Le Meur A-F (2010) Decor: A method for the specification and detection of code and design smells. IEEE Trans Softw Eng 36(1):20–36

Murphy-Hill E, Black AP (2010) An interactive ambient visualization for code smells. In: Proc. of the 5th ACM Symposium on Software Visualization, SOFTVIS. ACM, Salt Lake City, Utah, USA

Mäntylä M (2005) An experiment on subjective evolvability evaluation of object-oriented software: explaining factors and interrater agreement. In: Proc. of the 4th International Syimposium on Empirical Software Engineering, ISESE. IEEE, Noosa Heads, Australia

Mäntylä MV, Lassenius C (2006a) Drivers for software refactoring decisions. In: Proceedings of the International Symposium on Empirical Software Engineering, ISESE. ACM, Rio de Janeiro, Brazil

Mäntylä M, Lassenius C (2006b) Subjective evaluation of software evolvability using code smells: An empirical study. Empirical Softw Eng 11(3):395–431

Mäntylä M, Vanhanen J, Lassenius C (2004) Bad smells - humans as code critics. In: 20th IEEE International Conference on Software MaintenanceICSM 2004, ICSM. IEEE, Chicago Illinois, USA

Olbrich S, Cruzes DS, Basili V, Zazworka N (2009) The evolution and impact of code smells: a case study of two open source systems. In: Proc. of the 3rd International Symposium on Empirical Software Engineering and Measurement, ESEM. IEEE, Lake Buena Vista, Florida, USA

Olbrich SM, Cruzes DS, Sjoberg DIK (2010) Are all code smells harmful? a study of god classes and brain classes in the evolution of three open source systems. In: Proc. of the IEEE International Conference on Software Maintenance, ICSM. IEEE, Timisoara, Romania

Padilha J, Figueiredo E, Sant'Anna C, Garcia A (2013) Detecting god methods with concern metrics: An exploratory study. In: Proceedings of the 7th Latin-American Workshop on Aspect-Oriented Software Development(LA-WASP), Co-allocated with CBSoft. IEEE, Brasília, Brazil

Parnin C, Görg C, Nnadi O (2008) A catalogue of lightweight visualizations to support code smell inspection. In: Proc. of the 4th Software Visualization, SOFTVIS. ACM, Herrsching am Ammersee, Germany

Powers DMW (2012) The Problem with Kappa. In: Proceedings of the 13th Conference of the European Chapter of the Association for Computational Linguistics, EACL '12, Stroudsburg, PA, USA, pp 345–355

Rapu D, Ducasse S, Girba T, Marinescu R (2004) Using history information to improve design flaws detection. In: Proc. of 8th European Conference on Software Maintenance and Reengineering, CSMR. IEEE, Tampere, Finland

Riel AJ (1996) Object-Oriented Design Heuristics, 1st edn. Addison-Wesley Longman Publishing Co., Inc., Boston, MA, USA

Santos JA, Mendonça M, Silva C (2013) An exploratory study to investigate the impact of conceptualization in god class detection. In: Proc of 17th International Conference on Evaluation and Assessment in Software Engineering, EASE. ACM, Porto de Galinhas, Brazil

Schumacher J, Zazworka N, Shull F, Seaman C, Shaw M (2010) Building empirical support for automated code smell detection. In: Proc. of the International Symposium on Empirical Software Engineering and Measurement, ESEM. ACM, Bolzano-Bozen, Italy

Simon F, Steinbruckner F, Lewerentz C (2001) Metrics based refactoring. In: Proc. of 5th European Conference on Software Maintenance and Reengineering, CSMR. IEEE, Lisbon, Portugal

Sjøberg DIK, Yamashita A, Anda BCD, Mockus A, Dyba T (2013) Quantifying the effect of code smells on maintenance effort. IEEE Trans Softw Eng 39(8):1144–1156

van der Aalst WMP (2011) Process mining: discovery, conformance and enhancement of business processes. 1st edn., p. 352. Springer, Berlin

Van Emden E, Moonen L (2002) Java quality assurance by detecting code smells. In: Proc. of the 9th Working Conference on Reverse Engineering, WCRE. IEEE, Washington, DC, USA

Vinson NG, Singer Ja (2008) A practical guide to ethical research involving humans. In: Shull F, Singer J, Søberg DIK (eds) Guide to Advanced Empirical Software Engineering. Springer, London, pp 229–256

Whitehurst GJ (1984) Interrater agreement for journal manuscript review. Am Psychol 39(1):22–28

Wohlin C, Runeson P, Höst M, Ohlsson MC, Regnell B, Wesslén A (2012) Experimentation in Software Engineering. p 250

Zhang M, Hall T, Baddoo N (2011) Code bad smells: A review of current knowledge. J Softw Maint Evol 23(3):179–202

9

Improvement of IT service processes: a study of critical success factors

Thaíssa Diirr[*] and Gleison Santos

* Correspondence:
thaissa.medeiros@uniriotec.br
Graduate Program in Informatics
(PPGI), Federal University of Rio de
Janeiro State (UNIRIO), Av. Pasteur,
458, Urca, CEP 22290-240 Rio de
Janeiro, RJ, Brazil

Abstract

Maturity models and Information Technology (IT) service management models guide the definition and improvement of service management processes. Known approaches include ITIL, COBIT, ISO/IEC 20000, CMMI-SVC, and MR-MPS-SV. The implementation of these models results in benefits such as: increased user and customer satisfaction with IT services; financial savings due to less rework and less time used, and improved resource management and usage; improved decision making and optimized risk; and better alignment based on the business focus. However, some organizations find it difficult to use the models. This paper presents a study in which we identified critical factors for success and failure of the improvement of IT service processes. By doing a systematic mapping study and by snowballing, we were able to identify factors such as: project implementation strategy; support, commitment, and involvement; processes; and internal and external resources. Also, we analyzed our results using grounded theory procedures in order to facilitate their understanding.

Keywords: Critical success factors; Improvement of IT service processes; IT service management

Introduction

A service is a way of delivering value to customers, while facilitating the achievement of the results they want to obtain without having to deal with unnecessary and risky costs (SEI, 2010; Cartlidge et al. 2007). An Information Technology (IT) service is a set of resources, whether IT or non-IT, perceived by the client as whole, and maintained by an IT provider. Such services aim to satisfy one or more needs of a client and support the strategic goals of his business (Magalhães and Pinheiro, 2007).

In order to achieve good performance for the service provider and satisfy the client, it is necessary to develop and improve the practices involved with the services (SEI, 2010). In such a context, maturity models and IT service management models have been developed to guide organizations in the definition and improvement of service management processes. For instance, some of the already known and disseminated approaches are: ITIL (von Bon 2011), COBIT (ICASA, 2012), ISO/IEC 20000 (ISO/IEC, 2009, 2010a, 2010b, 2011, 2012), CMMI-SVC (SEI, 2010), and MR-MPS-SV (SOFTEX, 2012).

Several research papers (SEI, 2010; Cartlidge et al. 2007; and ICASA, 2012) have pointed out a series of benefits derived from adopting and implementing service management processes; for example: an increase in satisfaction with the services for both clients and users, higher productivity, improvement in economy by reducing workload and increasing the use of management resources, improvement in decision making, greater alignment between IT and the business goals, and appropriate management of the IT risks. However, there are organizations that suffer difficulties during the implementation of projects related to the improvement of IT service processes, and consequently they do not succeed (Jäntti, 2010; Pollard and Cater-Steel, 2009; Sharifi et al. 2008).

According to Tan et al. (2007, 2009) and Pollard and Cater-Steel (2009), some factors can influence and contribute to the success of an implementation project related to the improvement of IT service processes. These critical success factors are key aspects that must be achieved in order for the business to succeed, and, if not well performed, will make the achievement of the missions and goals unlikely within a business or project (Rockart, 1979 apud Pollard and Cater-Steel, 2009). Critical failure factors, or risk factors, can put the improvement of the IT service processes at risk, resulting in implementation failure (Ghayekhloo et al. 2009; Wan et al. 2008).

Even though Montoni (2010) consolidated critical success factors for the implementation of software processes through a systematic mapping study, we are not aware of a similar study having been performed in the field of IT services. Consequently, the goal of this paper is to identify critical success and failure factors in initiatives for process improvement in the field of IT services. Such information can aid organizations, that are willing to improve their IT services processes, to create implementation strategies with a higher chance of achieving success.

Besides this opening section, this paper presents seven more sections. In Section "Models for improvement of IT service processes" we present the theoretical background for improvement of IT service processes. In Section "Critical factors in improvement of IT service processes" we present a literature review of critical success factors, while in Section "Techniques for reference searching and for data analysis" we provide a discussion on the techniques for reference searching and data analysis used within our study. In Section "Protocol of the systematic mapping and snowballing", we describe the protocol for performing our study; in Section "Results from the systematic mapping study and snowballing" we provide the results from these studies; in Section "Comparison of critical factors in software process improvement" we present a comparison of the critical factors in software process improvement; and finally, in Section "Conclusions", we provide final remarks regarding this work.

Review

Models for improvement of IT service processes

The governance of IT services seeks to avoid the occurrence of problems in the delivery and operation of the services provided, in order to guarantee that their quality is perceived by clients and users (Magalhães and Pinheiro, 2007). Thus, many models for maturity and management of IT service processes have been proposed, which include approaches such as ITIL (von Bon 2011), COBIT (ICASA, 2012), ISO/IEC 20000 (ISO/IEC, 2009, 2010a, 2010b, 2011, 2012), CMMI-SVC (SEI, 2010), and MR-MPS-SV (SOFTEX, 2012). In the following paragraphs we provide a review of these models.

The Information Technology Infrastructure Library (ITIL) is a framework for better IT service management practices. It is composed of five books that cover the lifecycle of a service, including: business requirements analysis, design, migration to the operational environment, operation and improvement. The *Service Strategy* book guides service providers to build a strategy for delivering and managing services to support business requirements, while the *Service Design* book guides the design of appropriate IT services by considering business objectives. The *Service Transition* book offers guidance to ensure that service releases are implemented successfully into supported environments, and the *Service Operation* book guides the delivery of services to business users and customers. Finally, the *Continuous Service Improvement* book offers guidance for achieving improvements in service quality, operational efficiency, and business continuity, as well as to ensure the alignment of the service portfolio and business needs (von Bon 2011).

Control Objectives for Information and related Technology (COBIT) is a framework of good practices for effective governance and management over enterprise IT, that is based on five principles (meeting stakeholder's needs; covering the enterprise end-to-end; applying a single integrated framework; enabling a holistic approach; and separating governance from management) and seven enablers (principles, policies and frameworks; processes; organizational structures; culture, ethics and behavior; information; services, infrastructure and applications; and people, skills and competencies). The COBIT process reference model subdivides the IT-related practices and activities into two main areas: governance and management. The governance domain is: Evaluate, Direct, and Monitor; while the four management domains are: Align, Plan, and Organize; Build, Acquire, and Implement; Deliver, Service, and Support; and Monitor, Evaluate, and Assess (ICASA, 2012).

ISO/IEC 20000 is an IT service management standard that is composed of five parts: ISO/IEC 20000–1, ISO/IEC 20000–2, ISO/IEC TR 20000–3, ISO/IEC TR 20000–4, and ISO/IEC TR 20000–5. ISO/IEC 20000–1 specifies the requirements for planning, establishing, implementing, operating, monitoring, reviewing, maintaining, and improving the service management system (ISO/IEC, 2011). ISO/IEC 20000–2 and ISO/IEC TR 20000–5 present practices and an example of a management plan to achieve the requirements, respectively (ISO/IEC, 2012, 2010b). ISO/IEC TR 20000–3 provides guidelines for defining the scope, applicability, and conformity demonstration of the service management system (ISO/IEC, 2009). Finally, ISO/IEC TR 20000–4 describes a process reference model for service management, derived from the requirements described in ISO/IEC 20000–1 (ISO/IEC, 2010a).

The Capability Maturity Model for Services (CMMI-SVC) is a maturity model that focuses on companies supplying services and covers required activities for establishing, delivering, and managing services. Thus, there are two incremental paths that can be followed in order to achieve the process improvement: (a) Continuous, in which there is an improvement in an individual process or group of processes that are chosen by the organization; and (b) Staged, in which there is an improvement of a set of related processes already defined by the model. The Continuous representation allows the achievement of capability levels for the chosen process, while the Staged representation allows the organization to achieve evolutionary maturity levels. The capability levels are: (0) incomplete, (1) executed, (2) managed, and (3) defined. The maturity levels are:

(1) initial, (2) managed, (3) defined, (4) quantitatively managed, and (5) optimizing (SEI, 2010).

The Reference Model for Improvement in Service Processes or MR-MPS-SV (acronym derived from *Modelo de Referência de Melhoria de Processos de Serviços* in Portuguese) is a Brazilian maturity model for IT service provider companies which was created as part of the MPS.BR Program (Santos et al. 2012). The MR-MPS-SV focuses on microenterprises and small to medium-sized companies, and presents seven maturity levels, progressing from G to A: (G) partially managed, (F) managed, (E) partially defined, (D) widely defined, (C) defined, (B) quantitatively managed, and (A) optimizing. The division into seven levels enables the implementation and adequate assessment of microenterprises and small to medium-sized companies. Also, it can increase the visibility of the process improvement results in a shorter amount of time (SOFTEX, 2012).

Critical factors in improvement of IT service processes

Some research papers describe perceived critical success or failure factors during the implementation or improvement of IT service processes in provider organizations. For instance, Cater-Steel et al. (2006) present a case study with five organizations that implemented ITIL and, as a result, factors with a positive influence were identified; for example: support from managers to exert pressure towards change, engagement of the affected people, communication of results, reengineering of business processes, marketing campaigns to enhance acceptance and understanding, and the development of the people involved. Besides the above factors, the authors identified factors that had a negative influence; for example, lack of support from managers and resistance to cultural change.

Hochstein et al. (2005) present a case study involving six European companies that finished a project which involved implementing the ITIL. In their study they identified success factors such as employee support, understanding of service oriented processes, dissemination of quick gains, marketing campaigns to enhance acceptance and understanding, management support to exert pressure towards change, and training on a larger scale. They also identified failure factors such as the lack of understanding of the need for new processes.

Pollard and Cater-Steel (2009) compare critical factors that have a positive influence, which were identified in the literature, with factors related to the success of organizations working towards the improvement of IT service processes. Thus, some factors described in the literature were confirmed while others were added; for example, support from senior managers, training of employees, interdepartmental communication and collaboration, and use of external consulting and adequate tools. Wan et al. (2008) analyzed cases, visited companies, and reviewed the literature in order to study factors which have a negative influence on improvement initiatives. They verified 20 critical factors and, by analyzing the causal relationships among them, identified six root risk factors: (a) unclear project goals, (b) inadequate and ineffective communication between the teams, (c) senior leaders do not care about the project, (d) vague business strategy, (e) qualified team members leave the company, and (f) planning and designing of IT infrastructure are unreasonable.

The authors show that there is no consensus regarding which factors are capable of influencing the success of improvement initiatives for IT service processes. Montoni

(2010) presented a systematic mapping study that identified and consolidated critical factors that affect initiatives for improvement of software processes. He identified 12 critical factors and, associated with these factors, he identified 25 properties of critical factors for success. Moreover, in his study, he identified 59 categories for findings with a positive and negative influence — these categories characterize either the presence or absence of a property. The factors of "Processes"; "Support, commitment and involvement"; and "Skills of the organization's members"; cited by Montoni (2010) described almost 50% of the perceived occurrences and, therefore, were considered to be the most critical factors for achieving success in an improvement initiative for software processes. Furthermore, the other set of factors — "Implementation strategy for software process improvement ", "Resources", "Awareness of the benefits resulting from the process improvement implementation", "Organizational structure", "Conciliation of interests", and "Policy for recognition of collaboration in the improvement process" — were considered to be less critical due to the medium number of occurrences. Finally, due to the lower number of occurrences, the following factors were considered to be less influencing factors: "Respect for the consultants from the organization's members", "Acceptance of changes", and "Motivation and satisfaction of the organization's members". Although the above research provides an insight into success and failure factors in software process improvement initiatives, we are not aware of any similar work about critical success factors in the field of IT services. Therefore, this paper goes one step further by performing a study of this area. In the next section, we describe the techniques we applied in order to perform this study.

Techniques for reference searching and for data analysis

In our study, we used certain techniques to aid our investigation of critical factors. Through a systematic mapping study and snowballing we searched for literature references that contained reports of improvement initiatives in IT service provider organizations. Then, after collecting data from the identified papers, we used grounded theory (GT) procedures to perform analyses. In the following subsections, we will describe each technique.

A. Systematic mapping study

A systematic literature review (SLR) is a way of searching, evaluating, and interpreting the relevant papers for specific research questions, research areas, or topics of interest (Kitchenham, 2004). According to Kitchenham (2004), there are three main stages in the execution of an SLR:

- Review planning: In this stage, the researcher creates a review protocol containing the research question, search terms, paper selection criteria, and the data extraction strategy.
- Execution of the review: In this stage, the researchers perform a search of the databases, document the executed stages, and select the papers that possess evidence related to the research question. Then, they evaluate the quality of the papers and extract, monitor, and synthesize the data contained within the papers.
- Reporting of results: In this stage, the researchers write a report or document containing the results and findings from the SLR.

Systematic mapping studies use the same basic methodology as an SLR; however, they aim to identify all the research related to a specific topic and classify the primary research papers in that specific domain, rather than addressing the specific questions that a conventional SLR addresses (Kitchenham et al. 2010). This paper presents the protocol of a systematic mapping study based on the SLR protocol described by Kitchenham (2004).

B. Snowballing

Snowballing is a method for searching papers in the literature and it involves three steps (Jalali and Wohlin, 2012):

1. Gathering an initial set of papers from key journals and/or conferences related to the research topic;

2. Analyzing the references of relevant papers identified during step 1, in order to search for new important papers (backward snowballing);

3. Identifying and analyzing papers that cite the already selected papers (forward snowballing).

The analysis of the references is iterative until there are no new relevant references identified. It is worth noting that there are authors who suggest using snowballing starting from the references of papers that are identified in an SLR, as well as from the papers that are identified in the databases (Jalali and Wohlin, 2012). By complementing a review with snowballing, we intend to identify more relevant papers, increase the number of papers about the topic of interest, and complement and enrich the results presented by Diirr and Santos (2013).

C. Grounded theory

Grounded Theory (GT) is a scientific method that uses data collection and analysis procedures to create, elaborate, and validate substantive theories about phenomena and social processes (Bandeira de Mello and Cunha, 2003). A theory is a set of concepts that is related by relationship sentences and which, together, constitute a schema that can explain or predict a phenomenon. In other words, theories are derived from data that is systematically unified and analyzed through an investigative process (Strauss and Corbin, 1998).

Strauss and Corbin (1998) propose the following types of coding procedures for the GT method:

• Open coding: This is an analytical process in which concepts and categories are identified, and their properties and dimensions are discovered in the data. Thus, the data are divided, analyzed, and compared, and their central ideas are represented as concepts that allow the grouping of similar and significant events, incidents, actions, and objects in the data.

• Axial coding: This is the process of relating the categories and subcategories to form more precise and complete explanations about the phenomenon. The categories are developed systematically and then related so that they are more in-depth and more structured.

• Selective coding: This is the process of integrating and refining the theory by organizing the categories around a central explanatory concept that expresses the essence of the study's process. Also, possible flaws in the theory are solved and more categories are formulated.

Other authors have used GT to collect and analyze data in the context of papers related to improvement initiatives for software processes (Montoni and Rocha, 2010, 2011; Coleman and O'Connor 2008). Section VI.B explains how the GT method was applied to this work.

Protocol of the systematic mapping and snowballing

The goal of this systematic mapping study follows the paradigm of the Goal Question Metric (GQM) method (Basili et al. 1994) and consists of: *Analyzing* papers containing reports about improvement initiatives in IT service provider organizations, *with the purpose of* identifying and analyzing critical success and failure factors, *in relation to* the influence on the success or failure of improvement initiatives for IT service processes, *from the point of* view of organizations that implement improvements in IT service processes and the IT practitioners who are involved in such initiatives, and *in the context of* companies that provide IT services to implement improvements in their IT service processes.

As a result, we defined two research questions to be answered in order to achieve the described goal:

1. Question 1 Which factors have a positive influence on improvement initiatives for IT service processes?
2. Question 2 Which factors have a negative influence on improvement initiatives for IT service processes?

Regarding the scope of this research, we adopted the following criteria to select the search sources: (a) the source must be related to the topic being investigated; and (b) the source must either belong to one of the editors listed on the CAPES Journal Web Site (Portal de Periódicos da CAPES[a] in Portuguese), which is a virtual library that collects and makes available thousands of international scientific publications, or the source must be a symposium, conference, workshop, or similar, that is supported by the Brazilian Computer Society (SBC) — Sociedade Brasileira de Computação in Portuguese — and related to software quality (there is no specific event for IT services supported by SBC), in order to include Brazilian conferences not indexed by international search engines. It is worth noting that this research is restricted to analysis of the papers that were available until the date of its execution (May 2013). Also, we researched papers in English, since it is a language that has been widely adopted in the research area, and Portuguese, since this research was performed in Brazil and we wanted to consider papers published in national conferences.

We selected the Compendex and Scopus digital libraries because, based on other systematic mapping studies we have conducted, we consider their search engines to have good functionality and coverage. Furthermore, we considered that the imminent execution of the snowballing would reduce the risk of not considering other digital libraries such as IEEE and ACM. Also, we selected Brazilian conferences including the Brazilian Symposium of Software Quality (*Simpósio Brasileiro de Qualidade de Software* or *SBQS* in Portuguese) and the MPS Annual Workshop (*Workshop Anual do MPS* or *WAMPS* in Portuguese).

We used the following search string: (itil OR cobit OR "iso/iec 20000" OR cmmi-svc OR mps-sv OR "it service management" OR itsm OR "service oriented it management"

OR "gestão de serviços de ti") AND (implementation OR implantação OR adoption OR adoção OR "process improvement" OR "melhoria de processo") AND (factor OR fator OR factors OR fatores OR strategy OR estratégia OR strategies OR estratégias). The search string included synonymous terms in Portuguese because we considered Brazilian conferences in this research. The first set of terms refers to the IT service models described in Section "Models for improvement of IT service processes". Also, it uses the terms "IT service management", "itsm", "service oriented it management" and the Portuguese term "gestão de serviços de TI" to collect papers that either do not specifically mention one of these models, or that use other types of models. The second set of terms restricts the results to papers that report cases of the implementation/adoption of such models or cases regarding process improvement using those models. Finally, the third set of terms limits the results to papers that mention factors or strategies in the implementation or improvement of the cited processes. It is worth noting that the terms "(factor OR factors OR strategy OR strategies)" were used by Montoni (2010) for mapping the critical factors in software process improvement, thus being validated in such a context.

The selection of papers was done in three stages:

1. Selection and preliminary cataloging of the collected sources from the search string;
2. First relevant selection filter for the publications. This filter was designed by analyzing the abstract and applying the SC1 selection criterion — the paper must provide information about factors that have an influence on the success and failure of the improvement of the IT service processes;
3. Second relevant selection filter for the publications. This filter was performed by reading the complete text of the paper and applying the following selection criteria: SC2 — the paper must provide evidence that the presented factors originated from the analysis of studies, research, or case reports on improvement initiatives for service processes; SC3 — the paper must provide information about the factors that have an influence on the improvement initiatives for IT service processes, but not on the processes themselves; and SC4 — the paper must not report identical results from another study that have already been selected during the mapping.

After the third selection stage, we obtained a set of relevant papers. However, in order to complement the results obtained, we applied snowballing procedures to add any relevant papers that had not been identified during the exploration of the search string, but which were referenced by or referred to in any of the papers initially identified. Consequently, the following inclusion criteria were applied: IC1 — the paper is referenced or referred to in one of the papers that was retrieved and selected from the three selection stages; and IC2 — the paper satisfies the criteria from the second and third selection stages (SC1, SC2, SC3, and SC4). For each paper considered to be relevant, the following data was extracted: (a) publishing information, which consists of the title, author(s), date published, and publishing source; (b) abstract of the paper; (c) list of factors that positively influence improvement initiatives for IT service processes; (d) a list of factors that negatively influence improvement initiatives for IT services processes; and (e) origin of the identified factors.

After selecting and extracting data from the papers, we analyzed the data using GT procedures. Thus, we managed to perform two types of analysis — qualitative and quantitative. The qualitative analysis resulted in graphs generated through GT procedures and the discussion regarding the research questions, whereas the quantitative analysis resulted in: (a) a list of findings with a positive influence and the total number of occurrences; (b) a list of findings with a negative influence and the total number of occurrences; and (c) the list of critical success factors and the total number of occurrences.

Results from the systematic mapping study and snowballing

A. Research execution

After establishing the research protocol, we performed the systematic mapping study in May 2013. During the first selection stage, we used the search string in the Compendex and Scopus search engines. Also, we reviewed the papers from national conferences (SBQS and WAMPS). As a result, we identified 65 papers in Compendex and 54 papers in Scopus (41 papers were available in both digital libraries). None were identified in SBQS or WAMPS.

During the second selection stage, we read the abstract from each of the retrieved papers. Then, using the SC1 selection criterion we selected 14 papers. In the third stage, we read the full text of 13 of the 14 selected papers — one of the selected papers could not be downloaded. From this set of papers, one did not meet the SC3 selection criterion because it only presented factors that influenced the execution of the incident management process. Also, there were another 4 papers which did not meet the SC2 selection criterion, because they derived factors from the COBIT framework controls or a literature review, or did not present a description of the study from which the factors were found. Thus, using a systematic mapping study, we selected 8 papers which met the selection criteria.

Besides this initial set of analyzed papers, we read the title and abstract of papers that were retrieved using snowballing procedures. As a result, 12 papers were selected in the second selection process stage. In the third stage, since one paper was unavailable for download, we read the complete text of 11 of the 12 selected papers. After that, 3 papers did not meet the SC2 selection criterion, because they derived factors from a literature review. Also, one paper was discarded because it did not meet the SC3 selection criterion — it presented factors influencing IT service maintenance and operation — and one paper did not meet the SC4 selection criterion because the content about risk factors was identical to that presented in other papers. Thus, using snowballing, we were able to identify 6 papers which met the IC1 and IC2 inclusion criteria. Table 1 shows the 14 papers (8 using the systematic mapping study and 6 using snowballing) that were selected as a basis for the analysis of critical factors in the improvement of IT service processes.

From this set of papers we identified critical factors in two different approaches. The factors that were derived from empirical studies and researches were derived directly, whereas, if the reviewed paper described a case study of improvement initiatives, besides identifying factors that were explicitly indicated in the paper, we identified further factors from the content of the described cases. Also, some papers did not provide a specific section

Table 1 Final set of selected papers after performing the third selection step

Author(s) Year	Paper title	Name of the conference or journal in which it was published	Type of method in which the paper appeared (systematic mapping or snowballing)
Cater-Steel 2009	IT Service Departments Struggle to Adopt a Service-Oriented Philosophy	International Journal of Information Systems in the Service Sector	Snowballing
Cater-Steel and Pollard 2008	Conflicting views on ITIL implementation: managed as a project – or business as usual?	Information Resources Management Association (IRMA) International Conference	Snowballing
Cater-Steell and Tan 2005	Implementation of IT Infrastructure Library (ITIL) in Australia: Progress and success factors	IT Governance International Conference	Snowballing
Cater-Steel et al. 2006	Transforming IT service management- The ITIL impact	Australasian Conference on Information Systems, ACIS	Systematic Mapping
Hochstein and Brenner 2006	Implementation of service-oriented IT management: An empirical study on Swiss IT organizations	International Conference on Service Systems and Service Management, ICSSSM	Systematic Mapping
Hochstein et al. 2005	Service-oriented IT management: benefit, cost and success factors	European Conference of Information Systems, ECIS	Systematic Mapping
Iden 2009	Implementing IT service management: lessons learned from a university IT department	Information science reference	Snowballing
Iden and Langeland 2010	Setting the stage for a successful ITIL adoption: A Delphi Study of IT Experts in the Norwegian armed forces	Information systems management	Systematic mapping
Junior and Andrade 2010	Fatores Críticos de Sucesso e Benefícios da Adoção do Modelo ITIL numa Empresa de Telecomunicações	VII Simpósio de Excelência em Gestão e Tecnologia	Snowballing
Pollard and Cater-Steel 2009	Justifications, strategies, and critical success factors in successful ITIL implementations in U.S. and Australian companies: An exploratory study	Information Systems Management	Systematic mapping
Tan et al. 2009	Implementing it service management: A case study focusing on critical success factors	Journal of Computer Information Systems	Systematic Mapping
Tan et al. 2007	Implementing centralised IT service management: Drawing lessons from the public sector	Australasian Conference on Information Systems, ACIS	Systematic Mapping
Wan and Liang 2012	Risk Management of IT Service Management Project Implementation with Killer Assumptions	Technology and Investment	Snowballing
Wan et al. 2008	Empirical analysis on risk factors of IT service management project implementation	International Conference on Wireless Communications, Networking and Mobile Computing, WiCOM	Systematic Mapping

describing factors, and, therefore, we extracted factors from other sections such as lessons learned, discussions, and conclusions.

B. Analysis of the results

Using the data obtained from the review we were able to answer the research questions we defined above. We initially analyzed the obtained data using the open coding processes from the GT method. First, we identified quotes from the text of the papers which indicated factors associated with critical success or critical failure.

Table 2 Findings with a positive influence

Findings with a positive influence	Occurrences	Papers in which they were identified*
[Fi01] Existence of management support	13	[1–6],[8–12]
[Fi02] Commitment from the people involved in the project	6	[1],[4–8]
[Fi03] Dissemination of results	6	[4–8]
[Fi04] Adequate order for implementing the processes	2	[4],[8]
[Fi05] Project advertisement	9	[3–6],[8],[11]
[Fi06] People with the necessary knowledge are involved in the project	19	[2–10],[12]
[Fi07] Allocation of resources to the project	6	[2],[4–6]
[Fi08] Collaboration and communication in the organization	3	[2],[7],[10]
[Fi09] Focus on the customer	2	[10],[12]
[Fi10] Favorable culture towards the project	9	[1],[3–5],[7–11]
[Fi11] Use of external consultants	2	[9],[10]
[Fi12] Use of appropriate tools	4	[2],[9],[10],[12]
[Fi13] Benefits management	3	[5],[11],[12]
[Fi14] Change management	1	[12]
[Fi15] Adequate management of the project	11	[2],[5],[7–9],[11],[12]
[Fi16] Existing processes are adequate	11	[1],[2],[4],[5],[7],[8],[10],[12]
[Fi17] Good relationships with suppliers and consultants	2	[11],[12]
[Fi18] Adequate monitoring and control of the processes	7	[2],[4–6],[8],[12]
[Fi19] Adequate management of the organization	2	[1],[5]
Total	**118**	-

*[1] Cater-Steel (2009); [2] Cater-Steel and Pollard (2008); [3] Cater-Steell and Tan (2005); [4] Cater-Steel et al. (2006); [5] Hochstein and Brenner (2006) [6] Hochstein et al. (2005); [7] Iden (2009); [8] Iden and Langeland (2010); [9] Junior and Andrade (2010); [10] Pollard and Cater-Steel (2009); [11] Tan et al. (2009); [12] Tan et al. (2007).

Then, we also identified if there were similarities or differences among these quotes. From this initial analysis, we classified and separated our findings according to the subject and the type of influence it has (positive or negative) on improvement initiatives. These classifications were called "findings with a positive influence" and "findings with a negative influence", and yielded 33 categories in total. Table 2 and Table 3 show the findings with a positive and negative influence, respectively, and indicate in which paper these findings were located. Additionally, Table 4 and Table 5 present occurrences of some findings.

We performed the axial coding procedure in two iterations in order to establish more abstract categories for the codes of the findings. In the first iteration, the codes for the findings were grouped into 22 categories called "Properties of critical success factors". These properties group similar findings that differ only by the type of influence (positive or negative). Table 6 shows the occurrences of all properties of critical factors, grouping the 154 occurrences of findings within the papers. This total is the raw data found in the selected papers and initially grouped in the 33 findings. The findings grouped for each property are indicated in the same table. Additionally, during the second iteration, we aggregated the categories of the properties in a more abstract manner. Thus, there was a total of 8 categories of critical success factors that group properties related to a common topic: [Fa01] Processes; [Fa02] Support, commitment and involvement; [Fa03] Internal and

Table 3 Findings with a negative influence

Findings with a negative influence	Occurrences	Papers in which they were identified*
[Fi20] Lack of management support	1	[4]
[Fi21] Lack of commitment from the people involved in the project	2	[13],[14]
[Fi22] Resistance to change	5	[4],[5],[6]
[Fi23] Lack of appropriate tools	1	[4]
[Fi24] Inadequate processes	2	[14]
[Fi25] Inadequate order for implementing the processes	1	[14]
[Fi26] People involved in the project don't have the necessary knowledge	2	[14]
[Fi27] Problems in the understanding and the scale of the project	5	[13],[14]
[Fi28] Lack of collaboration and communication	3	[13],[14]
[Fi29] Problems in the allocation of resources to the project	3	[13],[14]
[Fi30] Problems in the management of the organization	5	[13],[14]
[Fi31] Difficulties in reaching agreement among the stakeholders	2	[14]
[Fi32] Difficulties with the improvement framework used	2	[5],[6]
[Fi33] Problems in project management	2	[13],[14]
Total	**36**	-

*[4] Cater-Steel et al. (2006); [5] Hochstein and Brenner (2006); [6] Hochstein et al. (2005); [13] Wan and Liang (2012); [14] Wan et al. (2008).

external resources; [Fa04] Skills of the people involved in the project; [Fa05] Structure and culture within the organization; [Fa06] Implementation strategy for the improvement project; [Fa07] Collaboration, communication and conciliation of the people involved; and [Fa08] Strategies for the advertisement of the project and the publication of its results. Table 7 shows the number of occurrences of critical success factors and the properties grouped for each factor.

In this analysis it was not necessary to perform the selective coding, since we were able to comprehend the critical success factors after the open and axial coding. In order to perform the selective coding it is necessary to validate all the categories and their relationships until we are able to achieve the theoretical saturation. This saturation indicates that the explanatory power of the theory is approximately null when more evidence is collected (Bandeira de Mello and Cunha, 2003). It is also important to note that, in order to perform the selective coding, it is necessary to collect more data, thus it is necessary for more papers to be published in the coming years. Figure 1 summarizes the analysis process.

After identifying all the categories, we counted the number of occurrences in the analyzed papers, aiming to identify which categories were the most cited. In order to establish relationships between the identified categories, we created a graph for each critical success factor. We used the connector "it is a property of" to relate the category codes of properties of critical success factors with the category codes of critical success factors. Also, we used the connectors "it is evidence of the presence of" and "it is evidence of the absence of" to relate the category codes of the findings with the category codes of properties of critical success factors. These connectors show a positive and negative variation, respectively, in the presence of a factor. Readers must take note that the codes presented in the graph are followed by two numbers which represent the groundness (foundation ground) and density

Table 4 Occurrences for some findings with a positive influence

Findings with a positive influence	Cater-Steel et al. (2006)	Hochstein et al. (2005)	Iden (2009)	Pollard and Cater-Steel (2009)	Tan et al. (2009)
[Fi06] People with the necessary knowledge are involved in the project	Basic training and development of the employees	Understanding of the service-oriented processes, implementing training on a large scale, encouraging the development of employees on a large scale	Training and specialization	Training and awareness of the employees	
[Fi01] Existence of management support	Management support to exert pressure over change	Management support to exert pressure		Support from high-level management	Support from high-level management
[Fi05] Project advertisement	Marketing campaigns for acceptance and understanding	Exhibition of quick gains to demonstrate service management utility; marketing campaigns for acceptance and understanding			Project Champion: Senior management who defend the project
[Fi02] Commitment from the people involved in the project	Engagement of the affected employees	Support from employees	High level of participation of the team in the change processes		
[Fi10] Favorable culture towards the project	Cultural change of the IT team, users, and clients		Acknowledgement of the need to improve the management of the employees	Creation of adequate culture for the ITIL	Change in the organization's culture
[Fi16] Existing processes are adequate	Reengineering of the business processes		Definition of a standard and flexible methodology for change processes	Definition of processes before tools	
[Fi15] Adequate management of the project			Production of deliveries in group meetings; definition of short schedule for the projects		Execution and governance of the project
[Fi18] Adequate monitoring and control of the processes	Continuous improvement to guarantee sustainable success	Continuous improvement to guarantee sustainable success for the project			

Table 5 Occurrences of some findings with negative influence

Findings with a negative influence	Cater-Steel et al. (2006)	Hochstein and Brenner (2006)	Wan and Liang (2012)	Wan et al. (2008)
[Fi27] Problems in the understanding and the scale of the project			The goals of the project are not clear	The goals of the project are not clear; analysis of the business demand is not sufficient; frequent changes in the client's demands; and the scale of the project is too big, which increases management difficulty
[Fi30] Problems in the management of the organization			Planning and design of the IT infrastructure are not reasonable; the company's business strategy is vague	Senior employees are imprudent when making decisions; the company's business strategy is vague; planning and design of the IT infrastructure are not reasonable
[Fi29] Problems in the allocation of resources to the project			High turnover of team members	Highly qualified members leave the team; there are not enough fundamental resources; vague definition of the responsibilities of the teams on both sides (client and provider)
[Fi22] Resistance to change	Resistance to cultural changes	Lack of acceptance; lack of understanding of the need for new processes		
[Fi21] Lack of commitment from the people involved in the project			Indifference from the leader	Senior employees do not care about the implementation of the project

(theoretical density) of the code. The groundness is the number of times that the code was mentioned in the papers, while the density describes the number of relationships that the code has with other codes. Figures 2, 3, 4, and 5 show the graphs with the categories and relationships regarding the factors: [Fa01] Processes; [Fa02] Support, commitment and involvement; [Fa03] Internal and external resources; and [Fa07] Collaboration, communication, and conciliation of the people involved. The figures present the properties related to the factor and the findings with a positive and negative influence that were grouped in each property. For instance, in Figure 1 it can be seen that the type of finding with a positive influence — [Fi16] Existing processes are adequate — and the type of finding with a negative influence — [Fi24] Inadequate processes — show the presence and absence of the property "[P11] Process adequacy", respectively. Furthermore, the properties "[P08] Processes monitoring and control", "[P11] Process adequacy", and "[P18] Adequate order for the implementation of the processes", are related to the factor "[Fa01] Processes".

Comparison of critical factors in software process improvement

When analyzing the critical factors identified by Montoni (2010) for software process improvement, and comparing them with the critical factors for service processes, we managed to identify some similarities and differences. In fact, the factors "Processes", "Support, commitment and involvement", and "Skills of the people involved in the

Table 6 Occurrences of properties of critical success factors

Properties of critical success factors	Occurrences	Related findings
[P01] Management support	14	[Fi01],[Fi20]
[P02] Experience and skills of those involved in the project	21	[Fi06],[Fi26]
[P03] Adequate management when running the project	13	[Fi15],[Fi33]
[P04] Project advertisement	9	[Fi05]
[P05] Allocation of resources to the project	9	[Fi07],[Fi29]
[P06] Favorable culture towards the project	14	[Fi10],[Fi22]
[P07] Adequacy of tool support	5	[Fi12],[Fi23]
[P08] Monitoring and control of the processes	7	[Fi18]
[P09] Collaboration and communication within the organization	6	[Fi08],[Fi28]
[P10] Focus on the client	2	[Fi09]
[P11] Process adequacy	13	[Fi16],[Fi24]
[P12] Relationships with providers and consultants	2	[Fi17]
[P13] Dissemination of results	6	[Fi03]
[P14] Existence of an external consultant	2	[Fi11]
[P15] Adequate management of benefits	3	[Fi13]
[P16] Adequate management of changes	1	[Fi14]
[P17] Commitment from the people involved in the project	8	[Fi02],[Fi21]
[P18] Adequate order for the implementation of the processes	3	[Fi04],[Fi25]
[P19] Adequate understanding and scale of the project	5	[Fi27]
[P20] Adequate management of the organization	7	[Fi19],[Fi30]
[P21] Agreement among the people involved	2	[Fi31]
[P22] Adequate framework for process improvement	2	[Fi32]
Total	**154**	-

project" or "Skills of the members of the organization", appear in both studies. In Montoni's (2010) study, these three factors were considered by the author to be the most important, due to the total number of occurrences in comparison with the other factors. In our study, two criteria were used to determine whether or not a factor is highly important: total number of occurrences and occurrences in all selected articles. Therefore, we considered highly important factors to be either the ones with a high number of occurrences in relation to other factors or the ones which occur in all

Table 7 Occurrences of critical success factors

Critical success factors	Occurrences	Related properties of critical success factors
[Fa01] Processes	23	[P08],[P11],[P18]
[Fa02] Support, commitment, and involvement	22	[P01],[P17]
[Fa03] Internal and external resources	16	[P05],[P07],[P14]
[Fa04] Skills of the people involved in the project	21	[P02]
[Fa05] Structure and culture within the organization	21	[P06], [P20]
[Fa06] Implementation strategy of the improvement project	24	[P03],[P15],[P16], [P19],[P22]
[Fa07] Collaboration, communication, and conciliation of the people involved	12	[P09],[P10],[P12],[P21]
[Fa08] Strategies for the advertisement of the project and the publication of its results	15	[P04],[P13]
Total	**154**	-

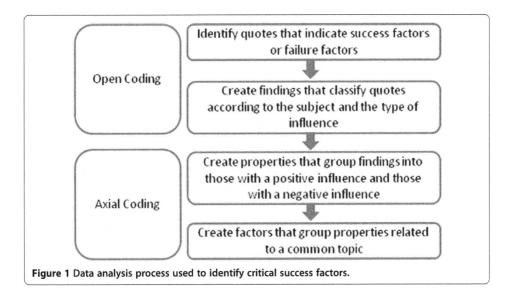

Figure 1 Data analysis process used to identify critical success factors.

selected articles. On the other hand, factors of medium or low importance are factors with a medium or low number of occurrences. Therefore, in terms of the number of occurrences, the factors "Processes" and "Support, commitment and involvement" were considered to be highly important, while the factor "Skills of the people involved in the project" would be a factor of medium importance. However, considering its appearance in all reviewed papers, the factor "Support, commitment and involvement" is considered to be the most critical. Also, in the present study, properties regarding skills of the members of the organization who implement the improvement, as well as the skills of the consultants, were grouped in the same factor. However, Montoni (2010) grouped the skills of the external consultants into the factor "Respect for the consultants by the organization's members" which also includes good relationships and trust between the organization and the consultants. This factor was not structured in our study and the properties related to the relationship among the people involved were grouped in the factor "Collaboration, communication and conciliation of the people involved". It is worth noting that the factor "Motivation and satisfaction of the members of the organization", which is indicated in Montoni's (2010) research, was also not structured in our analysis, since we only verified general properties about the commitment of the employees.

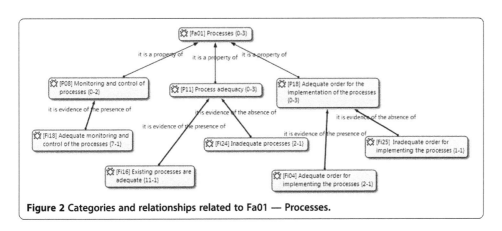

Figure 2 Categories and relationships related to Fa01 — Processes.

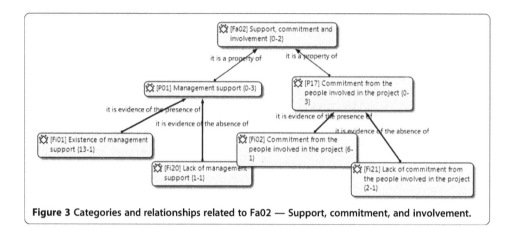

Figure 3 Categories and relationships related to Fa02 — Support, commitment, and involvement.

In this paper, the factor "Internal and external resources" was considered to be of low importance due to the total number of occurrences. This factor also considers the use of external consultants in the project. According to Montoni (2010), the factor "Resources" was evaluated as a factor of medium criticality. However, the properties related to the use of consultants were grouped in the factor "Skills of the members of the organization" which was evaluated by Montoni (2010) as a highly important factor.

In both studies there is a factor related to the management of the improvement implementation as a project. The factor "Software process improvement implementation strategy" defined by Montoni (2010) was considered to have a medium level of influence. However, in our study, the factor "Implementation strategy of the improvement project" was considered to be the factor with the greatest influence due to the number of occurrences. Also, in both studies there are factors that relate to the dissemination of the obtained results and the advertisement of the improvement project to the people involved. Thus, the factor "Strategies for the advertisement of the project and the publication of its results" was structured in our research and was considered to be of low criticality, while in Montoni's (2010) research the factor "Conscientization of the benefits of the implementation of the improvement processes" was considered to have a medium level of influence.

The factor "Structure and culture within the organization" was defined in our study as a factor with a medium level of influence and it is related to the management,

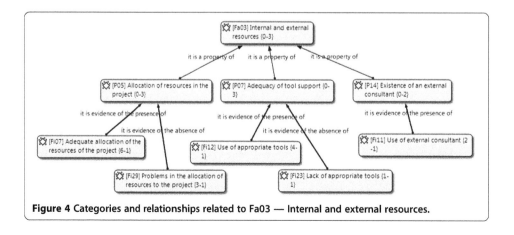

Figure 4 Categories and relationships related to Fa03 — Internal and external resources.

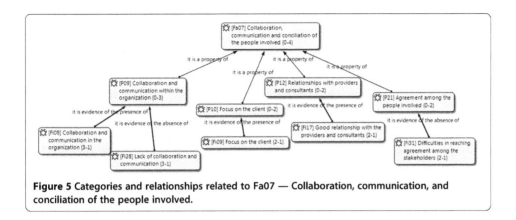

Figure 5 Categories and relationships related to Fa07 — Collaboration, communication, and conciliation of the people involved.

structure, planning, and cultural properties of the organization that is implementing the improvement project. Montoni (2010) presented the factors "Organization structure" and "Acceptance towards change", with a medium and low level of influence, respectively. Such factors are related to similar contexts (with the exception of culture in methodologies and processes, which was considered by the author in the factor "Processes").

Finally, in this paper, the factor "Collaboration, communication, and conciliation of the people involved" was considered to be of low criticality. The factors "Conciliation of interests" and "Policy for recognition of collaboration in the improvement process", which were defined by Montoni (2010) and considered to have a medium level of influence, contain similar issues (except for the relationship with the external consultants that was grouped by the author in the factor "Respect for the consultants by the members of the organization").

Conclusions

This paper described a study of critical success factors in improvement initiatives for IT service processes. We performed a systematic mapping study and snowballing and applied GT procedures for analysis purposes. By analyzing critical factors, we intend to assist organizations in developing strategies for the implementation of improvements for IT service processes, indicating features that could guide the success of such initiatives.

Some factors were considered to be more relevant and highlight the need for strategies for implementation of the improvement project which involve the execution and governance of the project, the management of benefits and changes, the understanding and the scale of the project, the adequacy of the improvement framework used, and management support and commitment of the people involved in the project.

We also identified other factors with less influence which relate to: organizational structure and culture (business strategy, planning, favorable culture towards the improvement project); experience and commitment of the people involved in the project; resources and team allocation; external consultants and tools of the project; strategies for the advertisement and acceptance of the project, and the dissemination of its results; and collaboration, communication and conciliation between the teams, clients, external consultants, and providers.

In this paper we also compared the identified factors with the critical factors of improvement initiatives for software processes. Despite some differences regarding the degree of importance, we perceived many similarities regarding the related context of the factors. Also, the identified factors indicate similar concerns that could be applied to both types (software and services) of improvement initiatives. However, there are still few reports regarding influencing factors for the improvement of IT service processes. The CMMI-SVC and the MR-MPS-SV are recent (released in 2009 and 2012, respectively) and their adoption, given the required time, could aid in the comprehension and implementation of improvements in these types of processes.

The use of snowballing reinforced the perceived critical success factors from the systematic mapping study and the positive and negative findings from the additional papers were able to be distributed into the 8 existing factor categories. Also, although some factors had a different number of occurrences and even changed between the categories for medium and low importance, the factors of "Processes" and "Implementation strategy of the improvement project" still had the highest number of occurrences after performing the snowballing. Furthermore, the factor "Support, commitment and involvement" continued to be the only one to appear in all selected publications, and its number of occurrences increased, evolving from a medium to a high level of criticality, which confirmed its relevance.

It is worth noting that, as a procedure for guaranteeing the quality of our research, another researcher, with a high level of experience in performing and reviewing similar studies, evaluated the protocol and its execution. We made adjustments and achieved a consensus regarding the performed analyses. Nevertheless, there are threats to the validity of our study. For instance, there are some papers that might not be available in the analyzed sources, and, therefore, might not have been considered during the systematic mapping study or snowballing (e.g., theses and dissertations). This can affect the generalization of our results, generating a threat to the external validity (Wohlin et al. 2000) of the study. Also, the composition of the search string can be a threat to the construction validity, since some papers might not contain the chosen terms. Such a threat was minimized by performing the snowballing, because it was not necessary for the selected papers to satisfy the search string. Moreover, using snowballing we could access papers that were indexed in sources other than the Scopus and Compendex digital libraries. Some of the selected papers were indexed in the IEEE, ACM, and DBLP, while others were not indexed in any of the main search bases. Another threat to the conclusion validity (Wohlin et al. 2000) is that some papers briefly describe the factors, or just mention them. Thus, having just a brief description of the factors in such papers can influence our understanding and the adequacy of the category to which they might belong. Finally, a threat to the internal validity (Wohlin et al. 2000) is the qualitative analysis of the summaries during the first selection stage of the papers, which, if not properly performed, could have resulted in us discarding relevant papers. However, we minimized this threat by performing this analysis from the point of view of two different researchers. In this case, we guaranteed that, in order to discard a paper, the researchers must agree that the provided information does not satisfy the inclusion criteria.

As a future work, we intend to execute a systematic mapping study and snowballing protocol again in the coming years in order to collect more data and achieve the theoretical saturation through GT selective coding. Furthermore, we intend to investigate the perception of the identified factors by the employees of the organizations that use IT service improvement models. Thus, we intend to confirm our findings and verify their applicability. Another future possibility with this research is the definition of a process line for strengthening the software services in software factories. Such a process line would consider the factors identified as critical. We expect that, by using the process line, organizations will be able to derive processes that guide software companies and diminish problems related to the occurrence or the absence of the critical success factors described in this paper.

Endnote
[a]http://www.periodicos.capes.gov.br/

Competing interests
The authors declare that they have no competing interests.

Authors' contributions
The research described in this paper is part of TD's MSc dissertation. GS is TD's advisor. All authors participated in the definition of the systematic mapping study and the snowballing described in this paper.TD conducted the study and GS provided guidance and also reviewed the result in order to guarantee its quality. All authors participated in the writing of this paper. All authors read and approved the final manuscript.

References
Bandeira De Mello R, Cunha C (2003) Operationalizing the method of Grounded Theory in Researches of Strategy: techniques and analysis procedures with support of ATLAS/TI software. Paper presented at the 1st Encontro de Estudos em Estratégia, Curitiba, pp 18–20. May 2003. (in Portuguese)
Basili VR, Caldiera G, Rombach HD (1994) The Experience Factory. In: Marciniak JJ (ed) Encyclopedia of Software Engineering. John Wiley & Sons, New York
von Bon J (2011) ITIL - A Pocket Guide - 2011 Edition. Van Haren Publishing, Netherlands
Cater-Steel A (2009) IT Service Departments Struggle to Adopt a Service-Oriented Philosophy. International Journal of Information Systems in the Service Sector 1:69–77
Cater-Steel A, Pollard C (2008) Conflicting views on ITIL implementation: managed as a project – or business as usual? Paper presented at Information Resources Management Association International Conference. IRMA, Ontario. May 2008
Cater-Steell A, Tan W-G (2005) Implementation of IT Infrastructure Library (ITIL) in Australia: Progress and success factors. Paper presented at IT Governance International Conference, Auckland. Nov 2005
Cater-Steel A, Toleman M, Tan WG (2006) Transforming IT service management- The ITIL impact. Paper presented at the 17th Australasian Conference on Information Systems. ACIS, Adelaide, pp 6–8. Dec 2006
Cartlidge A, Hanna A, Rudd C, Macfarlane I, Windebank J, Rance S (2007) An introductory overview of ITIL v3. IT Service Management Forum, United Kingdom. http://itsmfi.org/files/itSMF_ITILV3_Intro_Overview.pdf
Coleman G, O'Connor R (2008) Investigating software process in practice: A grounded theory perspective. J Syst Software 81:772–784
Diirr T, Santos G (2013) Critical Success Factors for Information Technology Services Processes Improvement: A Systematic Mapping. Paper presented at the 12th Simpósio Brasileiro de Qualidade de Software – SBQS, Salvador, pp 1–5. Jul 2013. (in Portuguese)
Ghayekhloo S, Sedighi M, Nassiri R, Latif SG, Tirkolaei HK (2009) Pathology of organizations currently implementing ITIL in developing countries. In: Proceedings of the 2nd International Conference on Computer and Electrical Engineering. ICCEE, Dubai, pp 28–30. Dec 2009
Hochstein A, Brenner W (2006) Implementation of service-oriented IT management: An empirical study on Swiss IT organizations. Paper presented at International Conference on Service Systems and Service Management. ICSSSM, Troyes, pp 91–97. Oct 2006
Hochstein A, Tamm G, Brenner W (2005) Service-oriented IT management: benefit, cost and success factors. Proceedings of the 13th European Conference on Information System. ECIS, Regensburg, pp 26–28. May, 2005
ICASA (2012) COBIT 5 – Control Objectives Management Guidelines Maturity Models: A Business Framework for the Governance and Management of Enterprise IT. Information Systems Audit and Control. Association, USA
Iden J (2009) Implementing IT Service Management: Lessons Learned from a University IT Department. In: Cater-Steel A (ed) Information Technology Governance and Service Management: Frameworks and Adaptations, 1st edition. Information Science Reference, Hershey, New York
Iden J, Langeland L (2010) Setting the Stage for a Successful ITIL Adoption: A Delphi Study of IT Experts in the Norwegian Armed Forces. Information Systems Management 27:103–112

ISO/IEC (2009) ISO/IEC TR 20.000-3: Information Technology – Service Management – Part 3: Guidance on scope definition and applicability of ISO/IEC 20.000-1. International Standard Organization/International Electrotechnical Commission, Switzerland

ISO/IEC (2010a) ISO/IEC TR 20.000-4: Information Technology – Service Management – Part 4: Process reference model. International Standard Organization/International Electrotechnical Commission, Switzerland

ISO/IEC (2010b) ISO/IEC TR 20.000-5: Information Technology – Service Management – Part 5: Exemplar implementation plan for ISO/IEC 20.000-1. International Standard Organization/International Electrotechnical Commission, Switzerland

ISO/IEC (2011) ISO/IEC 20.000-1: Information Technology – Service Management – Part 1: Service management system requirements. International Standard Organization/International Electrotechnical Commission, Switzerland

ISO/IEC (2012) ISO/IEC 20.000-2: Information Technology – Service Management – Part 2: Code of practice. International Standard Organization/International Electrotechnical Commission, Switzerland

Jalali S, Wohlin C (2012) Systematic Literature Studies: Database Searches vs. Backward Snowballing. Proceedings of the ACM-IEEE international symposium on Empirical software engineering and measurement. ESEM, Sweden, pp 19–20. Sept 2012

Jäntti M (2010) Lessons Learnt from the Improvement of Customer Support Processes: A Case Study on Incident Management. In: Bomarius F, Oivo M, Jaring P, Abrahamsson P (ed) Product-Focused Software Process Improvement. 10th International Conference, PROFES 2009, Oulu, Finland, Jun 15–17, 2009. Lecture Notes in Business Information Processing, vol 32. Springer, Heidelberg, p 317

Junior V, Andrade J (2010) Critical Success Factors and Benefits of ITIL Model Adoption in a Telecommunication Company. Paper presented at 7th Simpósio de Excelência em Gestão e Tecnologia. SEGeT, Resende, Out. *in Portuguese*

Kitchenham BA (2004) Procedures for Performing Systematic Reviews. In: Keele University Technical Report TR/SE-0401 and NICTA Technical Report 0400011T.1. Software Engineering Group Department of Computer Science and Empirical Software Engineering National ICT, Australia. Ltd. http://citeseerx.ist.psu.edu/viewdoc/summary?doi=10.1.1.122.3308. Accessed 17 Sept 2013

Kitchenham BA, Budgen D, Brereton OP (2010) The value of mapping studies - A participant-observer case study. Paper presented at 14th International Conference on Evaluation and Assessment in Software Engineering (EASE), Keele University, UK, pp 12–13. April 2010

Magalhães IL, Pinheiro WB (2007) IT service management in practice: an approach based on ITIL. Novatec, São Paulo (in portuguese)

Montoni MA (2010) A research on critical success factors in software processes improvement initiatives. PhD Thesis, Universidade Federal do Rio de Janeiro - UFRJ. in Portuguese

Montoni MA, Rocha ARC (2010) Applying Grounded Theory to Understand Software Process Improvement Implementation. Paper presented at 7th International Conference on the Quality of Information and Communications Technology - QUATIC 2010, Portugal. 17 Sept - 2 Oct 2010

Montoni MA, Rocha ARC (2011) Using Grounded Theory to Acquire Knowledge About Critical Success Factors for Conducting Software Process Improvement Implementation Initiatives. International Journal of Knowledge Management 7:43–60

Pollard C, Cater-Steel A (2009) Justifications, strategies, and critical success factors in successful ITIL implementations in U.S. and Australian companies: An exploratory study. Inf Syst Manag 26(2):164–175

Rockart JF (1979) Chief executives define their own data needs. Harv Bus Rev 57(2):81–93

Santos G, Kalinowski M, Rocha AR, Travassos GH, Weber KC, Antonioni JA (2012) MPS.BR Program and MPS Model: Main Results, Benefits and Beneficiaries of Software Process Improvement in Brazil. Paper presented at 8th International Conference on the Quality of Information and Communications Technology – QUATIC 2012, Lisbon, pp 3–6. Sept 2012

SEI (2010) CMMI for Services - CMMI-SVC. Software Engineering Institute, Pittsburgh

Sharifi M, Ayat M, Rahman AA, Sahibudin S (2008) Lessons learned in ITIL implementation failure. Paper presented at the International Symposium on Information Technology – ITSim, Kuala Lumpur, pp 26–28. Aug. 2008

SOFTEX (2012) Reference model for services process improvement. Associação para Promoção da Excelência do Software Brasileiro, Brasil. http://www.softex.br/mpsbr. (in Portuguese)

Strauss A, Corbin J (1998) Basics of Qualitative Research: Techniques and Procedures for Developing Grounded Theory. SAGE Publications, London

Tan W-G, Cater-Steel A, Toleman M (2009) Implementing it service management: A case study focussing on critical success factors. J Compu Info Syst 50(2):1–12

Tan WG, Cater Steel A, Toleman M, Seaniger R (2007) Implementing centralised IT service management: Drawing lessons from the public sector. Paper presented at 18th Australasian Conference on Information Systems. ACIS, Toowoomba, pp 5–7. Dec 2007

Wan J, Liang L (2012) Risk Management of IT Service Management Project Implementation with Killer Assumptions. Technol Invest 3:48–55

Wan J, Zhu S, Wang Y (2008) Empirical analysis on risk factors of IT service management project implementation. Paper presented at the 4th International Conference on Wireless Communications, Networking and Mobile Computing – WiCOM, Dalian, pp 12–14. Oct 2008

Wohlin C, Runeson P, Höst M, Ohlson M, Regnell B, Wesslén A (2000) Experimentation in Software Engineering: An Introduction. Kluwer Academic Publishers, Norwell - USA

10

Method-level code clone detection through LWH (Light Weight Hybrid) approach

Egambaram Kodhai[1][*] and Selvadurai Kanmani[2]

* Correspondence:
kodhaiej@yahoo.co.in
[1]Research Scholar, Department of
CSE, Pondicherry Engineering
College, Puducherry, India
Full list of author information is
available at the end of the article

Abstract

Background: Many researchers have investigated different techniques to automatically detect duplicate code in programs exceeding thousand lines of code. These techniques have limitations in finding either the structural or functional clones.

Methods: We propose a LWH (Light Weight Hybrid) approach combining textual analysis and metrics for the detection of method-level syntactic and semantic clones in C and Java projects. This approach has been experimenting for the detection of all four types of clones by a specific set of metrics assessment and textual comparison. A tool named CloneManager has been developed in Java to support the experiments carried out and to validate the proposed approach.

Results: A benchmark dataset widely referred in the literature and medium to large size open-source projects developed in C or Java. Java is used for the experiments.

Conclusions: The results show that the proposed approach is able to detect all four types of clones accurately with the precision and recall values ranging from 88% to 100%.

Keyword: Clone detection; Function clones; Source code metrics; String-matching

1 Introduction

Copying code fragments and then reusing them through the paste option with or without minor modification or adaptation is called "Code Cloning" and the pasted code fragment is called a "clone". Most of the software systems comprise a substantial quantity of code clones; typically 10–15% of the source code in large software systems are part of single or more code clones (Kapser and Godfrey 2006).

In literature, (Bellon et al. 2007) has classified and defined four types of clones. A number of techniques have been proposed for the detection of type-1, type-2, and type-3 clones as per the definition of clone literature. However, for type-4 clones called semantic clones, very few attempts were made with limitations to detect them (Marcus and Maletic 2001; Komondoor and Horwitz 2001; Krinke 2001; Gabel et al. 2008; Liu et al. 2006). So far, there is a lack of technique for the detection of all four types of clones in literature.

Clones may be useful from different points of view (Kapser and Godfrey 2008). Clones carry important domain knowledge and thus studying clones may assist in understanding it (Pate et al. 2011). Moreover, the software clone research has promoted academic-industrial collaboration. Software Practitioners used to copy and modify the existing project's clones frequently to meet the needs of the clients and users in their new projects (Petersen 2012).

A number of clone detection techniques have been proposed in literature. Among them, Text-based techniques are lightweight and are able to detect accurate clones with higher recall values, where recall refers to the overall percentage of clones exist in the source code that have been detected by the clone detector. However, it failed to detect suitable syntactic units (Bellon et al. 2007). Token-based techniques are fast with high recall, but failed in precision. Precision refers to the quality of clones returned by the clone detector. Parser-based techniques are worthy in detecting syntactic clones. However, they give low recall values (Bellon et al. 2007). Metric-based techniques are able to detect syntactic as well as semantic clones with high precision values. They are also very fast in detecting both syntactic and semantic clones. However, they fail to detect some of the actual clones (Bellon et al. 2007). PDG (Program Dependency Graph) based techniques are able to find more semantic clones, where PDG is a directed graph which represents the dependencies among program elements in a program. However, sub-graph comparisons are very costly (Koschke et al. 2006). These limitations in existing methods provide a path to investigate hybrid or combinational techniques in order to overcome them.

Although numerous techniques and tools have been proposed for code clone detection (Kamiya et al. 2002), only little has been known about, which detected code clones are appropriate for refactoring and how to extract code clones for refactoring. A technique that helps to process the code clones is called Refactoring. Refactoring is defined as "restructuring an existing body of code, altering its internal structure without changing its external behaviour" (Fowler 1999). By refactoring the clones detected, one can potentially improve understandability, maintainability and extensibility and reduce the complexity of the system (Fowler 1999).

The granularity of clones can be free with no syntactic boundaries or fixed within predefined syntactic boundaries such as method or block (Roy and Cordy 2007). Clone granularity is fixed at different levels, such as files, classes, functions/methods, begin-end blocks, statements or sequences of source lines.

Clone detection techniques have been proposed with free granularity, mostly with more than six lines of code (Kamiya et al. 2002; Koschke et al. 2006). On the analysis of different clone detection techniques, most of the matches tend to be methods/functions of 1-5 lines of code. Most of these methods are setter/getter functions which are valid set of clones. Only limited detectors used function clones as granularity. Function/ Method clones are simply clones that are restricted to refer to entire function or method. Function/Method clones appear to be the most promising points of refactoring for all clone types. They are larger and tend to have a significant amount of code in common.

The techniques that return only Function/Method level clones are suitable for architectural refactoring as they represent a meaningful code segment. It is not so in the case of detecting clones with fixed number of lines in a continuous unsegmented file of code. Tools have been proposed in the literature, which analyses these clones further to extract meaningful codes for refactoring support (Kapser and Godfrey 2006; Ueda et al. 2002; Zibran and Roy 2013). Function/Method clones are the meaningful clones which are also useful for software maintenance and evolution phases. Thus, it motivates researchers to fix the granularity as function/method level (Mayland et al. 1996; Roy and Cordy 2008).

In this paper, a LWH (Light Weight Hybrid) approach has been proposed with a combination of textual comparison and metrics computation. As there is no need for external parsing, this approach is of light weight. Moreover, a model has been arrived to detect syntactic and semantic clones which will cover all four types of clones. For experimental validation, a tool has been developed using the proposed LWH approach to detect method/function level clones for both C and Java projects. This tool has been developed in Java and it has been named as CloneManager. Experimental results show that, the proposed tool CloneManager is efficient and accurate in detecting all types of clones.

This paper is presented in five major sections. Section 2 discusses the literature review for clone detection. Section 3 introduces the basic definitions and background details of code clone detection. The detailed implementation of the proposed method as a tool is elaborated in Section 4. Section 5 summarizes the experimental results. Section 6 concludes the paper.

2 Literature review

There has been more than a decade of research in the field of software clones. To understand the growth and trends in different dimensions of cloning research, we carried out a quantitative review of related publications. Clone detection research has proved that software systems have 9%-17% of duplicated code (Zibran et al. 2011). (Thummalapenta et al. 2009) indicated that in most of the cases, clones are changed consistently and for the remaining inconsistently changed cases, clones undergo independent evolution. Effective code clone detection will support perfective maintenance. Up to the present, several code clone detection methods have been proposed (Petersen 2012; Al-Batran 2011; Leitner et al. 2013). Comparison and evaluation of code clone detection techniques and tools have been carried out by (Bellon and Koschke 2014; Bellon et al. 2007) and (Roy and Cordy 2007; Roy et al. 2009).

A clone detection process is usually done by converting the source code into another form that is handled by an algorithm to detect the clones. A rough classification is then carried out depending on the level of matches found. Token-based techniques (Li et al. 2006; Leitao 2004; Basit et al. 2007) use a similar sequence matching algorithm. However, its accuracy is not that adequate as the normalization, and also token conversion process may bring false positive clones in result set. Many of the clone detection approaches have used Abstract Syntax Tree (AST) and suffix tree representation of a program to find clones (Evans et al. 2009; Evans and Fraser 2005; Greenan 2005; Pate et al. 2011; Koschke 2012). Some of the clone detection techniques use an AST that is generated by a pre-existing parser. (Baker 1997) describes one of the earliest applications of suffix trees for the clone detection process. An algorithm based on feature-vector computation over AST was applied by Lee et al. (2010) to detect similar clones. However, all of them use parsing, which results in heavy-weighted approach.

Lighter weight techniques were proposed in the literature without the use of parsing namely text-based techniques and metrics-based techniques. Text-based techniques (Wettel and Marinescu 2005; Ducasse et al. 1999) are investigated by comparing two code fragments with each other to find longest common subsequences of same text/

strings to detect clones. Though these techniques detect clones they are not low in precision values. Metric-based techniques identify a set of suitable metrics to detect a particular type of clone. By a quantitative assessment of the metric values in the source code, the clone detection is done. (Kapser and Godfrey 2004) chaos Cyclomatic complexity as the corroboration metric. However, they have only proved that their technique works well to locate the clone segments across several versions of a software system using a very small test set.

Hybrid techniques were also proposed in the literature. (Marco Funaro et al. 2010) proposed a hybrid technique using Abstract Syntax Tree to identify clone candidates and textual methods to discard false positives. (Leitao 2004) also proposed a hybrid approach with the combination AST and PDG. Both approaches use parsing which results in heavy-weight. As text-based techniques preserve higher recall, metrics-based techniques preserve higher precision and both of them are light-weight, a hybrid technique with the combination of textual analysis and metrics, is experimenting in this paper for the detection of all four types of clones.

3 Background

Clones may be compared on the basis of the program text that has been copied. A related definition of cloning was described by (Bellon et al. 2007), who defined the types of code clones based on the degree and type of similarities.

Textual similarity

- **Type-1** is an exact copy without modifications (except for whitespace and comments).
- **Type-2** is a syntactically identical copy; except some changes in variable name, data type, identifier name, etc.
- **Type-3** is a copied fragment with further modifications. Statements can be changed, added or removed in addition to variations in identifiers, literals, types, layout and comments.

Functional similarity

- **Type-4** Two or more code fragments that perform the same computation, but implemented through different syntactic variants.

Table 1 illustrates the four types of clones. The clone pair (a, b) is of type-1 which have exactly the same code except the alignment, space and comment. The clone pair (a, c) is of type-2 which have minor differences in function names and parameters. The clone pair (a, d) is of type-3 with additional statements in code, as they need not be

Table 1 Illustration of four types of clones

Source code(a)	Type-1 clone(b)	Type-2 clone(c)	Type-3 clone(d)	Type-4 clone(e)
int main() { int x = 1; int y = x + 5; return y; }	int main() { int x = 1; int y = x + 5; return y;//output }	int func2() { int p = 1; int q = p + 5; return q; }	int main() { int s = 1; int t = s + 5; t = t/++s; return t; }	int func4() { int n = 5; return ++n; }

functionally similar. The clone pair (a, e) is of type-4 clones with no similarity in code, but the output of the functions are same.

The results of the code clone detection are presented as clone pairs and clone clusters.

- **Clone Pair (CP) or Code Fragment (CF):** pair of code portions/fragments that are identical or similar to each other.
- **Clone Cluster (CC) or Clone Class or Clone Set (CS):** the union of all clone pairs that have code portions in common.

The quality of clone detection by any tool is assessed by two key parameters precision and recall as defined in Figure 1.

Precision
Precision is the ratio of the number of correctly detected clones to the total number of detecting clones by the proposed tool.

Recall
Recall is the ratio of the number of correctly detected clones by the proposed tool to the total number of actual clones in the project by reference values.

4 Methods

This section describes the proposed LWH approach for automatic detection of function clones in C or Java source code. A tool CloneManager has been developed in Java in order to experiment the proposed approach. This tool accepts a C or Java source project as the input and separates the functions/methods present in it. A built-in hand-coded parser (Moonen 2001) is used to process these methods following an island-driven parsing approach (Moonen 2001). Having identified the methods, different source code metrics is computed for each method and stored in a database. With the help of these metric values the near equal methods are extracted and are subjected to textual comparison to detect potential clone pairs.

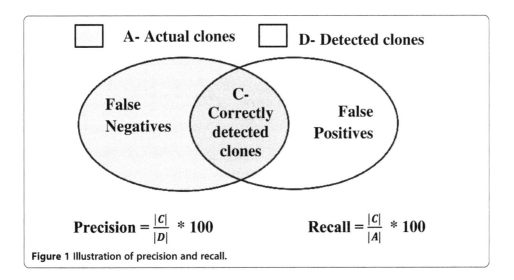

$$\text{Precision} = \frac{|C|}{|D|} * 100 \qquad \text{Recall} = \frac{|C|}{|A|} * 100$$

Figure 1 Illustration of precision and recall.

The overall process is carried out in three major stages: Pre-processing, detection and post-processing. Figure 2 shows the overall system diagram of the proposed system. The following subsections, explain the steps in each of the stages.

4.1 Pre-processing

This stage includes the process of comment, white space removal and source code conversion or standardization (formatting). All files are scanned for filtering the uninteresting statements such as comments and white spaces. The final step is re-structuring of the code into a standard form which is needed for establishing clone fragments similarity (Ducasse et al. 2006). This helps in the identification of the cloned methods, thus yielding a significant gain in the Recall. Figures 3 and 4 illustrates the removal of comments and white spaces and statement standardization.

4.2 Method detection

Another potentially useful analysis could be to extract the methods alone, as the granularity is method-level. The standard form of source code scans for the detection of methods of adopting an 'island-driven parsing' (Moonen 2001). In order to extract isolated phrases or to detect certain features of a text island parser is used instead of a full-fledged parser.

It is a grammar-based method for extracting parts of a program as required from unwanted parts which need not be precisely parsed. In the island driven parsing system

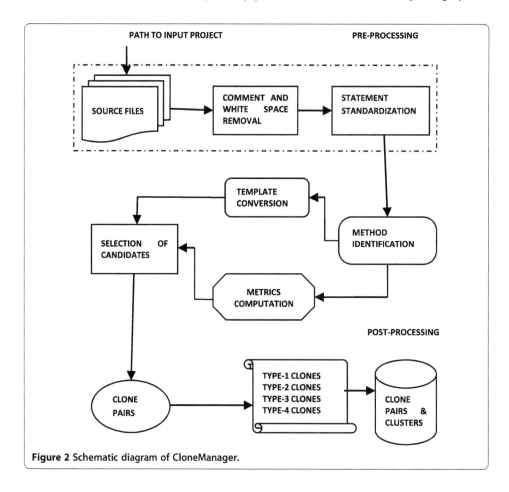

Figure 2 Schematic diagram of CloneManager.

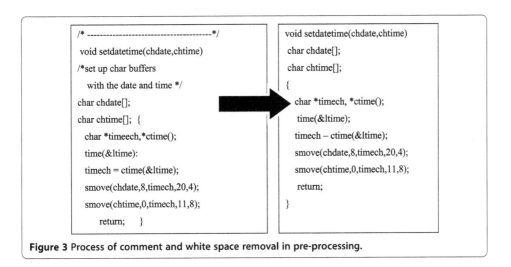

Figure 3 Process of comment and white space removal in pre-processing.

(Moonen 2001), parsing does not start at the beginning of the word network, but rather can start at confident regions within the network, at places known as islands. It provides a mechanism to find out the required elements to be compared.

Using this approach, the method definitions are extracted and collected by means of a hand-coded parser and saved for further reference. An interesting fragment is the piece of code that can be parsed and reduced to a nonterminal, method declaration. This approach takes text files and returns the structured fragments containing methods. For each method, it keeps track of the exact location within the file. An extracted method consists of a list with three elements such as (i) the method name (ii) the file name and the methods start and end positions (iii) the method content.

4.3 Template conversion

In addition to the standardization of source code, template conversion is exploited. This converts the original source code into a new form, having a uniform pattern for

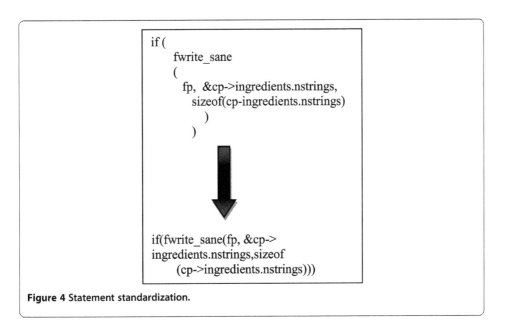

Figure 4 Statement standardization.

the permitted equivalent constructs between the clone pairs of the same type. An equivalent constructs contain invariant and variant parts as defined below.

- The invariant is part of the source code construct which is not expected to change between the clone versions.
- The variant is part of the source code constructs which are allowed to have changes among clone versions.

In this tool, variant part has been employed for detection of type-2, type-3 and type-4 clones.

4.3.1 Template conversion for type-1 and type-2

For type-2, as per the definition of literature the function identifiers, variable names, data-types, etc., are the only allowed differences in functions. Hence, to minimize the differences between the code fragments we bring out a uniform intermediate representation of the source code.

In case of type-2 detection, clone methods may contain a difference in the identifiers, literals, types, white space, layout and comments. To match all these differences, a common template is arrived. For instance, to avoid name differences, the names of the identifier are converted into common name as X and all the data-type declarations are converted into common data-type namely DAT. Figure 5 shows the template conversion for type-2 clones.

4.3.2 Template conversion for type-3 and type-4

In type-3 and type-4 clone detection, various constructs like iterations and branches may also change between clone methods. A slightly different form of representation is needed to be generated. Thus the following representations help in generalizing the various deviations and constructs and in identifying the various types of cloned methods.

4.3.2.1 Iterative equivalence The control looping structures are *for, while* and *dowhile*. The three patterns present in looping are initialization, condition and increment/decrement; these are separated and written, each in a separate line. The common template form *iteration* helps in replacing the above three patterns. Both open braces and close braces are neglected while writing due to the changes in the order of the statement changes in order and nested statements in the source code. Table 2 shows the different types of variants among the source code. Figure 6 shows the template conversion for type-3 & type-4 clones.

4.3.2.2 Conditional equivalence The conditional structures are *if, else* and *elseif*. In these statements, the conditions are separately written in new line following the template form *selection*. The nested operations are split separately and rewritten in each new line. In case of the ternary operator "?:" the condition and other statements are separately printed in order to get the similar pattern.

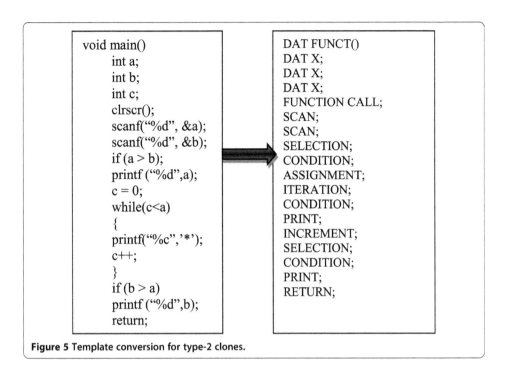

```
void main()                    DAT FUNCT()
    int a;                     DAT X;
    int b;                     DAT X;
    int c;                     DAT X;
    clrscr();                  FUNCTION CALL;
    scanf("%d", &a);           SCAN;
    scanf("%d", &b);           SCAN;
    if (a > b);                SELECTION;
    printf ("%d",a);           CONDITION;
    c = 0;                     ASSIGNMENT;
    while(c<a)                 ITERATION;
    {                          CONDITION;
    printf("%c",'*');          PRINT;
    c++;                       INCREMENT;
    }                          SELECTION;
    if (b > a)                 CONDITION;
    printf ("%d",b);           PRINT;
    return;                    RETURN;
```

Figure 5 Template conversion for type-2 clones.

4.3.2.3 Input equivalence The input statements such as *scanf, system.in, input.read-line*. In these statements, the variable alone will follow the template form *read*. For the multiple inputs, single input statements are separately written on each line as illustrated in Table 2.

4.3.2.4 Output equivalence The output statements such as *printf, system.out*. In these statements, the output variables alone follow the template form *write*. The print statements which are just printing any comments or statements are neglected. Also the multiple outputs, single print statements are separately written on each line.

4.3.2.5 Declaration equivalence The declaration statements start with keywords such as *char, int, long int, double, float, and string*. In this case, multiple declarations in a single statement are split and written, with each line as a single declaration statement. Table 2 shows the conversion of multiple declarations into single declaration.

4.3.2.6 Braces The braces are used in the programming languages for grouping the statements of looping and nesting. Both the open and close braces are neglected while writing due to the changes made in ordering.

4.4 Metrics computation
The previous method detection step produces a set of methods. In this step, we calculate the metric values for each of these methods to extract the potential clone pairs. A set of 12 count metrics has been proposed for the detection of these cloned methods.

Table 2 Types of variants among the source code patterns

S.No	Equivalence category	Possible constructs	Proposed pattern
1	Iterative equivalence	for	iteration
		while	<initial>
		do-while	<condition>
			<incre/decre>
2	Conditional equivalence	if	selection
		else	<condition>
		else-if	
		?:	
		switch	
3	Input equivalence	scanf	read <variable>
		system.in	
		input.readline	
4	Output equivalence	printf	write <variable>
		system.out	
5	Declaration equivalence	int	Multiple Declaration
		char	to Single line declaration
		float	
		double	*Example*
		string	int x
			int y
		Example	int z
		int x,y,z	char c
		char c,s	char s
6	Braces	{ }	Braces are removed in the code

Metrics, which are calculated using the simple counting formula are called as count metrics. These count metrics have been proposed for each type of cloned methods based on the necessity. Table 3 gives the list of metrics used for the detection of clones and their descriptions are briefed as follows:

1. **No. of Lines:** This indicates the number of effective lines of code in each method presents between the '{' and '}', indicating the start and end of the function definition.
2. **No. of Arguments:** This indicates the total number of arguments passed to the method irrespective of the data-types and the order of the arguments passed.
3. **No. of Local Variables:** The count value of the number of local variables declared within the function definition is represented by this metric. The number of variables used by the function or the number of global variables or the number of times the variables are used is not considered.
4. **No. of Function Calls:** This value gives a picture of the number of function calls made by the method. It is usually a measure of the flow of control in a source code and it gives an overall view of the functionality of both the defined and the called methods.

```
void main()                    void main()                    void main()
{                              {                              int a;
int a,b,c,max;                 int a,b,c,max,i;               int b; int c;
int i;                         printf("enter the value of a:");   int max;
printf("Enter the values of    scanf("%d",&a);                int i;
a,b,c:");                      printf("enter the value of b:");   scan a;
scanf("%d%d%d",                scanf("%d",&b);                scan b;
&a,&b,&c);                     printf("enter the value of c:");   scan c;
if((a>b)&&(a>c))               scanf("%d",&c);                selection
{                              if((a>b)&&(a>c))               a>b;
printf("%d is Greater",a);     printf("%d is Greater",a);     selection
}                              if((b>a)&&(b>c))               a>c;
if (b>a)                       printf("%d is Greater",b);     print a;
{                              if(a>b)                        selection
if(b>c)                        max=a;                         b>a;
{                              printf("Maximum is %d",max);   selection
printf("%d is Greater",b);     i=0;                           b>c;
}                              while(i<max)                   print b;
}                              {                              selection
max =(a>b)?a:b;                printf("*");                   a>b;
printf("Maximum is             i++;                           max = a;
%d",max);                      }                              print max;
for(i=0; i<max;i++)            getch();                       iteration
{                              }                              i=0;
printf("*");                                                  i<max;
}                                                             i++;
getch();                                                      getch();
}
```

Figure 6 Template conversion for type 3 & type 4 clones.

5. **No. of Conditional Statements:** This includes the conditional statements in each method like the number of 'if', 'else if' and 'else' statements, etc., defined in the method. It is considered important as it determines the overall semantics of the method.

6. **No. of Iteration Statements:** This gives a count of the iterative control structures used within the method definition. Statements defining "while", "do" and "for" are considered in this metric. These are also important in identifying the pattern of execution of the method.

Table 3 Metrics applied to methods

S.No	Metrics
1	No. of Lines
2	No. of Arguments
3	No. of Local Variables
4	No. of function Calls
5	No. of conditional statements
6	No. of iteration statements
7	No. of Return Statements
8	No. of Input Statements
9	No. of Output Statements
10	No. of Assignments through Function Calls
11	No. of Selection Statements
12	No. of Assignment Statements

7. **No. of Return Statements:** It gives the number of return structures defined within the method. It indicates the number of exits present within the method definition.

8. **No. of Input Statements:** The various types of input statements used in the method to obtain the values of variables, the choice of the user, etc., are identified and counted. These play a vital role in judging the similarities between various methods.

9. **No. of Output Statements:** Similar to the count of input statements, the output statements also make a significant contribution to the analysis of the content of the method. Simple output statements used for the purpose of formatting the output and information texts are neglected while the valid values and results from the method passed to the buffers, console, etc. are taken under consideration.

10. **No. of Assignments through Function Calls:** This metric count the number of variables which gets the value by the assignment of a return value from a function call. These give an exclusive classification for the variables and their values and hence are taken into interest.

11. **No. of Selection Statements:** This metric is used for identifying selection statements in each method which include conditional operators, cases, etc. These statements along with the conditional statements produce branches and are hence analyzed to find out the pattern of execution of the method.

12. **No. of Assignment Statements:** This metric gives the count of the number of assignment statements in each method that modify the values of the various variables used in the method. The statements may be simple assignments, arithmetic expressions, unary operators, etc.

Apart from these 12 count metrics, four more metrics are also used. The features examined for these metric computations are, Global and local variables defined or used, Functions called, Files accessed, I/O operations and defined/used parameters passed by reference and by value.

Let **S** be a code fragment. The description of the four metrics which are additionally used is given below. A detailed description is present in literature (Adamov 1987, Fenton 1991, Moller 1993). Note that these metrics are computed compositionally from statements, two functions (in C) and methods (in Java).

13. S COMPLEXITY(S) = $FAN\ OUT(S)$

    where $FAN\ OUT(S)$ is the number of individual function calls made within S.

14. D COMPLEXITY(S) = $GLOBALS(S)/(FAN\ OUT(S) + 1)$

where, $GLOBALS(S)$ is the number of individual declarations of global variables used or updated within **S**. A global variable is a variable which is not declared in the code fragment **S**.

15. MCCABE(S) = 1 + d, where d is the number of control decision statements in **S**.

16. ALBRECHT(S) = $\begin{cases} p1 * VARS\ USED\ AND\ SET(S)+ \\ p2 * GLOBAL\ VARS\ SET(S) + \\ p3 * USER\ INPUT(S) + \\ p4 * FILE\ INPUT(S) \end{cases}$

where,

$VARS\ USED\ AND\ SET(S)$ is the number of data elements set and used in the statement **S**,

$GLOBAL\ VARS\ SET(S)$ is the number of global data elements set in the statement **S**,

USER INPUT(S) is the number of read operations in statement **S**,

FILE INPUT(S) is the number of files accessed for reading in **S**.

The factors p1, .., p4, are weight factors. The values chosen are p1 = 5, p2 = 4, p3 = 4 and p4 = 7. These values are chosen according to the literature (Adamov 1987).

All 16 metrics are calculated for each method and stored for comparison and extraction processes. For type-1, type-2 and type-4, a constraint is posed that a cloned method pair must have an identical set of metric values. Thus, the database records containing identical metric values for method pairs are shortlisted for the type-1, type-2 and type-4 clone detection. The metrics are computed for each of the methods and are compared to be shortlisted by the formulas as indicated in Table 4.

4.5 Type-1 clone detection

With the shortlisted set of methods that are obtained, a textual comparison of the method pairs in the formatted and normalized code is done to identify the exactness of the extracted pairs. As per the definition, exact copy and paste of source code without any modification is called as type-1 clones. Methods having an exact equality score, which means, number of similar lines must be equal to the total number of lines in the method, are declared as type-1 cloned methods. The methods with same computed metric values and same as a textual comparison are declared as clone pairs. The detection criteria used for the identification of types of clones are tabulated in Table 4.

4.6 Type-2 clone detection

Type-2 cloned methods are syntactically identical code fragments except for variations in identifiers, literals, types, white space, layout and comments. Hence the textual comparison is performed on the template code created by the tool. The methods with the same computed metric values and same patterns for template comparison are short listed as clone pairs. The comparison in the template identifies type-1 cloned method along, with type-2 cloned methods. So they need to be removed separately. Further, for this reason textual comparison with original source code is compared to identify the differences in the parameters.

4.7 Type-3 clone detection

Copied code fragments with further modifications like statements can be changed, added or removed are considered as type-3 clones. In this case Range values of the calculated metrics are considered rather than the original values due to the wide variation in the syntactical structure of the methods. Thus to identify the clones, two different Range of metric values is identified which are suitable to detect type-3 clones. These

Table 4 Criteria for clone types detection

Clone type	Standardized source code		Template code
	Metrics comparison	Textual comparison	Template comparison
Type-1	Same	Same	-
Type-2	Same	Difference in Parameters	Same
Type-3	Range1 >=90%	-	Range2 >=85%
Type-4	Same	No match	Same

Range values are calculated for the methods in pairs. Range1 is the ratio of the actual metric value to the average metric value in the methods which are suspected to be clones.

$$\text{Range1} = \frac{\text{Actual metric value of method} * 100}{\text{Average metric value of methods}}$$

If any method is having more than 90% value for Range1, they are shortlisted under the possibilities for type-3 method clones. Then Range2 is calculated as the ratio of equal number of lines which are similar to the suspected method by the total number of lines in a method in the template code.

$$\text{Range2} = \frac{\text{No. similar lines in a method} * 100}{\text{Total no. of lines in a method}}$$

The method pairs having more than 85% values of Range2 in template methods are declared as type-3 clones. In the literature, there is no clear range specified for type-3 clones. The Range1 and Range2 values are equal for type-1, 2 and 4. Hence, for type-3 range has been explored with different values from 85% to 100%, and arrived this threshold value as a range after so many trial rounds.

4.8 Type-4 clone detection

Type-4 clones are the results of semantic similarity between two or more code fragments. In this type of clones, the cloned fragment is not necessarily copied from the original. Two code fragments may be developed by two different programmers to implement the same kind of logic, making the code fragments similar in their functionality. Thus the semantics of the cloned fragments remain the same while the structural and syntactical representation may show changes.

For type-4, first the two considered methods are taken and their computed metric values are considered. If the computed metric values are same for these two methods, then they are compared with the template methods. If they are also same, then the textual comparison of the source code is checked. If they are completely different, then they are categorized under type-4.

4.9 Post-processing

The output from the previous phase is in the form of clone pairs. The results of the tool CloneManager are given as clone pairs and clone clusters. The identified clone methods called as "potential clone pairs", are then clustered separately for each type and the clusters are uniquely numbered. *Clustering* is the process of grouping the clone pairs into classes or clusters so that clone pairs within a cluster are highly similar to one another, but are very dissimilar to clone pairs in other clusters. These clone pairs and clusters of all four types of clones are stored each in a text file separately.

5 Results and discussion

To validate the proposed LWH approach, the performance of the tool CloneManager is assessed for detecting the function clones in a number of open source systems. Based on the literature, Bellon's benchmark dataset (Bellon et al. 2007) has been chosen for code clone data which provides the details of reference set for eight software systems. For the remaining unclassified data, clone details are collected through manual verification process. Moreover, the experiments are carried out and presented as guidance provided by Wohlin et al. (2012).

5.1 Experimental setup

To evaluate the tool, source code of seven C projects and seven Java projects have been used. The experimental analysis has been carried out with a medium sized C project Weltab 11,000 lines to a large sized C project called Linux with 6,265,000 lines. Table 5 gives the size details of the projects, namely # files: number of files in the project, KLOC: number of thousand lines of code in the project and #methods: number of functions/methods in the project.

(Bellon and Koschke 2014; Bellon et al. 2007; Koschke et al. 2006) also measured the precision (refer section 3) and recall (refer section 3) of clone detection tools. Bellon created a benchmark set of clones by random sampling and evaluating a random subset of the union of clones detected by all clone detection tools in the study. This resulted in an oracled set of clones known to be true positives. Each reference clone was classified into one of three types: exact clones (Type-1); parameterized clones (Type-2); and clones with additional changes (Type-3). Six clone detection tools were used in the study: Dup (token-based), CCFinder (token-based), CloneDr (AST sub–tree), Duplix (PDG), CLAN (AST metrics), and Duploc (normalized lines of code).

Bellon's work produced the results for four C projects, namely Cook, Postgresql, Snns, Weltab and four Java projects, namely Eclipse-ant, Java netbeans-javadoc, Eclipse-jdtcore, J2sdk-swing. Finally, the precision and recall values in percentage are measured for each project by all the tools. Moreover, in literature, some researchers have used Bellon's benchmark for evaluation of their technique (Koschke et al. 2006; Selim et al. 2010; Hotta et al. 2014). Hence, in order to evaluate the proposed tool CloneManager, Bellon's benchmark has been adopted. For the remaining six projects, manual validation is carried out for the purpose of evaluation.

Table 5 Overview of the open source projects used by CloneManager

Language	Project name	#files	KLOC	# methods
C	Cook	287	70	1362
	Apache-httpd-2.2.8	496	275	4301
	Postgresql	314	202	4669
	Snns	138	94	2201
	Weltab	39	11	123
	Wget	23	17	219
	Linux-2.6.24.2	9491	6265	154977
Java	Eclipse-ant	161	35	1754
	EIRC	54	11	588
	Java Netbeans-Javadoc	97	14	972
	Eclipse-jdtcore	582	148	7383
	JHotDraw 5.4b1	233	40	2399
	Spule	50	13	420
	J2sdk-swing	414	204	10971

5.2 Results

The results of the experiments are summarized, in this section. It presents the numbers of clone pairs and clone clusters detected for different categories of clone types by our proposed tool CloneManager. In Table 6, the third column is the clone type-1 with the number of detected clone pairs and the clone clusters. Columns 4, 5 and 6 hold the same set of data for type-2, 3 and 4 respectively.

From the data presented in Table 6, the following observations were made.

- Linux with 6265,000 lines has only 39119 clone pairs in total. On the other hand, J2sdk-swing with only 204,000 of lines has 27559 clone pairs in total. This shows that, the number of lines in the projects is not directly proportional to the number of clone pairs.
- The smallest size project in our observation was Weltab with 11,000 lines. However, it had 333 clones in total.
- It is interesting to note, Wget has no type-1 matches, which means that they do not have exact functions in the code. The size of Wget is 17,000 lines. Moreover, they have the least number of clone pairs 17 in total.

On comparing the clone types obtained it has been observed that the no. of clones in type-2 clones is higher than type-1 clones and less type-3 clones; all projects have the least number of type-4 clones. This shows us that, the number of clones increases as the type increases and falls down for the type-4. In other words, the number of clones increases in textual similarity and decreases in functional similarity. These observations lead to an interesting inference: programmers do not write code with different logic for the same external behaviour.

On analysing the experimental results it has been observed that, on average, above 15% of the methods in open source Java code is type-1 clones, whereas only above 2.5% of C

Table 6 CloneManager: number of detected clones pairs and clone clusters

S.No	Project name	Type-1		Type-2		Type-3		Type-4	
		Clone pairs	Clone clusters	Clone pairs	Clone clusters	Clone pairs	Clone clusters	Clone pairs	Clone clusters
1	Cook	18	5	157	30	280	98	7	3
2	Apache-httpd-2.2.8	183	107	242	143	711	276	10	4
3	Postgresql	28	4	240	42	530	203	7	3
4	Snns	109	63	160	86	495	191	9	4
5	Weltab	46	8	115	11	160	20	12	5
6	Wget	0	0	4	2	11	2	2	1
7	Linux-2.6.24.2	5953	1505	7386	2265	25767	7918	13	5
8	Eclipse-ant	363	92	372	96	426	119	10	4
9	EIRC	117	35	119	35	149	47	6	3
10	Java Netbeans-Javadoc	193	80	199	83	304	110	8	3
11	Eclipse-jdtcore	1427	323	5573	587	4378	660	15	7
12	JHotDraw 5.4b1	291	137	299	142	598	208	10	4
13	Spule	60	11	69	14	113	19	4	2
14	J2sdk-swing	8115	516	8205	558	11209	843	30	14

functions are type-1 clones. Thus it shows that function clones appear more in open source Java code than C. After analysing the detected clones, it is observed that this is due to the large number of 'small getter and setter methods' in Java programs which are not present in C. From overall analysis, it has been observed that the level of cloning is found to be less in C than Java projects. Also, it is found that C projects have very less type-1 clones, less than 10% in some and to a large extent independently of the system size.

As a result of all these analysis, it could be inferred that,

- Most of the Java systems have significantly fewer clone clusters than clone pairs, indicating the fact that there are many pairs of functions in the systems that are similar to each other.
- Average number of clone pairs per clone cluster is more or less consistent for C and Java systems for different clone types.
- C systems show a faster growing ratio for type-3 clones than the Java systems, indicating the fact that there might be more type-3 clones in the C than the Java systems.

5.3 Procedure to determine reference data

The Bellon's benchmark (Bellon and Koschke 2014) results are used for the tool evaluation. Bellon's benchmark has evaluated 8 projects for different tools (Cook, Postgresql, Snns, Weltab, Eclipse-ant, Java netbeans-javadoc, eclipse-jdtcore and J2sdk-swing). He has evaluated experimental result with the manually evaluated values as reference values, which was only 2%. However, he produced his complete experimental results for all projects. Thus the results are taken from his benchmark, assuming that they are accurate. The complete results of Bellon's tool experiment are available at http://www.bauhaus-stuttgart.de/clones/. For the remaining six projects (Apache-httd-2.2.8, Wget, Linux-2.6.24.2, EIRC, Jhotdraw 5.4b1 and Spule), which are not available in Bellon's benchmark, manual evaluation was carried out with the help of semi-automated tools.

Using the standardization tool named fscodeformat64, both C and Java codes are standardized. Comments above the methods are examined carefully, which informs the method description. This helps to analyse the methods, with similar semantic methods, may be type-4 clones. These methods alone are extracted separately and by checking external behaviour, type-4 clones are detected. All the methods are extracted by removing the other codes by simple program developed in Java. The methods with similar codes are detected using another simple program. They are counted as type-1 clones and extracted separately in a file. Then the manual process is carried out to detect the type-2, 3 clones.

Two students in a batch are allocated for the manual detection of clones for 2 open source projects. They took 15 days training from the faculty, before starting their work. They took six months to complete this task. Two batches are allocated in parallel and thus 14 students helped to evaluate this work manually and took 21 months to complete this task. Moreover, one batch students' results are also verified by the other batch, mutually. Finally, to cross check the accuracy of these manual processes, some samples clones have been picked from the reference set of data and monitored whether these clones have been detected by the students. To carry out this evaluation process, misclassification is calculated as follows

Table 7 Misclassification report for sample clones

Project	Actual clones [A]	Detected clones [D]	Correctly detected clones [C]	False negatives [N]	False negatives in %	False positives [P]	False positives in %
Cook	14	14	14	0	0	0	0
Apache-httpd-2.2.8	20	20	19	1	5	0	0
Postgresql	11	11	11	0	0	0	0
Snns	14	15	14	0	0	1	6
Weltab	10	10	10	0	0	0	0
Wget	8	8	8	0	0	0	0
Linux-2.6.24.2	20	20	20	0	0	0	0
Eclipse-ant	15	15	14	1	6	0	0
EIRC	13	13	13	0	0	0	0
Java Netbeans-Javadoc	10	10	10	0	0	0	0
Eclipse-jdtcore	16	16	16	0	0	0	0
JHotDraw 5.4b1	24	24	24	0	0	0	0
Spule	15	16	15	0	0	1	6
J2sdk-swing	21	21	21	0	0	0	0

1. *False negative in* $\% = \frac{[N]}{[A]} * 100$
2. *False positive in* $\% = \frac{[P]}{[D]} * 100$

Where False Negative [N] = Actual clones [A] – correctly detected clones[C] which reports the number of clones failed to be detected.

False Positive [P] = Detected Clones [D] – correctly detected clones[C] which reports the number of clones wrongly detected as clones.

Actual clones [A] are the reference clones.

The Table 7 shows the misclassification report for the sample clones considered. From the Table 7, it is clear that the manual detection of clones is merely correct.

Table 8 CloneManager: precision and recall of type-1 clones

Project name	Actual clones (A)	Detected clones (D)	Correctly detected clones (C)	Precision %	Recall %
Cook	18	18	18	100	100
Apache-httpd-2.2.8	203	192	183	95	90
Postgresql	28	29	28	96	100
Snns	118	110	109	97	92
Weltab	46	46	46	100	100
Wget	0	0	0	-	-
Linux-2.6.24.2	6764	6470	5953	92	88
Eclipse-ant	382	374	363	97	95
EIRC	124	117	117	100	94
Java Netbeans-Javadoc	196	205	193	94	98
Eclipse-jdtcore	1603	1585	1427	90	89
JHotDraw 5.4b1	303	296	291	98	96
Spule	61	60	60	100	98
J2sdk-swing	8820	8196	8115	99	92

Table 9 CloneManager: precision and recall of type-2 clones

Project name	Actual clones (A)	Detected clones (D)	Correctly detected clones (C)	Precision %	Recall %
Cook	160	160	157	98	98
Apache-httpd-2.2.8	252	249	242	97	96
Postgresql	250	252	240	95	96
Snns	161	170	160	94	99
Weltab	115	115	115	100	100
Wget	4	4	4	100	100
Linux-2.6.24.2	7774	8116	7386	91	95
Eclipse-ant	379	422	372	88	98
EIRC	126	132	119	90	94
Java Netbeans-Javadoc	207	199	199	100	96
Eclipse-jdtcore	6057	5686	5573	98	92
JHotDraw 5.4b1	321	299	299	100	93
Spule	71	73	69	94	96
J2sdk-swing	8728	8918	8205	92	94

5.4 Evaluation of the tool CloneManager

From the standard benchmark results, a reference set is obtained for the evaluation of the parameters precision and recall. These values have been evaluated for all four types of clones and are given in Tables 8, 9, 10 and 11 respectively.

Table 8 shows the precision and recall values of type-1 clones for all the projects. Column 2 holds the number of actual clones (A) from the reference set for all the projects. Column 3 holds (D) the number of detected clones by our tool CloneManager. Column 5 holds (C) the number of correctly detected clones by our tool. Then, values for the two parameters precision and recall are computed using the formula given in Figure 1.

Table 10 CloneManager: precision and recall of type-3 clones

Project name	Actual clones (A)	Detected clones (D)	Correctly detected clones (C)	Precision %	Recall %
Cook	291	291	280	96	96
Apache-httpd-2.2.8	807	756	711	94	88
Postgresql	576	552	530	96	92
Snns	526	505	495	98	94
Weltab	160	160	160	100	100
Wget	11	11	11	100	100
Linux-2.6.24.2	28007	27411	25767	94	92
Eclipse-ant	448	426	426	100	95
EIRC	161	152	149	98	92
Java Netbeans-Javadoc	304	330	304	92	100
Eclipse-jdtcore	4864	4378	4378	100	90
JHotDraw 5.4b1	643	629	598	95	93
Spule	126	113	113	100	89
J2sdk-swing	12052	12737	11209	88	93

Table 11 CloneManager: precision and recall of type-4 clones

Project name	Actual clones (A)	Detected clones (D)	Correctly detected clones (C)	Precision %	Recall %
Cook	8	7	7	100	87
Apache-httpd-2.2.8	11	11	10	90	90
Postgresql	7	7	7	100	100
Snns	10	10	9	90	90
Weltab	13	13	12	92	92
Wget	2	2	2	100	100
Linux-2.6.24.2	14	14	13	92	92
Eclipse-ant	10	10	10	100	100
EIRC	6	6	6	100	100
Java Netbeans-Javadoc	9	8	8	100	88
Eclipse-jdtcore	17	17	15	88	88
JHotDraw 5.4b1	11	11	10	90	90
Spule	4	4	4	100	100
J2sdk-swing	31	32	30	92	95

From the data presented that has been given in Tables 8, 9, 10 and 11, it could be seen that, CloneManager has resulted in higher values for precision and recall for all the clone types. As precision and recall are the best parameters for the evaluation of clone detection tools, it could be concluded that the proposed CloneManager is found to be an effective tool for detecting all types of clones. Figures 7 and 8 shows the precision and recall values in graph for all the projects. Finally the result of the Linux project shows that the tool CloneManager is able to detect clones even for larger systems in size. This proves that the tool CloneManager is also scalable.

5.5 Comparison with existing tools

In literature, there are two approaches with method-level granularity: CLAN (Mayland et al. 1996) and NICAD (Roy and Cordy 2008) which is closely comparable to our own. In this section, the proposed tool has been compared with CLAN and NICAD. The first tool considered for analysis is the CLAN clone detection with metrics based clone detection technique and method-level granularity. CLAN gathered different metrics for code fragments and compared these metric vectors instead of comparing the code

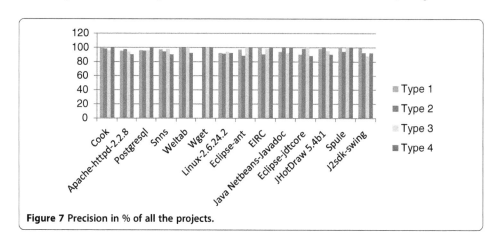

Figure 7 Precision in % of all the projects.

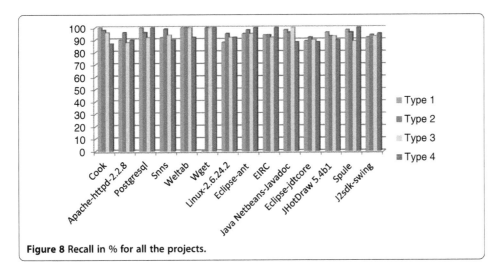

Figure 8 Recall in % for all the projects.

directly. An allowable distance (for instance, Euclidean distance) for these metric vectors can be used as a hint for similar code.

The second is NICAD (Roy and Cordy 2008) a parser-based, language specific, lightweight approach using simple text-line comparison which finds function clones with the aid of TXL. TXL (Cordy et al. 2002) is a programming language specifically designed for manipulating and experimenting with programming language notations and features using source to source transformation.

Because of limited space, only one system presented here. We have chosen Weltab, because some of the earlier experimental tools have used it to evaluate their work. The tool CloneManager ran successfully for all the projects in Table 5. The comparison of the results of all the projects with these two existing tools is done in the same way as Weltab. 321 clone pairs for type-1, 2, 3 were obtained altogether using the proposed LWH approach, while CLAN has obtained only 101 match clone pairs. Moreover, the CloneManager tool further classified clones pairs as clone clusters. In addition, type-4 clones are also detected by the tool CloneManager. The results obtained by these two existing tools are presented in Table 12 along with the computed values for the proposed tool CloneManager.

NICAD reported 8 exact-match and 20 near-miss clone clusters which are nothing but the type-1 and type-3 clone clusters found in Weltab. The implemented proposed method, have obtained similar results. NICAD having claimed to have obtained 100% when compared with Bellon's benchmark results, which concludes that the proposed method has also accomplished the same output.

Though NICAD has proved to effectively detect the function clones, the initial phases employ an external parser. Whereas, the proposed method uses a hand-coded parser,

Table 12 Comparison of clone pairs and clone clusters for Weltab

TYPE	CLAN	NICAD		CloneManger	
	Clone pairs	Clone pairs	Clone clusters	Clone pairs	Clone clusters
Type-1	46	46	8	46	8
Type-2	27	-	-	115	11
Type-3	28	160	20	160	20
Type-4	-	-	-	12	5
Total	101	206	28	333	44

Table 13 Comparison of run-time with NICAD and proposed tool CloneManager

Projects	NICAD in minutes	CloneManager in minutes
Cook	5.13	5.01
Apache-httpd-2.2.8	18.21	16.12
Postgresql	9.59	8.48
Snns	5.23	5.09
Eclipse-ant	1.57	1.35
Java Netbeans-Javadoc	0.42	0.38
Eclipse-jdtcore	17.43	16.02
JHotDraw 5.4b1	2.48	2.05
J2sdk-swing	35.24	30.37

external lexers or parsers have not been deployed. Moreover, NICAD tool did not classify the clones types-1, 2 or 3 as specified in the literature. Instead of that, the tool fixed some threshold value. If the threshold value is 0.0 then Roy called it as exact clones (type-1). Then Roy matches with threshold value 0.10, 0.20, 0.30 and called it as 10%, 20%, 30% of dissimilarity in the clones respectively. It is able to detect near-missed clones (type-3) but fails to detect type-2 and type-4 clones.

From the Table 13, shows the comparison of the run-time of the proposed tool CloneManager with the NICAD tool. It is easier to notice from the Table that the time taken by the proposed tool is lesser than NICAD. Thus the proposed tool proves to have time complexity better than NICAD.

Table 14 shows the comparison of the Precision and Recall parameters of the tool CLAN with the proposed tool CloneManager. In Table 14 T1, T2, T3 stands for type-1, type-2, type-3 respectively. The projects which have Precision and Recall data are taken from the standard Bellon's benchmark. Moreover, the data were only available for type-1, type-2 and type-3. From the Table it is observed that the proposed tool CloneManager is very high in Precision and Recall.

5.6 Threats to validity

In this section, the various factors that threaten the validity of our results are summarized. The common guidelines (Yin 2002) are followed for empirical studies.

Table 14 Comparison of the tool CLAN with the tool CloneManager

Projects	CLAN						CloneManager					
	Precision %			Recall %			Precision %			Recall %		
	T1	T2	T3	T1	T2	T3	T1	T2	T3	T1	T2	T3
Cook	33	10	3	4	16	12	100	98	96	100	98	96
Postgresql	9	2	0	0	19	11	95	95	96	100	96	92
Snns	8	11	4	11	6	2	96	94	98	92	99	94
Weltab	15	35	0	33	6	0	100	100	96	100	100	98
Eclipse-ant	11	9	0	5	20	0	97	88	100	95	98	95
Java Netbeans-Javadoc	7	6	6	33	9	13	94	100	92	98	96	100
Eclipse-jdtcore	4	4	0.8	4	53	12	90	98	100	89	92	90
J2sdk-swing	7	7	0.2	69	25	1	99	92	88	92	94	93

5.6.1 Internal validity

Threat of internal validity corresponds to the ability of our experiments to link the independent and dependent variables. The threat may be revealed through experimental or human errors. Bellon's benchmark was used as a reference set for the comparison of detecting clone results. The Bellon reference corpus was manually built by Bellon using only 2% of the clones suggested by the six clone detectors. For unbiased comparison, it is necessary to rebuild the clone references by considering the results of all clone detectors, which is beyond the scope of this paper.

We carried out manual analysis to verify the correctness of the clone detection using semi-automated tools/manual. The manual assessment can be subject to human errors. However, all the participants of this work are graduate students carrying out projects in the area of software clones. Thus we trust that each one has agent expertise to keep the plausible human errors to the minimum.

5.6.2 External validity

Threats to external validity are about how to generalize our results. We had done our comparison with 14 open source projects of various size and application domains that are written in two popular programming languages C and Java. However, this does not declare that the findings can be held true for other programming languages. Moreover, we planned to explore more systems written in various programming languages.

5.6.3 Construct validity

Construct validity threats are related to the relation between theory and observation. It corresponds to the suitableness of our evaluation parameters. We mainly focused on the precision, recall and run-time for the evaluation of our tool. These evaluation parameters measured high in precision & recall values and low in run-time values. However, the usage of the memory is slightly higher, as our approach uses the intermediate results such as generating templates in two different methods. Moreover, it will not affect so much as we can see the vast development of physical storage capacity and speed of access growing rapidly day-by-day.

6 Conclusion

In this paper, we have proposed a LWH approach to detect method-level clones for both textual similarity and functional similarity types with the computation of metrics combined with simple textual analysis technique. We could improve the precision and reduce the total comparison cost of avoiding the exponential rate of comparison by using the metrics. Since the string matching/textual comparison is performed over the shortlisted candidates, a higher amount of recall could be obtained. The early experiments prove that this method can do atleast as well as the existing systems in finding and classifying the function clones in C and Java.

As a future work, first we have planned to enhance the technique for Web Static pages. Second, we have also planned to enhance the tool for clone removal by using the refactoring technique. Third, if there are some simple modifications in the source code, then the clone has to be detected in the whole software from the scratch. It surely takes the same or more time to do the same process. This time can be reduced to a considerable extent, by making it to retain the previous clone detection results with the intermediate values and thus produce the results in a fraction of time for the next revisions. Next we have planned to enhance our tool with this incremental process.

Appendix A

The details of the open source projects chosen for the experimentation and evaluation of the clone detection tool CloneManager, is as follows

1. **Cook** is a tool for constructing files. It is given a set of files to create, and recipes of how to create them.
2. **Apache HTTP** Server project develops and maintains an open source HTTP (Hypertext Transfer Protocol) server for modern operating systems, including UNIX and Windows NT (New Technology).
3. **PostgreSQL** (Database) runs on many different operating systems.
4. **SNNS** (Stuttgart Neural Network Simulator) is a neural network simulator originally developed at the University of Stuttgart.
5. **Weltab** which is a Vote tabulation system.
6. **Wget** a free software package for retrieving files using HTTP, HTTPS and FTP, the most widely-used Internet protocols.
7. **Linux** is the open source operating system.
8. **Eclipse Ant** is the premier build tool for Java developers, and Integrating Ant with Eclipse provides a good solution for web development.
9. **Eight IRC (EIRC)** will be an Internet Relay Chat(IRC) client in windows that will also be translated to Swedish hopefully.
10. **JavaNetbeans- javadoc** tool provides an easy way to write API documentation for source code and software projects using the Java programming language.
11. **Eclipse-jdtcore** - The Java model is the set of classes that model the objects associated with creating, editing, and building a Java program.
12. **JHotDraw** is a Java GUI framework for technical and structured Graphics.
13. **Spule** stands for "secure practical universal lecture evaluator". Spule is a program to automatize the evaluation of lecture polls.
14. **J2sdk-swing** provides many enhancements to the existing graphics package.

Appendix B

The comparative results of the tool CloneManager with CLAN and NICAD tools for all chosen open source projects, are presented in the following tables (Tables 15, 16, 17, 18, 19, 20, 21, 22, 23, 24, 25, 26, 27 and 28).

Table 15 Clone pairs and clone clusters for cook

TYPE	CLAN	NICAD		CloneManager	
	CP	CP	CC	CP	CC
Type-1	-	7	5	18	5
Type-2	200	-	-	157	30
Type-3	249	280	98	280	98
Type-4	-	-	-	7	3
Total	449	287	103	462	136

Table 16 Clone pairs and clone clusters for SNNS

TYPE	CLAN	NICAD		CloneManager	
	CP	CP	CC	CP	CC
Type-1	100	109	63	109	63
Type-2	108	-	-	160	86
Type-3	110	495	191	495	191
Type-4	-	-	-	9	4
Total	318	604	254	773	344

Table 17 Clone pairs and clone clusters for Postgresql

TYPE	CLAN	NICAD		CloneManager	
	CP	CP	CC	CP	CC
Type-1	200	7	7	28	4
Type-2	200	-	-	240	42
Type-3	530	530	203	530	203
Type-4	-	-	-	7	3
Total	830	537	210	805	252

Table 18 Clone pairs and clone clusters for Weltab

TYPE	CLAN	NICAD		CloneManager	
	CP	CP	CC	CP	CC
Type-1	46	46	8	46	8
Type-2	27	-	-	115	11
Type-3	28	160	20	160	20
Type-4	-	-	-	12	5
Total	101	206	28	333	44

Table 19 Clone pairs and clone clusters for Eclipse-ant

TYPE	CLAN	NICAD		CloneManager	
	CP	CP	CC	CP	CC
Type-1	10	363	92	363	92
Type-2	54	-	-	372	96
Type-3	24	426	119	426	119
Type-4	-	-	-	10	4
Total	88	789	211	1171	311

Table 20 Clone pairs and clone clusters for Eclipse-jdtcore

TYPE	CLAN	NICAD		CloneManager	
	CP	CP	CC	CP	CC
Type-1	1030	1427	323	1427	323
Type-2	6050	-	-	5573	587
Type-3	3031	4378	660	4378	660
Type-4	-	-	-	15	7
Total	10111	5805	983	11393	1577

Table 21 Clone pairs and clone clusters for Netbeans-javadoc

TYPE	CLAN	NICAD		CloneManager	
	CP	CP	CC	CP	CC
Type-1	28	193	80	193	80
Type-2	28	-	-	199	83
Type-3	29	304	110	304	110
Type-4	-	-	-	8	3
Total	85	497	190	704	276

Table 22 Clone pairs and clone clusters for J2sdk-swing

TYPE	CLAN	NICAD		CloneManager	
	CP	CP	CC	CP	CC
Type-1	936	8115	516	8115	516
Type-2	936	-	-	8205	558
Type-3	937	11209	843	11209	843
Type-4	-	-	-	30	14
Total	2809	19324	1359	27559	1931

The following projects are compared to NICAD tool alone, as the data was not available for CLAN tool.

Table 23 Clone pairs and clone clusters for Apache-httpd 2.2.8

TYPE	NICAD		CloneManager	
	CP	CC	CP	CC
Type-1	183	107	183	107
Type-2	-	-	242	143
Type-3	711	276	711	276
Type-4	-	-	10	4
Total	894	383	1146	530

Table 24 Clone pairs and clone clusters for wget

TYPE	NICAD		CloneManager	
	CP	CC	CP	CC
Type-1	0	0	0	0
Type-2	-	-	4	2
Type-3	11	2	11	2
Type-4	-	-	2	1
Total	11	2	17	5

Table 25 Clone pairs and clone clusters for Linux

TYPE	NICAD		CloneManager	
	CP	CC	CP	CC
Type-1	5953	1505	5953	1505
Type-2	-	-	7386	2265
Type-3	25767	7918	25767	7918
Type-4	-	-	13	5
Total	31720	9423	39119	11693

Table 26 Clone pairs and clone clusters for EIRC

TYPE	NICAD		CloneManager	
	CP	CC	CP	CC
Type-1	117	35	117	35
Type-2	-	-	119	35
Type-3	149	47	149	47
Type-4	-	-	6	3
Total	266	82	391	120

Table 27 Clone pairs and clone clusters for JHotDraw

TYPE	NICAD		CloneManager	
	CP	CC	CP	CC
Type-1	291	137	291	137
Type-2	-	-	299	142
Type-3	598	208	598	208
Type-4	-	-	10	4
Total	889	345	1198	491

Table 28 Clone pairs and clone clusters for Spule

TYPE	NICAD		CloneManager	
	CP	CC	CP	CC
Type-1	60	11	60	11
Type-2	-	-	69	14
Type-3	113	19	113	19
Type-4	-	-	4	2
Total	173	30	246	46

Competing interests

The authors declare that they have no competing interests.

Authors' contributions

KE carried out the systematic reviews, identified the issues in the existing work. KE and KS designed architecture and implementation of the proposed algorithms. The dataset collection, experiments and result analysis are conducted by both KE and KS. The format of the manuscript was decided by KE and KS. The manuscript was prepared by KE, corrections and reviews are made by KS. Both authors read and approved the final manuscript.

Authors' information

Mrs. Kodhai. E is currently working as Associate Professor in the Department of Information Technology at Sri Manakula Vinayagar Engineering College affiliated to Pondicherry University, Puducherry, India. She has completed her M.C.A from Cauvery College for women, Trichy affiliated to Bharathidasan University, Trichy and M.E. in Computer Science and Engineering from Vinayaka Mission's Kirupananda variyar Engineering College, Salem. She has more than 14 years of experience in teaching in various engineering colleges. She is currently pursuing her Ph.D in Software Clones. Her Research interests include Software Maintenance and Evolution. She has published more than 30 papers in international conference and journals.

Dr. Kanmani. S received her B.E (CSE) and M.E (CSE) from Bharathiar University, Coimbatore, India and Ph.D from Anna University, Chennai, India. She is working as Professor in the Department of Information Technology at Pondicherry Engineering College. She has published nearly 63 research papers. She is currently a supervisor guiding 8 Ph.D scholars. She is an expert in Software Testing. Her areas of interests include Software Engineering, Genetic algorithms and Data Mining.

Acknowledgements

We appreciate the insightful comments from the three anonymous reviewers. Their comments were very helpful for us to improve the paper. We also express our thanks to Pondicherry Engineering College for their support in performing this research.

Author details

[1]Research Scholar, Department of CSE, Pondicherry Engineering College, Puducherry, India. [2]Department of IT, Pondicherry Engineering College, Puducherry, India.

References

Adamov R (1987) Literature review on software metrics. Institute of computer science, University of Zurich, Zurich

Al-Batran B, Sch¨atz B, Hummel B (2011) Semantic clone detection for model-based development of embedded systems. Model Driven Eng. Languages and Syst. 6981:258–272

Baker BS (1997) Parameterized Duplication in Strings: Algorithms and an Application to Software Maintenance. SIAM J on Computing 26(5):1343–1362

Bellon S, Koschke R (2014) Detection of Software Clones: Tool Comparison Experiment. URL: http://www.bauhaus-stuttgart.de/clones/. Accessed 29 Jan 2014

Bellon S, Koschke R, Antoniol G, Krinke J, Merlo E (2007) Comparison and Evaluation of Clone Detection Tools. IEEE Transactions on Software Engineering 33(9):577–591

Basit H, Pugliesi S, Smyth W, Turpin A, Jarzabek S (2007) Efficient Token Based Clone Detection with Flexible Tokenization. In: European Software Engineering Conference and Symposium on the Foundations of Software Engineering (ESEC/FSE'07). ACM, Croatia, pp 513–515

Cordy JR, Dean TR, Malton AJ, Schneider KA (2002) Source Transformation in Software Engineering using the TXL Transformation System. J Information and Software Technology 44(13):827–837

Ducasse S, Nierstrasz O, Rieger M (2006) On the effectiveness of clone detection by string matching. J on Software Maintenance and Evolution 18(1). doi:10.1002/smr.317, http://scg.unibe.ch/archive/papers/Duca06iDuplocJSMEPaper.pdf

Ducasse S, Rieger M, Demeyer S (1999) A Language Independent Approach for Detecting Duplicated Code. In: 15th International Conference on Software Maintenance (ICSM'99). IEEE, Oxford, England, pp 109–118

Evans W, Fraser C (2005) Clone Detection via Structural Abstraction. Technical Report MSR-TR-2005-104. Microsoft Research, Redmond, WA

Evans WS, Fraser CW, Ma F (2009) Clone Detection via Structural Abstraction. Software Quality Journal 17:309–330

Fenton E (1991) Software metrics: a rigorous approach. Chapman and Hall

Fowler M (1999) Refactoring: improving the design of existing code. Wesley, Addison

Funaro M, Braga D, Campi A, Ghezzi C (2010) A hybrid approach (syntactic and textual) to clone detection. In: 4th International Workshop on Software Clones. ACM 2010 ISBN 978-1-60558-980-0, Cape Town, South Africa, pp 79–80

Gabel M, Jiang L, Su Z (2008) Scalable Detection of Semantic Clones. In: 30th International Conference on Software Engineering. ICSE 2008, Leipzig, Germany, pp 321–330

Greenan K (2005) Method-Level Code Clone Detection on Transformed Abstract Syntax Trees using Sequence Matching Algorithms. Student Report. University of California, Santa Cruz, Winter. available at http://users.soe.ucsc.edu/~ejw/courses/290gw05/greenan-report.pdf

Hotta K, Yang J, Higo Y, Kusumoto S (2014) How Accurate Is Coarse-grained Clone Detection? Comparision with Fine-grained Detectors. In: Eight International workshop on software clones. Electronic Communications of the EASST, Antwerp, Belgium

Kamiya T, Kusumoto S, Inoue K (2002) CCFinder: A Multi-Linguistic Token-based Code Clone Detection System for Large Scale Source Code. IEEE Computer Society Transactions on Software Engineering 28(7):654–670

Kapser C, Godfrey M (2004) Aiding comprehension of cloning through categorization. In: International Workshop on Principles of Software Evolution. IEEE Computer Society, Kyoto, Japan, pp 85–94

Kapser CJ, Godfrey MW (2006) Supporting the analysis of clones in software systems: Research articles. J of Software Maintenance: Research and Practice 18(2):61–82

Kapser C, Godfrey MW (2008) Cloning considered harmful: Patterns of cloning in software. Empirical Software Engineering 13(6):645–692

Komondoor R, Horwitz S (2001) Using Slicing to Identify Duplication in Source Code. In: 8th International Symposium on Static Analysis. SAS 2001, Paris, France, pp 40–56

Koschke R (2012) Large-Scale Inter-System Clone Detection Using Suffix Trees. In: European Conference on Software Maintenance and Reengineering. IEEE Computer Society Press. University of Szeged Congress Centre (SZTE TIK), Szeged, Hungary, pp 309–318

Koschke R, Falke R (2006) Frenzel P (2006) Clone detection using abstract syntax suffix trees. Working Conference on Reverse Engineering, IEEE Computer Society Press, In

Krinke J (2001) Identifying Similar Code with Program Dependence Graphs. In: 8th Working Conference on Reverse Engineering. WCRE 2001, Stuttgart, pp 301–309

Lee M, Roh J, Hwang S, Kim S (2010) Instant code clone search. In: Fundamental of Software Engineering, pp 167–176

Leitao A (2004) Detection of Redundant Code Using R2D2. Software Quality Journal 12(4):361–382

Leitner A, Ebner W, Kreiner C (2013) Mechanisms to Handle Structural Variability in MATLAB/Simulink Models. In: Favaro J, Morisio M (ed), vol 7925. ICSR 2013, LNCS, Pisa, Italy, pp 17–31

Li Z, Lu S, Myagmar S, Zhou Y (2006) CP-Miner: Finding Copy-Paste and Related Bugs in Large-Scale Software Code. IEEE Transactions on Software Engineering 32(3):176–192

Liu C, Chen C, Han J, Yu P (2006) GPLAG: Detection of Software Plagiarism by Program Dependence Graph Analysis. In: 12th ACM SIGKDD International Conference on Knowledge Discovery and Data Mining. pp 872–881

Marcus A, Maletic J (2001) Identification of High-level Concept Clones in Source Code. In: 16th IEEE International Conference on Automated Software Engineering. ASE 2001, Coronado Island, San Diego, CA, USA, pp 107–114

Mayland J, Leblanc C, Merlo E (1996) Experiment on the Automatic Detection of Function Clones in a Software System Using Metrics. In: International Conference on Software Engineering 96. IEEE and ACM, Berlin, Germany

Moller K (1993) Software metrics: a practitioner's guide to improved product development. Hall, Chapman and

Moonen L (2001) Generating Robust Parsers using Island Grammars. In: 8th Working Conference on Reverse Engineering (WCRE'01). IEEE Computer Society, Washington, DC, USA, p 13

Pate J, Tairas R, Kraft N (2011) Clone Evolution: a Systematic Review. J of Software Maintenance, Research and Practice

Petersen H (2012) Clone detection in Matlab Simulink models. Master's thesis. Tech. Univ. Denmark

Roy CK, Cordy JR (2007) A survey on software clone detection research. Tech. Rep. 541. Queen's University, Kingston, Canada

Roy CK, Cordy JR (2008) NICAD: Accurate Detection of Near-Miss Intentional Clones Using Flexible Pretty-Printing and Code Normalization. In: 16th IEEE International Conference on Program Comprehension. IEEE Computer Society 2008, Amsterdam, The Netherlands, pp 172–181

Roy CK, Cordy JR, Koschke R (2009) Comparison and evaluation of code clone detection techniques and tools: A qualitative approach. Science of Computer Programming 74(7):470–495

Selim GMK, Foo KC, Zou Y (2010) (2010) Enhancing Source-Based Clone Detection Using Intermediate Representation. Working Conference on Reverse Engineering, In

Thummalapenta S, Cerulo L, Aversano L, Penta MD (2009) An empirical study on the maintenance of source code clones. Empirical Software Engineering 15(1):1–34

Ueda Y, Kamiya T, Kusumoto S, Inoue K (2002) Gemini: Maintenance Support Environment Based On Code Clone Analysis. In: 8th IEEE Symposium on Software Metrics. IEEE Computer Society 2002 ISBN 0-7695-1339-5, Ottawa, Canada

Wettel R, Marinescu R (2005) Archeology of Code Duplication: Recovering Duplication Chains From Small Duplication Fragments. In: 7th International Symposium on Symbolic and Numeric Algorithms for Scientific Computing (SYNASC'05). 115f, Timisoara, Romania

Wohlin C, Runeson P, Höst M, Ohlsson MC, Regnell B, Wesslén A (2012) Experimentation in Software Engineering. Springer Berlin, Heidelberg

Yin RK (2002) Design and methods. ICSM'00, 3rd edition. IEEE Computer Society 2002 ISBN 0-7695-1819-2, Montreal, Quebec, Canada

Zibran M, Roy CK (2013) Conflict-aware Optimal Scheduling of Code Clone Refactoring. IET Software 7(3):167–186

Zibran M, Saha R, Asaduzzaman M, Roy C (2011) Analyzing and forecasting near-miss clones in evolving software: An empirical study. In: International Conference on Engineering of Complex Computer Systems. IEEE Xplore Digital Library, Las Vegas, USA, pp 295–304

11

BugMaps-Granger: a tool for visualizing and predicting bugs using Granger causality tests

Cesar Couto[1,2*], Marco Tulio Valente[2], Pedro Pires[2], Andre Hora[3], Nicolas Anquetil[3] and Roberto S Bigonha[2]

*Correspondence:
cesar@decom.cefetmg.br
[1] Department of Computer Science, UFMG, Belo Horizonte, Brazil
[2] Department of Computing, CEFET-MG, Belo Horizonte, Brazil
Full list of author information is available at the end of the article

Abstract

Background: Despite the increasing number of bug analysis tools for exploring bugs in software systems, there are no tools supporting the investigation of causality relationships between internal quality metrics and bugs. In this paper, we propose an extension of the BugMaps tool called BugMaps-Granger that allows the analysis of source code properties that are more likely to cause bugs. For this purpose, we relied on the Granger Causality Test to evaluate whether past changes to a given time series of source code metrics can be used to forecast changes in a time series of defects. Our tool extracts source code versions from version control platforms, calculates source code metrics and defects time series, computes Granger Test results, and provides interactive visualizations for causal analysis of bugs.

Results: We provide an example of use of BugMaps-Granger involving data from the Equinox Framework and Eclipse JDT Core systems collected during three years. For these systems, the tool was able to identify the modules with more bugs, the average lifetime and complexity of the bugs, and the source code properties that are more likely to cause bugs.

Conclusions: With the results provided by the tool in hand, a maintainer can perform at least two main software quality assurance activities: (a) refactoring the source code properties that Granger-caused bugs and (b) improving unit tests coverage in classes with more bugs.

Keywords: Bug analysis tools; Software metrics; Causality tests

1 Background

A number of software analysis tools has been proposed to improve software quality (Nierstrasz et al. 2005; Hovemeyer and Pugh 2004; Wettel 2009). Such tools use different types of information about the structure and history of software systems. Basically, they are used to analyze software evolution, manage the quality of the source code, compute metrics, check coding rules, etc. In general, such tools help maintainers to understand large amounts of data coming from software repositories.

Particularly, there is a growing interest in analysis tools for exploring bugs in software systems (Hora et al. 2012; D'Ambros and Lanza 2012; Sliwerski et al. 2005; Dal Sassc and Lanza 2013). Such tools help maintainers to understand the distribution, the evolutionary behavior, the lifetime, and the stability of bugs. For example, Churrasco is a web-based tool for collaborative software evolution analysis (D'Ambros and Lanza 2012).

The tool automatically extracts information from a variety of software repositories, including versioning systems and bug management systems. The goal is to provide an extensible tool that can be used to reason about software evolution under different perspectives, including the behavior of bugs. Other visualizations were also proposed for understanding the behavior of bugs, including system radiography (which provides a high-level visualization on the parts of the system more impacted by bugs) and bug watch (which relies on a watch metaphor to provide information about a particular bug) (D'Ambros et al. 2007). Hatari (Sliwerski et al. 2005) is a tool that provides views to browse through the most risky locations and to analyze the risk history of a particular component from a system. More recently, the tool in*Bug (Dal Sassc and Lanza 2013) was proposed to allow users navigating and inspecting the information stored in bug tracking platforms, with the specific purpose to support the comprehension of bug reports.

Despite the increasing number of bug analysis tools, they typically do not provide mechanisms for assessing the existence of correlations between the internal quality of a software system and the occurrence of bugs. To the best of our knowledge, there are no bug analysis tools that highlight the possible causes of bugs in the source code. More specifically, there are no tools designed to infer eventual causal relations between changes in the values of source code metrics and the occurrence of defects in object-oriented classes.

In this paper, we propose and describe the BugMaps-Granger tool—an extension of the BugMaps tool (Hora et al. 2012)—that supports detection of causal relations between source code metrics and bugs. The tool provides mechanisms to retrieve data from software repositories, to compute source code metrics, to generate time series of source code metrics and defects, and to infer causal relations between source code properties and defects. Moreover, BugMaps-Granger provides visualizations for identifying the modules with more bugs, the average lifetime and complexity of bugs, and the source code properties that are more likely to cause bugs. More specifically, our tool relies on the Granger Causality Test (Granger 1981) to identify causal relations between time series of source code metrics and defects. This test evaluates whether past changes to a given time series of source code metrics can be used to forecast changes in a time series of defects. The proposed tool has the following features:

- The tool automatically extracts source code models of a target system from its version control platform in predefined time intervals.
- The tool generates time series of twelve source code metrics and time series with the number of defects in each class of the target system.
- The tool computes the Granger Test considering the metrics and defects time series to highlight possible causal relations.
- The tool integrates models extracted from the source code with models representing the number of bugs.
- The tool provides a set of interactive visualizations to support software maintainers in answering questions such as: (a) Which are the modules with more bugs? (b) What is the average lifetime of bugs? (c) What is the complexity of bugs? (d) What are the source code properties that Granger-cause bugs in a given module?, and (e) What are the metrics with the highest number of positive Granger tests?

The ultimate goal of BugMaps-Granger is to predict the changes in the source code that are more likely to cause defects. For example, with our tool in hand, a maintainer (before making a commit with changes to a given class) can verify whether such changes affect the values of source code metrics that, in the past, Granger-caused defects. If the changes significantly affect these metrics values, the maintainer can, for example, perform extra software quality assurance activities (e.g., she can conduct more unit testing or perform a detailed code inspection) before executing the commit.

In a previous conference paper, we described an exploratory study on using Granger to predict bugs (Couto et al. 2012). Recently, this paper was extended with a concrete approach that relies on Granger Tests to trigger alarms whenever risky changes are applied in the source code (Couto et al. 2014). A preliminary version of BugMaps—without any support to Granger Tests—is described in a short paper (Hora et al. 2012). Later, we proposed a second version of this tool, which we called BugMaps-Granger, including support to Granger Causality (Couto et al. 2013a). In the present paper, we extend this initial work on BugMaps-Granger by including a more detailed presentation on the tool and a case study, with two large open-source systems (Eclipse JDT Core and Equinox Framework).

2 Implementation

The execution of the BugMaps-Granger tool is divided into two phases: preprocessing and visualization. The preprocessing phase is responsible for extracting source code models, creating time series, and applying the Granger Test to compute possible causal relations between source code metrics and bugs. In the visualization phase, the user interacts with the tool. For example, he can retrieve the most defective classes of the system and visualize the source code properties that Granger-caused bugs in such classes.

BugMaps-Granger is implemented in Moose (Moose platform 2014), which is a platform for software and data analysis (Nierstrasz et al. 2005). Figure 1 shows BugMaps-Granger's architecture, which includes four modules: model extraction, time series creation, Granger Test module, and visualization module.

In the following subsections, we describe the modules of this architecture:

2.1 Model extraction

This module receives as input the URL associated to the version control platform of the target system (SVN or Git) and a time interval to be used in the analysis of the bugs. To extract the source code models, the module performs the following tasks: (a) it extracts

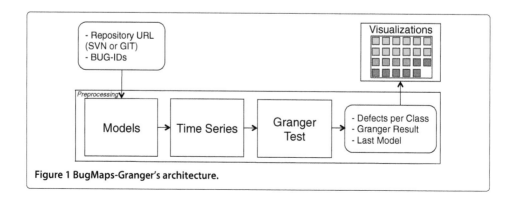

Figure 1 BugMaps-Granger's architecture.

the source code versions from the version control platforms in intervals of bi-weeks; (b) it removes test classes, assuming that such classes are implemented in directories and subdirectories whose name starts with the words "Test" or "test"; and (c) it parses the source code versions and generates MSE files using the VerveineJ tool (Ducasse et al. 2011; VerveineJ parser 2014). MSE is the default file format supported by the Moose platform to persist source code models.

2.2 Time series creation

To create the time series of source code metrics, this module receives as input the models extracted by the previous module. For each class of each extracted model, the module relies on the Moose platform to compute eleven source code metrics including six CK metrics (proposed by Chidamber and Kemerer 1994) and five others, such as lines of code, FAN-IN, FAN-OUT, etc. Table 1 shows the source code metrics considered by the tool. In a second step, this module stores the computed metric values in CSV files. Basically, for a target system S and a metric M, this module creates a CSV file whose lines represent the classes of S and the columns represent the bi-weeks considered when extracting the versions of S. A cell (c, t) in this file contains the value of the metric M, measured for the class c, in the bi-week t.

To create the time series of defects for each class, the module receives as input a CSV file containing the bugs (IDs and creation dates) collected from the bug tracking platforms (e.g., Bugzilla, Jira, Mantis, etc.). Basically, the module maps the bugs to their respective commits, using the mapping strategy presented in details in (Couto et al. 2012; Couto et al. 2014). Next, the source code files changed by such commits are used to identify the classes changed to fix the respective bugs.

2.3 Granger test module

This module applies the Granger Causality Test considering the metrics and defects time series. To apply the Granger Test, the module relies on Algorithm 1. In this algorithm, `Classes` is the set of all classes of the system (line 1) and `Defects[c]` is the time series with the number of defects (line 2). The algorithm relies on function d_check (line 3) to check whether the defects in the time series `d` conform to the following preconditions:

Algorithm 1 Applying the Granger Test

```
 1:  for all c ∈ Classes do
 2:      d = Defects[c];
 3:      if d_check(d) then
 4:          for n = 1 to NumberOfMetrics do
 5:              m = M[n][c];
 6:              if m_check(m) then
 7:                  granger(m, d);
 8:              end if
 9:          end for
10:      end if
11:  end for
```

Table 1 Source code metrics considered by BugMaps-Granger

	Metrics	Description
1	WMC	Weighted methods per class
2	DIT	Depth of inheritance tree
3	RFC	Request for class
4	NOC	Number of children
5	CBO	Coupling between object class
6	LCOM	Lack of cohesion in methods
7	FAN-IN	Number of classes that reference a given class
8	FAN-OUT	Number of classes referenced by a given class
9	NOA	Number of attributes
10	LOC	Number of lines oxf code
11	NOM	Number of methods

- P1: The time series must have at least 30 values. The motivation for this precondition is the fact that classes that only existed for a small proportion of the time frame considered in the analysis do not present a considerable history of defects to qualify their use in predictions.
- P2: The values in the time series of defects must not be all equal to zero. The motivation for this precondition is that it is straightforward to predict defects for classes that never presented a defect in their lifetime; probably, they will remain with zero defects in the future.
- P3: The time series of defects must be stationary, which is a precondition required by the Granger Test (Fuller 1995).

Suppose that a given class c passed the previous preconditions. For this class, suppose also that M[n][c] (line 5) is the time series with the values of the n-th considered source code metric, $1 \leq n \leq$ NumberOfMetrics. The algorithm relies on function m_check (line 6) to test whether time series m—a time series with metrics values—conforms to the following preconditions:

- P4: The time series of source code metrics must not be constant. In other words, metrics time series whose values never change must be discarded, since variations in the independent variables are the key event to observe when computing Granger causality.
- P5: The time series of source code metrics must be stationary, as defined for the defects series.

Finally, for the time series m (source code metrics) and d (defects) that passed preconditions P1 to P5, function granger(m,d) checks whether m Granger-causes d (line 7). In practice, to apply the test, BugMaps-Granger relies on the function *granger.test()* provided by the *msbvar* (MSBVAR package 2012) package of the R system.

It is worth mentioning that we previously performed an extensive study to evaluate the application of Granger Causality Test on software defects prediction (Couto et al. 2014). Basically, we focus on answering questions such as: (a) How many time series pass the preconditions related to defects (preconditions P1, P2, P3)? (b) How many time series pass the preconditions related to source code metrics (preconditions P4 and P5)? (c)

How many classes present positive results on the Granger Test? (d) What is the number of defects potentially covered by Granger? To answer these questions, we used a dataset including time series of source code metrics and defects for four real-world systems (Eclipse JDT Core, Eclipse PDE UI, Equinox Framework, and Lucene) (Couto et al. 2013b).

2.4　Visualization module

This module receives the following input data: a file containing the bugs mapped to their respective classes and the Granger results, a model extracted from the last source code version, and the source code itself of the system under analysis. From this information, the module provides four interactive visualization browsers:

- Two browsers are used for analysis. The first one deals with the classes, the number of bugs, and the Granger results of the system under analysis (called Granger browser) while the second one deals with the complexity of the bugs (called Bug as Entity browser).
- Two browsers are used to rank the classes and the metrics most involved with bugs.

Such browsers are implemented using visualization packages provided by the Moose Platform. Basically, the visualizations are based on Distribution Map, a generic technique to reason about the results of software analysis and to investigate how a given phenomenon is distributed across a software system (Ducasse et al. 2006). Using a Distribution Map, three metrics can be displayed through the height, width, and color of the objects in the map. In our maps, rectangles represent classes or bugs and containers represent packages.

Figure 2 shows the Granger browser, which has four panes: visualization of classes and packages (top left), measures (top right), Granger results (bottom left), and source code (bottom right)[a]. Metrics, source code, and Granger results are updated according to the selected class in the classes and packages pane.

Figure 3 shows the Bug as Entity browser which is composed by two panes: visualization of classes and packages (left pane) and bugs (right pane). When a defective class is selected, the bugs in the class are colored in black (in the right pane). In contrast, when a bug is selected, the classes changed to fix this bug are colored in black (in the left pane). BugMaps-Granger also shows a list of classes ranked by the number of defects and the number of Granger tests with a positive result.

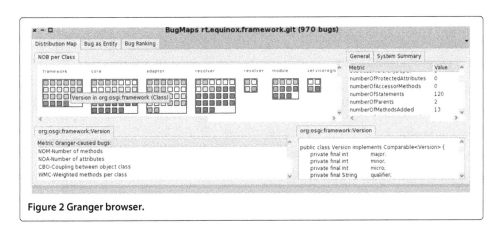

Figure 2 Granger browser.

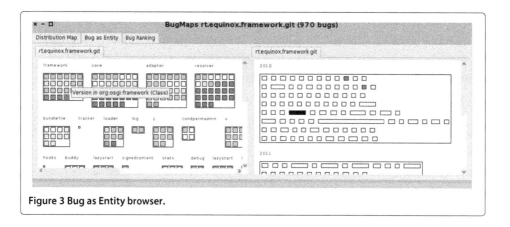

Figure 3 Bug as Entity browser.

3 Results and discussion

In this section, we provide an example of use considering data from the Equinox Framework and Eclipse JDT Core systems collected during three years. For Equinox Framework, the tool extracted 79 source code versions in intervals of bi-weeks, including 417 classes, from 2010-01-01 to 2012-12-28. For Eclipse JDT Core, the tool extracted 78 source code versions in intervals of bi-weeks, including 2,467 classes, from 2005-01-01 to 2007-12-15. In a second step, for each class, the tool created eleven time series of source code metrics (for each metric in Table 1) and one time series of defects. Finally, for each pair of time series (source code metrics and defects), the tool applied the Granger Test to identify causal relations. We analyzed the Granger results for both systems according to the proposed visualizations, as discussed next.

3.1 Granger

In this map, the rectangles are the classes of the target system, as illustrated in Figure 4. The color of a class represents the number of bugs detected through its history ranging from green to red (the closer to red, more bugs the class had in its history). By selecting a defective class, the bottom pane is updated showing the source code metrics that Granger-caused bugs in this class. Particularly, Figure 4 provides an overview of the distribution of the bugs in the Equinox Framework system. We can observe that the `resolver` package contains a significant number of classes with bugs. Moreover, for the class `org.eclipse.osgi.internal.resolver.StateImpl`, we can observe

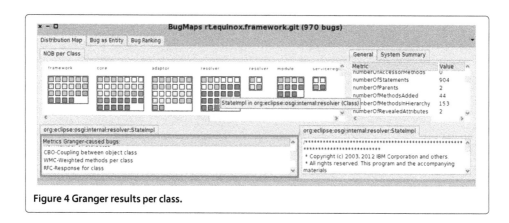

Figure 4 Granger results per class.

that the source code metrics that Granger-caused bugs were CBO (Coupling Between Object), WMC (Weighted Methods per Class), and RFC (Response for Class).

The Granger browser can also be used to avoid future defects. For example, with this result in hand, a maintainer (before making a commit with changes to the `StateImpl` class) can verify whether such changes heavily affect the values of source code metrics that Granger-caused defects in the past (in our example, the metrics that Granger-caused defects were CBO, WMC, and RFC). If the change affects these metrics, the maintainer can for example perform extra software quality assurance activities in this class (like unit testing or code inspection).

3.2 Bug as entity

As illustrated in Figure 5, this map represents bugs instead of classes. The color of a bug represents its lifetime, i.e., the number of days the bug remained opened. Blue denotes a bug that was still open at the end of the considered time period. Moreover, white denotes a bug that was open for a short time. Similarly, yellow is used for a bug that was open up to three months, and red for a bug that was opened for more than three months. The width of a bug representation denotes its complexity, measured as the number of classes changed to fix the bug. Bugs are sorted according to the date they were created.

Figure 5(a) shows the bugs of the Equinox Framework created in 2010. We can observe that all bugs from 2010 were fixed (i.e., there are no bugs in blue), that only two bugs remained open for more than three months (bugs going to red), and that complex bugs (long width) are dispersed in time. Figure 5(b) shows the bugs of the Eclipse JDT Core created in 2005. Similar to the Equinox Framework, all bugs were fixed and few bugs remained open for more than three months. In addition, most bugs have low complexity (short width). However, in a detailed analysis, we can also observe that the highlighted bug (ID 89096) is quite complex. More specifically, the developer team changed 75 classes in

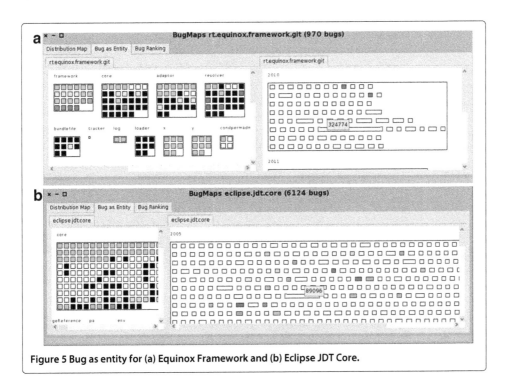

Figure 5 Bug as entity for (a) Equinox Framework and (b) Eclipse JDT Core.

order to fix this particular bug, which is related to a performance problem in the resource bundle mechanism (a requirement scattered by the classes of the JDT Core).

3.3 Bug ranking

Figure 6 shows examples of the Bug Ranking browser which is composed by one grid with two columns: class names (first column) and number of defects during the time frame considered in the analysis (second column). The figure shows the classes ranked by the defects for the Equinox Framework and Eclipse JDT Core systems during the period of three years. For the Equinox Framework, the two classes with more defects are `osgi.internal.module.ResolverImpl` and `osgi.framework.internal.core.Framework`. The `ResolverImpl` class—which has more than 2,000 lines of code—is an important class responsible for resolving the constraints of the bundles (JAR components) in a system that follows the OSGi standard (Tavares and Valente 2008). The `Framework` class also has more than 2,000 lines of code and represents the core OSGi Framework class. For Eclipse JDT Core, the top-ten classes with more defects include classes such as `org.eclipse.jdt.core.dom.AST` and `org.eclipse.jdt.-internal.core.JavaModel`. The `AST` class represents an abstract syntax tree node factory and the `JavaModel` class is responsible for managing projects in the Eclipse workspace.

3.4 Granger ranking

For each valid time series of source code metrics, Figure 7 shows the number of Granger tests that returned a positive result. For example, the number of CBO time series with a

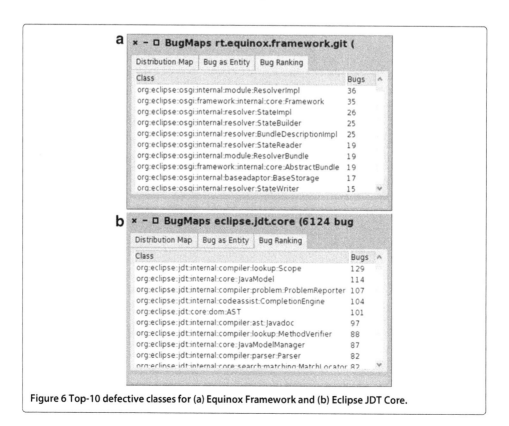

Figure 6 Top-10 defective classes for (a) Equinox Framework and (b) Eclipse JDT Core.

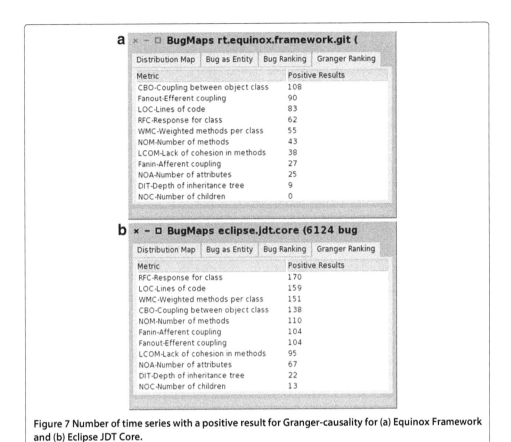

Figure 7 Number of time series with a positive result for Granger-causality for (a) Equinox Framework and (b) Eclipse JDT Core.

Granger-causality with defects was 108 and 138 series for Equinox Framework and Eclipse JDT Core, respectively. As can be observed, the metrics with the highest number of positive Granger tests were CBO, FAN-OUT, LOC, RFC, and WMC for Equinox Framework; and RFC, LOC, WMC, and CBO for Eclipse JDT Core. On the other hand, the metrics with the lowest number of positive results were DIT and NOC for both systems.

Based on these results, we can conclude that metrics related to complexity (WMC), coupling (CBO, RFC, and FAN-OUT), and LOC tend to impact in the occurrence of defects in the Equinox Framework and Eclipse JDT Core systems, at least according to Granger. Conversely, metrics related to inheritance—such as DIT and NOC—tend to have a small influence in the occurrence of defects.

4 Conclusion

In this paper, we described a tool that infers and provides visualizations about causality relations between source code metrics and bugs. The BugMaps-Granger tool extracts time series of defects from such systems and allows the visualization of different bug measures, including the source code properties that Granger-caused bugs. The ultimate goal of BugMaps-Granger is to highlight changes in the source code that are more subjected to bugs, and the source code metrics that can be used to anticipate the occurrence of bugs in the changed classes. With this tool in hand, maintainers can perform at least two main actions for improving software quality: (a) refactoring the source code properties that Granger-caused bugs and (b) improving unit tests coverage in classes with more bugs.

As future work, we intend to extend BugMaps-Granger with other internal software quality metrics, including metrics associated to violations in the static architecture of software systems, as revealed by the DCL language (Terra and Valente 2009) or the ArchLint tool (Maffort et al. 2013), for example. Another possible research thread concerns the relations between defects and code smells. In this case, we intend to start by investigating the relations between defects and methods located in inappropriate classes (i.e., feature envy instances), as revealed by the JMove recommendation system (Sales et al. 2013). In addition, we plan to extend BugMaps-Granger with a new functionality for alerting maintainers about the future occurrence of defects. We intend to implement this tool as a plug-in for version control platforms, like SVN and Git. Basically, this new tool should trigger alarms whenever risky changes are committed to version control platforms.

5   Availability and requirements

To execute BugMaps-Granger, the requirements of the target system are:

- Java-based systems.
- Identifiers and creation dates of bugs stored in a CSV file.
- URL or directory path of the version control platforms (SVN or GIT).

Additional information about BugMaps-Granger:

- **Project name:** BugMaps-Granger.
- **Project home page:** http://aserg.labsoft.dcc.ufmg.br/bugmaps/.
- **Operating system(s):** MacOS, Linux, and Windows.
- **Programming language:** Java, Smalltalk, and R.
- **License:** BugMaps-Granger is an open source project, distributed under a MIT license.

Endnote

[a] Since most of our visualizations make heavy use of colors, we provide high-resolution versions of these figures in a companion website: http://aserg.labsoft. dcc.ufmg.br/bugmaps.

Competing interests
The authors declare that they have no competing interests.

Authors' contributions
CC and MTV worked on the design and implementation of the tool and also wrote this manuscript. PP worked on the implementation of the preprocessing and visualization modules of the tool. AH and NA participated in the implementation of the first version of the tool (Hora et al. 2012). In this second version, they provided technical support on the Moose platform and revised the manuscript. Finally, RSB revised the manuscript. All authors read and approved the final manuscript.

Acknowledgements
This research is supported by grants from FAPEMIG, CNPq, and CAPES (Brazil) and INRIA (France).

Author details
[1]Department of Computer Science, UFMG, Belo Horizonte, Brazil. [2]Department of Computing, CEFET-MG, Belo Horizonte, Brazil. [3]RMoD Team, INRIA, Lille, France.

References
Chidamber SR, Kemerer CF (1994) A metrics suite for object oriented design. IEEE Trans Softw Eng 20(6): 476–493

Couto C, Silva C, Valente MT, Bigonha R, Anquetil N (2012) Uncovering causal relationships between software metrics and bugs. In: 16th European Conference on Software Maintenance and Reengineering (CSMR). IEEE Computer Society, USA, pp 223–232

Couto C, Pires P, Valente MT, Bigonha R, Anquetil N (2013a) BugMaps-Granger: A Tool for Causality Analysis between Source Code Metrics and Bugs. Brazilian Conference on Software: Theory and Practice (CBSoft), Tools Session, Brazilian Computer Society, Brazil

Couto C, Maffort C, Garcia R, Valente MT (2013b) COMETS: A Dataset for Empirical Research on Software Evolution Using Source Code Metrics and Time Series Analysis. ACM SIGSOFT Softw Eng Notes 38(1): 1–3

Couto C, Pires P, Valente MT, Bigonha R, Anquetil N (2014) Predicting software defects with causality tests. J Syst Soft. doi: http://dx.doi.org/10.1016/j.jss.2014.01.033

Dal Sassc T, Lanza M (2013) A closer look at bugs. In: 1st Working Conference on Software Visualization (VISSOFT). IEEE Computer Society, USA, pp 1–4

D'Ambros M, Lanza M, Pinzger M (2007) A bug's life: Visualizing a bug database. In: 4th International Workshop on Visualizing Software for Analysis and Understanding (VISSOFT). IEEE Computer Society, Canada, pp 113–120

D'Ambros M, Lanza M (2012) Distributed and collaborative software evolution analysis with churrasco. Sci Comput Program 75(4): 276–287

Ducasse S, Girba T, Kuhn A (2006) Distribution Map. In: 22nd International Conference on Software Maintenance (ICSM). IEEE Computer Society, USA, pp 203–212

Ducasse S, Anquetil N, Bhatti MU, Hora A, Laval J, Girba T (2011) MSE and FAMIX 3.0: an Interexchange Format and Source Code Model Family. Technical report, RMOD - INRIA Lille - Nord Europe, Software Composition Group - SCG

Fuller WA (1995) Introduction to Statistical Time Series. John Wiley & Sons, USA, pp 546–663

Granger C (1981) Some properties of time series data and their use in econometric model specification. J Econometrics 16(6): 121–130

Hora A, Couto C, Anquetil N, Ducasse S, Bhatti M, Valente MT, Martins J (2012) Bugmaps: A tool for the visual exploration and analysis of bugs. In: 16th European Conference on Software Maintenance and Reengineering (CSMR Tool Demonstration). IEEE Computer Society, USA

Hovemeyer D, Pugh W (2004) Finding bugs is easy. SIGPLAN Notices 39(12): 92–106

Maffort C, Valente MT, Anquetil N, Hora A, Bigonha M (2013) Heuristics for discovering architectural violations. In: 20th Working Conference on Reverse Engineering (WCRE). IEEE Computer Society, USA, pp 222–23

Moose platform (2014). http://www.moosetechnology.org

MSBVAR package (2012). http://cran.r-project.org/web/packages/MSBVAR/index.html

Nierstrasz O, Ducasse S, Grba T (2005) The story of Moose: an agile reengineering environment. In: 10th European Software Engineering Conference (ESEC). ACM, USA, pp 1–10

Sales V, Terra R, Miranda LF, Valente MT (2013) Recommending move method refactorings using dependency sets. In: 20th Working Conference on Reverse Engineering (WCRE). IEEE Computer Society, USA, pp 232–241

Sliwerski J, Zimmermann T, Zeller A (2005) Hatari: Raising risk awareness. In: 10th European Software Engineering Conference (ESEC). ACM, USA, pp 107–110

Tavares A, Valente MT (2008) A gentle introduction to OSGi. ACM SIGSOFT Softw Eng Notes 33(5): 1–5

Terra R, Valente MT (2009) A dependency constraint language to manage object-oriented software architectures. Softw: Pract Exp 32(12): 1073–1094

VerveineJ parser (2014). http://www.moosetechnology.org/tools/verveinej

Wettel R (2009) Visual exploration of large-scale evolving software. In: 31st International Conference on Software Engineering (ICSE). IEEE Computer Society, USA, pp 391–394

Permissions

List of Contributors

Hugo Melo
Informatics and Applied Mathematics Department (DIMAp), Federal University of Rio Grande do Norte, Natal, Brazil

Roberta Coelho
Informatics and Applied Mathematics Department (DIMAp), Federal University of Rio Grande do Norte, Natal, Brazil

Uirá Kulesza
Informatics and Applied Mathematics Department (DIMAp), Federal University of Rio Grande do Norte, Natal, Brazil

Demostenes Sena
Informatics and Applied Mathematics Department (DIMAp), Federal University of Rio Grande do Norte, Natal, Brazil

Wesley KG Assunção
Federal University of Paraná (UFPR), DInf, CP: 19081, CEP: 81531-980 Curitiba-PR, Brazil

Márcio de O Barros
Applied Informatics Department, Federal University of Rio de Janeiro State, CEP: 22240-090 Rio de Janeiro-RJ, Brazil

Thelma E Colanzi
Federal University of Paraná (UFPR), DInf, CP: 19081, CEP: 81531-980 Curitiba-PR, Brazil.
Informatics Department (DIN), State University of Maringá (UEM), CEP: 87020-900 Maringá-PR, Brazil

Arilo C Dias-Neto
Institute of Computing, Federal University of Amazonas, CEP: 69077-000 Manaus-AM, Brazil

Matheus HE Paixão
Optimization in Software Engineering Group (GOES. UECE), State University of Ceará, Fortaleza, Ceará, Brazil

Jerffeson T de Souza
Optimization in Software Engineering Group (GOES. UECE), State University of Ceará, Fortaleza, Ceará, Brazil

Silvia R Vergilio
Federal University of Paraná (UFPR), DInf, CP: 19081, CEP: 81531-980 Curitiba-PR, Brazil

Marcos Kalinowski
Federal University of Juiz de Fora, Rua José Kelmer s/n, Juiz de Fora 36.036-330, Brazil

Stefan Biffl
Institute of Software Technology and Interactive Systems, CDL-Flex-, Vienna University of Technology, Favoritenstr. 9/188, Vienna 1040, Austria

Rodrigo Oliveira Spínola
University of Salvador, Rua Doutor José Peroba 251, Salvador 41.770-235, Brazil

Sheila Reinehr
Catholic University of the State of Paraná, Rua Imaculada Conceição 1155, Curitiba 80.215-901, Brazil

Henrique Rocha
Department of Computer Science, UFMG, 31.270-901 Belo Horizonte, Brazil

Guilherme de Oliveira
Department of Computer Science, PUC Minas, 30.535-901 Belo Horizonte, Brazil

Humberto Marques-Neto
Department of Computer Science, PUC Minas, 30.535-901 Belo Horizonte, Brazil

Marco Tulio Valente
Department of Computer Science, UFMG, 31.270-901 Belo Horizonte, Brazil

Carlos Simões
Synapsis Brasil, S.A., Rua São Pedro n 181, CEP 24.020-054 Centro, Niterói, RJ, Brasil

Mariano Montoni
ProMove – Business Intelligence Solutions, Rua da Assembleia, No 10, Sala 2805, CEP 22.011-000 Centro, Rio de Janeiro, RJ, Brasil

João Felipe Silva Ouriques
Equal Contributors Federal University of Campina Grande, Aprigio Veloso 882, 58429-900 Campina Grande, Brazil

Emanuela Gadelha Cartaxo
Equal Contributors Federal University of Campina Grande, Aprigio Veloso 882, 58429-900 Campina Grande, Brazil

Patrícia Duarte Lima Machado
Equal Contributors Federal University of Campina Grande, Aprigio Veloso 882, 58429-900 Campina Grande, Brazil

Fadel Toure
Software Engineering Research Laboratory, Department of Mathematics and Computer Science, University of Quebec, Trois-Rivières, Quebec, Canada
Department of Computer Science and Software Engineering, Laval University, Quebec, Canada

Mourad Badri
Software Engineering Research Laboratory, Department of Mathematics and Computer Science, University of Quebec, Trois-Rivières, Quebec, Canada

Luc Lamontagne
Department of Computer Science and Software Engineering, Laval University, Quebec, Canada

José Amancio M Santos
Department of Technology, State University of Feira de Santana, Transnordestina avenue S/N - Feira de Santana - Bahia, Feira de Santana, Brazil

Manoel Gomes de Mendonça
Mathematics Institute, Federal University of Bahia, Ademar de Barros Avenue, S/N, Salvador - Bahia, Salvador, Brazil
Fraunhofer Project Center for Software & Systems Eng., Ademar de Barros Avenue, S/N Salvador - Bahia, Salvador, Brazil

Cleber Pereira dos Santos
Information Technology Department, Federal Institute of Bahia, Araujo Pinho Avenue, 39, Salvador - Bahia, Salvador, Brazil

Renato Lima Novais
Information Technology Department, Federal Institute of Bahia, Araujo Pinho Avenue, 39, Salvador - Bahia, Salvador, Brazil

Thaíssa Diirr
Graduate Program in Informatics (PPGI), Federal University of Rio de Janeiro State (UNIRIO), Av. Pasteur, 458, Urca, CEP 22290-240 Rio de Janeiro, RJ, Brazil

Gleison Santos
Graduate Program in Informatics (PPGI), Federal University of Rio de Janeiro State (UNIRIO), Av. Pasteur, 458, Urca, CEP 22290-240 Rio de Janeiro, RJ, Brazil

Egambaram Kodhai
Research Scholar, Department of CSE, Pondicherry Engineering College, Puducherry, India

Selvadurai Kanmani
Department of IT, Pondicherry Engineering College, Puducherry, India

Cesar Couto
Department of Computer Science, UFMG, Belo Horizonte, Brazil
Department of Computing, CEFET-MG, Belo Horizonte, Brazil

Marco Tulio Valente
Department of Computing, CEFET-MG, Belo Horizonte, Brazil

Pedro Pires
Department of Computing, CEFET-MG, Belo Horizonte, Brazil

Andre Hora
RMoD Team, INRIA, Lille, France

Nicolas Anquetil
RMoD Team, INRIA, Lille, France

Roberto S Bigonha
Department of Computing, CEFET-MG, Belo Horizonte, Brazil

Printed in the USA
CPSIA information can be obtained
at www.ICGtesting.com
JSHW051430221024
72173JS00006B/1427